12w

5/15

Douglas Lockhart lectured in religious studies at the Franklin School of Contemporary Studies and has worked as a freelance journalist. He is the author of *Jesus the Heretic* and three novels, *Sabazius*, *The Paradise Complex* and *Skirmish*.

THE DARK SIDE OF

G O D

*A Quest for
the Lost Heart of
Christianity*

Douglas Lockhart

ELEMENT

Shaftesbury, Dorset • Boston, Massachusetts
Melbourne, Victoria

© Element Books Limited 1999
Text © Douglas Lockhart 1999

First published in the UK in 1999 by
Element Books Limited
Shaftesbury, Dorset SP7 8BP

Published in the USA in 1999 by
Element Books, Inc.
160 North Washington Street
Boston, MA 02114

Published in Australia in 1999 by
Element Books and distributed
by Penguin Australia Limited
487 Maroondah Highway, Ringwood,
Victoria 3134

Cover design by Mark Slader
Design by Roger Lightfoot
Typeset by WestKey Limited, Falmouth, Cornwall
Printed and bound in Great Britain by
Creative Print and Design, Ebbw Vale, Wales

British Library Cataloguing in Publication
data available

Library of Congress Cataloging in Publication
data available

ISBN 1 86204 458 9

Contents

Acknowledgements   xi
Prologue   1

PART ONE: DARKNESS VISIBLE

1 THE CHALLENGE   11
The Holy Roman Catholic Church replaces the Roman
Empire, turns imperial, develops a mythology of
intelligent evil, flexes its pontifical authority in the
extermination of heretics and sets the pace for Hitler's
final solution
The Historical Backdrop   12
God's Shadow   19
Evolution of the Devil   21
The Delusion of Separateness   23

2 LES FLEURS DU MAL   25
The problem of origins, the repercussions of a Church
turned monarchical, and the attempt to cling to a vision
of Jesus untouched by twentieth-century scholarship
Double Disaffection   27
Apostolic Continuity   29
The Alien Dimension   31
Tug-of-war Theology   32
A Bucketful of Deceits   37
The Blood Relatives of Jesus   38
Forged Documents   46
Full Circle   49

3 THE HISTORICAL WHITEWASH   52
   The Church imaginatively extends the Gospels, invents the
   idea of Apostolic Succession, and successfully undermines
   the intellectual development of the Western world

   Robbing Paul to Pay Peter   54
   Strange Amalgamations   56
   The Legend of Peter   61
   The Cosmic War on Earth   65

4 THE DARK RENAISSANCE   67
   The revival of learning, the Church's grand delusion that
   it is engaged in a cosmic war, and the challenge of
   theology to the Western intellectual tradition

   The Revival of Learning   69
   The Un-dark Middle Ages   72
   The Progress of Roman Christianity   76

5 THE FATAL THREAD IN MODERNISM   81
   The Church's imaginary field of Satanic energy, the
   Teilhardian idea of consciousness as a general
   phenomenon in nature, and the necessity to go beyond
   childish things

   Back to Father 'Bones'   84
   Torn Between Realities   85
   Matter and Consciousness   90
   Mental Adjustment   96

6 A VEIL ACROSS THE FACE OF TRUTH   98
   The Church's traditional notion of intelligent good and
   intelligent evil, the squabble over whether Satan should
   be treated as a metaphor or as an entity, and the
   Christian community's refusal to deal with the fatally
   flawed side of its own collective psyche

   The World of the Compact   101
   Procedural Mistakes   105
   The Archangel Michael   109

7 SATAN AND JESUS 113
*The abduction of Jesus in the wilderness by Satan, the
Church's tendency to demonize what it does not
understand, and the curious fact that it was the very best
of the Christian communities who deserted the ship of
faith for the ship of understanding*

The Suppressed Gospel of Thomas 117
History and Mythology 118
The Satanic Indictment 121
The Demonic Cloud 122
The Heretics 125
Radical and Ultra-radical Christians 127

8 THE WINSOME DOCTRINE 133
*The Church's belief that its traditional answers are true
to reality, that answers found outside of the Church must
necessarily be inadequate, and the fact that there are now
two distinct Christianities in existence*

Crisis 139
Back to the Siblings 143
Two Christianities 145
Abraham's Dilemma 150

PART TWO: DARKNESS INVISIBLE

9 THE BEATING HEART 157
*The historical background to Jesus' life and ministry,
his rejection of doctrinal extremism, and the reversal
of his role as inaugurator of the End Time*

The Apocalyptic and the Prophetic 159
Love and Hate 164
The Incarnate Christ 168

10 THE NAZARENE COMMUNITY 170
*The problem of Christian scholars mistaking the
Nazarenes for Christians, the mystery of Paul's trip to*

Arabia, and the further mystery of there being two
Gospels of Jesus

The Myth Maker	174
The Resurrected Jesus	178
The Kingdom of God	181
Paul and James	183
Paul and the Phantom Jesus	187

11 IN THE NAME OF '*IS*'?   191
    The name 'Jesus', its sacred significance in relation to the
    Nazarenes and the Christians, and the conquering,
    revealing, sacrificing, dying and reappearing
    Jesus-archetype in Jewish history

Nomina Sacra/Nomina Divina	193
Historical Confusion	197
The Agreement	199
The True Prophet	201
Promotion/Demotion	205
The Day of Reckoning	209

12 WITH OUR MOTHER'S MILK   211
    The calibration of our minds towards accepting
    conscious sleep as natural, and the fact that many of the
    Gnostic sects sprang from the same Nazarene
    background

The Gnostics	213
The Mandean-Nazarenes	216
The Mysterious Race of Perfect Men	219
The Dilemma of the Nazarenes	223
The Fragmentation of the Nazarenes	226
The Regrouping of the Nazarenes	228

13 THE PERSONAL GOD   233
    Human consciousness, the development of the self and
    the central nervous system's organization of the
    archetypes

The Origins of Our Spiritual History 233
The Still Small Voice 234
The Process of Breakdown 240
The Hebrews 246
The Textual God 250

14 THE TRANSFIGURATION 253
Sensibility, passion and reason in the service of a
ritualistic dream – a dream of perfect freedom for the
human spirit
The Humanity of Jesus 256
Contradictions and Contrasts 259
Back to the Kingdom of God 262
The Outer and the Inner 266
An Inhuman Theology 268
The True Church 271

15 THE PARAGON DISMANTLED 275
The attempt to defuse the mythology of Jesus being
literally God, the theology of hyperbole used to stop him
from becoming properly human, and the redefinition of
transcendence
The Profoundest Mystery 279
The Essence of Christianity 287
The Crunch Point 289
The Final Picture 291

Epilogue 295
Notes 304
Bibliography 314
Index 321

Acknowledgements

Once again I am indebted to my partner Robin Mosley for her support and ongoing editorial efforts on my behalf; Thelma Mosley for her careful reading of the completed manuscript; my editor John Baldock for his encouragement and many helpful suggestion re content and structure; and Michael Mann, Chairman of Element Books, for his unswerving belief in my work. Thanks also to the many people at Element who gave of their expertise, and to the many scholars whose works I have consulted, and without whose efforts my own understanding could not have reached maturity. Anything of a scholarly nature achieved herein is due to their prodigious efforts, any mistakes, oversights or general inadequacies the result of my own shortcomings.

Author's Note

In an eighty-four page leather-bound Latin text entitled *De Exorcismiset Suplicationbus Quibusdam*, the Catholic Church claims to have presented a more subtle and sophisticated definition of evil for the millenium. This is a welcome reappraisal containing some serious adjustments to previous thinking, but as Church officials are quick to point out, it supports Pope John Paul II's recent assertion affirming the devil's existence. Fundamentally, nothing has really changed. The devil is still interpreted as an 'entity' with the power to possess. Human beings are still seen as vulnerable to intelligent forces of evil. The medieval vision which underpins this text is still operative in spite of major advances in medicine and psychiatry.

The Church may accept that many cases of exorcism in the New Testament reflect mental illness and not possession, but the present pope continues to believe that in a small percentage of cases possession did occur, and still occurs today. Bishop Carrado Balducci, one of Italy's famous exorcists, admits that out of every 1000 cases only 6 are probably ever genuine, but that is enough to keep the doctrinal clock ticking. Few Catholics may agree with him, but when all is said and done, the Church is not governed by opinion, but by doctrine, and doctrine claims that a literal spirit of evil is abroad in the world and has to be combated.

This suggests that in spite of an updating of language, and an attempt to accommodate the modern world, the old fear of things that go bump in the night is alive and well. Superstition still plays a large part in Catholic doctrine, and I have attempted to analyse such thinking in *The Dark Side of God*. It is therefore my hope that it will assist others to construct a vision in tune with reality, so avoiding the possibility of psychological and intellectual distortion.

Douglas Lockhart
Tasmania, 1999

When you approach a town, you shall lay seizure to it, and when the Lord your God delivers it into your hand, you shall put all its males to the sword. You may, however, take as your booty the women, the children, the livestock, and everything in the town – all its spoils – and enjoy the spoil of your enemy which the Lord your God gives you. In the towns which the Lord your God is giving you as a heritage, you shall not let a soul remain alive.   DEUTERONOMY 20:12–16

And they warred . . . as the Lord commanded and slew all the males. And they slew the Kings . . . and took all the women and their little ones . . . And Moses was wroth . . . and said unto them. Have ye saved all the women and the little ones alive? Now therefore kill every male among the little ones, and kill every women that hath known man by lying with him. But all the women and female children that have not known a man, keep alive for yourselves.   NUMBERS 31:7–18

A blessing on them who seized your babies and dashed them against rocks.   PSALM 137:9

. . . the Catholic Popes were also acting in accordance with the dictates of the Old Testament Lord of hosts. In consequence, hundreds of thousands of Moslems and Jews, and women and children, were sexually tortured, slaughtered, spitted, and roasted alive, and their cities and villages pillaged and set ablaze. All in the name of God and Christ.

RHAWN JOSEPH

. . . despite the 'infallible' proclamations of the Catholic Church, mass murder, torture, rape, pedophilia, and the castration of young boys were probably not what Jesus Christ had in mind when he preached his gospel.   RHAWN JOSEPH
Neuropsychiatry, Neuropsychology,
and Clinical Neuroscience

Prologue

The dark side of God is the underlying theme of this book, for that is the side which confounds and scares and bedevils us, one might say. For who can not be interested in a God who so often decides to be absent when most needed? Jesus had to deal with this absent God on the cross, and many other Jews have given up their religion as a result of the Holocaust. Equally, many Christians have turned their backs on Christianity because they sensed the absence of God as indicative of there being no God at all. No God at all. Nothing recognizably intelligent to regulate the extraordinary forces of the universe, or soften the drives of the human mind. Nothing at all to fall back on when life spits out its nastiness and love crumples in the face of anger, resentment and unfaithfulness. No God at all. Just a great silence and an emptiness.

But not quite empty, this universe, this strangely shaped chunk of space and time. A self with consciousness holding the whole scary edifice together, and a planet so infested with life that one can only marvel at its fecundity. So the next question is: Why life? And the question after that: Why anything? Why sight and hearing and love? Why horses and dung beetles and birds of paradise? Why self-consciousness? And why death? Why the death of all life after a little flutter, a little span of minutes, months or years? And most important of all, why evil? Why the concentration camps and the suffering? Or are such questions basically meaningless? Is there perhaps no point in asking them at all in the face of cosmic indifference, natural catastrophe and the vagaries of human nature?

If there is no God, no intelligible force behind the whole extraordinary edifice, then how has it all come about? How did the Big Bang result, for instance, in me sitting on a chair in a dressing gown having a cup of tea with the morning paper spread out before me? Looked at in this way, the idea of processes of increasing complexity explaining every aspect of life seems inadequate, and that in spite of the fact that such processes have obviously been at work. We incline to the suspicion that something very strange lies behind it all, something mysteriously intelligent. But as all the hard evidence suggests not just an absent God, but no God at all, then we are left, like our little planet, suspended in an emptiness, a darkness and a terrible silence.

Just the white noise of space and a planet in trouble because of over-population, acid rain, rampant pollution, stock piles of atomic weapons and the virus of sectarian ideas run riot. No God at all. Just genocide, starvation, torture, murder, self-interest and shoddy sentiments to juggle with. Quite an evil place, really, this planet Earth, when one is honest with oneself. A concentration camp in its own right where the inmates are murdered by degree, by life. All the beauty merely an interesting backdrop for this rabid little play to work itself out to the end. The end will be some kind of cataclysm, we are told, the collision of our planet with a comet, the dying of our sun, the Big Bang in reverse. Like us, our planet, and even the universe, has only so long to live. So in an attempt to combat the emptiness, explain the darkness and reinterpret the silence, we invented religion. God is there in spite of everything suggestive of the contrary. It is not his fault that cars crash or children suffer or love dies. He was the creator, the instigator, and he has a majestic plan for the whole edifice, a purpose, a playing out of events to a conclusion simply too big for our small minds to grapple with. Even death is part of the puzzle; we will go on after death and be made to face the consequences of our deeds while alive – the afterlife is an interrogation session.

The Christian baseline is this: Jesus died on the cross to redeem all human beings from their sins; all we have to do is accept this glorious fact, live a Christian life, and everything is fixed up for all eternity. What could be simpler? Those beyond the confines of Christendom with more exotic religious notions are . . . well, mistaken. Hindus and Buddhists are very nice people, but . . . Jews and the followers of Islam are equally nice, but . . . and anthropologists, sociologists, biologists, physicists and mathematicians are all very nice and terribly clever, but . . . Christianity is really where it is all at – not to understand this is not to understand anything at all.

What must be understood, Christians tell us, is that in spite of being made by God the world is in the grip of an all-encompassing evil. The world is not evil in itself, it is in the grasp of evil; and the whole extraordinary business of being alive is the working out of a plan of Salvation conceived in the mind of God before the creation of our world. We are, unwittingly, engaged in a battle between good and evil, between love and hate, between God and the Devil. Evil is not simply the result of bad or inadequate perception in action; it is an immensely powerful and independent force or energy lying behind the breakdown of our lives and our societies. There is an archetypal dimension to evil which can invade and control our lives.

Christian orthodoxy generally handles this message with some dexterity, allowing for metaphor, and much else; but those of a traditionalist persuasion are forthright both in their literal acceptance of such ideas, and in their condemnation of those who do not accept their premise as basic and self-evident. So there is a split in Christian ranks as to how such a message should be conveyed and the result is a theological and intellectual debate of some ferocity. It does not matter to which section, or side, of Christianity one belongs, the debate is evident. Whether Catholic or Protestant, every congregation has its hardliners, its liberals, its radicals, its fence-sitters and on top of it all have appeared apologists for a re-evaluation of Christianity in the light of recent historical and scientific research which sets many a believer's teeth on edge. Such believers have a ready answer for those demanding a fair go on the level of academic or scholastic probing: evil forces are behind all such approaches. Complex theories which undermine the enchanting stories of Scripture and attack the Christian message are quite obviously inspired by God's antagonist, the Devil. To say that Christ's death on the cross does not mean what the Church says it means, is to be in the clutches of an evil power.

In relation to Catholicism, the historical underpinnings for such a state of affairs is not hard to identify; there is no need to travel further back than the reign of Pope Pius X (1903–14) to discover why such a head-in-the-sand attitude toward scholarship and any form of learned debate exists. What Jesus really believed and taught was of no interest to Pius and those closest to him, only what the Church taught *about* Jesus and his teachings – 'tradition' was all. So afraid did this Pope become as the Modernists closed in on facts which the Church wanted neither to know nor to be made known, that he encouraged the formation of a spy ring, a Secret Service within the Vatican over and above that of those members of the hierarchy who spied on members of the hierarchy itself.¹ Fear of heresy among the learned was the reason for such measures, and the witch-hunting which ensued halted all Catholic scholarly efforts to keep pace with modern learning. In fact Catholic scholarship had later to work at a frenzied pace to make up for the wasted years.

As is only to be expected, there are those who persist in presenting a sanitized image of Pius, those who would have us believe that any priest who questions his Church is automatically a traitor. So Joseph Brasher, SJ, can speak of '. . . priests, infected with bad philosophical ideas and worse theological ones . . . striving to make modernism prevail against the Church'.² Furthermore, modernism should not be confused with a devotion to, say, television or to atomic research, that's a blind. No, modernism is much more dangerous: it is the liberal adaptation of the dogmas of faith to the fads of the day. So the writings of leading modernists were banned and an encyclical and a decree published to help tear such thinking out by the roots. This was followed by the demand that every priest take an oath against Modernism, a move which completely stifled the movement for reassessment and reinterpretation.

Pope Pius X died on 20 August 1914. It is said that miracles took place as the people thronged around his tomb. Beatified by Pius XII in June 1951, this bulwark against the development of a Christianity capable of making informed decisions was canonized in May 1954.

Things have changed dramatically since those days; or so we are led to believe. The argument used by grassroots Catholics to disarm people such as myself is to say that there is much, much more to Catholicism than a few stuffy old bishops and cardinals with their heads turned back to front. All is well with the monolith; it groans a bit, complains a bit, but it is fundamentally steady. The people at the bottom of the pile, the ordinary Joes, are way ahead of the hierarchy in Rome. The Pope may rumble, even ramble, on about this and that but little attention is paid to his pronouncements. Yes, he's still head of the Church, and is to be respected, but few educated people accept what he believes about contraception and much else. So it is to the educated rank and file that one must look to find out what the Church actually believes, for it is among these radical Catholics that one finds the most advanced spiritual ideas and practices in daily use, and it is among these same doers that the Church's future is being forged.

I think that this view is basically correct, but it has to be pointed out that the radical Christians of the Church's early historical period believed something alarmingly similar. In receipt of experiential knowledge which revealed their Church, even then, to be overly reliant on intellectual constructions of spiritual reality, those adventurous souls were made to submit to Rome's authority. It was either that or be named heretic and suffer the penalty for not following the established line of thinking. Some paid lip service and kept what they knew to themselves; others were outspoken agents for change and paid the price. Some disappeared into monasteries and kept their discoveries under close wraps. Today, the price for overt heresy is not the same as it was then (burning people at the stake, torturing them, or putting them to the sword in the name of Jesus is now considered to be in bad taste), but the Church's desire to reinstate something of its old authority is never far from its mind. It is unlikely that the old punishments will ever be brought back, but the hierarchy has both the capacity and desire to turn the clock back and should not be underestimated. In fact, I think that such a move is now seriously under way on a number of fronts; the writing on the wall is plainly visible and the hierarchy of the Roman Church is running scared.

What this means is that the Church will once again attempt to stifle the processes of spiritual growth and development and replace such natural expressions of the human spirit with a return to lifeless dogma. Aware of this tendency, the psychologist Carl Jung wrote in 1979 that: 'The advocates of Christianity squander their energies in the mere preservation of what has come down to them, with no thought of building on to the house and making it roomier.'[3] This aptly describes the problem, and it signals an attitudinal pattern which will, I believe, become more and more evident as we move towards the year 2000, with its inbuilt end of the millennium fears. For if the Church is anything, it is consistent; it believes in 'belief' with a passion, returning to its circumscribed world of dogma and the Creed whenever it feels threatened. As it is now constantly under threat due to a world-wide revival of interest in the historical origins of Christianity, the only path left open to it is back into the dim shadows of medieval certainty.

Why should this be? Why should the Church react in such a fashion? What is it afraid will be discovered that makes it so nervous? First, there must be the fear that its so widely and for so long acclaimed continuity of doctrinal authority from apostolic to sub-apostolic to patristic Church will finally be revealed by scholars to be a nonsense. The claim is, in essence, a fabrication based on New Testament documents tampered with and interpreted in such a fashion as to obscure the rampant discontinuity between such very different periods of religious expression. There is also the constant threat of material coming to light which further reveals Jesus for what he really was: a human being, an ordinary man of flesh and blood who donned the mantle of the Jewish Messiah and, as such, was rejected by the religious establishment of his day. He was not God in person setting in motion a process of Salvation earmarked to become a fixed system of belief in a Church envisaged by himself before the foundation of the world. Investing everything in those two claims, the Church is forever apprehensive that its inflated opinion of its own importance, and its similarly inflated portrayal of Jesus, will finally collapse. And rightly so, for the myth is not only exhausted, and therefore vulnerable, it is also now disintegrating as a result of its own inherent extravagance.

Dr Hugh Schonfield describes the basic lie told by the Church as a 'thumper'; in fact such a thumper that few have seen fit properly to question its claim that it is in receipt of the 'true tradition of the Apostles'.[4] At first glance, everything seems to be in its place; but a second or third glance reveals all kinds of historical anomalies. The standard view is that the Apostolic gave way to the sub-Apostolic, the sub-Apostolic, after losing focus, to the patristic. But it wasn't like that at all. By claiming an imagined mantle of Apostolic authority through a bogus connection with the Apostle Peter, and unwilling to hand authority back to the Nazarenes when this group of sectarian Jews recovered from the Roman invasion of Judea, the Church took control of the Jesus myth and progressively changed it until it fitted neatly into the Greco-Roman mind-set. Disallowing and replacing Nazarene dynastic authority – that is, the monarchical succession stemming from Jesus and his brother James – with the purely invented notion of an episcopal succession through Peter as first Pope, it further muddied the waters by presenting a Jesus whose identity and intentions were so utterly at odds with Nazarene sensibility that these sectaries took to writing their own propaganda by way of defence. And so the derogatory term 'apocryphal gospels' came into existence, to describe primary documents of great historical importance which were being dismissed as mere curiosities.

This was not the last time the Church would be involved in propaganda, in forgery and textual subterfuge; it would go on to perfect the art and bring the whole weight of its magisterial imagination to bear on the problem of tidying up loose ends, filling in blanks and creating new vistas of historical self-promotion. Peter de Rosa records that by the mid-1100s the Code of Canon Law was 'peppered with three centuries of forgeries and conclusions drawn from them'.[5] Which is to say that not only were there multiple forgeries in existence by that time, but that whole echelons of theology and Curial Law were built on those forgeries. Nor would the game stop there; it continues up to the present and results in such an explosion of doctrinal fiascos that even to consider them results in intellectual vertigo.

It is not thought 'nice' to accuse the Roman Catholic Church of such skulduggery, at least not in so many words. But I am not concerned with being nice, I'm concerned with the fact that Catholicism has wilfully distorted the picture of its own origins and growth to such an extent that all one can do is gasp at its cupidity. Paranoid in its desire to be thought of as carrying God's truth without any hint of deviation, this Great Church, as it is often called, has lied its way through the centuries and been one cause of some of the most hideous episodes known to humanity. Patently false in its claims to both sanctity and wisdom, it has nevertheless exercised such control over the Western imagination that its early stages of growth have not been examined with the thoroughness they deserve. So we must travel the highways and byways of history and examine the most unlikely happenings in the most unlikely of places before even a glimpse of what has been going on in the name of Jesus Christ can be uncovered. For it is in the dim light of the early centuries, and of medieval times, and even of our own 'enlightened' century, that we find stark evidence of the Church's long-term policy of deception. Not always a conscious policy, but clever enough and sustained enough to warrant real doubts as to its spiritual integrity.

As already stated, the underlying theme of this book is to explore the dark side of God. Such a side undoubtedly exists, manifesting itself in our psyches, in our individual natures, in nature itself, and in the institutions we create. We are more than we seem, and there is more to the world we inhabit than is immediately obvious. At first glance everything is as it ought to be; at a second glance we are confronted by the embryonic realization that everything is just a touch more complicated than we first thought. By the third and fourth glance we are caught up in a series of mysteries so demanding that we fear we will never make sense of our lives at all; from there on in we have to brace ourselves for the final struggle, the final onslaught of doubt and fear and incomprehension. *That* is the challenge of our lives, of our physical, mental and spiritual existences, to partake of this extraordinary journey of exploration and not to stop too soon. The danger we face is the danger of giving in to inadequate explanations, inadequate formulations of knowledge and experience because they cause us less pain. Or so we think. I would argue that in the end they cause us the greatest pain of all, the pain of knowing, deep within, that we have lied to ourselves, and to the world.

Ultimately we may not arrive at the answers we have so diligently searched for, the answers we have hoped for. But I believe that it is better to have tried and failed than not to have tried at all. And I have a suspicion, born from experience, that to step out on such a journey is in itself to set in motion a mystery that is profound in its own right.

PART ONE

Darkness Visible

CHAPTER ONE

The Challenge

The Holy Roman Catholic Church replaces the Roman Empire, turns imperial, develops a mythology of intelligent evil, flexes its pontifical authority in the extermination of heretics and sets the pace for Hitler's final solution

Some years ago I read an account of Jewish families being herded into a concentration camp. Straight from a ghetto, and after an horrendous train journey in cattle trucks, without food or sanitation, these hapless individuals stumbled out into the light to face even greater horror: the horror of a system specifically designed to exterminate them. Incomprehensible as this may now seem, such intent was then abroad in the world and most people know of at least one story sufficiently terrible to thickly underline the depth of degeneration reached. Some of the individuals involved in perpetrating such horror later admitted to real stress as they went about their business; all was not ruthless efficiency. The hierarchy in Berlin were well aware of the strain their specially trained units were under as they battered and butchered the inhabitants of the concentration camps. The camp administrators and staff obviously became brutalized to an alarming degree, but there were times when at least some of them seem to have buckled under the weight of trying to fulfil the extraordinary wishes of the Third Reich. Ultimately, no judgement can be passed on those who revelled in their butchery without remorse, for who can guess at the pathologies they carried, at the aberrant states of consciousness they considered normal, at the blanking-out mechanisms of psyche operative as they blindly obeyed the dictates of superiors to whom a strangely twisted ideology had become God.

Since its beginnings, Christianity has considered evil closely related to intelligent but destructive forces on some other level of being. At its theological heart, Christianity continues to believe in some such arrangement and the Third Reich is conceived of as having attempted to harness these negative forces. Believing himself to be a type of Messiah (a fact now admitted to by scholars), Adolf Hitler hoped to liberate men and women from what he considered their principal weakness, lack of will, and it was this vision of the human will both liberated and channelled which quickly gave rise to policies of subjugation and control not seen since the heyday of the Roman Empire, well not entirely, since the Church itself had engaged in similar practices the moment it acquired a strong, secular arm. The principal difference between the two systems was that the Church wanted human beings to submit their wills to God's will, whereas Hitler wanted them to submit their wills to *his* will. Quite a different focus one might think; but not so different when one realizes that God's will actually meant the Pope's will. For was not the Pope God's representative on Earth? Was he not the channel through which Christ himself made known his doctrinal wishes? This had become the Catholic standpoint in the early centuries and, in a curiously oblique fashion, Hitler saw himself as the spiritual force that would both correct and complete the papacy's exhaustive attempt to bring the whole of humanity into a state of obedience.

THE HISTORICAL BACKDROP

The Church which replaced the Roman Empire developed a theology of the human will subservient to God through Christ and his Church which men like Hitler came to envy and copy. So, in a strange way, the Christian Church, the Roman Empire and the Third Reich are all part of the same puzzle, each progressively influenced by the other and curiously linked in style, ceremonial and symbol. God and not the Devil may reign over this Church, but the dark side of that God is never far off in the shape of rules and dogmas which are to be obeyed and believed in without question.

What is not generally realized is that the Church 'Christianized' ancient Rome's imperial ideology, borrowed such terms as 'diocese', 'prefecture', 'vicariate' and 'consistory', incorporated court ritual into its forms of worship, adopted an autocratic attitude, refocused the whole bag of tricks on Jesus and made him into a holy ruler beyond the skies. Never again would Jesus be seen as he had once been; instead he became a kind of divine emperor who

stamped each pope's reign with approval. Seated on purple cushions and treated, eventually, as a universal cosmic emperor who
just happened to be the Son of God, the Jesus of the gospels
melted clean away. Armed with impressive insignia, privileges and
secular dignity, the ministers of this new Roman order progressively created for themselves an aura of authority sanctioned from
above. So successful were they in this operation that Hilaire Belloc
wrote of the Roman Empire that it had never perished at all, but
had simply been transformed into the Catholic Church. Thomas
Hobbes was of the same opinion; he saw the Roman Church as
the ghost of the deceased Roman Empire.

During the first three centuries of the Church's existence, the
bishops of Rome were elected in much the same way as bishops
elsewhere, but from the fourth century through to the eleventh,
the election of Rome's bishops (not universally recognized in the
West as 'popes' with papal authority until the eleventh century)
turned into a purely political affair. Up until the fifth century the
'elections' were controlled by the Roman emperors and by
the eleventh century the papacy was virtually the family possession of the counts of Tusculum. In his *Anatomy of the Catholic
Church*, Gerard Noel succinctly sums up this situation: 'Temporal
rulers stopped at nothing to secure the appointment of their
chosen candidates. Coercion was freely used as was, on occasion,
forcible deposition and imposition.'[1] All was not as it seemed.
Tusculum control of the papacy only came to an end when
Benedict IX was bribed so handsomely that he voluntarily
abdicated St Peter's throne.

The closing of the first millennium saw the beginning of a state
of affairs within the Church which beggars the imagination: popes
were done to death in various ways, imprisoned, caught in inces-
tuous relationships and brought to their deaths through amorous
excess. Men who were not even in holy orders became pope;
family dynasties ran the papacy; anti-Semitic behaviour was rife.
Noel sums up the situation thus: 'In what direction could the
Christian community look to be saved from drowning in a
cesspool of debauchery and political intrigue?'[2] Harsh words. In
the fourth century Sylvester I claimed absolute 'primacy' for
himself; in the fifth Leo the Great pushed the notion of papal
supremacy much further by reinstating the heathen imperial title
Pontifex Maximus. From that moment on Rome's bishops classified themselves as supreme high priest, and began to function with

ever greater daring. Carrying a manufactured authority, the papacy's extraordinarily conceited notion of itself grew steadily until in 1846 Pius IX excelled all of his predecessors and introduced the notion of papal infallibility. Convinced that some mighty oracular power was at his disposal, he assumed total control of the Church and made his college of advisory bishops obsolete. As they are still.

By the time of the German Third Reich, the Church under Pius XI was well ahead of that regime in its brutal treatment of the Jews; it is on record that when Hitler talked with Bishop Berning of Osnabrück in 1936, he intimated that he saw no difference whatsoever between the Catholic Church and National Socialism, and explained that he was only doing what the Church herself had done for fifteen hundred years. By 1179 the Third and Fourth Councils of the Lateran had codified the Church's attitudes and made Jews wear a badge of shame, forbade them to interact with Christians, kept them out of administration and trade and locked them into ghettos at night. Countless thousands were slaughtered during the Crusades and, as the Catholic historian Peter de Rosa records, millions suffered and died horribly down the ages as a result of disastrous theology.[3]

In 1209, at the instigation of Pope Innocent III, 30,000 knights from northern Europe descended on southern France with the intention of rooting out what was termed the Great Heresy. As a result, the whole territory was laid waste. Richard Leigh has described the situation as the first case of genocide in European history.[4] Town after town fell to Innocent's advancing army, the people being slaughtered *en masse*. In the town of Beziers alone 15,000 men, women and children were put to the sword. The whole of the Languedoc fell, Perpignan, Narbonne, Carcassonne and Toulouse going the way of Beziers. Called a 'Crusade', and lasting an astonishing forty years, Christian knights killed Christians, Jews, Cathar heretics and anyone else who stood in their way. The Crusaders did not differentiate; all who stumbled into their path suffered the same fate. Backed, eventually, by the ecclesiastical tribunal, or Inquisition, under the watchful eye of Domingo de Guzman, a Spanish churchman and founder of the Dominican Order, the cruelty was refined, no less than 100,000 Cathar and Cathar sympathizers being tortured and burned.

In such a fashion was the way for Hitler's Final Solution prepared, and the Church has not yet properly acknowledged her role in the persecution of the Jews, a persecution which, as de Rosa has made clear, makes the cruelties of Hitler pale in comparison with the cruelties attributed to Christian theologians and contemplative monks. Dark indeed was this God who whispered his wishes into the ear of popes and cardinals; and highlighted now since John Paul II announced his desire that the Church consider closely its treatment of the Jews throughout the last two millennia. Examining the behaviour of the Church towards the Jews from the earliest days of Christianity to the present, and including a special study of the Holocaust, a special 26-member commission composed of clergy and academics is to determine whether accusations such as Peter de Rosa's are to be taken seriously or not.

Catholics cocooned in their theologically constructed faith believed that the Church had all the answers, and that these answers could not and should not be tampered with. There was no other teacher than the Church. God had sanctioned the Church, and deviance from what the Church taught should be condemned as heresy and punished. It was as simple as that. In 1907 those who dared question established Church thinking were brought to book, and the persecution of such thinkers continued until 1914, when Benedict XV was elected Pope. Finding himself on the previous pope's 'hit-list' as a suspected Modernist, Benedict suppressed this Inquisitional-type spy-ring and returned things to normal. But damage to the Church's capacity to redefine itself was already integral, and it would take the revolutionary presence of John XXIII to finally move the whole edifice towards a proper reassessment. Noel refers to this reassessment as 'the great going-back', by which he means that Catholic scholarship eventually got back on track and allowed the latest historical discoveries to seep into its consciousness.

In spite of this forging ahead, however, this apparent reassessment of her past, this seeming attempt to be open and responsible and reasonable, traditionalist views and beliefs of a medieval cast continued to control the Church. It could be said that the Church played a game with herself, a game which allowed her to store away her scholarly findings and initiate a highly controlled release of such findings to the seven hundred million men, women and children who formed her gigantic flock. So while there was a semblance of openness on the scholarly level, the method of handling the results of such scholarship were bound to the old premise that the 'faith' of the people must be safeguarded at all cost. No matter that such an approach could result only in confusion and perplexity; it was more important to have continuity than admit failure on the level of interpretations once considered beyond dispute. Whatever the findings of historians, anthropologists, archaeologists and others, the Church was the Church and she was not going to disappear. Her teachings about God, Jesus, the Virgin Mary, the Holy Spirit and the Devil, although hard to accept on many levels, remained the cornerstone of what had been, and would continue to be, the principal regulating religious force of the Western world. There was a further dimension to this, which scholarship, intellectual debate and ordinary secular intelligence were not able to penetrate, and it was the job of the Church to ensure that that dimension was not entirely eroded. Whatever the world might think of the idea, for the Church evil and good exist as opposing forces, and Christ's life and death are our only conduit towards comprehending what that might mean.

In 1976, the great explorer and writer Laurens van der Post pinpointed a logical anomaly in relation to the above. 'The coming of Christ,' he observed, 'had abolished neither the darkness nor the Devil. They existed, still active and valid as ever in life.'[5] This was an important observation; nothing had changed in relation to good and evil except the creation of a theological escape hatch through which every single human being had to pass in order to avoid damnation and the torments of hell. As this close friend of Carl Jung's came to realize, God's world was still full of 'an old night and unrepentant evil'. Whether we liked it or not, evil was a living element of reality with which we each personally had to deal; and it seemed that that was how God wanted it. The crucifixion of Jesus, in spite of an elaborate 'victory' theology created over the centuries, had not quite fulfilled its earlier promise. John's gospel had Jesus promise that his death on the cross would result in the prince of this world (Satan) being cast out; but Satan had been as active as ever after the event, and this suggested a delayed fulfilment. Paul believed that the power of the Devil had been destroyed by Jesus' death; but this was flatly contradicted by passages showing that the Devil had continued in his role of devouring beast. So it was not an immediate victory that Christianity had won over evil, it was a victory to come as the Book of Revelation made clear. Only the Second Coming of Christ would initiate the casting of Satan and his hosts into the lake of fire and brimstone.

Satan's 'hosts' were composed of fallen angelic beings and the human beings seduced by them. The lesser angels who followed Satan into exile were now 'demons' and the human beings in his pay were, for want of a better word, 'Satanists'. The only problem with all of this was that the angels said to have followed Satan, then called Lucifer ('light-bearer'), into exile, had apparently done no such thing. According to the Jewish Apocrypha they had fallen in love with the daughters of men long after Lucifer's fall, taken them to wife and fathered children of great historical renown. As a result, impiety had taken root on the Earth and God had to destroy almost everyone on earth with a great flood. In the Book of Enoch, God chains his lusting angels in the 'dark places of the earth' to await judgement and by inexplicable means their gigantic progeny turn into evil spirits, or demons. In the Books of Adam and Eve, written in the last quarter of the first century, and believed to be either Christian in origin, or influenced by Christianity, Satan incites other angels to disobey, and all are cast out of Heaven. So went the topsy-turvy stories of how evil had come to this beautiful earth of ours and one can only wonder at the mythological contradictions, not to mention the unresolved issue of how angels from a non-physical dimension could experience sexual attraction.

According to Christian teaching, one tenth of all the hosts of Heaven followed Satan down to our realm, and this exodus, along with what appears to have been a subsequent migration of angelic beings to Earth for purely carnal reasons, leaves one with the impression of a God curiously ignorant of his angels' needs. Heaven riddled with pride and carnality? What kind of place had Heaven become that such a change in character and atmosphere could have taken place? And why hadn't the ringleaders been dealt with sooner? And what of the physical aspect; were these beings somehow human in spite of their divine origins?

The angels of the Old Testament were called *malachim* – literally, 'emissaries' – and constituted a kind of divine postal service between Heaven and Earth. Prior to the destruction of Sodom and Gomorrah, angels of a distinctly anthropomorphic type had appeared to Lot and although human in appearance had been immediately recognized as angels. In spite of looking human, there seems to have been something about angels that gave them away, some recognizable characteristic or capacity which earmarked them as *different*. Appearing as if by magic seems to have been one such characteristic; arriving physically above the heads of their contactees another. Abraham, we are told, had to 'raise his eyes' to look at three men who appeared; and he asks them not to pass over him, and then invites them to wash their feet, rest and eat. Curious stuff. Having done so, these angels then journey on to Sodom and the task of mass destruction they had come to execute.

Many centuries later, Augustine of Hippo would maintain that the Devil and his angels were expelled from Heaven and cast into darkness. By this, he did not mean the bowels of the Earth, but the Earth's atmosphere. This was the realm mysteriously given to them by God and, although a prison in comparison with Heaven, it constituted a vast area within which, and from which, they could exercise their desire to subvert the human race. Having once been angels, they could not be robbed of that status, merely demoted; they would retain their angelic bodies, their ethereal natures *and* their extraordinary powers. Lords of the 'upper air', they could move around as they had once done on God's behalf, with speed and surprise on their side. As can be imagined, the contest between fallen angel and human being was really no contest at all; at least not until Jesus appeared on the scene. After his redemptive death on the cross, Satan and his angelic horde could no longer push human beings around: the name of Jesus was all they needed to put Satan and his minions to instant flight.

With regard to this, Norman Cohn has put his finger on one very important aspect: the later Christian exaggeration of, and morbid interest in, the demonic. The dark fascination filling medieval descriptions of things Satanic is quite lacking in the disputations of the early Church Fathers. In fact Origen was convinced that Satan's power was actually lessening in strength; for when a Christian successfully stands up to a demon in the name of Jesus, and wins, he believed that that demon lost its power to tempt another and had to return to hell. By the late Middle Ages this kind of confidence had been undermined and all but forgotten. Satan was by then everywhere, in every dark nook and cranny, and he had successfully broken through and enlisted the help of human individuals to corrupt the faith from within the Church itself. Heresy-mongers flourished, and their often subtle rearrangements of the faith were designed to lead whole sections of the Church astray. And so was born that attitude which feared knowledge and remained aloof from the whisperings of a rudimentary science. The myth of a Church uniquely in possession of

eternal truths was what had to be believed, and God help anyone
who contradicted that carefully elaborated idea with a few ideas
of their own!

This brings us back to the reign of Pius X, during which all
books and magazines produced by Roman Catholics were censored prior to publication and priests had to obtain permission to
write to or for a newspaper. In fact, Pius instigated such a purge
of scholars' investigations that the effects were still being felt fifty
years after his death, creating a situation within which censorship
was commonplace. Père Lagrange, in scripture, and Louis
Duchesne, in history, were made to toe the papal line. In particular, Duchesne was forced to give up his chair at the Institut
Catholique in Paris and his seminal book on the origins of
Christianity was placed on the Index.[6] Even Angelo Roncalli (the
future Pope John XXIII) came under suspicion of being a
Modernist. The result of it all was a Church massively out of step
with the modern world and its decisive historical and scientific
discoveries. The next handful of popes did little to correct the
situation, and even Pius XII, a forerunner of John XXIII in many
of his ideas, failed to move the Church away from absolutism.
Jesus remained crowned, seated on purple cushions, his
autocratic stare focused on an imaginary past. The Church dupli-
cated that stare by remaining aloof, unapproachable and beyond
criticism as it contemplated its future.

GOD'S SHADOW

The human mind is capable of sustaining a terrible darkness, and
this darkness, for both Laurens van der Post and Carl Jung, was
related to a fundamental archetypal force with a troubling double
aspect – God, it seems, has a 'shadow' of some proportions. In
spite of much Old Testament evidence to the contrary, the Church
was convinced that God and the Devil were separate forces in
keen opposition, and that through Christ she had the means to
control the Devil. As someone who wished to destroy Christianity
utterly and replace it with a religious organization of his own,
Hitler was a 'Satanist' by definition; he believed in opposing forces
battling on some alien dimension of existence for all eternity.[7] As
there was plenty of evidence to place Hitler in the esoteric, or
occultist, camp, that in itself was interpreted as a fundamental

proof that the Church's theology of evil accurately reflected a hidden reality. No thought was given to the fact that Hitler's occult vision was only possible because the Church had invented that vision; and no thought, either, to the fact that two such inventions in collaboration did not necessarily constitute a reality. But real enough in effect, in intention; as if a reality to believers on both sides of the fence.

In a letter written by the occultist Adolf Lanz in 1932, Hitler is described not only as a 'pupil', but in prophetic tones described as someone who '. . . will one day be victorious and develop a movement that makes the world tremble'.[8] Hitler came to power one year later. Lanz, a renegade Cistercian monk of six years' standing, had founded a racialist organization called the Order of the New Templars (Ordo Novo Templi), and based its philosophy on the legends of the Holy Grail. In his book, *Occult Reich*, J H Brennan states that this new Order was deeply interested in the concept of an Aryan master race, and that for reasons of purity it introduced the idea of selective breeding. Heinrich Himmler saw to it that Lanz's ideas were put into brutal practice, and his suggested methods for dealing with inferior races were incorporated into Nazi strategy. If this fact alone is not sufficient to convince one of an occult background to Hitler's thinking, then Adolf Lanz's choice of a flag bearing a swastika, in 1907, should be enough to sway opinion in that direction.

Impressed by the Church's ruthlessness down the centuries, Hitler copied that organization's basic shape and format on the political level, and with surprising thoroughness proceeded to house the whole hierarchal structure within a recognizable religious framework. Consciously designing the *Schutzstaffeln* (SS) units on the Society of Jesus, he left it to Himmler to develop this elitist group into a magically oriented order of super-obedient troops. Striving to control the human will through rigorous discipline and a breakdown of all sentiment, the Third Reich followed the Church's historical lead and began to harness the libidinal energy of the German people. Viewing Hitler as another Christ, as a modern Saviour who would free the human psyche from the sin of weakness (the Church's version of this was 'the weakness of sin'), the new Reich, like the Church, conceived of a kingdom without limit, a kingdom within which every knee would bow. In a strange twist of theology and mythology, the Führer's dark system of belief and methods of subjugation were unnervingly similar to that of the Church which proudly carried the symbols and titles of the old eagle-bedecked Roman Empire. Schooled in an occult system based on complex religious reasoning, every frightful thing conceived of and initiated by Hitler was a reflection of what the Church *in the name of Christianity* had itself inflicted on the world over the centuries. Of course, she had also done much good during those centuries, to delight the eye, gladden the heart and provide security in the face of a God so often felt to be absent. And the Third Reich intended, no doubt, to be just as kind and sensitive and supportive of its own as the Church had ever been.

But something else needs to be said in relation to this uncomfortable parallel between Church and Third Reich, for just as those who helped further Hitler's ends have denied any personal responsibility, claiming that they were simply 'obeying orders', so, too, have those who have furthered the more questionable objectives of the Church. The contortions undergone by the Church as she contemplates the quality of her relationship to the Jews over the last two thousand years are interesting to watch, and one wonders if her self-evaluation will prove any better than that of those who followed the orders of their political masters in Germany. The Church's interim document on the *Shoah* (Holocaust) betrays a mind-set incapable of facing historical reality, so it is highly unlikely that her final statement on its treatment of the Jews will be of any greater quality.

EVOLUTION OF THE DEVIL

At the theological level, Christianity spoke of an evil being of great power, a being in constant opposition to the Supreme Deity. Dante had described this being as a giant with three heads, coloured red, yellow and black, and down the centuries numerous descriptions of this being had held the human imagination in sway. More importantly, however, there resided behind such descriptions the idea of a once great angel of God fallen from the Divine presence, whose whole *raison d'être* was the moral destruction of the human race. And herein lay the heart of the puzzle, for how had such an august being fallen away from God when he was neither tainted by a physical nature, nor in receipt of human emotions? How had the sin of pride arisen in a mind with direct and constant access to the Supreme Being? Both Milton and Goethe saw Satan as a tragic, yet heroic and even reasonable, man of the world; and J B Priestley, along with Christopher Marlowe, had Satan capable of physical manifestation. This suggested that Satan, in a manner not yet properly understood, had a physical aspect. The popular notion of him was of a horned figure dressed in a one-piece suit of red and complete with pitchfork and cloven hooves. This image strongly influenced the public imagination, reducing what had once been considered a very dangerous being indeed to the level of a pantomime character whose kingdom was at the Earth's fiery centre.

So God, through Jesus, struggles with Satan, his one-time friend, companion and helper, and the world is split into two camps which must forever relentlessly oppose one another. In Satan's kingdom, the powers of darkness prevail; Christ's sole mission is the destruction of that kingdom. Unlike Yahweh in the Old Testament, the God of the New Testament is confronted by a Satan no longer in his pay, as it were, but by a being formidable in power and totally separate from himself. In the Old Testament Satan is one of God's courtiers, and as Norman Cohn observes, his achievement is that he forces God's hand against an innocent man, namely Job. But in the tale itself Job knows nothing of Satan; he ascribes his intolerable condition to God, and the reason for this may be that the prologue carries a theological view at variance with the story's main text. In earlier times the God of the Old Testament would have had no trouble with the role of tempter, but later this duty is passed over to Satan, and then separated from God altogether. Cohn points to a parallel story development about God tempting King David in 2 Samuel 24 (probably early tenth century) with a repeat of the same story in 1 Chronicles 21 (probable fourth century), where responsibility is switched from God to Satan. In the whole of the Old Testament, it is this text alone which suggests that Satan is himself a principle of evil, and it is the only time that the noun *śatan* (adversary) becomes a proper noun.[9]

With the development of monotheism in the Old Testament, the tribal God Yahweh eventually underwent a metamorphosis and emerged as omnipotent, omniscient and omnipresent. As such, there was no room for a serious counteractive evil of any dimension. So strenuously were these characteristics of God affirmed, that evil paled into insignificance. Satan, when he appeared at all, was God's accomplice, not his antagonist.

Norman Cohn interprets this state of affairs thus: 'Satan, in fact, developed out of Yahweh himself, in response to changing ideas about the nature of God.'[10] But after the incident between God and King David, the Jews developed what Cohn terms '. . . a new, complex and comprehensive demonology':[11] the age of the apocalyptic with its clear-cut dualism, its revelations and ambitions for the future was now the name of the game.

THE DELUSION OF SEPARATENESS

A different, more humanistic explanation for the existence of Satan is put forward by Geoffrey Hodson in *The Kingdom of the Gods*. Here, Satan is the personification of the 'I-making impulse from which arises the delusion of separateness'.[12] The Satan of popular theology and public imagination is little more than an excuse, a scapegoat to be blamed for the errors into which we all fall. This is a sophisticated approach to the question of what Satan or the Devil or Lucifer might mean; but it does not fully explain the idea of a being of concentrated demonic power as believed in by many Christians, and by others of a different religious persuasion. There is, under certain circumstances, it seems, something incredibly tangible about evil; which suggests that at its most concentrated it is more than a mere mode of perception, and sometimes a *presence which overpowers*. Exactly what this presence signifies is difficult to determine, but one thing is sure, and that is that once sensed, it is impossible to any longer consider it innocuous. The presence of evil is a truly terrifying experience which can neither be ignored, nor satisfactorily diluted by psychological theory. In fact it is sometimes so powerful that even the Church may fail when trying to deal with it.

But how can there be a Devil, a tangible and concentrated force of evil, if there is no God, indeed, if the capital 'D' devil is no more than a personification of the I-making impulse? And if the Devil is the opposite of God, and there is no God, then does that not automatically disallow the existence of the Devil? For if God is truly absent, truly non-existent and not merely in hiding, then it is axiomatic that the Devil too does not exist. Then again, if evil is merely the absence of good, as some Christians believe, then the very absence of the font of all good must surely initiate a monstrous evil into existence. This is of course to form an illegitimate mix of ideas, but this is the mix most of us carry at the back of our minds, and it gets us into endless trouble. The popular Christian theory of evil, dependent as it is on a God 'out there somewhere', and therefore in some unimaginable fashion an object, yet simultaneously not an object (otherwise God too would be bound by cosmic events), unwittingly promotes a topsy-turvy conception of evil which elevates it beyond its station, makes it concrete and in so doing reduces human beings to no more than playthings between gigantic opposing forces beyond time and space. So the question is: how can God be defined as all good if he allows an evil only marginally less powerful than himself to exist for purposes of ultimate victory? If an intelligent evil can constantly bedevil our minuscule hopes and aspirations, and on occasions subject us, like Job, to unbearable physical and mental torture, then the mind behind such a state of affairs has without doubt similar pathologies to our own. And this should come as no surprise, for is it not said that we are made in the image of God?

So is the Christian God mad? Is he perhaps insane? Or have we simply been misinformed about his mentality and habits? Could it be that the apparent absence of God has a significance far beyond the notion of desertion or non-existence? Could it be that the dark side of this creator God of ours has not been properly understood; indeed, that good and evil and the complex relationship between them constitute a mystery which we have to reinterpret for purposes of survival? In his engrossing and provocative book, *The Disappearance of God*, Richard Elliott Friedman suggests that we are at a crossroads, and must decide how to proceed on to our destiny.[13] But what exactly must we do or think or be to earn such a destiny? That is the question we have to ask, and our answer should be robust enough, compassionate enough and intelligent enough to avoid exclusiveness. If our answer is other than that, if we fall into exclusiveness, into narrow-mindedness and prejudice and self-opinionated certainty, then we have surely failed in our task. Exploration, not declaration, is the tack we need to take.

CHAPTER TWO

Les Fleurs du Mal

The problem of origins, the repercussions of a Church turned monarchical, and the attempt to cling to a vision of Jesus untouched by twentieth-century scholarship

On 12 March 1622, five Spaniards were canonized by Pope Gregory XIII; one of the five was Ignatius Loyola, founder of the Society of Jesus, better know as the *Jesuits*. A statue of Ignatius Loyola stands in the entrance hall of the Jesuit Curio in Rome, sporting a metal halo and a look suggesting ecstasy, but as the writer/broadcaster Macdonald Hastings suggests, it does not capture the man's true image or spirit. According to Hastings, Ignatius' true spirit does not rest in pious evocation '. . . but in his successors, the flesh and blood Jesuits who carry on his mission'.[1] Having been educated by the Jesuits, Hastings' remarks carry an insider's authority.

The new militant Order of dedicated priests created by Loyola was much admired during his lifetime, but his religious innovations were later considered dangerous. Accused of being secretly Protestant in orientation, the Jesuits were suppressed in 1773 by Pope Clement XIV, newly elected and in the pocket of the Bourbon princes who, in turn, were greatly influenced by the Jesuits' greatest enemy – European Freemasonry. But the Jesuits were not so easily got rid of. Under new names, they regrouped, and in Russia and Prussia continued to exist due to the refusal of Catherine and Frederick to promulgate the Pope's decree. Clement XIV died one year later, and his successor, Pius VI, promised a near-future restoration of the Order, a restoration inaugurated by Pius VII on 7 August 1814.

The word 'Jesuit' carries a special aura. The Ignatius Rule of the Jesuits demanded a level of obedience recognized as more severe and demanding than any other – an obedience sometimes referred to as 'corpse-like', a term taken from Ignatius Loyola's own notion of unconditional obedience being as unresisting as that of a cadaver. Today, Jesuit neophytes are men of mature judgement, often with university degrees, who already carry respect in the community; not 'beardless boys' straight from Jesuit school (to quote Macdonald Hastings). Things have changed. Jesuit candidates are now chosen by committee, one member being by necessity a psychiatrist. And if, for some reason, you decide to leave, you can; all you need do is apply to be released from your vows. Hastings tells us that one of the remarkable things about the Society of Jesus is that its members reflect every level of opinion, although they of course conform on the essentials of the faith.

But not always. Jesuit liberalism of thought was directly challenged as recently as 1981 by Pope John Paul II. Unhappy with the Order's attempt to fulfil Vatican II's agenda of radical reform, John Paul imposed Father Paolo Dezza, a nearly blind 79-year-old priest, on the Jesuits as Superior General. By way of reaction, and in conjunction with seventeen other leading Jesuits, the distinguished theologian Karl Rahner requested that the Holy Father permit them to elect their future Superior General without interference, but it was not to be. Blind obedience to the Pope's will on all matters was what Ignatius Loyola had promised, and blind obedience was what John Paul now demanded from the Society of Jesus; his choice of Paolo Dezza was perhaps an unconscious metaphor.

Freemasonry and powermongering may well have caused the downfall of the Society in 1773, but it seems that there was something inherently dangerous about Jesuit thinking from the very beginning. Ignatius himself was arrested and acquitted twice for heresy prior to entering the priesthood. This fact is mentioned without elaboration in the many texts on the saint's early life, and leaves one wondering what exactly it was about Ignatius Loyola's thinking that caused the religious authorities to arrest him. Acquitted he may have been, but he must have sufficiently nudged the line of orthodoxy to get treated in such a fashion. The later accusation that he and his Order were secretly Protestant in orientation suggests a freeing-up of theological attitudes. Whatever the case, the Jesuits have produced some interesting thinkers, and the present pope's reaction to the Order in 1981 suggests that they are again under close scrutiny.

DOUBLE DISAFFECTION

Two Jesuits who have used the special release clause and set aside their vows are Malachi Martin and Peter de Rosa. Martin withdrew from the Order in 1964, de Rosa in 1970, but for very different reasons and with very different results. During 1988, Peter de Rosa published *Vicars of Christ*, an historical study of the papacy's darker side, and in the same year Malachi Martin published *Hostage to the Devil*, a study of demonic possession and exorcism today.

Peter de Rosa left the Jesuits and the priesthood to marry and have children and to write his stinging attack on the papacy; Malachi Martin left because he felt the Society of Jesus had betrayed the Roman Catholic Church and undermined the authority of the very papacy de Rosa describes as 'rotten to its historical core'. This is not to inflate de Rosa's study; it is a devastating read which reveals the papacy as never having had the right to exercise supreme authority at any time. The book was appreciated for its honesty and seriousness by many Catholics, and has became a bestseller, attracting both admiring and damning comment from many quarters.

For example: Professor H J Richards of the University of East Anglia stated that *Vicars of Christ* was an alarming book because it '. . . contained so much that I did not know and should have known'. Having previously looked only at the brighter side of the papacy, Richards admits to finding de Rosa's pitiless search of its dark side 'shattering'. From the *Dublin Evening Herald* came a similar reaction, de Rosa being likened to a devil's advocate who opens the stained glass window and reveals that the Church's teachings were too often '. . . shaped by the whims of corrupt, despotic and fanatical popes'. The *Irish Times* followed suit, with Father Michael Keane quoting Hilaire Belloc and suggesting that the Church had to be divine otherwise it would not have lasted a fortnight considering the knaves who ran it; and Bill Ratchford of the BBC World Service reminded us that '. . . claims of infallibility mixed up with personal sexual impasses have had and could have dire consequences for millions of people'. To the *Sunday Press* de Rosa's exhaustive study of the papacy's dark side was a spellbinding historical account; to the *Birmingham Post* it was sombre and disturbing; and to the *Sunday Tribune* de Rosa was a writer of unusual breadth and talent. But to ex-Jesuit Peter

Hebblethwaite of the *Sunday Times*, the book might as well have been commissioned by the Protestant Truth Society. To a scornful and dismissive Philip Caraman, SJ, *Vicars of Christ* was no more than 'a binful of garbage'.

So who is Peter de Rosa? Well, he turns out to have been a Professor of Metaphysics and Ethics at Westminster Seminary, and Dean of Theology at Corpus Christi College, London. A binful of garbage? Was this evaluation by fellow Jesuit Philip Caraman a carefully considered lash of the academic whip, or was it founded on some other factor? On the fact, perhaps, that de Rosa had left the priesthood altogether, married and fathered two sons? Obviously a subversive in need of correction! Professor Richards' summation of de Rosa's far-ranging research into pontifical naughtiness completed the picture: the author had not only left the priesthood and married, he had also written *Vicars of Christ* '. . . in quest of a better perspective'. Being fundamentally a plea for reform, and not just an unprincipled attack on a venerable institution, de Rosa's study echoed Pope John XXIII's desire for change and was not written in a spirit of antagonism. Peter de Rosa confirms that this is so in a special note to the reader where he says: 'Though, like Dante, I stress here the dark side of the papacy, it is the work of a friend not an enemy.'

In contrast to this eye-opener of a study, Malachi Martin's book launches the reader into an experience of what I can only describe as 'medieval sensibility'; a sensibility held by Martin to be superior to that of the Renaissance mind, which he describes elsewhere as 'alienated'.[2] With a degree in Semitic languages and Oriental history, and parallel studies in Assyriology at Trinity College, Dublin, this one-time professor at the Vatican's Pontifical Biblical Institute almost takes one's breath away with his mixture of Stephen King-like reconstructions of demonic possession in the twentieth century. With turns of phrase as chilling as any I have ever read, Martin hatches his five-pronged plot of intrinsic evil and reveals to us a world ever-teetering on the edge of diabolical infringement, the description of which novelists interested in the genre could read to their stylistic benefit. Yet I was impressed by this book, impressed by its extraordinary ability to evoke deeply ingrained fears, and was not at all surprised when I eventually discovered that Martin, like myself, was also a writer of fiction.

So on the one hand we have Peter de Rosa's fact-laden replay of the papacy, a replay which not only questions the whole idea of papal authority from its inception, but a replay which reveals a Church darkly capable of inventing reasons to cement that authority in place for all time; and on the other we have Malachi Martin's exposition on the diabolic which places the Church at the very heart of all things spiritually sane, and demands that we take seriously the Catholic Church's claim to be founded on truths which cannot ultimately be questioned. So we are confronted with a dilemma, the dilemma of reconciling diametrically opposed views of the same institution, and have to ask ourselves whether it is possible that such an institution, simultaneously fraudulent and truthful, can be relied upon to speak truthfully rather than fraudulently about the serious issues which presently concern Western society.

The conventions of religion, like the conventions of politics, are essential for human happiness; at least that's the view promoted by Macdonald Hastings. I'm not so sure. Peter de Rosa's study suggests that the Catholic Church, governed as it is by a single person claiming divine authority, cannot be trusted to handle the delicate questions facing all of us as this century reaches its close. Whereas Malachi Martin's basic premise not only reinforces reliance on Church directives, it also upholds the idea of the Catholic Church as a profound source of spiritual healing, and the pope as a spiritually potent figure whose authority should not be doubted. In Martin's estimation, Vatican II did away with much of the Church's ancient symbolism, and as a result opened its doors to what he terms 'a vacuum of indifference'; and this from someone who was a close associate of John XXIII, and was apparently sympathetic to some of the changes initiated by that extraordinary pope. De Rosa, on the other hand, feels that the whole process of Vatican II did not go far enough. In de Rosa's terms, John XXIII was not, as some conservatives believe, 'a crypto-communist who opened a window and let in a hurricane', he was a man of courage and insight who pushed the Church towards a necessary reassessment of its role in the world.

APOSTOLIC CONTINUITY

So what of the Catholic Church's present stance? Is this Church capable of the ferocious honesty required to re-make itself, to question its own historical formation and reformulate its doctrinal position in terms of the reality we are now fast realizing is much more complicated and daring than anyone ever guessed? Or do we have to look elsewhere for the answers that will either save us or damn us by their unexpected originality? Forever teased by reality, we may eventually have to admit that our most adventurous answers to the questions conceived to ultimately matter may be utterly inadequate, and that we are all of us in dire need of a new perspective, a new conceptual orientation in the face of cosmic detachment. Jesus may have hung on the cross and cried out to a God who seemed to have abandoned him, but that cry may not mean quite what we have been led to believe it meant.

If he were still alive, the Christian philosopher Etienne Gilson would take me to task for daring to question Christianity's continuing efficacy in the twentieth century; and I have little doubt that he would interpret the result of Peter de Rosa's efforts in much the same manner as Philip Caraman. Convinced that the Christian life offered a radical solution to *all* of life's problems, Gilson, with that almost admirable capacity for faith and the kind of reasoning that accompanies it, dismissed past attacks on Christianity's theological credibility as nothing more than a misunderstanding of the Christian mystery. This view is shared by Malachi Martin. In fact the result of the latter's possession studies is a series of remarkable statements about life and living which, when analysed, reveal a mind utterly convinced of the existence of intrinsic evil and the Church's divine role in combatting it. Playing subtle games with both language and meaning, Martin's *fleurs du mal* open out into a truly terrifying vision where demon entities play hide-and-seek with often ill-prepared priests who sometimes discover that they too are possessed. No one is safe; and one can only assume that such reasoning applies equally to the Church's pontiffs.

Like Gilson, Martin seems to believe in a spiritual, theological and historical continuity from Jesus through the Apostles to the present age. In spite of the odd hiccup or two, this continuity is to be accepted by all Christians as divinely set in motion and perpetually sustained by divine approval. Darwinian theory, the laws of physics and the mysteries of the human brain are to be ignored in favour of a view where demonic forces wait to pounce on unsuspecting individuals. In some inexplicable fashion evil is bound closely to this world in the form of negative forces and entities whose whole *raison d'être* is the blanking out of the

Christian message. But when confronted with the name of Jesus such forces and entities must eventually fall back or submit, and in submitting vanish again into the hinterland of reality from whence they came. This hinterland is 'hell', we are told, the now laughed at domain of the Devil, and it constitutes a domain, a mode of existence utterly devoid of the presence of God. Whether we like it or not, the name 'Jesus' is the only name before which such entities will bow; and that only if the name is pronounced by someone properly *possessed by the spirit of Jesus.*

Beyond time and history and culture, the occupants of this pitiless sphere constantly seek to enter time, history and culture through the mind's back door. Through a tearing of the psychological and psychic fabric of individual minds which consciously reject the Christian message, the Devil, in one guise or another, eventually makes his entrance and takes up residence. Unwittingly possessed by evil in an often hidden and subtle manner (their reason for the rejection of the Christian message in the first place), such individuals live out their life mostly oblivious to the fact that they are slowly drifting away from everything wholesome. Naturally at war with Christianity, and with the better aspects of themselves, they eventually succumb to the evil within and are invisibly united with that evil at their death.

Terrifying stuff. The kind of writing that makes one's flesh creep. The kind of thinking that makes one wonder if time has slipped and the medieval ages have returned. So what of Peter de Rosa's historical criticisms of the Church and its popes? Is he then a secretly possessed individual whose mind, torn and infiltrated by evil forces, cannot help but attack God's church through the manipulation of historical data? Is it for this reason that the Jesuit Philip Caraman refers to de Rosa's book as 'garbage'? I think not. If asked, I think Caraman would state that de Rosa's historical overview is simply 'over the top', and that only a balanced depiction of the Church's history can do that extraordinary edifice justice.

THE ALIEN DIMENSION

So what is my point? It is this: where does one draw the line? At what point does an educated man like Malachi Martin start talking possession? If demonic possession is a fact of life as this ex-Jesuit believes, how does he differentiate between the facts of history or science and the twisted reasoning of evil spirits driving the human mind towards abnegation, towards negative formulae and interpretations where everything concerning human beings and their world is used to undermine belief in God?

Or is it simply that the many scientific negatives we are forced to acknowledge concerning the nature of the universe, and the nature of our own natures, is the price we have to pay for venturing too close to the information systems intrinsic to biological life and the make-up of the cosmos? Might we not be teetering on the edge of finally comprehending, of finally admitting that we really are alone, that God and Devil and Church and everything we call 'spiritual' is no more than a dream, a way of handling our fear? Or is such thinking the direct result of the spiritual vacuum we consider natural, but which is actually created by the Devil's subtle infiltration of society at all levels?

Ignatius Loyola would have agreed with Malachi Martin on this question. Martin believes that the Devil roams the world with the conscious intention of destroying the image of God wherever it might appear, and Loyola was equally convinced that 'Lucifer' was the main enemy. On having drawn a picture of Loyola as someone who, like St Paul, had ascended to the 'Third Heaven' and participated in '. . . the most hidden secrets of divinity for which human language has no words,'[3] Martin goes on to describe how this saint perceived things, and reveals a mind convinced that demons had been scattered throughout the world to bind men with chains of sin.[4] How depressing. It is even more depressing to think that Ignatius Loyola was still in the grip of such ideas *after* having tasted of the secrets of the Divine. Or was this the whole point, the ultimate proof that the Church had always been right: that there really was an alien dimension to this life about which the secular mind knew virtually nothing.

TUG-OF-WAR THEOLOGY

This, basically, was the Church's stance in relation to a theology which did not reflect the known world. We were expected to believe that it was her knowledge of this alien dimension which vindicated, say, the views of popes such as Pius X; he had had no choice but to blast the Modernists because he *knew* what they did not seem to understand, that the Church of Jesus Christ was the world's only real bulwark against evil. This was the baseline of it all, the Church's *raison d'être* which could be perceived only through the eyes of faith, the new eyes which opened automatically when God's majestic blueprint was superimposed on the whole extraordinary affair of life and living.

The only problem with this view was that the Modernists too were people of faith, good Catholics to whom the historical reality of Jesus and what he had taught was paramount, and their idea of God's blueprint was quite different from that of their opponents. Had not Pope Benedict XV ended up on the same hit-list as those considered theologically suspect? The very fact that he had become pope suggested factions within the Vatican to whom a tug-of-war theology capable of leaning either way was normal. Some might believe that nothing could, nor should, change; just as many thought the exact opposite, yet not strongly enough to really upset the applecart. Knowledge on the historical and scientific levels capable of radically changing the face of Catholic Christianity was available, but its eye-dropper distribution ensured that everything trundled on much as before.

It is Malachi Martin's thesis that the halls of higher learning are inadvertently subverting human intelligence, that intellectual reasoning, psychological subtlety, philosophical logic and historical evidence have no relevance whatsoever in the face of direct psychic attack and the covert manipulation of our world by demonic forces. Our detailed knowledge of world and self is nothing more than accumulated trash in the face of such a reality.[5] Even theology is useless when the flames of evil advance across the threshold of being. This is strong stuff. Evil is very, very powerful, it would seem. The Devil can tear priests apart during an exorcism – some even die. Some are left partly empty inside, empty and staring, shocked so deeply by their encounter with evil that the rest of their lives is a constant vigil, a 'watching' for the evil one to appear. Usurped in their imagination, the world seems to close down and leave them alone with 'an old and unrepentant evil'.

Now this is in itself rather odd, for did not Christ's death on the cross overcome evil once and for all? So by what mechanism, or law, or system of spiritual permission does the Devil continue to infiltrate the world Christ died for? How does he get from his domain (hell) to our domain (the planet Earth) without God and his remaining angels noticing? And as there are so few cases nowadays of demonic possession, of Church-authenticated appearances of the Devil as a possessing spirit, are we to assume that he and his spawn have changed tactics and, on the whole, prefer a subtler methodology, an invisible undermining of the human spirit through knowledge unsalted by faith and belief? And if this is the case, then why break out into our world every so often in the form of raging, cursing spirits? No, there's something wrong here, something is not quite right in the theological mix. For why should some Catholic priests have to forfeit their own spiritual welfare (for all eternity?) on behalf of the possessed souls they help release? Is the Devil still so powerful that God must stand by helplessly and allow his servants to be plucked out of his hand at death because of some mishandling of events during an exorcism? Malachi Martin suggests as much in many a veiled passage, and one can only wonder at the kind of reasoning behind such statements.

And there's more, much more.

An exorcist must be officially sanctioned by the Church, for '. . . any power he has over Evil Spirit can only come from those officials who belong to the substance of Jesus' Church'.[6] This Church can be either Roman Catholic, Eastern Orthodox or one of the Protestant Communions. Now this seems to be a fair and equable distribution of power between the differing congregations, but we later learn that Protestant ministers generally defer to Catholic priests when it comes to exorcism because of the Catholic Church's longer track record: such ministers have little or no idea on how to approach Evil Spirit. And it's just as well that they do defer, for in such engagements there is always a victor and a vanquished, and whatever the result, the contact is always '. . . in part fatal for the exorcist'. Pillaged in his deeper self by the process, something in him dies a little, and the withering of this deep something within is because he has had to face the opposite of all humanness, namely intrinsic evil. Or could it be that he has simply abandoned himself to reasoning processes which he knows deep down he ought to have rejected? Could that be it? Would his deeper self not wither a little under such conditions?

It is only after allowing for mental or physical disease, or for chemical abnormalities, and only after stringent psychiatric probing that an exorcist will now define another human being as possibly possessed. Because, for reasons not given, reported cases of possession over the last hundred years have decreased, the

French priest and exorcist Henri Gesland admitted in 1974 that out of 3,000 cases since 1968, only four had been deemed truly demonic. Martin counters with a statement from one T K Osterreich to the effect that possession is an extremely common phenomenon, but adds incomprehensibly '. . . cases of which abound in the history of religion'; which is to say no more than we already know, and which Martin eventually admits are claims more often due to causes other than possession.

In *Hostage to the Devil* there is a section titled 'Father Bones and Mister Natch' which carries the reader deep into Malachi Martin's understanding of demonic possession. Of more immediate interest, however, are some of Martin's statements concerning Father David 'M' Bones himself (Bones was a nickname), and his educational attainments before his ordeal of attempting to exorcise a possessed priest. After being ordained in 1947, after seven years' study, Father David was asked by his bishop to consider another two terms of study: the diocese needed a professor of anthropology and ancient history, and they believed he was their man. But first he would need to take a doctorate in theology to offset the temptations of the scientific approach to knowledge – 'doctrine' would be his haven of safety.

This was because of Teilhard de Chardin, that intellectual ascetic and First World War hero who expected Christians to accept Darwinian evolution alongside their Catholic faith. Thought earlier to be a kind of twentieth-century Aquinas, de Chardin had fallen into disgrace by the 1950s because of his refusal to intellectually kowtow to the ecclesiastical mind. Silenced, exiled, and forbidden to either publish or lecture (shades of Hans Kung), de Chardin's attempt to explain the mysteries of the Catholic faith in more comprehensible terms was rejected out of hand. Oddly enough, the rational fire driving de Chardin had come from none other than Ignatius Loyola, father of the Jesuits and patron of what Martin calls 'the lone and the brave'. Captured in his imagination by Ignatius and by St John of the Cross, de Chardin becomes what Martin stingingly calls '. . . the ready-made darling for the bankrupt Catholic intellectuals of his century'.[7] And he isn't finished; he adds: 'Teilhard was neither strong food to satisfy real hunger nor heavenly manna for a new Pentecost. He was merely a stirrup cup of heady wine.'[8]

To explore de Chardin's highly synthesized system of thought is not my intention here; rather, I wish to pursue Malachi Martin's system of thought and highlight what is without doubt a unique mind clinging to an antique vision: the vision of a Jesus untouched by twentieth-century scholarship. That is exactly what we will do at intervals throughout this book; we will attempt to measure ideas such as Peter de Rosa's against the beliefs and opinions of this powerful conservative thinker. For like Pius X, or Pius XII, Martin wants to purge our minds of *all* 'dangerous ideas'; that is, he wants to rid us of ideas capable of creating a climate of opinion within which the Church's age-old version of Jesus is abandoned, and its offer of spiritual salvation through this Jesus disregarded. For the idea that human origins started in some remote period is too much for this old Catholic warhorse to tolerate: Jesus is not some fancy Omega Point in the evolution of man, he is the creator of it all, and as such is both Alpha and Omega. Father David Bones will have to make a journey into virtual unbelief before the truth of this matter begins to dawn, and the story of this priest's search for and confrontation with Evil Spirit is the substance of Father Bones and Mister Natch's interaction.

The question that disturbs Father David is one which occurs as he attempts to finish a paper for a conference on de Chardin's unearthing of the fossil *Sinanthropos* in China: is evolution as much a fact as the salvation of us all by Jesus? An Old School question, and foolish, yet it keeps on bothering him, and that in spite of the fact that he is surrounded by fossils, by chipped skulls and anklebones, by fauna fossils embedded in ancient rock. There, to bamboozle him further, the plaster busts of Solo Man, Rhodesian Man, Neanderthal Man and Cro-Magnon Man. He feels anger at the unfairness of it all. Why does a *choice* have to be made? Can he not have evolution *and* Jesus? So the process of doubt continues, and he passes his exams, and becomes convinced that there are no reliable records about Jesus written during Jesus' own lifetime. There is only what men and women believed about Jesus. The pomp and splendour of Rome cannot be superimposed on Jesus' little life without the absurdity of it all surfacing; there is simply no relationship between the life of Jesus and the glory of papal Rome.

But Father David's Modernist approach to life and religion is soon to be undermined; the possession of a fellow priest, and the eventual realization that he himself is possessed, will blow all of that nonsense out of his head. Raw experience will reveal unimaginable complexities of the spirit, and the final revelation will be that evil is 'neutral', and because neutral, baleful. Beauty and harmony and meaning cannot exist when the senses are invaded, when all that one is begins to waste as if in an Arctic wind.

In such a fashion does Malachi Martin build his case against modern knowledge, against scholarship, against research of any kind which might suggest a point of view other than that of the old and tried Catholic Church. In a truly extraordinary avalanche of language he records and evokes evil with such alacrity that one can almost taste the sulphur, and we learn that only one thing is real, the 'autonomous will'. So the question is: How many choices had Father David made freely in his life before that night of terror and realization? Had he ever really chosen anything without outside stimuli, without background memory, without the push from acquired tastes and persuasions, without reason, or cause, or motive? This is the question he has to answer, and the answer to that question is a resounding No. So what does he do? He chooses to believe of course. After a long and trying period he cries out: 'I choose . . . I will . . . I believe . . . Help my unbelief . . . Jesus . . . I believe I believe I believe.'[9] In that moment it's all over. He is safe. He has come home again.

A BUCKETFUL OF DECEITS

Hostage to the Devil is the kind of book that could start a psychic epidemic, a return to attitudes and fears long since thought to be dead and buried, but only if writers like Peter de Rosa are not read with the seriousness they deserve. For if there is a defusing principle in all of this, a principle of sanity, it is the fact of the Church's extraordinary centuries-old manipulation of history and theology and the human mind for political reasons. There is nothing more sobering than a bucketful of deceits pulled up out of the historical depths and dumped in one's lap. All the pomp and splendour and apparent self-assurance of an organization perpetually reinventing itself for purposes of control can be laid bare when such deceits are laid out end to end.

Of course, this begs the question as to whether Peter de Rosa would ultimately disagree with Malachi Martin about such issues. It may well be that de Rosa has similar beliefs to Martin, for he was after all Dean of Theology at Corpus Christi for a time. To de Rosa, the questioning of papal authority may not necessarily undermine the theological possibility of the Devil's existence. What then of my case for identified historical deceits having a sobering effect, a defusing effect in relation to Martin's claim that evil has a concrete, entity-type life of its own? Does the existence of dud popes automatically disallow the existence of evil incarnate? Or might it be that another set of questions has to be asked? I suspect the latter rather than the former; and that in spite of the fact that the former must necessarily play an important role in our general perception of whether the Roman Church and its Protestant off-shoots have anything of value to say about evil. Dud popes have contributed to the Church's present state, and a study of those popes should not be avoided, but the core problem may lie elsewhere.

As it happens, Malachi Martin has himself written critically on Church history, and has made observations not dissimilar to those of Peter de Rosa concerning the failings of the Roman Church. In *The Decline and Fall of the Roman Church*, he outlines the growth of early Christianity in Rome and throws momentary doubt on the value of the Church's sudden and quite unexpected reversal of fortunes under the Emperor Constantine. As a result of Constantine's change of heart in the fourth century, Christianity was suddenly made respectable and carried triumphantly into the future on the back of the Roman eagle. The price paid for that sudden elevation to respectability and power was considerable. Martin's own words clearly capture the situation that arose: 'Once Constantine's favour placed Christians in a privileged position, the Christian focus narrowed from remote eternity to passing time and measurable space.'[10] That, I think, is put perfectly.

THE BLOOD RELATIVES OF JESUS

But alongside this surprising change in circumstances lay a little-known meeting in 318 between Pope Sylvester and those termed, in Greek, *desposyni*, the blood relatives of Jesus in charge of every section of the Jewish Nazarene Church throughout Palestine, Syria and Mesopotamia – a Church which did not pass as speedily into oblivion as many Church historians would like to think.[11] In fact the exact opposite was true. According to the Church historian Eusebius (a personal friend of the Emperor Constantine), the Jewish Nazarene Christian Church attracted large numbers of

Jews to its ranks; however, there was certainly a chaotic period
after the unsuccessful Jewish rebellion of 70 during which division
and controversy reigned.

So says the Jewish scholar Dr Hugh Schonfield, and Malachi
Martin concurs. The Jewish followers of Jesus, he tells us, created the Church's first major crisis through splitting into factions
from the very beginning. Schonfield goes further still, writing of
the Nazarenes as beset by '. . . grave internal problems, false
teachers, antinomianism, faction and rivalry, loss of confidence
in the Second Advent, persecution and apostasy'.[12] But what
Malachi Martin does not tell us is that the Nazarenes eventually
reorganized themselves, and Eusebius confirms this when he says
that after the uprising the family of Jesus, in conjunction with
those apostles and followers of Jesus still alive, chose Simeon
(after the death of Jesus' brother James) as titular head of the
Nazarenes, so recreating stability. Schonfield calls this family
dynasty the *desposyni* ('heirs') and remarks that twelve others
followed in turn whose names are preserved down to 132.[13] The
list is as follows: James, Simeon, Justus, Zaccheus, Tobias,
Benjamin, John, Matthew, Philip, Seneca, Justus II, Levi,
Ephraim, Joseph and Judas.

Nazarene communities were apparently still active in north
and east Palestine right up until the fifth century, and Schonfield
notes that the name of Jesus was now being used by both the
Jewish and Gentile Christians in the interest of policy. Further
and further magnified by the Roman Christians in particular,
Jesus became progressively more symbolic and representative of
ecclesiastical concerns.

More accurately termed the 'Orthodox Nazarene Church', this
Jewish-oriented Church of ancient Jewish-Arabian lineage was
virtually ignored by the early Greek-oriented Church at Rome.
However, once its own house was in order, its members watched
amazed as Rome's Christians redeveloped and added to Paul's
teachings. Dismissed in 318 with a regal curtness, the representatives of this the original Jerusalem Church were informed that the
centre of influence had long since shifted to Rome, that St Peter's
bones were not in Jerusalem, but in Rome, and that the admittedly
once powerful family dynasty of Jesus was no longer considered
apostolically important. Greek bishops should therefore be
allowed to replace those of the line of Jesus still holding to the
now defunct Nazarene dream of superiority.

Quite a slap in the face to those of Jesus' own family who, since the time of James the Just, had faithfully carried their message of Jesus to all and sundry! And this was the point: *their* Jesus was not Paul's Jesus. In his *Dialogue with the Jew Trypho*, Justin Martyr admits that there are two Christianities. Born in Samaria at Flavia Neapolis (modern Nablus), Justin studied philosophy before becoming a Christian. Martyred in Rome in 165, he followed Western Christianity's doctrine of Jesus as a divine being, but did not altogether condemn the Nazarene followers of Jesus for their very different doctrinal stance. They were entitled, he said, to observe the Mosaic Law if they so wished, but Gentiles should not be made to follow suit. In his estimation, Paulinist Christians were wrong to reject the Nazarenes, and they were equally wrong in their belief that these original followers of Jesus would not be saved. Associating with the Nazarenes as kinsmen and brethren, Justin revealed that the Paulinists were by this time denying the Nazarenes both hospitality and recognition, and that '. . . the old Faith of the Apostolic Church was now being treated as sectarian'.[14] To the Nazarenes, Jesus was an ordinary man anointed by election to be the Messiah, or Christ; he was *not* literally God in any shape or form. Despised by the Christians for not acknowledging Jesus' deity, the Nazarenes were shunned, and finally persecuted.

But just to complicate things, these Nazarenes were also sometimes referred to as 'Ebionites' (the poor), and in her provocative book *Putting Away Childish Things*, Uta Ranke-Heinemann (first woman professor of Catholic theology at the University of Essen) confirms that the radical Ebionites, or Nazarenes, were led by James, Jesus' brother, and that '. . . all the way into the second century they continued to choose their bishops from Jesus' family'.[15] But then she goes much further; she also confirms that these Ebionite-Nazarenes rejected Paul's Christology, particularly the notion of Jesus' death on the cross being a bloody act of atonement. Claiming Jesus as the Messiah, and rejecting animal sacrifices, they substituted water for blood in the Eucharistic meal, believed Jesus to have been an ordinary man born of ordinary parents, and argued that he had achieved his righteous state like any other sage or prophet. Writing against the Ebionite-Nazarenes, the Church Father Irenaeus correctly summed up their belief that Jesus was an ordinary man by saying that '. . . they destroy God's tremendous plan for salvation'.[16]

Indeed they did, and that's why Sylvester I dispersed them; he could see no way of reconciling the diametrically opposed beliefs of the two Jesus groups.

With wit and erudition, Professor Heinemann opens our eyes to what was really going on during the first and second centuries, and with skill reveals that Christian fairy tales have been changed into doctrines demanding absolute allegiance. Of course, she has paid the price for her honesty and integrity; she has been declared ineligible to teach theology by the Catholic Church. The writer Karen Armstrong – another strong-minded woman holding similar views – says of Heinemann that she has '. . . skilfully disentangled the web of contradictions and improbabilities that surround the Christian story'.[17] Yes, the Ebionite-Nazarenes interpreted Jesus' life and life-purpose in a quite different way from the Pauline-influenced Roman Christians, but it is perhaps somewhere between these seemingly irreconcilable points of view that the truth will be found. In literal terms, Jesus was neither the Son of God, nor God himself somehow transformed into a human body, but as an archetypal Messiah he does seem to have carried a new and expansive perception of reality which left everyone guessing.

The Jesus of the Nazarenes was the Messiah of Israel, the archetypal 'man' entitled to be called 'light Adam' or 'son of God'; but basically he was flesh and blood and as ordinary as anyone else. Not so the Jesus held up by the Roman Church. Elevated to God's right hand, he was about to be heralded as God's *actual* son, and by reasoning incomprehensible even to those who penned it, somehow God made manifest in the flesh. Such a claim, when news of it got out, must have appeared to be a form of lunacy to those of Jesus' dynastic family.

But rejected, this flick of the pontifical wrist. The representatives of the Jewish Nazarene Church stood their ground and demanded that the Roman Church recognize the *desposynos* as the Mother Church, the original Church. Banned from Jerusalem since the time of Hadrian (135), and still under that ban in spite of the Roman Church's changed position in relation to imperial Rome, they had not come to submit, but to correct a dangerous fallacy: Jerusalem was where the Church's heart was to be found, not Rome. The Roman Church, now in such a favoured position with the persecutors of Jews and the Nazarene followers of Jesus, should have Hadrian's ban lifted, revoke its confirmation of Greek bishops at Jerusalem, Antioch, Ephesus and Alexandria, and allow *desposynos* bishops to take over. Converted pagans with little appreciation of things Jewish were not the right choice; the true apostolic succession was Nazarene by right, by blood, and in relation to the Messiah had started with Jesus' full brother James, *not* Peter. The Roman Church, no matter how powerful, could lay no rightful claim to being the Mother Church. To say that Peter had broken with the Nazarene Church in 40 along with Paul was ridiculous; Peter had been of the Nazarene camp right from the beginning. There was no evidence whatsoever for his ever having been in Rome, never mind his having been pope for twenty-five years. When they had sorted all of this out, and come to their senses, and stopped playing pagan-type games with the Jewish Messiah, they should immediately resume the practice of sending donations to the *desposynos*; for as the dynastic heirs of Jesus they had the right to expect foreign-based off-shoots of the Nazarene Mother Church to continue what Hadrian had disrupted when he banned all Jews from entering the Holy City.

Malachi Martin tells us that this was probably the last known discussion between '. . . the Jewish Christians of the old mother church and the non-Jewish Christians of the new mother church'.[18] He goes on to show that Jewish Christians had no place in this new Greek-oriented church structure, and that the Jewish Christian Churches refused to be part of it. This is correct; but what is not correct is the use of the term 'Jewish Christians'; the Nazarenes were certainly Jewish, but it should be remembered that they were sectarian Jewish (they carried many beliefs at odds with orthodox Judaism), and that it was Paul's churches that eventually used the term 'Christian' to describe themselves. But the most important of Martin's statements is the following: 'By his adaptation, Sylvester, backed by Constantine, had decided that the message of Jesus was to be couched in Western terms by Western minds on an imperial model.'[19] That, basically, is the whole bag of tricks in one statement: the Christian revelation had been *adapted* to suit the whims of a renegade church with imperial ambitions.

The principal question is, why had nothing been done about Roman harassment of the Nazarene community? Why had the ban against the Nazarenes entering Jerusalem not been lifted? The Church at Rome was now in such a powerful position that a word in the Emperor's ear could have instantly secured the right for her Jewish brothers and sisters to return to Jerusalem. So why the blind eye and the deaf ear? Was it perhaps official policy that the Nazarenes should be ignored and left to their fate so as to allow the new administration in Rome to flourish unchallenged? Did the word 'Christian' simply not register in Rome's ear because of the word 'Jewish' preceding it? Or is it simply that the word 'Christian' was never used in relation to these Nazarene followers of Jesus at any time, and that it was this that allowed the early Christians at Rome to ignore the plight of the Jerusalem Mother Church? Plenty of time had elapsed since Constantine's change of heart, which rather suggests that being of the original Jewish Nazarene Church now meant absolutely nothing to Sylvester and his Greek-minded supporters; it was not their concern that any Jew found entering Jerusalem would be instantly executed. Paul, it had to be understood, had broken with the Nazarenes first over circumcision and the dietary laws, then over his more daring theological reinterpretations of Jesus' importance. By the end of the first century the restored, and by then predominantly Greek-oriented, church at Rome had rescued these more daring notions about Jesus, inflated them still further and unsteadily set sail for the future. When that future came, it contained the quite unexpected change of mind by the Emperor Constantine, and resulted in a church previously doomed to persecution, obscurity and probable obliteration being made the religious model for the whole Roman Empire.

The Nazarene representatives received by Sylvester in Rome in 318 would not have left anyone in doubt about their history, about their view of Paul, or about their right to be accepted still as the Mother Church. As far as they were concerned, the Nazarene Church was the legitimate centre of the so-called Christian spiritual cyclone, and not to recognize this as true was to be downright dishonest; without Constantine's favour this Church, and not the Roman Church, would have been Christianity's spiritual spearhead. Anyone who knew anything about the Church's early history knew that the Church at Jerusalem had been run by the Nazarenes right up until 135, that they had left the Holy City only once in 102 years (due to the city's capture by Titus in 70) and that in the year 72 they had returned to Jerusalem and stayed there until Hadrian's ban. Since then, Nazarene churches had been set up throughout Palestine, Syria and Mesopotamia, and these churches constituted the true Church of Jesus, the true succession and bloodline, the survival of which was now in Sylvester's hands owing to continued

Roman aggression towards the Jews. This surely must have been the tenor of the conversation, for why else would these Nazarenes have demanded that Sylvester revoke the confirmation of Greek bishops in Jerusalem, Antioch, Ephesus and Alexandria, and replace them with *desposynos* bishops?

Thus, not only had the Church at Rome become something other than a simple holy community, it had also been in receipt of a timely visit from representatives of the original Nazarene Church which, at the very least, ought to have created a bond between the two Jesus-based organizations. Martin's approach to this situation is two-fold. He suggests that a church left in the catacombs of Rome would have achieved little, and that the eventual collapse of the *pax romana* (the 'peace' Rome offered to those who became her willing subjects) was only successfully replaced by the 'peace of Christ' because of the Church's new-found security under Constantine. Without that curious relationship, persecuted Christians bound to obscure strata of society could have done very little to change their world, and would have had to wait until the resurrection of Jesus to achieve their dream of a renewed world. If Sylvester *had* given in to Jesus' relatives, then '. . . the appeal of Christianity as a universal way of life would have been restricted to a small number of Jews or an impotent and doomed minority in the great urban centres'.[20] Everything would have collapsed; all hope would have died. The Roman world would have disintegrated and European civilization would not have arisen.

So runs the stock excuse for the creation and continuation of a Church that even in Sylvester's time had donned imperial raiment, taken on the autocratic attitudes of the caesars and begun systematically to create and eliminate heretics. So runs the reasoning, that it is *this* Church, *this* Greek hybrid of original Nazarene Christianity that in the future will have the right to claim power over demons in the name of Jesus because of Apostolic lineage. Lineage? Apostolic? If, as just about every Church historian admits, Peter's 25-year episcopate in Rome is sheer fantasy, and if over the centuries the papacy was bought and sold and subject to the vicissitudes of human nature like any other organization, then by what stretch either of reasoning and or of imagination can the Catholic Church claim legitimate, meaningful Apostolic Succession?

The answer to this question is that she can do no such thing, and this makes null and void her many, many claims to an over-arching spiritual authority. For how can an organization with such a track record claim authority over anything, or anyone, never mind over Satan and his demons? To make the Apostle Peter the foundation of such claims is, as Peter de Rosa shows so effectively, to make a nonsense both of the Gospels and of the early Church Fathers' comprehension of the Gospels. There is simply no justification whatsoever for believing that Peter was awarded the title of 'Rock', that he was given the 'keys of heaven and earth', and that by succession subsequent bishops of Rome acquired the same spiritual power. De Rosa is clear and precise on this point: there *was* no Petrine 'office', no 'inheritance' from Peter mentioned in early Church documents. Not one Church Council between the fourth and the fifteenth centuries makes anyone other than Christ the Rock of Salvation. All of the early Church Fathers were of the same opinion: Christ, not Peter, was the Rock on which the Church was founded, neither is there any mention anywhere of a transference of power from Peter to any other bishop.

More telling still is a statement made in 1150 by Gratian, the Church's greatest canon lawyer: 'Peter,' says Gratian, confronting his Church with an uncomfortable fact, 'compelled the Gentiles to live as Jews and to depart from Gospel truth.'[21] Here then is the crux of the matter: Peter was not ultimately persuaded by Paul's rejection of things Jewish, his rejection of things Nazarite and Nazarene, he remained a Nazarene, a Jewish follower of Jesus and observer of the Law to whom the Greek-oriented beliefs of the Church at Rome would have been quite unacceptable. More relaxed in his behaviour than James the Just he certainly was (an openness learned from Jesus himself, no doubt), but it was to James as head of the Nazarene Community that he would have continued to look after the crucifixion. De Rosa concurs: 'The Catholic Church had made it a point of faith that popes are successors of St Peter as Bishop of Rome. But Peter never had that title; he was only invested with it centuries after he died.' And on the equally important point of Peter's Jewishness he adds: 'Naturally, he would have had immense moral authority in the Jewish-Christian community in Rome but, unlike Paul who was a Roman citizen, he would have been a foreigner there.'[22] De Rosa's use of 'Jewish-Christian community' in this context should not be read as referring to Paul's Christian community, but to an extension of the Jerusalem Nazarenes. There were two Jesus communities in Rome, and after Nero's great fire of 64, they were at doctrinal loggerheads.

FORGED DOCUMENTS

Unlike secular historians, Church historians cannot help but slant their interpretation of history in the direction of a God who had salvation in mind since the beginning of time itself. Following Eusebius, they claim that the promise made to Abraham was fulfilled in Christ; that is, the divine plan of salvation can be detected within world history. Working from Abraham to Christ to Constantine, Eusebius argued that Jesus appeared on Earth at the time of the Roman Empire's zenith so that news of God's salvation could eventually reach the greatest number of people: there simply had to be a Constantine to make it all possible. The fact that there was a Constantine was certain proof that God had been at work through the Emperor. So, through a theology of history closely allied to things both political and convenient, Constantine as the first Christian Emperor of Rome came to embody the image of God on Earth – an idea that curiously embodied both Emperor worship and the cult of the sun – and the union of Empire and Church became an 'anticipation of the millennium', to use the words of the historian Joseph Vogt.

In his book, *The Decline of Rome*, Vogt draws our attention to *The Donation of Constantine*, a document dated 30 March 315, but actually composed during the papacy of Stephen III (752–7) to convince Pepin, king of the Franks, that he should defend the Church against the Lombards. A forgery through and through, *The Donation* claimed that Constantine, suffering from leprosy, had had a vision in which Saints Peter and Paul had told him to contact Pope Sylvester. Healed as a result of obeying this heavenly command, Constantine had in gratitude handed over his palace to Pope Sylvester and made the entire Western Empire subservient to the Holy See. The sacred See of Blessed Peter was to be exalted above the Empire and the Emperor's throne, and Sylvester made ruler of Antioch, Alexandria, Jerusalem, Constantinople and *all* the churches of the world. Heady stuff. This document was accepted without a quibble until 1440, when Lorenzo Valla, a papal aide, proved beyond all doubt that *The Donation* was a fraud. Valla's book was published in 1517, the same year that Luther raised his voice against papal indulgences, and in spite of *all* independent scholars agreeing with Valla, the Papacy continued to deny any skulduggery for the next few centuries. Professor Ranke-Heinemann refers to *The*

Donation as '. . . a swindle, a handmade-homemade inside job, an ecclesiastical forgery'.[23]

King Pepin, however, was very impressed when he read *The Donation*; for it appeared to prove beyond doubt that the Pope was successor to both Peter and Constantine. All power on Earth indeed; and behind the scenes the power of Heaven to back it up. Routing the Lombards, Pepin dutifully handed over the lands mentioned in *The Donation*, thus making the Holy See all-powerful at a single stroke.

In his summing-up of the Constantine era, de Rosa, like Malachi Martin, refers to a 'loss of innocence'. But then he parts with Martin, talking of Constantine's cynical use of Christ, and of Sylvester's equally cynical acquiescence in the falsification of the Gospel message. 'From then on,' he says, 'Catholicism flourished to the detriment of Christianity and of Jesus who wanted no part in the world of power and politics.'[24] Alas, the Church had taken a different route, a route that would see forged documents being created on demand.

By 1187 the forging of documents had become a profitable business, with a whole school of forgers toiling to produce ratification of Gregory III's ambitions; there was even a policy of making old documents say the reverse of what they actually said. Amusingly, de Rosa points out that some of these earlier documents were forgeries in their own right, and states that this school of forgers '. . . treated all papers, forged or genuine, with a completely impartial dishonesty'.[25] With the ability to invent history through the forging of imposing-looking documents complete with papal seals, and with the added ability to instantly insert such fabrications into Canon Law, the Catholic Church systematically recreated its past and ended up believing its own lies.

De Rosa is rightfully merciless when dealing with this extraordinary situation, and reveals that during the mid-twelfth century the *Decretum*, or Code of Canon Law, was '. . . peppered with three centuries of forgeries and [the] conclusions drawn from them'.[26] One such conclusion was that the pope was superior to, and the 'source' of, all laws without qualification; a fact noted by de Rosa as suggesting that he was by definition equal to the Son of God. Here then was the Church we had to have, the institution created by God through Constantine to shed light on a darkened world.

Malachi Martin is also intrigued by the relationship of Pope Sylvester and the Jewish (Nazarene) Christians. He interrupts his narrative to speculate that: 'As he lay dying, perhaps Sylvester's chief regret would have been having so churlishly dismissed the blood relatives of Jesus. Some of those Jewish Christian *desposyni* must have borne facial characteristics that Jesus himself would have had.'[27] A possibility indeed, considering that the family dynasty of the Nazarenes had, at the time of Jesus' crucifixion, been led by Jesus' flesh and blood brother James (not Peter), and from that point onwards predominantly by other members of the same family. Keeping to the theologically necessary line that James the Just was Jesus' cousin, and not his actual brother as the New Testament states, Martin holds this group of Nazarene representatives at arm's length, but cannot but admit that the issue dealt with that day '. . . was nothing less than the whole nature of the church'.[28]

Indeed it was, and taken seriously enough for Sylvester to provide sea travel for the group as far as the Roman port of Ostia. It is certainly indicative of something serious that they refused to 'sit' when requested. No record of the meeting was kept, but their reason for being there was, apparently, 'very well known to everyone', and their attitude was certainly not one of subservience. Martin further describes the *desposyni* as '. . . that most hallowed name . . . respected by all believers in the first century and a half of Christian history'.[29] This was certainly not so in the centuries that followed, it seems, and particularly not during the reign of Pope Sylvester I.

As shown in my previous book on Christian origins, *Jesus the Heretic*, ecclesiastical historians are able to bear witness to the fact that the original apostles and elders and the relations of Jesus were originally the controlling force of the whole early Church, and that this so-called Jewish Christianity considered Pauline Christianity an heretical offshoot. Hugh Schonfield is of the same opinion, and writes that the early Nazarene government, although the legitimate authority, could not '. . . effectively exercise control of Christian affairs' due to being marked as anti-Roman. This created a vacuum which Christianity in other parts of the Empire began to fill. So, slowly, the Roman Church took on the mantle of leadership, and eventually produced the necessary propaganda to undermine and finally replace Nazarene dynastic authority. Schonfield adds, caustically: 'According to the view which prevailed the Catholic Church of the new orthodoxy was the inheritor of the true tradition of the

Apostles, an assertion which illustrates the power of a lie if it is a thumping big one.'[30]

FULL CIRCLE

Macdonald Hastings pinpoints the relevant issue when he says: 'it is surely untrue that the challenge of our age is atheism . . . What so many have ceased to have faith in is not God but the human organisations which claim, with divine authority, to instruct us how to reach Him.'[31] This, to my way of thinking, is the core problem. The mess the Church has got itself into down the centuries has without doubt resulted in some peculiar doctrinal shifts, in anomalies of judgement and curious outbursts of bravado, but the underlying problem goes much, much deeper. For that problem has to do with the Church's basic premise of existence, its fundamental doctrinal ground plan, its miraculously conjured into existence belief in itself as divinely appointed, as having the right to dictate the shape and content of our spiritual lives.

Malachi Martin may believe that European civilization would have collapsed if Roman Christianity had not taken its chance with the Emperors, that Christianity as a universal way of life would '. . . either have been restricted to a small number of Jews or an impotent and doomed minority in the great urban centres',[32] but this does rather suggest a God lacking in imagination, a God incapable of having realized his ground plan in some other way. To say that another great civilization could not have arisen in the place of the one shaped and influenced by Roman Catholicism is arrant nonsense; a civilization of some kind would have arisen automatically, and it may even have been rather better than the one we have ended up with.

The whole history of the human race is concerned with the ebb and flow of civilizations, many of which have been highly sophisticated. In any case, Martin cannot have it both ways, for it is deep secular learning that he appears to blame for our spiritually alienated natures, and that he links with diabolic purposes. If this is indeed the case, then it appears that the Roman Catholic Church is ultimately responsible for every nastiness that has ever happened in the West, and in terms of argument that is about as silly as it is possible to get. It should be remembered that it was the Church's bedfellow Constantine who '. . . halted the anti-intellectual trends which had set in under so many of the soldier-emperors'.[33]

Dismissing a religious philosophy such as Buddhism as 'disembodied', and therefore incomplete, Martin directs us instead to Ignatius Loyola's ardent desire to meet the risen Christ in his glorified body, to venerate that body, to kiss and adore its wounds with hands and eyes. In desiring this Loyola had discovered the secret of Christian mysticism, a secret which has eluded people such as Aldous Huxley, Teilhard de Chardin and Thomas Merton.[34] Martin freely admits that such thinking is a stumbling block for the non-Christian mind, and earmarks his stance as the touchstone by which what is authentically Christian can be identified. Amidst the welter of religions shouldering one another in the market place, Christianity ought to stand out as the religion which balances spirit with matter – the human body cannot and should not be ignored.

In her discussion of another God-struck Ignatius – Bishop Ignatius of Antioch in 110 – Uta Ranke-Heinemann observes that this much-lauded martyr was in fact a religious maniac. Describing him as 'a reckless self-destroyer, a neurotic seeker of martyrdom, and a religious masochist',[35] she aligns him with other Catholic saints who have been morbidly addicted to the idea of an excruciating death on behalf of their beliefs. This brings us back to Ignatius Loyola and his ardent desire to kiss Jesus' bloody wounds and adore them with his eyes. Is this the same kind of body-mysticism that Bishop Ignatius experienced as he wish-fulfilled his own bloody end? Described by Malachi Martin as 'the secret of Christian mysticism', this ability to identify emotionally either with Jesus' suffering or (I can only presume) physically suffer unbearable pain in the same fashion, is held up as a 'secret' to be rediscovered. This is what makes Christian mysticism different from, indeed superior to, any other.

Peter de Rosa is also interested in the human body, in the suffering human body; *Vicars of Christ* is dedicated, humbly and with penitence, to all the victims of the Jewish Holocaust.

So we come full circle, for to what can we attribute such evil dealing? The Devil? The Church's closed-lipped policy on Nazism right until the end of the war? Human beings so devoid of religious faith and belief that their store of ordinary secular knowledge is insufficient to sustain their sense of the human? Or to a God who does not care, a God so far off, so distant as to be virtually non-existent? Or a God simply nowhere to be found at all. Should we perhaps double back to Malachi Martin's description of Father David Bones as 'lacking an autonomous will'? Devilish indeed the human mind bereft of a proper will, a proper centre from which to view self, world and other; but hardly in league with the Devil because of such devilish behaviour. Ultimately it does not matter to what one blindly conforms, to what one is unquestioningly obedient; it only matters that one wakes up out of such a condition and does not simply exchange one shadow-bound system of conformity for another without noticing.

In an attempt to deal with these questions, this puzzle, this nightmare, the Church has elevated Jesus the Nazarene to astonishing heights and, as a result, her mental perambulations over almost two thousand years of history draw us into a system of reasoning so strange, so anciently connected and so psychically intuitive, that in spite of everything to the contrary we cannot altogether ignore what she has to say. Mistaken she certainly is in many of her grand theological and historical pronouncements, in her assessment of herself as an unimpeachable Apostolic Succession originating in the Jewish period, but her pointing finger, weighed down with gold and silver and precious stones, may not be completely without direction. In spite of herself, and not because of herself, she may yet be shown to carry the rudiments of a vision of value to us all.

CHAPTER THREE

The Historical Whitewash

The Church imaginatively extends the Gospels, invents the idea of Apostolic Succession, and successfully undermines the intellectual development of the Western world

Malachi Martin holds that European civilization would not have arisen without the Church and her many and curious doctrines, but this is an eccentric view of European history and not borne out by the facts. The truth of the matter is that the Church wiped out almost everything of value in paganism so as to establish its unique point of view, and in doing so systematically eradicated critical thought, progress in medicine and the arts, areas of creative exploration which had already reached a high level of development. In his quite excellent book *Binding the Devil*, Roger Baker states that 'The intellectual development of Europe was arrested for a thousand years'.[1] Here then is the opposite view from that held by Martin, a view with which I personally concur. Martin believes that without Christianity no great European civilization would have arisen; Baker suggests that because of Christianity's early dealings with her pagan neighbours whole echelons of intellectual development already under way were either retarded or obliterated.

By 395 all pre-Christian religious forms had been banned and classified as criminal; by 600 the Church was seriously debating whether or not women could be considered human. Were not labour pains an obvious punishment from God for having indulged in sex? Should not baptism be considered an exorcism of the Devil from the newly born child? Didn't unbaptized babies go straight to hell and suffer for all eternity? Weren't pagans just devil-worshippers in disguise? This was the state of affairs established after the death of Constantine, and it was all due to a Church which believed itself divinely appointed and guided by the Holy Spirit. How convenient. God, not man, was dictating policy, and he would dramatically escalate his restrictions on human behaviour and thought until the whole of Western society obeyed the divine will. Dark indeed this God, dark and resentful and heavy-handed and to become yet more heavy-handed as the centuries rolled on. Pagans and heretics alike would suffer the Church's growing intolerance and confidence in herself and, as God's appointed judge on Earth, she would further tighten her systems of control through highly imaginative extensions of the Gospel message.

As far back as 1968, Dr Hugh Schonfield admirably summed up the situation in *Those Incredible Christians*: 'Christianity as we know it,' he said, having spent most of a long life studying Christianity, 'must not be imagined to be identical with what Jesus taught about himself and what his immediate Apostles proclaimed. Catholic Christianity is based on a radical deviation, which progressively by dubious ways and means was converted into an orthodoxy.'[2] So said the only Jewish scholar who was allowed to work on the Dead Sea Scrolls when they were first discovered; and today there is a growing number of scholars who are equally aware of the historical whitewash the Church has engaged in to ensure its survival.

To believe that the God of whom Jesus spoke was capable of inflicting such misery, such stupidity, such mindless nonsense on the whole of European civilization is to be in the clutches of a neurosis. To accept unquestioningly that this God worked in such a manner, and not to suspect that it was human beings and not God who were fabricating such policies, is to be in need of psychological help. To argue that God had to work through the frailties and limitations of human beings is to overlook the fact that this God had been capable, during New Testament times, of giving very precise instructions in all matters through a discarnate Jesus. Visions of the risen Lord had been frequent, and information of a very precise nature had crossed from Heaven to Earth without hindrance. Which is to say that a species of television channel complete with sound had been available to the Apostles (particularly Paul), a channel one would have expected to remain open to those of the so-called Roman apostolic succession. Unless of course things had not been quite so clear-cut during the days, the years, the centuries that followed the death of the original Nazarene-affiliated Apostles, but merely a dull repetition of earlier uncertainties. And so we return to the question of God's existence, of his interest in, and his love for, this little world of ours. If so far off that the Church was quite beyond his control and guidance, what then the purpose of the whole affair? Or was there simply no God out there at all to regulate the Church's growing pomposity and paranoia?

ROBBING PAUL TO PAY PETER

In order to get events in a contemporary perspective, we should remember that the Emperor Constantine murdered Crispus, his son by his first wife, drowned his second wife in the bath, killed his nephew, and after an oath of safe-conduct killed his brother-in-law. Playing the political game to the hilt, the embryonic Roman Church ignored such lapses, willingly accepted his politically motivated sponsorship, and swiftly reversed his policy of religious tolerance – the very policy which had allowed the Church to emerge from the catacombs in the first place. Once in control, she immediately denied religious freedom to others, a policy continued over the centuries, and by 1648 was blithely condemning the Peace of Westphalia for allowing citizens the right to hold religious views at variance with their sovereign. By 1870 Vatican City was no more than a police state, complete with spies and inquisitors. Now many churchmen will invoke the 'human frailty clause' and argue that these good Christians only acted in such a manner because of the times in which they lived; but this argument is not acceptable. Why would the Lord of Hosts set up a fiasco of such proportions? Why reveal yourself and talk clearly in one century, then for the next nineteen mumble in a dark and incomprehensible manner?

Of more immediate and rewarding interest are the unusual facts surrounding the appearance of the Nazarene Christians at the court of Pope Sylvester I in 318. These are facts seldom talked about by Christian historians for reasons which are already self-evident. There was a moment of uncertainty for Sylvester as those Jewish Nazarene Christians knocked the dust off their sandals and headed for home. As he lay dying a moment of regret, perhaps, for his curt dismissal of these family members and their so, so foolish proposals.

But had he done the right thing in sending them away in such a manner? What would have happened if they had somehow managed to settle their differences, if through frank discussion and the practice of Christian humility they had properly explored those differences? What then? Would the combined strength of the two churches have been enough to temper the hypnotic notion of using the Roman Empire and its immense strength and glamour to win the world for Christ? One can imagine a shrug from the dying man, and a wistful smile; useless to dream such a dream. These Nazarenes probably did carry the stamp of Jesus' own countenance, but everything had moved too fast and gone too far by then for reconciliation to be possible: the Nazarene Jesus was no longer the Jesus known and worshipped by the Christian community at Rome, *that* Jesus was now a stranger.

Hugh Schonfield lays out the puzzle of the Nazarene Christians with some dexterity. He tells us that after the fall of Jerusalem and the destruction of the nation's infrastructure by the Romans in 70 CE, the churches which managed to regroup had been only too pleased to receive 'the propaganda of Roman Christianity'.[3] Helpful counsel in the form of communications from Apostles such as Peter would not have been recognized as forgeries; the fact that such communications were received from Rome itself would have ensured their acceptance. Did this not prove beyond doubt that God was still working on behalf of His people? How else could the new seat of Christian authority have ended up in Rome, in the lion's den itself? And was not the Blessed Peter's name to the fore, showing continuity with those who had known Jesus in person? In the light of Peter's acceptance of Paul as a brother in the Lord, as a visionary acceptable to the whole Church, should not his extended theology be accepted as authentic?

Peter de Rosa points out that Roman pontiffs 'claim to be successors not of Peter *and* Paul but of Peter alone. The New Testament speaks of Peter as the Apostle to the Jews.'[4] Interesting. So why an apostolic succession from Peter when it was obviously on Paul's teachings that the Roman Church was founded? Again, why Peter, when by way of apostolic succession among the Nazarenes Jesus' brother James, and not Peter, was the heir from which any such succession arose? Was there perhaps a double game being played here, the game of continuity through Peter, an actual apostle of Jesus', and by such means a tapping by proxy into the Nazarene Church's status without actually having to recognize the real succession? Succession both was and is extremely important to Rome, and it is my contention that she built her own succession on an intentional blurring of the boundaries between those two factors. For it cannot be denied that the Church at Rome was founded not on the teachings of Peter, who was an Apostle to the Jews, as the New Testament clearly states, but on the teachings of Paul, through whom a completely independent authority was set up. And an authority whose independence was striking because of its claim to be guided by Jesus from Heaven through the auspices of the Holy Spirit. Who could argue with that? As Schonfield says: 'In due course any doctrine which the Church found it desirable to proclaim as Catholic Truth could be attributed to this guidance, even when there was no warrant for it in the New Testament itself.'[5] This, one can only surmise, was the source of such notions as that of women not being full human beings.

As one would expect, and given the above circumstances, letters emanating from Rome reflected not only anti-Jewish sentiments, but by circuitous arguments implied that the original apostolic body had been superseded. Schonfield says that most of the Christian communities in receipt of such epistles saw no reason to throw out instructions received from the Apostles prior to the war with Rome; but he adds: '. . . a time of grave uncertainty . . . called for an agonising reappraisal; but it was not evident that the situation required a wholesale abandonment of former positions.'[6] Members of Jesus' own family were still around, together with many others still alive who had heard the original teachings. Yet here were letters with Peter's name on them. What were they to think? To whom should they turn? And so, as Schonfield skilfully shows, compromise between the eastern and western sources of information took place, a collating of often diametrically opposed religious ideas into a series of strange stories and equally strange doctrinal amalgamations.[7]

STRANGE AMALGAMATIONS

One such strange amalgamation of ideas was that Jesus was the politically explosive Jewish Messiah, descended from David and sent to rescue Israel from the Romans; at the same time he was the divine Son of God, come to save all humankind, a mission above politics. Another collation was Paul's apparent dismissal of Jesus' genealogy as unimportant with the Nazarene insistence that his genealogy, like theirs, was the most important aspect of his life. What to make of the idea that their mutual Lord had been born of a virgin by miraculous means, yet was the predestined King of the Jews through Joseph, his legal father? In spite of revision, the Book of Revelation described Jesus as the 'Lion of the tribe of Judah', and the 'Root of David', claims that were anti-Roman by any definition. Furthermore, a serious slip in the verses following the 'Lion of Judah' claim revealed one of the most important doctrinal errors of all time. The passage reads: 'The dominion of the world has become the dominion of our Lord and his Messiah, and he shall reign for ever and ever.'[8] Our Lord *and* his Messiah? Quite obviously 'Lord' stands not for Jesus, but for God, and Jesus is unequivocally separated from God as his Messiah. And in the Epistles everything was topsy-turvy with James and Jude attacking Paulinist doctrine and Peter, of all people, upholding it. So the two Christianities battled it out, slowly merging into what eventually appeared to be epistemological harmony.

The problem was that the Nazarene Mother Church, regarded as dangerous by Judaism, and continually persecuted by the Romans, could do little to halt such a process. Attempts had been made by Hegesippus in the second century to collect earlier traditions of the Christian east and the Christian west, but the surviving records were fragmentary. The real problem was not just general Roman persecution and resentment against the Nazarenes from the Jews for having helped incite, along with other sectarians, a Roman attack, but a policy of persecution by the Romans directed specifically against members of Jesus' family; for it was they, the Romans realized, who would fan the flame of insurrection back into life. This view seemed to be contradicted by the fact that the Nazarenes refused to join Bar Kochba's revolt against the Romans during the reign of the Emperor Domitian, but this refusal was only because of their complete faithfulness to Jesus as Messiah – to them Bar Kochba was a fake Messiah. It was this kind of faith in Jesus as the returning Jewish Messiah (a worrying notion to the Romans) that earned the Nazarenes recognition as a potentially dangerous family dynasty.

The facts suggest that by the end of the first century and during the first quarter of the second, the Nazarenes had little knowledge of doctrinal developments among the Roman Christians. When the dust settled, it may well have come as a complete shock to them to discover that a whole new view of Jesus had evolved as a result of this group's interpretation of Paul's teachings – teachings which even early on had caused the Apostles to question both his credentials and his motives. When it became evident that a challenge to such ideas should be mounted, they themselves had modified their beliefs and acquired what Schonfield refers to as 'eccentricities as a result of new teaching and relationships with remnants of Baptist, Essene, Samaritan and other sects of "Saints" of the pre-war period'.[9] Here then is the historical mix, and from the many clues embedded in it we realize that the Nazarenes considered Paul's teachings, or more accurately what the Roman Church had done with Paul's teachings, to be an idolatrous offshoot of Nazarene beliefs: Jesus as the Jewish God *in the flesh* was, as far as they were concerned, pure blasphemy.

This conflict between the Nazarenes and the Roman Church lasted for centuries, and the fact that it did so shows the depth of feeling involved on both sides. But it is a conflict demoted in most historical writings to no more than a difference of opinion between the Roman Church and the 'Jewish' (at one time Jerusalem-based) Church. Jewish. Not Nazarene. The edge is taken off the situation by simply ignoring the Nazarenes-cum-Ebionites and using the blanket term 'Jewish' to describe a much more complex situation. The problem with this is that the Jews also were against the Nazarenes, for it was the Nazarenes in conjunction with what Schonfield calls the 'Essean-Essene' (the Holy Ones of Israel) who had brought calamity on the nation with their severity and their apocalyptic hopes. The reason for this approach is probably due to the reaction of the Jews to what Paul early on began to teach for, as he admits and as was certainly the case, his teaching was 'heresy', and regarded as such by orthodox Jews. Again there is a curious blurring of boundaries, but the result is the same as before: the Nazarenes are made to evaporate. It is almost as if they had never existed, as if Jesus had never been known as 'Jesus the Nazarene'.

Or is there a still deeper reason, perhaps?

Schonfield notes (as does Professor Ranke-Heinemann) that Irenaeus attacks the Nazarenes as heretics, but calls them 'Ebionites', 'the poor'. This was a term used by both the Essenes and the early Christian Church to describe their position before God: 'poor' simply meant 'humble'. That the Ebionites were a closely allied offshoot of the Nazarenes, but with even stricter habits, is recognized by most scholars. It is known, for instance, that they were fanatical vegetarians and opposed to all animal sacrifice. Schonfield is aware of such differences, and says that 'it would be going too far on the available evidence to regard the Ebionites as a denomination wholly distinct from the Nazarenes'.[10] Irenaeus seems to agree, for when describing the Ebionites he describes exactly the Nazarene rejection of Jesus as being anything other than a normal man born by normal means. As if this is not enough, he also observes that the Ebionites used only the Gospel of Matthew and that they rejected the Apostle Paul as an apostate from the Law, the latter being the principal factor in the Nazarene case against Roman Christianity.

The point is this: the Nazarenes rejected Paul's highly imaginative theology concerning Jesus as the Christ and spent centuries combating those ideas. The later Nazarenes had documented proof to work from: the original *Gospel of Matthew* in Hebrew; the Hebrew or Aramaic *Gospel according to the Hebrews* (also reputed to be by Matthew); the Ebionite anti-Pauline *Acts of the Apostles*; and last but not least other forms of the Aramaic Gospel such as the *Gospel of the Twelve* or *According to the Apostles*. Schonfield speculates that the *Gospel according to the Hebrews* was probably a propaganda exercise specifically designed to 'counter the New Testament Gospels and undermine their effect on Jewish Christians by furnishing a document that was consistent with Nazorean teaching and tradition'.[11] Such a statement brings us ever closer to the historical reality, the reality within which another set of entirely different Gospels were in circulation. And not Nazarene translations of the canonical Gospels, but original Nazarene Gospels (Matthew, John and the Acts of the Apostles) which would later be rewritten by the Christians and parodied by the Jews.[12]

Dr Schonfield is explicit concerning Peter's role in the early Jewish Nazarene Church. He tells us that Peter was not the chief spokesman for that Church, and that he was never converted to Paulinism. James (Jesus' full brother) was 'chief representative of Jesus' in the early Christian (Nazarene) community, and modern belief to the contrary is the result of centuries of propaganda initiated by the Roman Christian community. Denigration of the original Nazarene authority 'invested in the Apostles of Jesus and members of his family' had been their aim, and they had successfully wrested that authority from Jesus' family by adopting

Peter and making him a convert to Paul's new, heretical Gospel. We then learn that the Nazarene refutation of all this is to be found in the *Clementine Homilies* and *Recognitions* and, although late in origin (probably fourth-century translations from Greek into Latin reflecting third-century problems), they carry information quite obviously written to counter Western propaganda concerning Peter. Which is to say that although these sections of the *Homilies* and *Recognitions* said to have been written by Peter were known forgeries, the statements made by this pseudo-Peter nevertheless accurately reflected Nazarene concerns at the time. On behalf of Nazarene outrage at the Apostle Peter being 'borrowed' by Rome and made into an advocate for Paul's ideas about Jesus, pseudo-Peter denounced the Western Church's attempt to reverse what he himself had said and done, and although he named no names, his references to the 'lawless and trifling preaching of the man who is my enemy', and to men 'telling their catechumens that this is my meaning, which indeed I never thought of', were too obvious to be interpreted in any other way.

In the *Recognitions*, pseudo-Peter condemned those who dared misrepresent him and railed against those offering an authority other than that of the Nazarene Council. This was direct and unmistakable. Teachers lacking Nazarene credentials were not to be believed; only teachers from the 'Jerusalem Church' carrying the testimony of 'James' the Lord's brother, or interestingly, 'whosoever may come after him', were to be believed. All teachers had to be approved by the Jerusalem Council; there were no other Apostles apart from the original twelve. There then followed an argument between Peter and Simon Magus (believed by some scholars to be an alias for Paul); once again the subject was an extended revelation through 'visions', and Peter's rebuke of this position was to say that those who trust in apparitions or visions or dreams were 'insecure'.

To my way of thinking this reflects enormous commonsense, the kind of commonsense one would expect from someone with a real handle on reality. To pseudo-Peter, talk of the Holy Spirit guiding the Church is not to be accepted; for it could easily be a deceiving spirit that was talking, and such a spirit could 'say of himself what he will'. Pseudo-Peter the writer may be called, but to my ear he sounds more like Sir Walter Scott lecturing a namesake of mine on the dangers of taking apparitions seriously.[13]

THE LEGEND OF PETER

As noted earlier, it is now a point of faith to believe that the popes are all direct successors of Peter as Bishop of Rome. But if Peter never had that title, and was never in Rome, then those claiming succession from him are claiming a meaningless authority. Some historians do allow Peter a period of three or four years in Rome on the basis of tradition alone, but there is no actual historical evidence to that effect, and certainly no evidence to suggest that he was ever in charge of that particular Christian community. Paul's journey to Rome is recorded in great detail, but there is no New Testament evidence, nor any historical evidence, that Peter ever went there. There is no allusion in Peter's Epistle to Rome; and when the word Rome is mentioned in the New Testament, Peter's name is never associated with it. All is legend. If he was Paul's superior, then why does he receive so little attention after Paul's arrival?

And how do we explain Paul's letter to the Roman Christians at the height of Peter's *alleged* episcopate in or around 58? Paul addresses his letter not to Peter, which protocol would have demanded had he been leading the church since 42, but to the general congregation. And what of the letter's ethical content? Paul writes that he longs to see them, for he wants to impart to them some spiritual gift so that they might be established. Established? In what? Paul's version of the Gospel? Now if Peter was in Rome at this time, then the letter is a calculated insult to this chief Apostle's ministry; it is either that or he simply wasn't there at all and Paul was free to write whatever he wished. And as in this letter he also states that he does not 'build on another's foundation', it is hard to imagine that this can mean anything other than the fact that Peter was neither in charge of the Roman Church, nor even physically in Rome.

In his detailed study of Roman Catholicism, Dr Loraine Boettner points out that 'Paul was writing this letter because no apostle had been in Rome to clarify the Gospel to them and to establish them in the faith.'[4] This means that not only was Peter not there, and until that point had never been there, but that these Roman Christians were at that time of a different theological stamp from those established by Paul elsewhere. Now it is not too difficult to see what this means. It means without a doubt that in 58 the church at Rome was still Jewish-Nazarene. Not until the great fire of Rome in 64, and the persecution of the

Roman Church by Nero as a result of that fire would the predominantly Jewish-Nazarene adherents of that church be put to flight.

Peter was married and his wife accompanied him on some of his missionary journeyings. Catholic parlance has it that Peter's wife was actually his sister, but like the problem of James being Jesus' full brother, it should be noted that in Greek the word for sister is *adelphe*, whereas the Greek word used in the New Testament is *gune*, meaning 'wife'. Paul says: 'Have we no right to lead about a wife that is a believer, even as the rest of the apostles, and the brethren of the Lord, and Cephas (1 Cor. 9:5) Even as the rest of the apostles? And Jesus' family heirs? And Peter? What now of his railing against marriage and the flesh and goodness knows what else? Could it be that the New Testament texts contain not two points of view, but three? That of the Jewish-Nazarenes, that of Paul, and that of the Roman Church as it eventually came to be? For in the above statement Paul is certainly at variance with that church when it comes to 'marriage'; and he is blatantly at odds with this church in as far as 'spiritual gifts' were eventually outlawed by the Roman Church as anarchic and undermining of the authority of the bishops. And he is also in conflict with the Jewish-Nazarene church at Jerusalem. In fact he agrees with hardly anybody about anything! He is out of step most of the time, and his seeming conformity with later Roman opinion is only because he has been thoroughly edited and made to fit into that quite original theological scheme – a scheme developed almost wholly out of his theological notions, it has to be admitted, but a scheme not of his actual making. Eventually sandwiched between two heavily opposed theologies, what Paul actually believed would be crushed out of existence to allow a hybrid form of Christianity to grow and develop, indeed to mushroom into the future backed by Rome's secular arm.

Most historians would not even allow Peter three or four years in Rome, for, surprising as it may seem, his name does not appear on the earliest lists of bishops of Rome. According to Irenaeus, the first bishop of Rome was Linus, and he was appointed by Paul, whereas the bishop after Linus, Clement, is said to have been chosen by Peter. De Rosa's comment is simply to say 'the mystery deepens'. Also Eusebius, Constantine's friend and apologist, does not say that Peter was ever Bishop of Rome; and that in spite of Jerome saying later that he did. In the seventeenth century King Charles II's chaplain, William Cave, corrected Jerome by saying that he had probably reported on a notion of his time quite without substance, 'no such thing being found in the Greek copy of Eusebius'. And in line with modern scholarship, de Rosa notes that in those early days of the Church the Apostles did not belong to any one church, but to the Church as a whole, the fact of Apostleship precluding them from being bishop of one place. 'Peter, too,' he says, 'whatever momentous decisions he made in Jerusalem, Antioch and elsewhere, remained an apostle of the entire community.'[15] This is the reason why Paul, who really was in Rome, did not become its first bishop, but helped appoint someone else.

Basic to this question of whether Peter was ever actually in Rome, never mind being the first Bishop of Rome, are the designated 'missions' taken on by Peter and Paul. In his Galatian Epistle (2:7–8) Paul speaks of being entrusted with the gospel of the uncircumcision, and of Peter's mission being that of the gospel of the circumcision. Which is to say quite clearly that Peter's mission was to the Jews, and that Paul's was to non-Jews, to Gentiles. Boettner supplies the details here, and we learn that Peter's area of mission was to the Jewish exiles in Pontus, Galatia, Cappadocia, Asia and Bithynia – in other words Asia Minor. More importantly his journeyings also took him as far east as Babylon, and it is from Babylon that certainly his first, and probably his second, epistle comes. Boettner points out that although there is no scriptural evidence for Peter ever having been in Rome, there is certainly 'a plain statement of Scripture that he did go east to Babylon'.[16]

But Catholic exegetes play the same game with the word 'Babylon' as they play with James' relationship to Jesus, and with words like 'wife' and 'sister' in relation to Peter; in an introductory note to 1 Peter, the Catholic Confraternity edition tells us that 'Babylon' is a 'cryptic designation of the city of Rome'. The reason for this curious rejection of what is *actually* written in 1 Peter is surely that in the *Book of Revelation*, Rome is referred to as 'Babylon'. But as Boettner is quick to point out, the *Book of Revelation* is apocalyptic; it is written in figurative and symbolic language. Peter's first epistle, on the other hand, is a straightforward letter in a matter-of-fact style. So why pretend that Babylon means Rome?

I think that the reasons are obvious.

The historical facts are that Jews had been living in Babylon since the time of the Exile; Josephus confirms that great numbers of them had settled there by the time of Jesus. It was therefore exactly the sort of place Peter would have headed for. And it should be noted that in terms of New Testament chronology, Peter was part of the Jerusalem Council described in Acts 15, and that that council had specifically to do with the presentation of the Gospel to the Jewish and Gentile communities. It is at this council, held in 54, that Peter and Paul are assigned their separate missions. Chronologically this fact alone shows that Peter was not in Rome at the time he was supposed to be, and as it is not long after this council that he is confronted by Paul over his conformity to Judaistic rituals (Gal. 2:11–21), it is highly unlikely that he went against his assigned mission and ended up at the very heart of the Gentile world.

Boettner asks the appropriate question: 'Would he [Peter] defy the decision reached by all the apostles and brethren from the various churches who met in the famous first Council in Jerusalem?'[17] I believe Boettner to be correct in his assumption that Peter would not have defied that Council; and I think him equally correct when he says that Peter's missionary work would have taken him in the opposite direction. Three factors emerge clearly from this: (1) the Nazarene church at Jerusalem controlled by Jesus' brother James was still running the show; (2) Paul was already straining at the theological leash and threatening to break away from the Jerusalem church altogether; and (3) the church at Rome was still Nazarene governed. Boettner later makes much the same point in relation to the Nazarenes: 'It is well known that during the time of the apostles and for generations later the Eastern cities and the Eastern Church had the greatest influence, and that the Roman Church was comparatively insignificant.'[18] The Nazarene church of Rome was in the lion's den and so not able to grow like the other churches. Long before the reformation of the Catholic Church Rome's claim to be the only true Church had been firmly rejected by the Eastern churches. The first councils had been held in Eastern cities and were composed mostly of Eastern bishops, and the principal patriarchates had been Eastern – namely, Jerusalem, Antioch and Alexandria. Only centuries later and after the breakup of the Roman Empire would Rome gain the ascendancy.

THE COSMIC WAR ON EARTH

Malachi Martin would have us believe that a cosmic war between God and Satan has been in process since the beginning of time. Not only are the Scriptures (and history) wrong and Catholic tradition right about Peter being in Rome and not in Babylon, but above and around and *in* this whole situation Satan-cum-the-Devil-cum-Lucifer is at work. Martin states this quite plainly:

> Through the sacrifice, death and resurrection of Christ, and by the founding of the Roman Catholic Church, God had made it possible for each man and woman to make godly choices in life, and by those choices to attain Heaven after death. In that cosmic and constant war, Christ was the leader of God's campaign; and Christ's personal, visible representative among men was the Roman pope. Lucifer's aim in the war – the aim of Satan as adversary – was to ensure that as many human beings as possible missed that eternal after-life goal.[19]

What an extraordinary statement! In a roundabout manner this is to say that the questioning of Peter's episcopacy in Rome is part and parcel of Satan's *raison d'être* to pin one's soul to his lapel – reject the pope – *any* pope – and you're in deep spiritual trouble. We are no longer dealing with tradition alongside history or scripture, we are now dealing with a capital 'T' Truth which cannot be contradicted – the myth has gone manic. And if we do contradict it? Well, hell and damnation will be the result. Christ is in Heaven with God, and the pope in Rome has a divine mandate to do whatever comes into his head to safeguard the Roman Church which God has personally founded. We are the 'cherished objective' of God *and* of the Devil, and it is in this light alone that we must comprehend the whole edifice of Church history as taught by the Catholic Church.

What we have to watch out for is the Devil's propaganda campaign. For just as God can communicate by immaterial, supernatural, and totally spiritual means through images and sense data, through external events, words and actions, Lucifer too can communicate his desires at the sense data level. Which is to say that all he can offer us is, metaphorically speaking, the apple of temptation, the hard sphere of sense data alone. For Lucifer is preternatural, not supernatural; he moves outside of the supernatural because that is God's exclusive domain. So ultimately it is our ability to make 'choices' or suitable 'acts of will' which determines our spiritual fate; and to be able to make such choices we should attempt to find out from which source the data is streaming.

Martin refers to the above view of reality as 'authentic Christian teaching', and points back to Ignatius Loyola as the man who resuscitated this now ignored perception of reality. We are to realize that we have lost our way, that the cosmic war is still going on, that the humanistic cry of the Renaissance heralded not light, but darkness.

CHAPTER FOUR

The Dark Renaissance

The revival of learning, the Church's grand delusion that it is engaged in a cosmic war, and the challenge of theology to the Western intellectual tradition

In *The First Jesuit*, Mary Purcell tells us that the genius of Ignatius Loyola displayed itself more fully in education than in any other sphere. Devising an educational plan from his experiences in the universities of Europe, he chose 'the golden mean between the old and the new, being always on the alert for what was good and useful in contemporary educational developments'.[1] Appraising the strengths and weaknesses of the older medieval and the newer Renaissance education, he learned how to 'adapt himself to the needs and interests of his times'. So said a certain Father Ganss, relied upon by Purcell to paint her picture of Ignatius' intellectual formation in a period of great change. Summarizing Ganss, she describes Ignatius as devoted to the 'harmonious development of the whole man with all his faculties, natural and supernatural'.[2]

Reading such words leaves one with the impression of a thoroughly balanced mind seeking the best for all. However, Malachi Martin's description of the same idealistic vision sounds slightly different: 'Programmatically,' says Martin, choosing a strange word with which to begin 'he [Ignatius] best achieved that goal ... by training his companions so that they could achieve the desired unification of many wills, each and all locked into a super-human spiritual ideal.'[3] Super-human spiritual ideal? From the difference of focus detectable in these conflicting descriptions, I could only presume that I'd confused two processes: (1) those who were to be trained, and (2) those who were going to do the training. Loyola himself seems to agree with this division. In his *Spiritual Exercises*, Purcell's 'harmonious development of the whole man' turns into: 'To arrive at the truth in all things, we ought always to be ready to believe that what seems to us white is black, if the hierarchical church so defines.' So much for the harmonious, balanced development of others; Ignatius is obviously talking of his super-obedient 'soldiers', and these soldiers – referred to by Malachi Martin as a papal Rapid Deployment Force – no doubt purveyed their likes and dislikes with conviction and certainty.

And the reason for this training of the will among Loyola's followers? Because public interest in the 'here and now', in the more 'exciting temporal life' of the early sixteenth century had swamped the age-old belief in the subtle war against God waged by Lucifer through his subverting of the human will. The Renaissance may have seemed light-struck to those who gloried in its humanist values, in its cult of the individual, in its profane pronouncements against God and Church, but it was actually a Dark Renaissance, a return to pagan values under the guise of freedom through thought and knowledge. Thus thinks Malachi Martin; and I dare say there are many who agree with him. For in spite of the great advances made during the Renaissance period, it can also be argued that the brilliance of social culture hid savage appetites and passions, and that the courtly refinement and spectacular literary and artistic achievements of the age cloaked many hideous deeds. Christian virtues were scorned. Diplomacy in the hands of human-ists created a network of intrigue and string-pulling at the highest levels. The society surrounding Ignatius Loyola became mundane, pagan and irreligious. The good of the past was sacrificed, its evil retained, in moral terms the future was ignored.[4]

But surely that was more or less the state of affairs long before the start of the Renaissance? What was so different? When the Renaissance finally came the Church was in a state of moral and spiritual collapse; centuries of debauchery, scandal and power-mongering had enfeebled it. And this, I think, is why Ignatius' élite team of teachers were finally directed not to the poor and needy, to the uneducated and deprived as first intended, but to the task (directed by the pope himself) of creating a dedicated phalanx of totally obedient leaders of men. The rampant modernism of the time could not be stopped, that was realized, but through a highly skilled teaching Order like the Jesuits the people could be recon-vinced of their spiritual plight and brought back to the fold. For although many had discovered that there was more to life than religious dogma, that there was a mental air to be breathed which was untainted by fear, superstition and corruption, at the back of this new-fangled freedom lay the machinations of Lucifer – a fact which only those enthralled by Lucifer could not detect. The Renaissance was therefore no more than a new phase of the war between God and his evil counterpart; it was not, as many believed, an indication that the Church had got things terribly wrong from the very beginning.

THE REVIVAL OF LEARNING

The transition from the Middle Ages to the modern period is a fascinating historical journey which, alas, we can only touch upon here. Suffice it to say that this transition contained many important ingredients, some of which are vital to our appreciation of the medieval mind and its enthusiastic search for truth on multiple levels. A fresh and invigorating stage of the human journey had been reached, and with it came a fuller consciousness than had previously been witnessed.

As the word 'Renaissance' means 're-birth', this has led some writers to interpret the Renaissance as a harking back to antique times; but according to the experts, the revival of learning which took place signifies a much broader canvas of research and discovery based on the release of vital energies which heralded a mental revolution. Yes, the pagan past would contribute greatly to the Renaissance thirst for art and literature, but at base it was a visionary movement with its eye on the future, not the past. Brilliant the past had certainly been, but to Renaissance thinkers the future spelt release from the gods, or from God, not a doubling back into an older, more primitive perception of reality. The recovery of the classics was certainly important, but in comparison with the more immediate factors of the decay of the Church, the breakdown of empire, the weakening of the feudal system throughout Europe, the earlier invention of paper, printing, gunpowder and the mariner's compass, what the classical authors revealed of ancient Greek and Roman culture took second place.

Thus the Renaissance was a time of transition, fusion, preparation and tentative endeavour, the last stage of that escape from ecclesiastical and feudal despotism which so characterized the Middle Ages. As men and women read the classics and realized that humanity had a great and glorious past, their confidence soared; for had not these men and women found a new, freer way to live, relate and express themselves? Such freedoms had been eroded at the whim of emperors and kings and popes, but what should be remembered is that in spite of having no Christian tradition, these pagans had created two great civilizations replete with works of literature, philosophy and art, and encouraged both enquiry and criticism within their societies. In fact, from a very early period, they had created civilizations which, in the view of Malachi Martin, could not have continued if Christianity hadn't merged with the Roman Empire; civilization would have come to an abrupt halt. Here then was a mirror-image for the future, a goal to be reached and refined with the energy of a people at last set free. And the start of this great mental revolution? Ironically, the fall of Constantinople to the Turks in 1453. The will and intellect of the people, harnessed now towards self-emancipation, towards the natural rights of reason and the senses, was to open a gap between Church, state and populace which would never again close.

Malachi Martin does not agree with this; to him 'self-emancipation' is a dirty word. And so too reason and the senses divorced from a theology which demanded total subjugation of intellect and feeling – subjugation to theological policies often blatantly at odds with everything sensible and humane. Without at any point seeming to consider that self-emancipation – termed 'self-centredness' by this ex-Jesuit – was utterly natural as a way of reaction to past subjugation of the human spirit, he tells us that the Jesuits rejected the Renaissance preoccupation with the 'grandeur of the self', their attention being directed always to just two things: 'the warfare between God and Lucifer for each individual, and the Pope's need of devoted servants'.[5]

On reading such a sentence, one cannot help but wonder which of these propositions came first, and whether the latter 'need' was somehow linked to the former problem. But Martin's point is basically straightforward; he is saying that individuals should know what kind of 'spirit' a situation or event contains. But by this he does not mean 'natural bias' or 'fashion of thought' or 'paradigm' but, quite literally, either 'the spirit of God' or 'the spirit of Lucifer'. We should not allow perception or analysis to function divorced from this polarizing theological view, for to do so is to fall foul of Lucifer's means of communication through the natural world. Sense data on its own is not innocent, it is by its very nature Lucifer's means to an end, that end being the creation of 'images and motives he [Lucifer] would like to see as the individual's interior intimates, the regulators of his decisions and actions'.[6] This is no metaphor; it is a challenge to the very fabric of the Western intellectual tradition.

Yet in spite of what Martin has said about self-centredness and self-grandeur, he then tells us that the 'power of the individual in all this is crucial'. We have the power to choose, the power wilfully to reject spiritually inadequate views of the world or self. For as Ignatius had discovered, whatever you deliberately allowed to develop in your 'inner theatre of consciousness' would eventually regulate your decisions and general mode of behaviour. Herein lay the power of the Jesuits, the secret of their extraordinary success: it was their willingness to sublimate the whims of the self on behalf of a greater vision. Here was the purpose of the *Spiritual Exercises*, and that purpose was 'to control what entered his consciousness . . . so that he could remain Romanist and activist'.[7] Romanist *and* activist? Apparently so. The Jesuit's ascetic training was based on rules, and more rules, and then more rules. Every move, every thought, was governed by a rule. Order and discipline was the secret of Jesuitical success. As can be imagined, a cool, rational detachment resulted, a trait sustained by rigorous self-analysis, which was either admired or feared by friend and foe alike.

Of course the whole exercise was for the 'greater glory of God' through the recognition that God and Lucifer were at war, and because the Pope needed devoted servants. These were the factors that differentiate it from, say, the attempts of *Reichsführer* Heinrich Himmler to create the Waffen SS. Martin is himself interested in this curious copy-cat organization, describing how Himmler put together a huge library about the Jesuit Order, and that he even dreamed of training his élite troops along Jesuit lines. Dreamed? I could have sworn he did exactly that. And when Martin goes on to say that Himmler's plan failed to produce that 'inner subjugation of the will and intellect that Ignatius had produced in his Jesuits', one can only wonder at such a statement. For if ever soldiers were brought to a state of 'cool, rational detachment', it was certainly Hitler's Waffen SS. Of course, one should question the word 'rational' in this context, but was it ever really rational to believe that some kind of cosmic war was going on between God and Lucifer, and to think that believing such a thing glorified God? Or was it more accurate to say that the *raison d'être* of *both* organizations had been a willingness to sublimate the whims of the self on behalf of what was believed to be a greater vision? SS combat troops may have taken part in foolish esoteric rituals based on Ignatius's *Spiritual Exercises* at Wewelsburg Castle in Westphalia, and the vision adopted no more than a curious blend of 'the new Nordic cult of Wotan, Siegfried, the Holy Grail, and the Teutonic Knights of old', as Martin records, but was there really any difference between such an esoteric line up and the Church's unquestioning notion of itself as divinely appointed by God to control what happened not only on Earth but also in God's good heaven? Hitler, it is agreed, was either mad or crazed to think of himself as a latter-day Messiah sent to liberate the German people from the sin of weakness, but popes believed something uncomfortably similar, and expected to be treated not only as sane, but as sensible and spiritually responsible – the 'weakness of sin' was after all nothing more than the 'sin of weakness' by another name.

And so, in 1936, Hitler could speak confidently to Bishop Berning of Osnabrück as having done no more than the Church itself had done for over fifteen hundred years; for had not both organizations the same basic vision, the vision of all humanity brought to a state of perfect subjugation? To believe such a thing was of course to misrepresent the Church in many, many ways; but could Hitler ultimately be blamed for such a view (whether cynically held or not) given that the Catholic Church had itself blithely killed so many hundreds of thousands of people in the name of Christ? No, there was a terrible darkness on both sides, and Hitler's darkness was only seen to be the more terrible because it had been perpetrated after rather than before the Renaissance. Like it or not, the Renaissance, in spite of its intellectual impiety and arrogant sense of self-importance, heralded a healthy change in human consciousness, and to read it any other way was, perhaps, to be in the grip of a disabling fear, a fear of things that go bump in the night.

THE UN-DARK MIDDLE AGES

Basically, the Renaissance symbolized the recovery of the human spirit. However, its many marvels of thought and perception did not materialize without much previous endeavour. After what is generally seen as a long period of bondage to oppressive ecclesiastical and political orthodoxy during the Middle Ages, European consciousness once more became liberal, practical and enthusiastic. Finding again some of the qualities exhibited by classical civilizations, but with an even more astute perception of the self and the world, human consciousness began to evolve a vision quite at odds with Church and state. From being dominated by an intolerant theology, and deprived of any positive knowledge, the medieval mind had indeed struggled to make philosophical and mathematical sense of the world, but had fallen back in disarray as Churchmen, backed by the awesome power of the Church, and wielding the same type of logic (shades of the Jesuits to come), argued that 'heaven' and 'hell' and 'salvation' were the only realities worth considering. Everything had to be measured against those realities; to speculate on anything for its own sake was to invite the world to loom larger than the creator of that world. Persecuted for trying to free philosophy from theological orthodoxy, Scotus Erigena and Abelard gained little support and were defeated. So too was Roger Bacon, condemned by the Franciscans because he presumed to know more than was allowable in terms of humility. The Fraticelli spiritualists, inspired by the mystic prophesies of Joachim of Flora, attempted to grasp something purer than rigid Latin theology could afford and were treated abominably as a result. The influential order of the Knights Templar suffered wholesale persecution because they, too, sought to evade the rigidity of the Roman Church.

In 1231, the Inquisition was born. Anyone opposed to the Church's teaching was condemned as a heretic and given into the hands of the secular authorities to be interrogated, tortured and burned. Repentance – the very heart of Christian teaching – earned one imprisonment for life. De Rosa states that in July 1233 Gregory IX appointed two full-time inquisitors, the first of 'a long line of serene untroubled persecutors of the human race'.[8] In a telling cameo we learn that in 1239 a bishop by the name of Moranis was accused of allowing heretics to live and multiply in his diocese. As a result, a certain Dominican by the name of Robert le Bougre was sent to Champagne to investigate. One week later the whole town was on trial, and on 29 May Bishop Moranis and 180 people went to the stake. Such fanaticism, it seems, was not uncommon, it having taken root after Gregory VII's reign. And no wonder, for between 1200 and 1500 all shades of difference in discipline and belief had been carefully removed by a series of papal laws – creative disagreement was officially taboo.

Yet as early as 384 torture had been denounced by a Roman synod, and in the seventh century judges had been ordered by Nicholas I to ignore any testimony procured by such means. Being beyond civil law, inquisitors could do whatever they liked, for as long as they liked, to whomever they liked. By direct papal command they were to have 'no mercy' on their victims; pity for heretics was defined as 'unchristian'.

De Rosa is implacably truthful in the face of such evidence. He says: 'Like the Nazi SS in the twentieth century, they were able to torture and destroy with a quiet mind because their superior officer – in this case, the Pope – assured them that heretics were a dirty, diseased and contagious foe that must be purged at all costs and by all means.'[9] I can only presume that it is observations such as this that made Philip Caraman, SJ, call Peter de Rosa's book 'a binful of garbage'. But one can only wonder why, for there is a great deal of damning evidence against the Church and the papacy for anyone with the patience and the stomach to seek it out. The excuse of 'human frailty', of 'these were ages of barbarity' does not wash here, not one little bit. For behind these vicious, arrogant and pathologically driven men of the cloth hung the Christ of Golgotha, the God-man who through the auspices of the Holy Spirit was supposed to be in charge of the whole operation.

Such deeds were certainly inspired from within, of that there can be little doubt; but not as a result of some whispering Christ, as anyone with an ounce of commonsense must realize. Rather, more by an ever-growing hydra-headed theology which ensnared and destroyed innocent human beings by its insidious presence. Even the acclaimed Dominican Thomas Aquinas succumbed to theological madness, for in his *Summa Theologia* he wrote:

> Though heretics must not be tolerated because they deserve it, we must bear with them, till, by a second admonition, they may be brought back to the faith of the church. But those who, after a second admonition, remain obstinate in their errors, must not only be excommunicated, but they must be delivered to the secular power to be exterminated.[10]

More terrifying, more chilling, however, is a statement by Dr Marianus de Luca, SJ, Professor of Canon Law at the Gregorian University in Rome who, in his *Institutions of Public*

Ecclesiastical Law (1901) was able to write that the Catholic Church 'had the right and duty to kill heretics'. For if they were imprisoned or exiled they would only corrupt others. There was therefore no option but to put them to death. 1901? And this statement was backed by a personal commendation from Pope Leo XIII![11] What can one say? Malachi Martin may dream of an age of faith, of a return to the 'good old days' when the Church had power and respect and authority, but for his sake as well as my own and Peter de Rosa's, I sincerely pray that it never comes about.

During October 1302, Pope Boniface VIII made the ever-growing claims of the papacy 'arrestingly specific', as Will Durant so charmingly puts it. Issuing the Papal Bull *Unam sanctum*, Boniface stated that there was but one true Church outside of which there was no salvation; that there was but one body of Christ, with one head, not two; and that Christ's representative on Earth was the Roman pope. But he didn't stop there; the Bull went on to say that there were two swords, or powers – the spiritual and the temporal – that the first was borne *by* the Church, the second borne *for* the Church by the king. But only under sufferance. Spiritual power was above temporal power, and in the light of this, *all men should be subject to the Roman pontiff.*

Without going into the complicated circumstances surrounding this outburst of spiritual bravado, suffice it to say that Boniface VIII, governed in his nature by a brutal cynicism, died one year later as a result of stretching the patience of his subjects too far. One incident will be sufficient to show the ruthless nature of this pope, a ruthlessness which caused Dante to bury Boniface head down in a fissure of rock in his Eighth Circle of Hell. At the storming of Palestrina where some of his enemies were besieged after questioning his legitimacy, he avenged himself by killing some six thousand of its inhabitants and utterly flattening the fortress – only the cathedral was spared. Nicknamed the 'Black Beast' for his deeds of tyranny, murder, adultery and much else, he was posthumously tried for practising ritual magic in or around 1310. Peter de Rosa adds a curious footnote to the volumes of information available on this infamous pope; he tells us that when the new St Peter's was completed in 1605, Boniface's tomb had to be moved. To everyone's horror it cracked open and revealed a body uncorrupted in spite of a lapse of three centuries.

THE PROGRESS OF ROMAN CHRISTIANITY

And so Roman Christianity 'progressed', having started humbly in the catacombs with care for the needy and a real humility due to much suffering on behalf of a high moral ideal. Thrust suddenly into the limelight and given unlimited prestige and resources before it had time to mature, before it could properly digest its future role in the world, it succumbed to the temptation of seeing itself as the only legitimate arbiter of the spiritual condition, and fell into the grotesque state of rationalizing its most brutal and devious actions as sanctioned from above – for surely God had ordained such a miraculous elevation? Constantine may even have sensed the direction about to be taken by the Church he had so rapidly elevated, for it is said that he cried out on his death bed: 'Not the sword! Not the sword! Knowledge!' Did he perhaps see the carnage to come, the intolerance, the greed, the brutality?

Speaking of the same tradition, Malachi Martin says: 'Was Constantine regretting it all? The wealth he had conferred on the Church, the power he had put at the Roman pontiff's disposal?'[12] But on further reflection he thinks not; it is more likely that, in an unrefined way, Constantine was attempting to say what a dying Augustine was to cry one hundred years later: 'Too late have I known thee, O beauty ever ancient, ever new!' Yet Martin asks the question, and in asking it shows that he is conscious of the possibility that something had gone wrong, or was about to go wrong, with the Church's method of functioning; a functioning related to Martin's previous speculation that Pope Sylvester's churlish rejection of Jesus' blood relatives could have been better handled. But in what way could it have been better handled? If Sylvester had not sent these Jewish-Nazarene Christians packing what then? A friendship? A relationship? A partnership? What then? A sharing of power? A whole new set of influences on the early Church? A completely different basic theology of Jesus' spiritual status? This thought is obviously at the back of Malachi Martin's mind, but it is never articulated. As he says, 'The Jewish Christians had no place in such a church system.'[13] The juggernaut of Roman Christianity was already on the move.

Later, in a different context, Martin recognizes that things could have been different; however, I cannot help but feel that I've been distracted from the main event when he explains that the Church's basic problem was Constantine, and that through supplying both the Eastern and Western branches of the Church with hypocritical religious reasons to split from one another (religious reasons backed by political and economic considerations), this Emperor effectively derailed the Church through the introduction of election methods which produced bitter, and sometimes violent clashes between prospective popes. As one pope lay dying, factional disputes filled the air, bishops, priests, deacons and sub-deacons facing up to nobles and the Roman Senate while the friends, kinsmen and families of ambitious candidates tried to sway the decision in their favour. As a result, blood was shed and people died in the name of the Church.

So we learn that at the election of Pope Damascus I in 366, no less than thirty-seven corpses littered the Liberian Basilica. Only occasionally were popes elected by their predecessor, force sometimes being used to ensure the result. In the final part of the process, the nominee had to be ratified by the Emperor, who more often than not produced his own candidate and expected him to be accepted without question. So, yes, Constantine was a primary influence on how things shaped up within the Church, but the question of Jesus' kinsmen just will not go away – their omission from this process of formation is, in my opinion, fundamental.

Throughout the centuries the Church promoted feeling and emotional attachment over intellectual development; yet at the same time there evolved a highly complex backcloth of theology linked to divine revelation. Through claims of divine revelation the Church cancelled out the strict requirements of intellect, and in organizing such revelations into dogmas backed by theology, held the mind of the faithful in thrall both by way of emotional projection and intellectual bemusement. And so 'doubt' became a sin, and the conflict with natural intellect arose, and a closure on philosophy took place. It did not matter what the question was, divine revelation had produced the answer, or if not, then the answer was to be found hidden somewhere in Scripture. In 307 Lactantius wrote: 'We who are instructed in the knowledge of the truth by the Holy Scriptures know the beginning of the world and its end.'[14] So the axis of concern was shifted from this world to the next, and the supernatural replaced history. By such means was investigation of natural causes discouraged and, as the historian Will Durant tells us: 'The advances made by Greek science through seven centuries . . . sacrificed to the cosmology and biology of Genesis.'[15]

However, it cannot and should not be denied that it was the
Roman Church which helped to hold things together during
the Dark Ages of barbarian invasion and cultural decline; the
destruction would certainly have been worse but for the Church
with its unwavering policy of faith over reason. The constant pro-
vision of supernatural sanctions to support social order, of a creed
created out of myth, miracle, fear, hope and love to tame the barbarian heart and quieten the brute mind eventually backfired, for
it was a policy which resulted, inadvertently, in a hostility towards
real learning. Seven centuries of Greek science all but vanished as
the Roman Church evolved; literature in the free, explorative
pagan sense went into decline – in spite of the aspirations of some
of the Church Fathers to keep the writings of Virgil and Cicero
alive. The historic function of Roman Christianity may have been
to re-establish the moral basis of society, but as it tangled with the
world of politics and power this promising premise gave way to a
stultifying egocentricity – the Christ of Faith, unleavened by
Nazarene realism, was running out of epistemological control.

Writing of the Renaissance and the Middle Ages in 1965,
Professor P Smith of Cornell University reminds us that in spite of
being dominated by an intolerant theology and deprived of positive knowledge, the 'native human instincts, [and] the natural
human appetites, remained unaltered and alive beneath the crust
of orthodoxy'.[16] All was not lost. But the dangers inherent in hallucinations of fancy, allegory and visions were real enough. Smith
captures the situation in these words:

> Man and the actual universe kept on reasserting their rights and
> claims, in one way or another; but they were always being thrust
> back again into Cimmerian regions of abstractions, fictions,
> visions, spectral hopes and fears, in the midst of which the intellect
> somnambulistically moved upon an unknown way.[17]

That describes exactly the dilemma faced by intelligent minds during that long dark night of the intellect. Numerous attempts were
made to lighten and enlighten, but each attempt was successfully
suppressed by a logic of Heaven and Hell and Salvation which
haunted the conscience like a nightmare, and still does. Smith adds
to this apt description the observation that the medieval problem
was that the age had lost 'the right touch on life'. This was what
was missing. And how beautifully put. No dwelling on rebellion
or lawlessness here; just a wistful noticing that the delicate touch

required to live a successful life or build a successful civilization had all but vanished. This was the problem; and the losing of this delicate human sensibility had resulted in the over-shadowing sphinx of theology sustaining superstition and stupidity to the detriment of real questions.

An attempt at intellectual and aesthetic escape was made in southern France during the thirteenth century; Emperor Frederick II was deeply influenced by the blooming of a gentle culture perfumed by poetry in Provence. The ecclesiastical and feudal fetters were momentarily broken. A rich and dextrous language developed which reflected the latest, most modern phase of medieval literature in Europe. Naturalism was released in what Professor Smith describes as 'the fabliaux of jongleurs, lyrics of minnesingers, tales of trouvères, romances of Arthur and his knights'. Passion and the enjoyment of life came bursting to the surface. And, curiously visible in Goliardic poetry, was the influence of pagan inspiration. In poem and in song the ancient gods of Greece and Rome were evoked in taverns, on the open road, in the forests. Those naughty gods of the ancients were no longer in exile, but back in the hearts and minds of men and women.

I have closely paraphrased Professor Smith's prose at this point to capture something of what he so movingly conveys in his excellent article on the Renaissance and the medieval preparation for that rebirth, and I can almost see Malachi Martin shudder at what I think he would consider the beginnings of the spiritual debauch to come. Along with Smith and de Rosa (and many another) Martin is fully aware of the state the Church had got itself into, and is honest to a fault in writing of that debacle; but he believes something inherently sinister to have resided in the resuscitation of the pagan vision. And that in spite of the fact that the revival of learning was not the root of the Renaissance at all, rather, it was the surfacing of the pent-up energies of natural human intelligence using whatever lay around. Once again Martin would wince; for the word 'natural' would to his ear suggest an unbalanced condition of soul and mind, mind having displaced soul and left it vulnerable to demonic attack.

But for the people of southern France this opportunity to continue the experiment in freedom and gentleness was short lived. In a re-thinking of age-old dogma, the Church 'preaching Simon de Montfort's crusade' and 'organising Dominic's Inquisition' bore down to exact vengeance for deviation by sword, fire, famine and pestilence. The people were driven back into the darkness of superstition to experiment, not with reality, but with sorcery and magic; for these were the only means left through which power over nature or insight into the mysteries surrounding human life could be attained. It did not matter that life had seemed sweet and ordinary, sensible and free of fear during those heady days of poetry, enquiry and love, what mattered was the realization that all of it was in the hands of Satan, and that the idea of innocent action at any level was a dark trick perpetrated by that great and terrible being. This attempt to throw off the shackles of a religious vision which had sufficed for so long was premature; the historical conditions were not yet unbalanced enough for the idea of universal monarchy, of an indivisible Christendom incorporating the Holy Roman Empire and the Roman Church to come apart. Reassessment and experiment and exploration were not yet fully possible; and that in spite of Frederick II's extraordinary attempt to initiate a Renaissance all of his own and single-handedly to topple the Pope from his lofty perch in 1250. It was an abortive Renaissance; but an inkling of what was to come!

CHAPTER FIVE

The Fatal Thread in Modernism

The Church's imaginary field of Satanic energy, the Teilhardian idea of consciousness as a general phenomenon in nature, and the necessity to go beyond childish things

In his spiritual testament written one month before his death, Pierre Teilhard de Chardin, SJ, speaks of 'energy being transformed into Presence'. But alas, as he tells us frankly, he is one of the few people to have witnessed such a transformation – the wonderful 'Diaphany' that has transfigured everything for him seems to be a closed book for other writers. And yet, in spite of having had a 'glorious vision' of energy undergoing fundamental change, he is no better as a person; he is still not at peace and cannot, through his actions, properly communicate the 'wonderful unity' encompassing him.

The words used are interesting; 'Diaphany', 'Glorious vision' and 'Wonderful unity'. And then a question from this remarkable Jesuit: 'Is there in fact a Universal Christ, is there a Divine milieu? Or am I, after all, simply the dupe of a mirage in my own mind?' But each time he thinks like this, each time he questions the authenticity of his 'Christic' (his vision of the cosmic Christ), three successive waves of evidence arise from deep within to sweep away any such fear: (1) *coherence* of mind and heart; (2) a *contagious power* which allows the love of God to erupt; and (3) the obvious *superiority* of such a vision over religious dogma. This is startling stuff, particularly the last point, but it is as nothing compared with a later statement suggesting that this 'superiority of vision' might spontaneously and explosively spread to others as in a chain reaction. For is it not the case, asks de Chardin, 'that the truth has to appear only once, in one single mind, for it to be impossible for anything ever to prevent it from spreading universally and setting everything ablaze'?[1]

Malachi Martin is more than sceptical about de Chardin's 'glorious vision'; he is openly scathing, and not without justification on occasions. He flatly rejects what this fellow Jesuit postulated in his writings about the spiritual evolution of the human race. In fact he singles de Chardin out for punishment in his book *The Jesuits*, stating that it is not possible to understand the change brought about in the Society of Jesus without a knowledge of de Chardin's thinking – a change which he describes as 'the almost perfected mode of recalcitrance to all and any papal wish'. Warming to his topic from this interesting standpoint, we learn that de Chardin was tall and aristocratic in bearing, distinguished and quick-witted, messianic in intensity and not unlike Charles de Gaulle in some aspects of his character and verbal delivery. We also learn that he consciously identified with the sixteenth-century astronomer, Galileo Galilei, that he possessed an arrogance of attitude that did not repel, and that he injected a new philosophy and a new excitement into an age already revolutionized by genetics and many other scientific discoveries. The only problem was that this new philosophy utterly contradicted Catholic teaching on creation; the Bible did not say anything about Adam and Eve being the apex of the animal creation – the Scriptures stated quite clearly that *homo sapiens* had resulted from a separate act of creation. The human soul had not 'evolved'; it had been 'breathed' into Adam as a direct gift from his creator.

The attempt by some Catholic scholars to reconcile evolution with official doctrine had, as a result, spawned a nightmare scenario, a hybrid theory of creation in which God had intervened in the evolutionary process and infused a soul into an already highly evolved animal. Orthodox Catholic teachings rejected such a view. De Chardin overcame this rejection by postulating an innate connection between matter and spirit – basic consciousness had existed in matter from the very beginning. And so not 'two', but 'many' human beings had exhibited a new level of self-consciousness in the beginning, and this process of development was now heading, in our century, for what de Chardin termed the 'Omega Point' of history. Christ was this Omega Point, but not the Christ called 'Jesus'. Rather, some figure of the distant future not properly defined by de Chardin in relation to the Christ of the Gospels.

Martin is not amused by this vague use of words. 'Obviously,' he says, tilting for the attack:

such a theory imposes either the abandonment or the complete transformation of all the basic doctrines of Roman Catholicism. Creation, Original Sin, the divinity of Jesus, redemption by Jesus' death on the cross of Calvary, the Church, the forgiveness of sins, the Sacrifice of the Mass, priesthood, papal infallibility, Hell, Heaven, supernatural grace – even the existence of the freedom of God – all must be reformulated, and perhaps abandoned in large part.[2]

But he is only just starting. He attacks de Chardin's notion of the 'Ultra-human', and with dexterity so describes his character and mind-set that almost every action, every statement, every thought takes on sinister overtones: de Chardin was against the cloistered life; de Chardin didn't like Christmas; de Chardin was feckless; de Chardin lacked gentleness and compassion and fair-mindedness and sensitive perception; and, finally, de Chardin was completely disillusioned with the Roman Catholic Church and its monstrous supernaturalisms.

At this point we can begin to get down to the grass roots of de Chardin's search for something beyond dogma and magical-type beliefs; but the invective housed in Martin's questioning of de Chardin's character should not go unnoticed. It is after all a pretty damning exercise to strip someone of all gentleness, compassion, fair-mindedness and sensitive perception. Considering how Martin has previously accommodated the austere, ultra-cool character of Ignatius Loyola, this relieving de Chardin of *all* the basic human qualities because of a surface coolness is perhaps to go too far. A cold fish he may well have been, but his writings reveal a mind on fire with a vision for humanity which even at its strangest is more balanced than some of the religious dogmas either rejected or modified by that mind. We should remember that Martin admits earlier that de Chardin's type of arrogance did not repel others; there was something deeply attractive about this man in spite of his odd personality traits.

Yet I can sympathize with Martin's exasperation with de Chardin, for one senses in his writings the use of religious terminology merely for its own sake. I mean by that that he had, possibly, jettisoned most, if not all, of the conceptions behind the religious language he utilizes. In some curious fashion, Christ is not Christ and God is not God in the sense generally held. Something else is going on in de Chardin's language; something deep and

troubling and confrontational is struggling to articulate its presence
through his spiritual imagination. And my use here of the word
'imagination' should not be seen as pejorative; I mean simply that
faculty which allows us to explore and extend our mental boundaries. De Chardin's vision of God has undergone dramatic change;
he's trying to highlight what most of us already know only too well:
the simple God of our childhood is long since dead, he has
evaporated like smoke and left us in the lurch. De Chardin puts it
this way: 'At the present moment in human history, no religion
explicitly and officially offers us the God we need.'

BACK TO FATHER 'BONES'

In *Hostage to the Devil*, Malachi Martin hits his novelistic stride
and carries us down into what he considers the Teilhardian
mystery in a new way. We are shown how the 'fabric of faith' is
stripped away in Father David Bones' life through too strong a
fascination with de Chardin's thinking. David falls into the trap of
suspecting that what he had previously thought of Jesus was too
small a concept. The 'complaints of reason' in David's head over
doctrines that do not fit with the findings of science constitute a
'fatal thread' born out of his acceptance of de Chardin's theories.
Due to such theories he can no longer put up with the break
between the world of 'nature' and Jesus as 'saviour'. In evolutionary terms, materiality and divinity are one; Jesus was not God
come down to Earth from Heaven, he was merely an off-shoot of
creation's travail towards perfection. Here then was the meaning
of how Jesus was simultaneously human and divine; he had
carried the divine element of self-consciousness potentially
resident in matter to its point of fullest expression.

As seen through the eyes of a Catholic traditionalist like
Malachi Martin, all of this is a horrendous deceit; it is a fundamentally Satanic reinterpretation of a stupendous Gospel truth
that should not be tampered with under any circumstance. It
does not matter that Catholic doctrine flies in the face of scientific descriptions of how the world works. It does not matter that
the evidence of palaeontology points unreservedly to there
having been many precursors of the human. It does not matter
that cyclotrons reveal an amazingly complex subatomic world. It
does not matter that every scientific discipline points in at least a

similar, if not an identical direction. All that matters is that one continues to believe, without question, without a flutter of doubt, in a Catholic interpretation of New Testament writings. The 'sacred' is locked up inside the pages of the New Testament, in the stories and dialogues of men and women dead these two thousand years, and the Catholic methodology of translating that sacredness from paper to life, from ancient story to modern mind and heart has to be accepted as having existed in the mind of God since before the foundation of the world.

De Chardin is not simply wrong, not simply mistaken; Martin sees him as in some sense possessed by diabolical forces which skewed his thinking away from revealed truth. That is the bottom line. On this basis, Martin's interpretation of my statement that something deep, troubling and confrontational was struggling to articulate its presence through de Chardin's spiritual imagination, will be that I have unwittingly intuited a terrible truth. De Chardin was possessed; he was spiritually numb and eventually incapable of detecting that 'possessing presence' in the depths of his own being. Energy was indeed transformed into 'presence', and this is the underlying reason why the Jesuit Order has succumbed to rebellion and disobedience.

TORN BETWEEN REALITIES

In *Hostage to the Devil*, Malachi Martin refers to de Chardin's thinking on seven occasions; in *The Jesuits*, on fourteen occasions. And each time he makes reference to this internationally acclaimed Frenchman, we gain access to Martin's thinking processes and witness the phenomenon of a highly educated mind bound to, and in the service of, Christian dogma. It is fascinating to listen to his tone, to pick up on his passionate sincerity, to feel the binding power of doctrine on his thinking. He can list reasons galore for not believing in something, and in the next breath declare belief in that very thing by way of faith or revelation. Whatever the hard facts of a situation, he can produce an escape route by pointing beyond these facts to miraculous intervention. Which is to say that he believes in a universe where the laws of physics are mere decoration. If God wants to intervene in human affairs, such laws can be suspended. And why not, he would argue. What's the good of being God if you can't have your own way?

But first of all, let's get the de Chardin in Malachi Martin's mind out into the open. What is this American Jesuit's overview of this French Jesuit's contribution to the sciences of palaeontology and anthropology? How does he rate his fame, influence, and character? Well, Martin describes de Chardin as an intellectual, an ascetic, a hero, a brilliant student, teacher and mystic, and goes on to paint him as a pioneer field worker, a discoverer of Pekin Man (*Sinanthropus pekinensis*), and a philospher who thought that matter, even primitive matter, was transfused with consciousness. Dedicated to the philosophy of Descartes, de Chardin's ability to 'answer inquisitorial questions with a flow of professional and technical detail'[3] is recorded, and his refusal to 'kowtow intellectually' to Church authority is described as having frightened the ecclesiastical mind.

All in all, quite a list of positive attributes, one would think, but immediately invalidated by his statement about Teilhard being the 'custom-built answer, the ready-made darling for the bankrupt Catholic intellectuals of his century'. Quite a barrage, that, and all because de Chardin helped others shake off the traditional shackles of Christian dogma. Condemned for his 'refusal to revolt when silenced by chicanery', de Chardin is likened to Joan of Arc, Francis Xavier and Simone Weil.

Condemned for his refusal to revolt when silenced by chicanery? What exactly does that mean? Does it mean that in spite of being wrong de Chardin is further condemned for having had the intelligence to keep his mouth shut when faced with trickery and fallacious methods of reasoning? If so, what exactly *is* Martin saying? Why this choice of words? What is his game plan in making such an extraordinary statement? And why is his work peppered with sentences such as this? Is some other part of his mind perhaps trying to inform him that his conscious evaluation of Catholic Christianity is questionable?

Malachi Martin's principal quarrel with de Chardin's thinking is that he allowed scientific theory to get in the way of revealed truth. Allow the beliefs and assumptions of science to stand as undeniable, or even highly probable facts, and the Church's teaching on creation, the human condition and the coming of Jesus as saviour become superfluous. Describing the gulf between these two approaches as an 'impassable' and 'impossible' gap, Martin derides those who think such a gap can be closed, and speaks of them as being in the clutches of a 'fatal flaw'. For in such a scheme, ultimately, God is no longer divine, Jesus is no longer a saviour figure, life is an evolutionary accident and human consciousness is no more than the 'culminating flower' of a process born among the gases and acids of outer space. We have emerged from nature, and Jesus is no more than the prototype for a new species of evolved human being.

Referring to a meeting between de Chardin and Father David Bones in 1955 (two months before de Chardin's death), Martin describes the man some have likened to a second Aquinas as exhibiting a strange simplicity. In fact, he speaks of de Chardin in such a fashion that he begins to take on a sinister and vacuous edge. Martin's description of the man is straightforward enough, probably accurate enough, but there is something elusive within or behind these words. And then there is the inscription written by de Chardin in *Le Milieu Divin*, the book brought by David to be autographed. This inscription, innocent in itself, is left in mid-air, so to speak, and later made into a reason for David to question the old Jesuit's state of mind. The words are innocuous, it might be argued, but deadly in their impact when all the pieces are finally presented. For the old Jesuit had written: 'They said I opened Pandora's box with this book. But they did not notice, Hope was still hiding in one of its corners.'[4] And in a description of de Chardin during this meeting (a description which makes one wonder if Martin was hiding in a cupboard complete with spyhole), Martin has him 'completely with David, totally present to him, taking in David's glance with a personable expression and a direct simplicity that almost embarrassed the younger man'.[5]

But instead of reading this situation positively, it is again left in mid-air and the impression given is of an old man who is curiously empty, perhaps even drained of intelligence in some untoward fashion. Clever writing. Once again Martin the novelist is at work, and the impressions build page by page towards a damning broadside which eventually changes the old anthropologist into an agent of the Devil. This is not, of course, said directly, but it is undeniably what Malachi Martin is driving at when he later describes Father David Bones' breakdown-cum-possession and makes the whole incredible experience the result of his having accepted the theories of Teilhard de Chardin.

So what exactly did Teilhard de Chardin believe in that warranted such a fear-ridden response? This is a complicated question and can be touched upon only lightly here, but it was undoubtedly his metaphysic of evolution which upset the ecclesiastical hierarchy. Christocentric this metaphysic may have been, but in the end it was a synthesis of ideas which bred suspicion, incomprehension, and finally anger among his peers. As with the theories of John Hick, de Chardin saw evolution as a process converging towards a final unity. And like Hick he also helped revitalize the ideas of Irenaeus and Duns Scotus over against those of Augustine without losing sight of the problem of sin so dear to Augustine's heart. He was a priest of the Roman Catholic Church and remained as such until the end of his days; and that in spite of the fact that he was eventually censored, silenced, exiled and forbidden to publish or lecture. But as Martin points out, his ideas 'ran through the intellectual milieu of Europe and America like mercury',[6] and these ideas continue to influence those thinkers who are dissatisfied with constipated theology and the sometimes arrogant dictates of science. Classified along with devout pioneers such as Pico della Mirandola, Ramon Llull and even Origen, de Chardin's originality of thought earned him much applause in some quarters, condemnation in others.

And all because he believed that materiality and divinity were one and the same thing. That was what could not be tolerated by orthodox Catholic thinkers. This recalcitrant Jesuit had had the audacity to amalgamate physical creation with the spiritual domain. Which is to say that the Church's carefully nurtured grand divide between the material and the divine was under threat, and that science and theology were being made to coalesce in an utterly indecent manner. That was the crux of the problem, and if allowed to mature as an alternative theology of the human spirit, this diabolical stitching together again of God and world would result in a new paganism, a pagan gnosticism placing the emphasis not on redemption through Christ's death on the cross, but on man's consciousness 'emerging from sheer materiality as automatically as a hen from an egg'.[7] This description of cosmic events is unthinkable in Christian terms. For if accepted even tentatively, then Jesus' divinity must also, as repercussion, be interpreted as having emerged from his human nature.

In *The Jesuits*, Teilhard de Chardin is singled out for special obloquy over the state of the Catholic Church in India. Focusing on a special meeting between John Paul II and some high-ranking clerics, Martin reveals some fascinating information on Vatican tensions, while at the same time concentrating on a report which summarizes Jesuit influence in India as an adulteration of Christian belief. Accused of having deformed the meaning of priesthood, baptism, the value of prayer, mortification and penance, the Society is also held responsible for undermining the value of the Eucharist, of discrediting belief in immortality, of diluting belief in Heaven and Hell, and of eroding the primacy of the Holy Father.[8] All in all, a most damaging catalogue of misdemeanours aimed directly at de Chardin's influence on Catholic intellectuals of the Jesuit variety. In view of this, it is not at all strange that a sturdy traditionalist like Malachi Martin froths at the mouth when de Chardin's name is mentioned, and in terms of his personal beliefs it is quite understandable.

Understandable it may be, but definitely not acceptable when this skilled writer and thinker carries his umbrage too far and presents de Chardin as a henchman of the Devil for daring to question, by way of reasoned argument, the contents of the Church's doctrinal suitcase. Or would the word 'baggage' not be better in this instance – for in essence is that not the whole point of this war of words, the doctrinal baggage lugged down the centuries by Christians because of a deeply embedded fear of their own inner darkness? And not only of the darkness, but also of the light. A fear of the mind and its illumination. A fear of the body and its utterly natural requirements. A fear of anything which directly challenges or confronts their pet paradigm – a paradigm where innocent human beings can be damned to the flames of hell for not carrying a particular belief-system in their heads. If it were not so dangerous, it would be laughable. But it is not laughable, it is pathetic, for ultimately it is much more than a war of words that orthodox Christians are engaged in. It is a war for the control of our innermost being, and as such a doctrinally driven Christianity is not a shield against diabolical infringement, but more probably a perfect example of it.

Now I do not mean to imply by this that Christianity is in any sense evil; that is, evil in the sense that de Chardin is made out to be evil by Malachi Martin. Merely that the behaviour of the Christian churches in relation to their own dogma is unacceptable to thinking people who have broken out of the doctrinal strait-jacket. And I do not mean by that people who have no spiritual life, no interest in spiritual things, no sense of God or the numinous. No, I am referring to ordinary people with a healthy sense of the spiritual who have not only categorically rejected Christianity's central thesis of Salvation through the cross, but also rejected the candypuff spirituality of the so-called New Age. There are a lot of thinking people who are awake in, and to, their intrinsic self, and it would appear that Teilhard de Chardin, whatever one might think of his spiritual-cum-scientific and social theories, was one of these awakened individuals.

This goes far to explain the disturbance in Malachi Martin's mind when he learns from Father David Bones of de Chardin's wide-open stare, of his expression of direct simplicity. Embarrassed indeed this already fearful young Jesuit who would in the end unravel psychologically and shout 'I believe, I believe, I believe' because of a deeply instilled and reinforced fear. And what are we to make of the fact that de Chardin's vision seemed to have ceased before his death, as Martin claims? We can read into Father Bones' description of this old palaeontologist a deep-seated fear of his own – the fear of a human presence rendered bare and immediate through authentic questioning. *That* is what is going on here, and the relegating of this marvellous old man to the spiritual scrapheap is, in my opinion, an act of character vandalism. For what Father Bones sensed in de Chardin was not a diminution of hope, but the presence of a man to whom faith was no longer an act of belief, but a laying bare of the self to what exists. Without realizing it, David had glimpsed de Chardin's soul.

MATTER AND CONSCIOUSNESS

The candypuff spirituality of the New Age is dismissed by most Christian churches as being exactly that, a spirituality which cannot in the end satisfy our deepest needs. Our cravings perhaps, but not our needs. Attacking the label 'Neo-Gnosticism' on the fandango of cultic groups which have appeared since the early 1960s (and before then, in the shape of Theosophy and such like), Christians glare disapprovingly from their Olympian perch – a perch consisting of doctrines so intrinsically daft in essence that they have caused a veritable exodus from the churches. Staring into the eye of science, reason and logic at every corner, most people have eaten of the fruit of the knowledge of good and evil and can no longer be fobbed off with tall stories. Christians with a little more sense have attempted to reinterpret ancient doctrine to suit this change in mentality, but such refurbishments generally fail due to mystification continuing to be the hallmark of the new versions proffered. On the whole these new versions are creations dripping with poetic licence. And so thinkers like N T Wright, the Dean of Litchfield, can confound us all by sandwiching history with theology in his book *Who was Jesus?* and expect to be taken seriously.

What then must we do? Should we return to the gospel stories and attempt to ignore the absolute implausibility of doctrines such as the Virgin Birth and the perpetual virginity of Mary? Should we plump for the more upbeat interpretations of the Dean of Litchfield? Or should we attempt to create a synthesis, as de Chardin and many another writer has tried to do since? Is it enough to place a Christocentric veneer of language on science and speak of super-organisms 'woven of the threads of individual men';[9] or should we bite the reality bullet and allow to wash over us the terrible feeling that we are, in the end, alone and responsible for our own lives? Teilhard de Chardin understood this dilemma only too well, hence his probing question as to whether there is in fact a Universal Christ or a Divine Milieu. But he experienced 'Energy becoming transformed into Presence', and so is able to rescue his thoughts. No aloneness here; this man has been nudged by 'something' which has unravelled his dependence on religious or scientific dogma.

Teilhard de Chardin's basic hypothesis was that matter and consciousness are bound together and that, although not measurable, consciousness is nevertheless 'organically and physically rooted in the same cosmic process with which physics is concerned'.[10] So consciousness is no chance eruption in nature – it is not simply a fortuitous event. It is there because it is a *general* phenomenon. It is essential. It is fundamental. It is what makes sense of it all. Without consciousness there would be no universe, and without the universe there would be no consciousness. This is to say that human beings are pretty special, for it is in them that consciousness has reached its most complex form. Small and insignificant we may be, but we are nevertheless an important part of a general thrust in nature towards ever more complex expressions of awareness. Consciousness belongs to all organized states of matter. Almost imperceptible in relation to low values of complexity, it 'gradually makes itself felt and finally becomes dominant when we reach high values'.[11] So there is no such thing as inert, brute matter in de Chardin's scheme of things, for matter and life are not opposed but complementary.

Enter Malachi Martin with a reversal of this view couched in the language of diabolism run rampant. It is not enough for Martin to disagree with de Chardin – he has to link the close relationship of consciousness and matter to an imaginary field of Satanic energy. For in the story of Father David Bones there is another priest, a certain Father Jonathan, who figures importantly in David's breakdown and his eventual brush with Satan. Handsome, intelligent, and with an attractive personality, this young man prepares for the priesthood, sells out to de Chardin's ideas as a result of his training in palaeontology under David, and in the end formulates an approach to Church doctrine which is utterly at odds with orthodox sensibility. The sacraments, for Jonathan, become no more than 'expressions of man's natural unity with the world around him',[12] Jesus' death on the cross is a return to nature and the universe. Perturbed by the news that Jonathan holds such views, David blames himself for not having more carefully guided this talented young man through Teilhard's notions. He ought to have realized the dangers involved, noted that Jonathan was crossing the 'thin and fragile line between Teilhard's view and a total denial of the divinity of Jesus'.[13] But he had not noticed; in fact he had begun to think along similar lines to Jonathan without fully realizing what was happening to him.

The writing is masterly as Martin pieces this jigsaw of possession and infection together. Visited by a force which instructs him as he goes about his business, Jonathan will progressively surrender his will until he has no more will to surrender. He will become a priest, but his mind by then will be in the service of 'serpentine thoughts', his will intertwined with 'fine tendrils' which cannot be shaken off. And all around him is the glorious world of colours, smells and textures which progressively infatuate his senses. And through and behind it all a 'coiled presence weaving slowly, possessively, with ease, lazily enjoying an acquired resting place in the shaded corners of his being'.[14] An ancient voice sounding deep within, asking him to 'let go', inviting him to be at peace. Then, finally, comes the moment of surrender as this invading force lays claim to him during Mass. He has a seizure as he stretches his hands out over the chalice. Tears, groans and urine ease from him as he stands there, rooted to the spot, his hands clamped down on chalice and wafer. Then he is suddenly flung backwards onto the marble floor and rendered unconscious before an astonished pastor and his two assistants. Epilepsy on his mother's side is blamed for the incident, but there is no truth in this claim. Father Jonathan's mother was not an epileptic.

This is indeed a far cry from de Chardin's experience of nature, of energy transformed into a presence, of the whole universe in evolution – a universe described as *concentrating upon itself*. Yet perhaps it is not all that different. Perhaps it is only a matter of mental focusing, of the way in which the mind is trained and directed to perceive reality. For it should be remembered that de Chardin and Father Jonathan were, first and foremost, Catholic priests, their mental paradigm Christ-centred, their inclination towards a religiously-oriented overview underscored by science and the arts. Jonathan was a gifted painter, poet and writer enamoured of the poet Shelley's fresh ideas about God from an early age. By pioneering a similar break with the Catholic orthodoxy's notion of God during the 1960s, Jonathan's contribution would be curiously New Age in feel and quality, a candypuff of spirituality with the elder Jesuit's Jesus as Omega Point placed on top like the fairy on a Christmas tree. This was not at all the diaphanous transformation of the world as experienced by de Chardin, more a bedazzlement of the mind and senses. Yet it was not all that dissimilar when the experiential visions of these two men are placed side by side. Grandiose ideas coursed through both minds. A new humankind for de Chardin; for Jonathan a new priesthood and a new Church that would replace both Catholic and Protestant institutions. These constructions of the younger priest are rooted directly in de Chardin's writings, but they are not so well contained intellectually; in fact, they are quite manic on occasions.

An old dread seeps into one's mind as one reads Malachi Martin's skilful prose – the dread of things that go bump in the night. As he brings the story of Father Jonathan to its climax, he pushes the question of what is happening to this man beyond the edge of credibility and into the realm of paranoia – his own. Receiving an invitation to spend three weeks with a party of friends in the Canadian wilderness, Jonathan accepts, and so sets in motion a train of events which will result in his being exorcised by Father David Bones. He takes to spending more and more time by himself while the others are hunting and fishing, and eventually wanders deep into the wilderness, 'looking for something or some place'.[15] It is not long before he finds what he's looking for – an S-shaped section of river bank where he experiences an electrifying sense of discovery. It is a beautiful place. The water is shallow, the sand of the riverbed soft, the surrounding boulders and rocks almost like black-cowled monks arranged in rows. Here then is his place of revelation and transformation, his 'opening in nature'.

It is all as he expects it to be. Stretched out face down on the sand he starts to dig with his fingers, shouting all the while *'Sacerdos! Sacerdos! Sacerdos!'* He wants to become a new priest for the New Time; as he lies there this process of transformation begins, first as an emptying, then as a flushing away of the man he had become. Under some form of compulsion he is made to walk into the water. In midstream he bends over to feel at the base of a rock for the 'veined heart of our world . . . where Jesus, the Omega Point, was evolving . . . and was on the threshold of emerging'.[16] Softly chanting the name of Jesus, he relaxes into the experience until all anticipation, forward-looking thought and emotion are 'wrapped up and contained in the now, the here-present'.[17] Then psychological disaster strikes. Withdrawing his now bleeding hands from the water, he looks at them lovingly, turns, wades back to the beach and heads at a zig-zagging trot through tall pine trees. Propelled by an inner force, he struggles up to a ridge where a small tree with low branches allows him to rest but on drawing back to look at this tree properly, is horrified to see that unlike the pines, this tree is nothing but a dead, barkless, lightning-blasted trunk with two stubby arms. It is a cross, and there is blood on it. Falling into a state of uncontrollable rage, he begins to curse the tree and everything it stands for. Breaking off first one of the stubby arms, and then the other, he tumbles down the slope and is rendered unconscious.

Malachi Martin makes an emotional meal of this incident and what follows. Yes, Father Jonathan has problems, that is pretty obvious, but his principal problem is not demonic possession, but the kind of Catholicism he has dined on since childhood. David too is undergoing the same troubling process, the same process of will-bending towards an accommodation of doctrines which contradict reality on every level imaginable. He does not experience seizures, but his mind will eventually seize up and threaten him with exactly what he expects – possession by evil. For David is a practising diocesan exorcist torn between the real-ities of palaeontology, anthropology and the literalist demands of his faith. Aware that palaeontology and the doctrines of the Church are at odds with one another, he nevertheless manages to continue with his priestly life and ignore the obvious, at least for a while. But when faced with an exorcism this seemingly easy alliance of incompatibles becomes difficult to handle; and when confronted by his bishop and asked point blank if evolution is as much a fact as the salvation of Jesus, this alliance finally breaks down. Jesus may have become the culmination of the evolutionary process for Teilhard de Chardin, but for Father David Bones such an arrangement is not sustainable. Neither is it for Father Jonathan. He too will crack wide open as the pressure towards doctrinal conformity is applied by way of progressively more confrontational exorcisms.

So we are left with Jonathan's mysterious seizures to bedevil our imaginations, and the fact that he lied about his mother being an epileptic. Everything is neat and tidy in Malachi Martin's mind as we move to the next possession story. But it is not quite as neat as he imagines, for there is a little more to these seizures of Jonathan's than meets the eye. His mother may not have been an epileptic, but as David discovered later, she too was prone to seizures. Martin makes no comment on this fact, except to record that David was 'relieved' to know that something of the kind ran in the family. But he himself is not relieved to hear this; he ignores the obvious implications and leaves us with the word 'seizure' reverberating on the page. For if not epilepsy, then what? That is the question he hints at but without actually posing it.

So are we to conclude that Jonathan's mother was also possessed by evil, and that the son was in receipt of this evil force from the mother? If not, then why separate the information on the mother's seizures from Jonathan's claim that he has inherited epilepsy from his mother? *That* is when we should have been informed that seizures ran in the family, not later. For this separation causes the word 'seizure' in relation to Jonathan to collapse into the word 'seizure' in relation to his mother, so making her seizures diabolical by inference. But since Martin offers absolutely no evidence that the mother is possessed and, indeed, she assists at Jonathan's final exorcism, then why should we accept the son's seizures as diabolical when it is perfectly obvious that such seizures are an inherited condition? Since Martin has already revealed that Jonathan had been prone to severe outbursts of uncontrollable temper as a boy, the evidence for a disturbed, rather than a possessed mind becomes the more tenable.

MENTAL ADJUSTMENT

After such a barrage of nonsense it is necessary to re-adjust one's perception of de Chardin and his work. For beneath all the obscure language lies a great truth, a truth capable of carrying us not only to the heart of matter, but to the heart of what matters in the deepest sense of presence, or identity. Teilhard de Chardin offers us a clue when he speaks of 'a precise and overwhelming sense of the general convergence of the universe upon itself'. And this is not, as Malachi Martin seems to think, a reference to the presence of nature, of the world usurping consciousness to the detriment of the divine. Rather, it is a fundamental perceptual capacity to detect the underlying unity of creation in a manner not yet developed in our societies. Such a capacity 'encompasses' de Chardin; it is a spontaneous breaking into perceptual focus of a gift we all possess, but do not know how to activate. Yet he admits that he has not been fundamentally changed by this sexperience. Looking at the humble, kneeling worshipper whose unsophisticated faith in the catechism produces more real charity and calm trust than he himself can muster, he recognizes both his failings and his inability to accept the old way. For Malachi Martin such a statement is self-explanatory: de Chardin's sophisticated perception of things could not produce the moral base that simple faith in the catechism could. *Ergo*, his perceptions were not spiritual at all.

To my way of thinking this kind of approach is both naive and inadequate; it smacks loudly of the simplistic and cannot be allowed to go unchallenged. But for all that, it is a conclusion reached with the deepest sincerity and backed by what seems to be irrefutable evidence on the moral level. For if God really were part of this opening up of the senses, then surely anyone who experienced it would be transformed for the better, changed instantly in their inner being like the early disciples, made into a new person devoted to the very doctrines that de Chardin's theories render obsolete. That is Malachi Martin's argument, and on the surface it is a good one. But when it is examined closely and made to bear the weight of human experience down the centuries, it is no argument at all. Yes, we are more than we seem, more than our science can fathom, more than our education can describe, but when all is said and done the path to spiritual and intellectual maturity has never been simple or straightforward.

CHAPTER SIX

A Veil Across the Face of Truth

The Church's traditional notion of intelligent good and intelligent evil, the squabble over whether Satan should be treated as a metaphor or as an entity, and the Christian community's refusal to deal with the fatally flawed side of its own collective psyche

William Peter Blatty's best-selling novel *The Exorcist* was published in 1972. The novel was seminal in its influence on the public imagination in relation to exorcism, and was soon followed by a visually arresting film. The story is that of a young girl harassed by poltergeist phenomena, but the tale soon explodes into really bizarre behaviour, a hospital scene having her cursing like a trooper in some ancient language. Strapped helplessly to a bed, her legs bearing grotesque scratch marks, the 12-year-old Regan MacNeil is treated to the best of the hospital's competence, but is eventually discharged in an unchanged condition. Removed to St Louis and into the hands of a priest who is given permission by his superiors to conduct an exorcism, the book moves inexorably towards its hair-raising conclusion.

For our purposes, however, it is the opening scene of both book and film that is of interest. In the film we are presented with a large archaeological dig somewhere in northern Iraq. In the book we learn that this dig lies somewhere between Mosul in the northwest, Erbil in the east, and Baghdad and Kirkuk in the south. The senior archaeologist is an elderly priest named Merrin; a priest with a heart condition and a deep knowledge of Assyrian mythology. In both film and book Merrin searches out an ancient limestone statue as big as himself and stands by it pondering things inexplicable. The statue is of Pazuzu, the personification of the southwest wind, its dominion sickness and disease. Blatty describes Pazuzu as having '. . . ragged wings; taloned feet; bulbous, jutting penis and a mouth stretched taut in feral grin'. All around lie the ruins of

Nineveh, city of the ancient Assyrians; the Temple of Nabu; The Temple of Ishtar; the palace of Ashurbanipal. The heat is horrendous. The wind is blowing. Two dogs are fighting savagely. Evil is in the air, in the place itself, embodied in stone, ready to reach out and contaminate the present from the distant past.

In *Hostage to the Devil*, Malachi Martin produces a series of verbal portraits of possessed individuals which are much more scary than anything Peter Blatty can muster in *The Exorcist*. In fact it could be said that Martin's ability to describe a possessed individual far exceeds anything yet created by novelists or filmmakers. Stephen King pales into insignificance next to Martin, whose chapter titles alone could win awards for originality. 'Father Bones and Mr Natch.' 'The Virgin and the Girl-Fixer.' 'Uncle Ponto and the Mushroom-Souper.' Great stuff. And within these chapters there is a vision of evil described so delicately that as one reads one can almost feel it seep from the pages. No doubt about it, Malachi Martin is a verbal craftsman, someone who can empathically enter the mind and experience of the supposedly possessed to such an extent that he seems to be describing not another's experience, but his own. I mean by this, not that he himself is possessed, but that he gets so close to those he presumes to have been possessed, and has such a clear and precise idea of what possession is and means, that he manages to capture the intrinsic horror and desolation of that mental state.

Perhaps *too* well, it could be argued. Perhaps his very ability to do descriptive justice to this strange condition of mind is his greatest failing, his Achilles' heel. For as Martin himself writes in connection with Pedro Arrupe, Father General of the Jesuit Order in the 1960s, Arrupe had acquainted himself so deeply with Modernist ideas that he had become seriously infected by the very ideas he was supposed to counteract as a Catholic priest.

Oddly enough, like the old priest Merrin in *The Exorcist*, Malachi Martin is also a expert in things Assyrian; he is a Professor of Assyriology and has a bachelor's degree in Semitic languages. And one can detect not only his interest in, but also his cast of mind concerning, the ancient past in *Hostage to the Devil* when dealing with possession-case number 4, designated: 'Uncle Ponto and the Mushroom-Souper.' Taking these factors together, what then might be at the back of Martin's mind when he informs us that in New York:

The millions of immigrants came from lands where their religion (mainly Christianity, with Jewish and Muslim minorities) had its roots deep in ancient pre-Christian cults. European and Middle Eastern pagan instincts were never rooted out; they were adopted, sublimated, purified, transmuted. In that mildewed baggage of morals, ritual practices, folk mores, social and familial traditions, the new Americans surely transported the seeds and traces of ancient, far-off powers and spirits which once held sway over the Old World.[1]

In my mind's eye I can see Martin standing with Merrin by the statue of Pazazu, its ragged wings silhouetted against a purple sky, its bulbous penis sticking out obscenely, the ruins of Nineveh and all that it once stood for looming in the background. For it is among this rich tapestry of nationalities transported to New York that a nine-year-old Jewish boy called 'Jamsie' eventually falls foul of 'Uncle Ponto', a disembodied 'face' which appears without warning. A 'funny lookin' face'; or, more accurately, 'a face with a funny look' which progressively haunts Jamsie until he seeks escape through exorcism.

Ponto is a spirit of some kind, we are told; Jamsie even considers the possibility of Ponto being from another planet. A description of Ponto is as follows: a large pointed head; heavy eyelids; no chin; no emotions that could be identified with; neither one colour nor another; hands like mechanical claws; a cat-like flexibility of body; a height of about four and half feet; bandy-legged with toes all the same length and size.

But there is more than Ponto around, so it seems. On one occasion Jamsie sees what he calls the 'Shadow' when visiting the Pinnacles National Monument. This is an extra. The Shadow moves from shadowy place to shadowy place and is quite separate from Ponto; but he eventually sees Ponto's face *in* the Shadow, along with that of his father and many others. Then comes the tying together of all the extraneous bits and pieces of Malachi Martin's spiritual vision: 'He [Jamsie] knew he had seen the father of all man's real enemies. The Father of Lies and the ultimate adversary of all salvation, of any beauty, of each truth throughout the cosmos of God's working.'[2] For the Shadow has momentarily revealed itself. It is abnormally tall and bulky, its body covered in black folds, its two arms raised at the elbow, the palms of its hands turned out towards him, its fingers clenching and unclenching. But more important still, in a sense, is the fact that its head is 'lifted up, thrown back . . . in a fixed haughtiness, a resisting pride'. Here, in full view – in spite of a certain blurriness – is the archetypal Satan, the Devil in person, God's adversary Lucifer standing revealed in the shadows as the most terrible shadow of all – the archetypal Shadow backgrounding *all* human evil and inadequacy.

THE WORLD OF THE COMPACT

The film *The Exorcist* was based on a supposed case of actual possession where a spirit of considerable malignancy was exorcised by Jesuits in 1949 – official reports show that no less that forty-eight people witnessed this exorcism, nine of them Jesuits. The little girl in the film – Regan MacNeil – was a little boy in real life, Robbie Manheim by name. Writing of this case with insider knowledge, the professional writer and one-time student of the Jesuits, Thomas Allen, explores Malachi Martin's notion of the Devil being a real person; that is, an entity of some sort capable of manifestation. With the benefit of a diary written by an eye witness, Allen records the story of Robbie Manhein's successful exorcism (there had been a previous attempt that failed) by Father William S Bowdern, SJ (principal exorcist), Father Raymond Bishop, SJ (assistant and diarist), and Father Walter Halloran, SJ (assistant). Allen describes the moment when he received a copy of the diary from Father Halloran: 'My hands were trembling when I tore open the package, which contained twenty-four, single-spaced typewritten pages. I began to read: *Satan . . . diabolical . . . a huge red devil*. I was reading the words of a witness!'[3] Later we learn that the Catholic Church views exorcism as a direct confrontation between Satan and Christ, the priest summoning up the power of Christ through prayer. We also learn that some Catholic priests are of the theological persuasion that during an exorcism Satan cannot exploit the sins of a priest that have been forgiven in confession, and that Catholic theology is formally linked, as one would expect, to 'angelology'.

Thomas Allen's mental footwork in the writing of this book is fascinating and highly informative. We are told that belief in the Devil is not held to be compulsory by some modern Catholic theologians. The more traditionally minded do accept the Bible as divinely inspired, and believe, in spite of modern psychological theory, that the Devil-cum-Satan-cum-Lucifer is a being whose literal existence must be accepted in conjunction with other biblical teachings. Modernists, on the other hand, are of the opinion that the Devil is nothing more than a metaphor, and as such cannot be made into an article of faith. The Apostle Paul was of a different persuasion; he conceived of two levels in relation to this question of the Devil's existence: (1) the law of God as related to the mind, or *inner man*; and (2) the law of sin as related to the body, referred to by Paul as *the flesh*. Allen tells us that this dual view frames the concept of diabolical possession.

So far so good.

The human body is the weak link in the chain; it is virtually an open door to evil unless the mind is fortified by faith in Christ's redemptive sacrifice. If no such faith has been established in the mind, or has been undermined or lost due to Modernist notions, then the way is wide open for evil, in varying degrees of intensity, to possess the body at any time. So why not everyone all of the time, if it's that easy? According to Allen, St Augustine holds the key to this theological dilemma: God does not allow the Devil to do whatever he likes, whenever he likes. Which suggests, of course, that God is himself responsible for the decision when someone is possessed by evil incarnate; either that, or there is a point in the life of a human being where they wilfully allow evil to enter into them and take control.

Malachi Martin is of the latter opinion. In his book *The Jesuits*, subtitled *The Society of Jesus and the Betrayal of the Roman Catholic Church* he paraphrases Paul VI's statement to the 31st General Congregation of the Jesuits about something called 'the world of the Compact', and reveals how Catholic traditionalists perceive the world, its cultures and its intellectual attainments. For to Martin the 'Compact' signifies two classes of people: those who do not believe in Christ's redemptive power, and who have given way to the Enemy, and those who have either not made up their mind about Christ, or who have not yet realized that there is anything about which they have to make up their mind. The latter are unfortunate because they have no real spiritual light to guide them. The former are either individuals deluded by knowledge of the world into believing that that is all that matters; or they are perhaps consciously part of 'a specific organisation dedicated to promoting Lucifer and Lucifer's cause.'[4]

This latter point of view, strange as it may seem, is in fact not at all strange when the spiritual perspective of Catholic Traditionalists is clearly defined. For in alignment with Ignatian teaching, such Traditionalists hold that the human condition is governed by two cosmic powers, what Malachi Martin has described as intelligent good and intelligent evil personified in God and Lucifer, and that we humans are caught in the middle of a life and death struggle between those diametrically opposed forces. Martin states that this struggle can be 'tracked and identified in the multiple details of complex human situations'.[5]

Oddly enough, the maiden speech of Father General Pedro Arrupe at the Second Vatican Council, held one year before General Congregation 31 got under way, reflected a view curiously similar to that of Pope Paul VI: and that in spite of the fact that Arrupe was a known Modernist with a liking for Teilhard de Chardin's *spirit of enquiry*. Arrupe had caused a sensation in the international media by suggesting that the cultural environment of the world in general was not only atheistic, but part of a 'perfectly mapped-out strategy' which had to be counteracted. It was suddenly not just a matter of the world being worldly; it was a matter of that world being either unconsciously or consciously part of a highly organized conspiracy to diabolically subvert human intelligence. The godless society was in control of the world's lines of communication, its international organizations and its finances, and this signified Luciferian intervention.

Tongue-in-cheek, Malachi Martin remarks that Arrupe's speech was worthy of Ignatius Loyola himself; then with a whiplash he tells us that no more than a month later Arrupe would do a backward flip, show his true colours, and scathingly attack the approach of Catholic missionaries in Africa and Asia, calling them 'myopic' and 'infantile'. Roman Catholic missionary work, founded as it was on the Traditionalist perspective, was for 'children and illiterates', according to Arrupe. Here then was the tip-off; Pedro Arrupe, Father General of the Jesuit Order, was not quite what he seemed.

Neither was Robbie Manheim.

Robbie's bed, so runs the story recorded in the diary kept by Father Bishop, SJ, becomes the focus of an unnatural force or power which causes furniture to move and scratching noises to be heard inside the mattress. And then, suddenly, without so much as a by-your-leave, this poltergeist-like force enters Robbie's body and possesses him. Well, almost; he isn't actually conscious of what is happening to him, and as such is not so much possessed as besieged from within. A Lutheran minister by the name of Schulze is called in; but he advises the family to seek psychiatric help – unlike Martin Luther, he no longer believes in diabolical possession. In any case, the mechanism for dealing with such a situation had long since been swept away, the rite of exorcism having been thrown out and replaced by 'prayer and contempt', because Luther didn't like to make a display of evil. And so Schulze organizes prayer circles at his church; but this has no effect on Robbie's condition. Allen tells us that for Schulze, as a Protestant pastor, possession and exorcism were medieval relics without currency. Conservative Protestants still believed in a personal Devil, but not Schulze; in his estimation there was a probable parapsychological answer to the phenomenon. In the end, however, it was not Schulze or his prayer circles who helped Robbie or his family; it was, we are led to believe, the indefatigable, Camel-smoking Father Bowdern, a 52-year-old Jesuit who, through the power of God, routed the enemy and sent him back to hell. But not without a fight; a fight which Father Bishop's diary describes in horrendous detail.

By the the end of Thomas Allen's book the reader is psychologically bedraggled; it is a harrowing tale as vividly told and as unnerving as Peter Blatty's novel based on the same bunch of facts. Facts? Well, who is to say? The supposed facts of the case slide in and out of focus. Forty-eight witnesses (nine of them Jesuits) plus a diary and special reports there might have been, but at the end of the whole frightening affair there were quite a few detectable contradictions to worry about. Father Bowdern, as chief exorcist, as the man in the hot seat, so to speak, will remain convinced that he has been dealing with Lucifer himself; but two of his Jesuit companions will not be so certain. Robbie will have dreamt that a big red devil was fighting to keep him from passing through iron gates at the top of a pit two hundred feet deep; vomit, sometimes in prodigious quantities, will have come out of Robbie's mouth and accurately caught those around him in the face in spite of his eyes being closed; unimaginable amounts of urine will have darkened the bed and words like HELL and SPITE will have appeared miraculously on the boy's chest; but when it's all over and this nine-year-old is back to normal, such events, in spite of their realism, their horror, their seemingly diabolical origin, will come under question. Was the cowled figure riding on a giant black cloud as seen by Robbie actually the Devil? Was the Latin spoken by Robbie during the exorcism positive proof that an ancient power had him besieged from within? The 'facts' suggest as much. But as we shall see, the 'facts' as recorded in Father Bishop's diary are not quite all they are made out to be. When the whole event was wrapped up and everyone had gone back to the comfortable insanity of their ordinary lives, there were those who remained unsure about the interpretation adopted.

PROCEDURAL MISTAKES

Before dealing with the testimony of those who doubted that Robbie had been besieged by the Devil in person, certain oddities of perception and behaviour as exhibited by Father Bowdern and Father Bishop have to be examined. For such oddities amply illustrate the mind-set of these men – a mind-set capable of making short-sighted, superstition-ridden judgements. For example, according to exorcist-type tradition a possessing or besieging demon should reveal its time of departure. Now on the very first night of the exorcism an X had appeared on Robbie's right leg, and both Bowdern and Bishop had decided that this meant the demon would leave Robbie in exactly ten days. Bishop reckoned the departure would take place on Thursday 24 March because it was the feast of the Annunciation, the day on which the Archangel Gabriel said 'Hail, Mary', and announced to the Holy Virgin that Christ would be incarnated. Bowdern, however, was not altogether in agreement with Bishop; he saw 25 March as the tenth day. Later, Bowdern sensibly reproached himself; he had been too literal in his mind-set – demons do not follow the liturgical calendar. He ought to have realized that. He had fooled himself. Indeed, he had. Yet he remained enamoured of numbers; he immediately began to speculate on the number 18, the most recent number to be singled out.

Harmless as some might see this incident, it reveals a basic gullibility, a mind-track locked into doctrine and dogma and exorcist formulae which rendered Bowdern and Bishop unreliable as witnesses. Perhaps this is why the Archangel Michael has to appear at the end of the whole affair and exorcise the demon for Bowdern; along with Bishop and many another he's simply lost the plot.

Next comes an unbelievable scene, in which Robbie, a nine-year-old in a serious mental condition, is taken from his home to the Alexian Brothers' Hospital: the Alexian Brothers are a Congregation of 'Cellites', an Order founded in the fourteenth century by monks at the time of the Black Death. In a wing reserved for mental patients, Bowdern arranges for the use of a 'security room' on the fifth floor; secrecy has been demanded by Bowdern's superiors. And so Robbie, at ten o'clock in the evening, and without his permission, is taken to this institution for the night so that his family can get some sleep. The boy's father accompanies the little party, and Robbie is put to bed. But the security room bed is not an ordinary one; it has straps hanging from it, and there are bars on the window and no doorknob on the inside of the door. Braced, as Allen says, for a night of horror, Bowdern is surprised when absolutely nothing happens: the boy is wide awake and in a state of fear. His eyes dart from bar to straps – the straps that now hold him fast. The boy, it seems, is more afraid of his surroundings than of the exorcism already being conducted by Bowdern. As it turns out, there is nothing to exorcise that night; Robbie remains alert and fearfully awake. Whatever is bothering him does not manifest itself.

This scene seems all right at first glance, but it carries some major flaws: Bowdern ought to have realized before he started the exorcism that Robbie was in a normal state of consciousness. The boy was awake. He was looking around him. He was strapped down tight and he was afraid. What on Earth were they going to do to him? Why had he been taken from his home? All of this ought to have been obvious to Bowdern; and if not to Bowdern, then certainly to those assisting him, particularly Robbie's father. The boy's father eventually spent a peaceful night sleeping in that room and was awakened by Robbie in the morning. And yet the exorcism continued, while the boy was fully conscious, with all its mystery and oddness witnessed by the boy who knew nothing about what went on when he was supposedly possessed and unconscious.

Once again Bowdern shows himself to be inept, unobservant, too caught up in his own affairs to read the situation accurately.

And as those with him are similarly blinkered to reality, the same criticism applies to them. On this occasion the exorcism may have taken only an hour to complete, but it was probably enough to deeply influence the conscious boy's perception of what was the matter with him. And the mistakes do not stop there; again and again Bowdern will consider the exorcism a probable success, only to find that he has miscalculated. And then he will pull out what he thinks of as his ace card; while the boy is conscious and in control he will start instructing him in Catholicism. The circle will now complete itself; the antiquated language and prayers and teachings of the Church will now become part and parcel of Robbie's exhausted and mentally unstable consciousness.

Robbie Manheim eventually returns to that fifth-floor security room, and the Alexian Brothers start a 24-hour adoration of the Blessed Sacrament in order to concentrate their prayers on Robbie's plight. But the stories that emerge do not tally; some have it that Robbie could arch his body backward until the back of his head touched his feet, but there's no mention of this in Bishop's diary, and Halloran states that no such thing ever happened when he was present. Others said that Robbie exhibited prodigious strength; Halloran denies this and states that the boy's strength was no more than that of an agitated adolescent. And neither did he speak a foreign language, or a dead language such as Latin. Father Albert Hughes, the young and inexperienced Jesuit exorcist who failed with Robbie, was convinced that he had heard him speak good Latin; but there is later no evidence of this whatsoever – in fact it is suggested that Robbie simply repeated, parrot fashion, what he heard these priests articulate over him. Halloran, in spite of having been an eye-witness to much of what went on, is quoted by Thomas Allen as having said: 'I should never feel comfortable or capable of making an absolute statement . . . I don't have the faintest idea why the Devil would need a possession.'[6] This is probably why Halloran cannot muster the emotional reactions he thinks necessary when witnessing this exorcism; deep down he no longer really believes in any of it. Or was he simply numbed by evil? Halloran himself posits this as a way out of his dilemma, but his other statements suggest no real belief in this either.

Equally dubious about the exorcism's merits is Father William Van Roo, a Jesuit priest in his postordination tertianship. Recognized as a brilliant theologian, Van Roo, whose special interest is the influence of Arabian philosophy on Thomas Aquinas, was later to shun demonology and complain that he had been drawn into an exorcism without having a chance to study the phenomenon. No instant conversion here. Van Roo is intellectually confounded by what he sees, but remains sceptical as to its causes. He describes his own reaction to the whole mad event quite dryly: 'I was a sort of monitor. I would sit at his bedside. I watched his eyes . . . It was all unpredictable; I can't recall a pattern.'[7] Not much of a theological reaction there, just an embarrassed drawing away from a situation that had got out of descriptive control. Allen puts it like this: 'Did demons possess Robbie? Or did religious belief mask a psychiatric phenomenon?'[8]

So what was going on? Multiple-personality? Tourette's syndrome? An obsessive compulsive disorder? Covering all these angles, Allen states that some multiple-personality patients believe themselves possessed by Satan, and that they exhibit: (1) a high susceptibility to self-suggestion; and (2) a quite amazing openness to hypnotic suggestion. This condition does seem to apply to Robbie; the exorcist's *suggestions* get exactly the kind of results that he expects. And following the classical Tourette's syndrome, Robbie does curse and swear like a seasoned trooper; but he recovers from this compulsion when the exorcism is over and, according to specialists, Tourette's syndrome is incurable. In relation to obsessive compulsive disorder (OCD), he does not seem to have suffered from the virus of manic religious scrupulosity as a result of his Protestant religious background. But the alacrity with which he takes to Catholicism under Father Bowdern's instruction should not be overlooked; and his sudden transformation from normal little boy to possessed little boy when confronted by the Station of the Cross showing, in particular, Jesus being stripped of his garments, may point either to the surfacing of too vivid a religious imagination (a probable base for OCD), or to sexual abuse in early childhood. The psychiatrist consulted by Allen is suspicious of this event, and seems to lean more in the direction of possible sexual abuse by way of explanation for Robbie's extraordinary mental condition than any other.

So it is not surprising that when Archbishop Ritter appoints a Jesuit professor of philosophy at St Louis University as an examiner of what went on during this exorcism, his findings show Robbie not to have been diabolically possessed at all. At the end of a thorough examination of witnesses under oath, it is concluded that there is no evidence whatsoever for supernatural or preternatural influences having played a part in the affair.

Allen's observation that religious belief may have masked a psychiatric phenomenon takes on further significance when one considers that the founder of the Jesuit Order, Ignatius Loyola, himself clearly describes an experience of religious behaviour answering exactly to what is now termed OCD. He describes his own obsessive compulsive disorder-type behaviour thus:

> After I have trodden upon a cross formed by two straws, or after I have thought, said or done some other thing, there comes to me from 'without' a thought that I have sinned, and on the other hand it seems to me that I have not sinned; nevertheless I feel some uneasiness on the subject, inasmuch as I doubt yet do not doubt.[9]

This condition does not seem to have been part of Robbie's bag of mental tricks; but given the religious credulity of Hughes, Bowdern and Bishop, it may well have played a part in their interpretation of what was taking place – their carrying of the traditional Catholic religious paradigm could well have compelled them to incite Robbie to react in the manner expected during an exorcism. It is blithely assumed that Robbie is the only one with a psychological problem, but that may not have been the case.

To believe wholeheartedly in exorcism requires a mind-set singularly divorced from consensus scientific reality at many strategic points. Now this does not automatically make that mind-set either wholly wrong or wholly stupid; but it can produce systems of interpretation which, although useful in the treatment of certain psychological conditions due to enculturation, are gross distortions of reality at the cutting edge. The cutting edge of reality is human consciousness, and it will be some time yet before the mysteries of that multi-levelled consciousness can with confidence be said to have been satisfactorily mapped.

THE ARCHANGEL MICHAEL

I mentioned earlier in the text that it was neither Bowdern nor Bishop who brought this sad tale to a successful conclusion, but the Archangel Michael. Inexplicably, Michael himself decides to intervene and bring the exorcism to a successful conclusion. This is an important point, for not all exorcisms are successful (some supposed demoniacs never recover), and if Michael can interfere in one, then why not in the rest? Why was Robbie Manhein singled out for special treatment? Was it because he was not properly possessed but only under siege, as Allen's book suggests? Was it because he was under siege and the exorcist was not getting it right that Michael had to intervene? All sorts of reasons could be put forward for the appearance of this august figure in Robbie's psyche, but it is not the reasons that interest me, but the reasoning itself; for to what exactly are we referring when we speak of the Archangel Michael? An actual Archangel come from God? Does God uphold the Catholic Church's extraordinary theological paradigm as Bowdern and Bishop and Malachi Martin wish us to believe?

At the very end of the exorcism Father Bowdern is reciting the ritual in a quiet voice while Robbie, eyes closed, roars with rage and spits in people's eyes. And then there is a change in his condition; he quietens, slips from a supposed trance state to a normal state and shows an interest in the ritual itself. Then he's back in trance and fighting them with everything he's got, his tongue flicking, his head moving with the gliding action of a snake's. He screams, arches, and becomes quiet again. All very convincing; in fact exactly what one would expect from someone inhabited by the Father of Lies whose very first choice of a body had been that of the wily serpent in the Genesis story. But at 10.45 in the evening a turning point comes and a new note is struck. A different kind of voice issues from Robbie, a clear, masterful voice. The voice names itself as no other than the Archangel Saint Michael himself, and this voice commands Satan and the other evil spirits inhabiting Robbie to leave in the name of *Dominus*. The voice is imperious; it will brook no argument; Satan has to leave immediately. Now! NOW! NOW! There follow the most violent spasms and contortions yet witnessed, a fight to the finish for seven or eight minutes followed by a great and sudden calm. Robbie, everyone knows for certain, has been released. And the boy is able to describe St Michael in detail: a beautiful figure with flowing, wavy hair standing in a brilliant white light. He is wearing a close-fitting white garment made of mail, and in his right hand there is a fiery sword. His left hand points down to a pit, or cave, and Robbie can see the Devil-cum-Satan-cum-Lucifer standing amidst flames surrounded by other demons. He is laughing. He charges the gate, but is sent scurrying back into his domain by a repetition of *Dominus!*

In bringing this extraordinary tale to its close, Thomas Allen completes it with a few well-chosen words: 'There is, I think, something of the fable to exorcism, if a fable is a veil thrown across the face of truth.'[10] I like that: *fable as a veil drawn across the face of truth*. But earlier Allen has made an even more telling remark. 'He was, I believe,' he says, trying to grapple with what had happened to Robbie, 'a victim of a strange, incomprehensible event, an unearthly event whose cultural and psychological roots are deeper than Christianity's.'[11] Psychologically deeper? Culturally older? Is Allen perhaps suggesting, like Malachi Martin, that powers or spirits *predating* Christianity somehow popped up in Robbie Manheim's life for the same reasons that Uncle Ponto popped up in Jamsie's? Or is he postulating something quite different? Is he perhaps saying that Christianity's interpretation of such an event may obscure rather than reveal what is going on? Neither priest nor psychologist really understands what such cases are about. The human psyche is a powerful instrument of perception and comprehension about which we as yet known very little.

And, bringing us full circle, Teilhard de Chardin taps into the same problem when he says: 'Is there a Divine milieu? Or am I, after all, simply the dupe of my own mind?' He thinks not; he believes he has experiential proof to the contrary. Alas, so does Malachi Martin and many another. But unlike those others, de Chardin is acutely aware that the religiously dogmatic life of his fellow priests houses many an illusion – a forcing of reality into a perceptual straitjacket. So what to make of a later conversation Allen has with a hard-headed Jesuit theologian which seems to steer everything back in the direction of Satan and God fighting it out inside Robbie Manheim's head? For he rounds off his tale with a tale – the tale of what is said to have happened in St Xavier's church the night Robbie was released from Satan's grip. According to several Jesuits who had gathered for a service on Robbie's behalf, 'the shadowed loftiness of the great soaring apse blazed with light. The Jesuits looked up and saw, filling the immense space above the altar, what Robbie said he had seen – St Michael, flaming sword in hand, defending the good and warding off evil.'[1]

So was the Jesuit professor of philosophy appointed by Archbishop Ritter quite mistaken in his verdict? Was it just a case of yet another Jesuit intellectual having been spiritually undermined by the thinking of someone like Teilhard de Chardin? And is the whole edifice of the Church, both Catholic and Protestant, literally 'going to the Devil' as Malachi Martin supposes? Or is this massive religious organization which spans the whole world finally disintegrating, not because of diabolical forces but because it simply refuses to deal with its own dark side, the fatally flawed side of its own collective psyche? This would seem to be the truth of the matter. And the Vatican hierarchy's present inability to deal with Monsignor Emmanuel Milingo's regular mass exorcisms in Rome must surely confirm the point I am trying to make.

CHAPTER SEVEN

Satan and Jesus

The abduction of Jesus in the wilderness by Satan, the Church's tendency to demonize what it does not understand, and the curious fact that it was the very best of the Christian communities who deserted the ship of faith for the ship of understanding

The supposition behind all exorcisms is that Satan is at large in the world; that is, he has the power to visit us, and tempt us. Jesus, so it seems, was no exception. In the Gospels of Matthew and Luke, Jesus is led into the wilderness by the spirit to fast and be tempted by the Devil, but like Robbie Manheim this tempting of Jesus by God's adversary may not be all it is made out to be. Jesus holds to his fast for an amazing forty days, and during this period undergoes the hallucinatory experience of being simultaneously in other locations, such as Jerusalem, and on top of a very high mountain from which he can see all the kingdoms of the world. Afterwards, as one would expect, he is very hungry, and we are told that 'angels' minister to his needs.

Now forty days may be a bit of an exaggeration, but there is no good reason to reject this story out of hand, at least not entirely. Fasting was after all part of Nazarene-cum-Nazarite practice, and Jesus, like his brother James, was a Nazarene – James being an ultra-strict Nazarene with strong Nazarite-Ebionite affiliations. In fact when referred to as 'Jesus of Nazareth', we ought really to read 'Nazarene'; for outside of the New Testament there is no record of there ever having been such a place as Nazareth in Palestine during Jesus' lifetime. And like anyone who fasts for a long period, perhaps *too* long a period, Jesus seems to have undergone that change of consciousness which attends such rigour. Many others have attested to this change of consciousness which comes through lack of food, and the description given by the Gospel writers accurately reflects the state of mind Jesus could eventually have experienced. The facts as recorded speak for themselves: Jesus was apparently seeing, hearing and experiencing on a quite different level of reality.

Or was it perhaps the writers who were seeing, hearing and experiencing on another level of reality?

Mark's Gospel contains the same wilderness temptation story, but Mark's version is thought to have been written ten or twenty years before those of Matthew's and Luke's, and is therefore considered the source document for this story. So it is interesting to note that Mark ties the whole episode up in a two verses; whereas Matthew and Luke expand Mark's cameo statement into 11 and 13 verses respectively. According to Mark, Jesus is driven into the wilderness by the Spirit and tempted for 40 days by Satan. When the ordeal is over, he is ministered to by angels. Matthew and Luke, on the other hand, seem to know what Satan actually said to Jesus, and what Jesus' replies were.

How is this possible? Is there another written source we don't know about? Or did Matthew and Luke merely elaborate imaginatively on a theme? Or could it be that what seems to be going on isn't in fact going on at all, and that these extended versions carry another quite different story thinly disguised as a supernatural interaction? Yes, Jesus is in the wilderness, and he has probably fasted, perhaps quite rigorously; but something else could be happening here – Mark makes no mention of a fast. Which allows us to conjecture that Jesus' hallucinatory state may not have been as hallucinatory as later recorded. For he is holding a conversation with someone described initially as 'the tempter', then as 'the Devil', then finally as 'Satan', and this conversation, in spite of the detail given, and in spite of the ever-expanding view of the original 'tempter', is too much in line with later developments in Christian theology to be taken at face value. The conversation between Jesus and this tempter is so forced, theologically, that we in turn are forced to seek a more conventional explanation for this remarkable wilderness incident.

But before getting to this more conventional approach, certain curious elements of this story should be highlighted, for amidst all the theology certain blunders have been committed that are worthy of comment. As Marcello Craveri observes in his excellent study, *The Life of Jesus*, the dignity of Christianity's founder is compromised by Satan's magical powers – he is whisked here and there without as much as a by-your-leave. Is this really the *Son of God* Satan is dealing with? Is this really God himself somehow extended into matter? Craveri speculates that the temptation might represent a spiritual conflict in Jesus' life at a critical moment; and then wonders if it may have been delirium due to prolonged fasting; or ecstatic suggestion or hallucination. These are quite valid approaches. But it is an earlier thought on the matter that might be the more accurate, for on considering the temptation story a possible invention of the Evangelists, he says, 'or whether the name of Satan was employed to represent a human agent under orders to corrupt Jesus'.[1] I warm to Craveri's reasoning at this point; the story could indeed reflect a conversation between Jesus and some human agent, a commander of the Zealot forces, for instance, trying to get this wayward Messiah on his side. Tempter indeed. But only 'diabolical' in his purpose and cunning. In this sense, the idea of spiritual conflict, of a critical moment in Jesus' life, collapses effortlessly into a sensible context.

The give-away, to my way of thinking, is Satan's claim to have the authority to give Jesus all the kingdoms of the world if he will worship him – this is much the same as saying that he will make him into a great and powerful king for the simple act of recognition. The promise might of course have been much more circumspect, not the *whole* world, but the whole *known* world. All he has to do is give up his pacifist ways and accept the speaker's view of things – recognize him and join with the militants. For that is what this passage comes down to; how else can Jesus end up as ruler of the known world unless he becomes Israel's new warrior Messiah and king? Israel is the context; we must never forget that. And how else can this actually happen unless Jesus changes into the warrior Messiah the sectarians are at that precise moment waiting for? The tempter is quite explicit: 'All this power will I give thee, and the glory of them: *for that is delivered unto me*; and to whomsoever I will give it.'[2] [emphasis added] This is not Lucifer speaking, it is not the Devil; it is someone acting like a devil, someone speaking with Luciferian intent and Zealot-like authority; it is, quite probably, a prominent sectarian leader carrying an invitation to Jesus as the man of the moment. And it's interesting that Jesus is 'driven' out into the wilderness to hear such demands; whether he likes it or not, this 'Satan' has to be listened to.

Apart from anything else, it should be pointed out that the Temple in Jerusalem did not have a pinnacle for Jesus to stand on; and there are no mountains in either Palestine or Judea high enough for even a major portion of the whole world to be viewed from. On the theological front, it should be noted that Satan does not use the term 'Son of God' at all; to be precise, he addresses Jesus not as *ho hyos Theou*, but as *hyos Theou*, which means only 'protected by God'.[3]

Professor Elaine Pagels has a quite different approach. She also notes that Matthew changes Mark's wordless contest with Satan into a dialogue, and she too posits another source for this particular incident; but with dexterity she sets out to prove that Matthew, writing after the destruction of Jerusalem, the Temple, and the whole Jewish infrastructure as a result of sectarian madness, caricatures Satan as a scribe, a 'skilled debater adept in quoting Scripture for diabolical purposes'[4] – it is the scribes and Pharisees who are being attacked in the guise of Satan. Pagels gives many excellent reasons for thinking this, and I for one have no problem with her theoretical working. But I still think the scenario I have presented has merit for the very reason that it reflects a probable historical event of much earlier vintage. And as Carsten Peter Thiede and Matthew D'Ancona have recently contested the dating of Matthew's Gospel, pushing it much further back, a political rather than a scribal scenario for this incident is perhaps more feasible. For me, Matthew's adding of words to the story glosses over a conversation had by Jesus in a quite different context; either that, or it is simply presumed that the reader will understand what is going on here.

The Nazarenes, along with other sectarians (including Christians), were later to be singled out for punishment by the Jewish orthodoxy; for they had dramatically miscalculated and failed to beat the Romans. And so they were classified as heretics, Jesus as the Christian Messiah being viewed by the sectarians as not just a failure, but also as a spiritual coward; he had after all refused to join them in what they believed to be the final battle against the Children of Darkness. I think that these Nazarenes were linked with the militants in the minds of the orthodox, and this confirms the existence of a militant branch of the Nazarenes, a branch which probably tried to enlist Jesus' help. Prayers against the heretical sectarians were later offered in the synagogues, and the Nazarenes were *specifically identified* alongside Christians and Zealots as responsible for the debacle. Named the *birkat ha-minum* ('benediction of heretics'), this prayer was designed to expose secret Nazarene and Christian followers of Jesus who were mixing with fellow Jews. This, of course, put the Nazarenes where they had always belonged, close to the sectarians and close to the militant forces which had ignited the whole ugly affair.

Back in 1959 Professor Kurt Schubert noted that Satan's three temptations were all eschatological in intention; that is, they belonged to the Rigorist, isolationist camp of political expectation, and as such strongly suggest that Jesus was being asked to put his messianic, miracle-working cards on the table. Schubert put it this way: 'Jesus was to prove himself to be the Messiah of the messianic movement.'[5] This allows us to read the text just as it stands, but we have to realize that its underlying intention is to demonize the questioner. As the demonizing process has been identified by scholars as belonging to the nationalists, the idea of Jesus' tempter being a Zealot commander is not at all far-fetched.

THE SUPPRESSED GOSPEL OF THOMAS

The New Testament scholar Helmut Koester has argued for the so-called apocryphal *Gospel of Thomas* to be recognized as a source document for the canonical Gospels; Elaine Pagels agrees, and argues along with Koester that the Gospels of Matthew and Luke resemble this controversial Gospel; Pagels then asks the obvious question: 'Why was this Gospel suppressed, along with many others that have remained unknown for nearly two thousand years?'[6] The answer given is that around 370 the Archbishop of Alexandria ordered Christians to destroy all such heretical writings. Heretical? Why heretical? Because like the *Gospel of Thomas*, they presented a view of Jesus almost diametrically opposed to that of the canonical Gospels – there was another Jesus, a quite different Jesus, lurking in the historical bushes. The Jesus of Thomas' Gospel parallels many statements made by the synoptic Jesus, but there are also statements which quite literally reverse Jesus' New Testament point of view. This fact, in conjunction with Koester's argument for Thomas' Gospel containing material which *predates* the Gospel, allows us to conjecture that the Jesus of the New Testament was either edited into his present shape fairly late in the day, or that coded language, which only the initiated could properly understand, was used from the very beginning. I suspect the latter; it is just possible that these texts are older than previously thought, and that the picture of Jesus being presented in the New Testament is much more complicated than at first supposed.

Paul's theology (when in fact it is his own) may appear to represent Jesus as in some sense 'divine', but there is just as much evidence in the New Testament pointing in the opposite direction, and this allows us to construct a middle-ground picture which helps focus the image. Paul's Jesus is an inflamed and inflated theological image; the Gospel Jesus is a sober, down-to-earth image of a man struggling to transcend fear and doubt. The Church of Rome's Jesus is the Gospel Jesus explained through Paul's eyes; Thomas' Jesus is the Jesus who sorts it all out, the Jesus who, in Elaine Pagels' words, 'urges people to seek direct access to God, unmediated by church or clergy'.[7] The Jesus of Thomas' Gospel does not ask for subservience from his followers; he asks them to dig deep within themselves as he has done – the Kingdom of God is not grounded in belief, but in knowledge of the self at the deepest level. In what Pagels refers to as 'sayings as strange and compelling as Zen koans', we hear Jesus say: 'If you bring forth what is within you, what you bring forth will save you. If you do not bring forth what is within you, what you do not bring forth will destroy you.' (NHC II. 45.29–33)

HISTORY AND MYTHOLOGY

Allowing for Professor Pagels' theoretical stance on the wilderness story, I would posit a further two levels; for I sense a mixing of history and ancient mythology bent to the twin purposes of distraction and supernatural elevation. Distraction in terms of the text's political importance being cleverly veneered over; supernatural elevation in terms of the ghostwriters' transposition of Jesus' very earthy messianic ministry on to a cosmic key. It is the only way these writers can overcome the problem of why Jesus' messiahship eventually failed, why he was rejected by his own people and crucified by the Romans as a common criminal. The story of Jesus is no longer the story of an ordinary man become the Messiah of Israel; it has been elevated to the level of a cosmic drama, inflated to the level of a divine/diabolical confrontation where good and evil battle it out in the lives of individuals and nations. The 'ordinary' has been banished; the 'extraordinary' has been established as daily routine; flesh and blood have been theologized into a literal amalgamation with deity; the capacity of individuals to seek God in their own depths transformed into *things to be believed about Jesus.* The question is, why should such a thing have happened? Yes, there was crisis, persecution; but surely something of the original Jesus managed to struggle through? It couldn't all have been a whitewash, a rearranging of materials to incite solidarity. Jesus had been special and that fact was stamped all over the apocryphal, as well as the canonical, Gospels.

Extraordinary things were spliced into the original Jesus story; but to this day the question of why such miraculous shadings were added remains a real question – Jesus seems to have so deeply affected those around him that tall stories became the coinage of most Christian thinkers. And amalgamated as he eventually was with a pagan-infused interpretation of Paul's highly evolved theological vision, it is not at all surprising that the new centre of Christian authority set up in Rome after the destruction of Jerusalem should have considered itself in receipt of a remarkable Truth. The later Roman Church, the new Roman seat of apostolic authority displacing the original Nazarene Mother Church, cannot in all honesty be accused of making up a new Jesus story just for the sake of it; but it can, as history clearly reveals, be accused of progressively manipulating an already hybrid story down the centuries for the sake of power.

Early Jewish belief had it that Satan was God's silent partner in moral affairs (witness the temptation of Job); it was believed that God allowed Satan to tempt and harass the inhabitants of the Earth for moral reasons. But as we have already seen in Chapter 1, this Old Testament scenario was eventually replaced with a view of Satan in which he ceased to be God's silent partner and became his moral adversary. It is however this former conception of Satan that arises in both Matthew's and Luke's Gospels, not the latter; Satan sounds as if his control of affairs is God-given, not wrested from God via human weakness. Basically, this old conception of Satan is the subject of these longer passages, and I believe that that is the mistake committed by these writers as they dressed up political confrontation as diabolical temptation. The story's offer of 'worldly power' in return for a reversal of Jesus' mind-set clearly reflects what lies hidden; and the mistake of going too far back into Jewish mythology in their attempt to conceal what is going on is, for me, a secondary proof that the ghostwriter of this text merely camouflaged a political argument with an ancient view of Satan which just happened to fit the circumstances. To put it simply, Satan was no longer viewed as having such a relationship to God in Jesus' day. Also, if it was accepted without question that Satan had the right to offer inducements of the magnitude proffered to Jesus, then God and Satan have to be seen as in league. Which suggests that Christianity, since its inception, has quite mistakenly interpreted the delicate relationship, or balance, between good and evil.

By the end of the wilderness temptation passages, what was in all likelihood a Zealot commander trying to persuade Jesus to submit to sectarian authority has been transformed into an event of cosmic proportions; an event made to serve all sorts of first- and early second-century Christian propaganda purposes. Jesus is no longer a pacifist, no longer a rogue Messiah making sectarian leaders and the rule-bound Jewish priesthood uncomfortable; he is now the Son of God to whom angels must minister. Identified with God come down to earth in human form, with a divine intelligence methodically working to some pre-ordained plan, whatever Jesus does or says takes on such significance that every verse in every chapter of the New Testament becomes a means to an end. And by linking the whole corpus with the Hebrew Old Testament, what is basically the history of a rejected Jewish Messiah and sectarian drop-out is transformed into the biography of Israel's war God become a man who eschews war. From that contradictory point onward, whoever disagrees with Jesus disagrees with God, and thus whoever disagrees with Jesus' disciples also disagrees with God. And from there anyone who disagrees with the Church set up in Jesus' name and run by those claiming to be the legitimate succession from his disciples is in disagreement with God. By the end of the New Testament story, no one will be safe from the writers' literalist touch. Judas Iscariot, the disciple who betrays Jesus, will, by definition, become the excuse for torture and murder on a vast scale; for this unfortunate individual is conveniently demonized with the words: 'Then entered Satan into Judas . . .'[8] and with this useful shorthand Christianity's future enemies will be demonized *en masse*. Jews, pagans, heretics – *all* will be classified as dupes of the Evil One and eliminated. On this score, thanks are due to the Jesus Seminar for finally debunking Judas' betrayal of Jesus for 30 pieces of silver.

THE SATANIC INDICTMENT

In her recent ground-breaking book *The Origin of Satan*, Elaine Pagels traces the evolution of the idea of Satan from its earliest origins to its later Christian interpretation. At first merely obstructive, Satan later changes into evil incarnate, becoming the Prince of Darkness. But as Pagels so carefully shows, the four Gospels take to condemning as 'creatures of Satan' anyone who disagrees with them, and the end result is that even Christians with a tangentially different view of Jesus are eventually described as 'satanic'. Thus is born the Christian Church's certainty, its seemingly indefatigable belief that what it decides to nominate as 'the truth' must necessarily be left to stand as the truth beyond all debate or criticism. It is God's will that the New Testament is the way it is, and no amount of scholarship or study or honest Modernist probing will ever undermine the Good News it contains.

Behind closed doors, or in the secret depths of their own minds, the educated, thinking clergy may well voice serious doubts about Jesus' divinity and much else, but before the public they mostly deny that any real problem exists. Alas, as anyone with a skerrick of commonsense knows only too well, the old, old story of the Gospels is a problem; in fact the whole New Testament is a problem. Jesus as he is offered to congregations all over the world is a problem. The form Western society has taken in conjunction with Christianity's growth and success is a problem. And, in particular, Christian fundamentalism is a problem; for at the heart of fundamentalist views, whatever their variety, hides the dread spectre of God's diabolical counterpart – Satan is alive and well in the twentieth century, and he is out to get YOU.

Professor Pagels is most enlightening about all of this; she has written a book which, according to Professor David Sperling of Hebrew Union College, 'helps us to understand the power of irrational forces that still need to be confronted in contemporary society'. And this is exactly what Pagels does manage to accomplish in her delicately constructed text; she shows how the sectarian demonization of Christianity's early enemies – Jews, pagans and heretics – shaped the Church's growth and allowed her to survive against all odds. But at what price has this monumental organizational and theological success straddled so many centuries? For as Malachi Martin and Peter de Rosa show clearly

in their separate historical accounts, the Church's early suc-
cesses, in conjunction with the favoured status conferred on
Christianity by Constantine, eventually produced a lethal
cocktail that was composed of power and authority backed by
unassailable certainty.

THE DEMONIC CLOUD

Pagans came to hate Christians because of their atheism; yet
another strange twist in an already twisted tale. They sincerely
believed that Christianity's growing success in converting their fellow pagans to the new faith would bring the wrath of the gods
down on their communities, and predicted both the destruction of
family life and loss of social cohesion if this hybrid Jewish cult
were allowed to spread unchecked. For from being a minority religion within Judaism, Christianity became (between 70 and 100) a
largely Gentile-cum-Diaspora movement due to orthodox Jewish
rejection and the earlier efforts of Paul among pagan communities. And just as the Jews were quickly demonized for rejecting the
up-dated Good News of Paul, so also were pagans eventually
demonized for not recognizing Jesus the Jew as Son of the only
real God in existence – the Jewish one. Complicated. And made
more so by the fact that the Christian view of the pagan gods was
not only that they did not exist, but that what did exist were
demons mistakenly worshipped as gods. That was quite a slap in
the face for non-Christians and it produced a backlash.

What happened at the time is hard for us of the twentieth century to fully appreciate; we simply do not hear the word 'demon'
in quite the same way. And the word 'demonize', as we have come
to use it, has almost completely lost any connotation with demons
in the real sense. In the real sense? That's the catch; we don't really
believe in demons any longer. But the early Christians did believe
in them and some, as we saw in the last chapter, still do.

Recapturing that earlier belief in, and fear of, demons is no
easy task; but it can be accomplished by empathetically entering
the Christian mind of that period. No, that's not quite right; what
we have to do is enter the Christian *imagination*, for it is there,
in the dim, preternatural light of a mental cosmology given over
to Satan and his angels, that we stumble into the terror. Terror?
The terror of living on a planet in the throes of a cosmic war.

What has to be understood is that the whole climate of Christian opinion was locked into a vision of things where God and Satan battled it out for supremacy allied to a *still developing* theology of Jesus' crucifixion and resurrection. As a result of this, daily events took on an unusual significance, being interpreted in the light of this belief system. This is to say that everything 'said' or 'thought' or 'done' was subject to internal scrutiny. Satan was never far off; his angels-cum-demons were always at hand to lead the unwitting astray.

But there is a single point where all of this falls into a clear and terrifyingly real perspective, and that point is in the Roman arena. It is there that we see this belief system at work with astonishing success. Arrested for not sacrificing to the Emperor, many Christians managed to sustain a quiet fortitude in the face of unbelievable barbarity. So much so that Justin, a student of philosophy in Rome around 140, was startled to witness Christians being torn apart by wild animals with the kind of equanimity generally associated with philosophers. And not only that, for these unfortunates, he discovered, were not even educated Christians, but illiterate tradespeople. By inexplicable means, these simple Christians had 'tapped into a great, unknown source of power', to use Elaine Pagels' words. Pagels clarifies this situation by revealing that the incredible confidence of these early Christian martyrs lay primarily in their certainty that their deaths would advance God's victory over the forces of evil, forces that inhabited the minds of Roman magistrates as they condemned Christians to death. It is impossible for us fully to savour what having a belief system like this really felt like, but knowing something of what lay behind such acts of courage does allow us to at least partially penetrate their mystery.

And so we are left with a vision which presupposes unseen energies forcing human beings to do their enigmatic will; a view endorsed by the pagan world itself. According to Pagels, Justin 'realises with a shock that Socrates himself had said the same thing the Christians are saying – that all the gods Homer praises are actually evil energies that corrupt people'.[9] But it was not seen in quite this way by the pagan world; their gods weren't evil, just capricious. But Justin can now see through this subterfuge, for wasn't Socrates himself charged with atheism, just like the Christians, and given hemlock to drink? And so, in Justin's mind, there arises a form of proof for the Christian point of view: the irrational hatred being exhibited against the Christians was merely a symptom of the very thing the Christians were describing – demons were in control of the pagan mind.

But not only the pagan mind; orthodox Jews too were under the thrall of Satan in Christian opinion. In fact everyone not in agreement with Christianity was eventually perceived in such a light. The word 'light' is the operative one, for like the wilderness holy ones, the Essean-Essene, Christians saw themselves as 'sons of light', the pagan nations and orthodox Jews as 'sons of darkness'. Blanketing everyone with Satanic intention, Christians came to see themselves as besieged by evil. The battle lines were drawn, the great cosmic conflict between God and Satan was now being fought out in the streets and back alleys of Rome. Relentlessly persecuted by all and sundry, the Roman Christians scratched a living, kept a low profile, and methodically lived their message out into the populus. If educated, they ran the constant risk of discovery, but could at least claim for themselves a clean, quick death; if uneducated, there was less chance of discovery, but the risk of a brutal death prefaced by torture.

There is absolutely no doubt that these Roman Christians were utterly sincere in their faith; in fact the word 'sincerity' is not really sufficient to describe the kind of faith they possessed. Their patience, good works and perseverance in the face of what must often have appeared to be insurmountable odds is quite staggering. One is reminded of Teilhard de Chardin's comment that he himself did not measure up, in moral terms, to someone of simple faith. But as can be imagined, not all of them managed to hold their simple faith in place when arrested and tortured. Some crumpled under the brutality and named their associates, betrayed their brothers in Christ and died in stark terror of what the afterlife would bring. Some did sacrifice to the gods, to the Emperor, and lived to tell the tale. Not all Christians walked or crawled into the arena with a beatific smile on their face, as Hollywood would have us believe. And many Christian Gnostics did not end up in the arena at all; tongue in cheek, they happily sacrificed to the Roman gods and got off without as much as a curt word. It is known that the behaviour of these Gnostic Christians caused much consternation among the regular variety. The regular variety? Yes, there were 'regular' and 'irregular' Christians, and the irregular ones were yet another category of demonized individual.

THE HERETICS

Everything depended on whether you followed the party line or not; if you veered from the accepted code of behaviour, ritual and interpretation of gospel events, you were out. It was as simple as that. Questions were utterly forbidden. Jesus may have said: 'Seek and ye will find, knock and it will be opened unto you', (Matt. 7:7) but such an argument did not prevail with the leaders of the Christian community as it developed at the end of the first century. Elaine Pagels describes this attitude in detail in her book on Satan's origins, and what she reveals is that dissident thinkers did not have a chance of being heard. And it is at exactly this point that we stumble upon the transition point between a church governed by apostles, and a church governed by deacons, priests and bishops.

Things had changed; the days of the itinerant apostle were over. Christian communities were now on their own and subject to the pressures of the pagan world on all sides. And like all rapidly growing communities, the Christian community was also subject to internal pressures. Pagels cites a letter written by Clement to Christians in the Greek city of Corinth around 90, a letter in which he reveals much of what was going on during this period. Sections of the Church were in an uproar, it seems, over heavy-handed behaviour from leaders such as Clement; leaders who seem to have decided that what they nominated as 'the truth' was utterly beyond question. And to cement their supposed apostolic authority in place, such leaders resorted to writing their own Scriptures; that is, they created letters (Epistles) supposedly written by some of the apostles themselves. In these letters they contrived events to show that certain individuals had received the necessary apostolic blessing to make them heirs of these Apostles.

Of such a nature was Peter's first Epistle, and Paul's Letters to Timothy. Ordained an 'overseer' or 'bishop' by Paul, Timothy is made Paul's legitimate successor, and as such allowed to wield Paul's portion of apostolic authority. There was a good reason for this transferral of power, for it is in these supposed Letters to Timothy that Paul makes childbearing the chief task of women, so barring them from occupying positions of power in the Church. Professor Heinemann remarks: 'Women in particular are given all sorts of pious directives in both the presumably false and the certainly false letters of Paul. And down through history

the Church has toiled tirelessly to get women to take such exhorta-
tions to heart.'[10] Women should obey their husbands, learn silence
and submissiveness, and keep silent when men are around.
Childbearing is their destined lot. In her witty and provocative
book, *Putting Away Childish Things*, Professor Ranke-Heinemann
sums up this situation with characteristic force. Suggesting that
some kind of warning against forgeries ought to be printed on the
New Testament, she says: 'Perhaps it would cut down on the use of
the expression "Word of God", not just for false Letters but also
for the genuine ones. For all their genuineness, not one of them has
ever been anything more than the word of man.'[11]

Referring to those Christians who did not agree with him as
self-willed people who had initiated a 'horrible and unholy rebellion', Clement rails against their rejection of the 'clergy', and in
the process lets slip that the dissidents considered such appointments an 'innovation'. Clement's reaction to such a charge is to
quote Paul's Letter to Timothy in the hope that this forgery, this
conveniently created piece of propaganda, will cancel dissident
objection; for is it not because of such apostolic successions that
the Church's consensus truth claims must be accepted? The irony
of the situation is that Matthew and Luke, virtual contemporaries
of Clement, had just revealed in their gospel reconstructions that
the Jewish priesthood had been Jesus' principal enemy – the house
of cards was shaking.

By the second century this dispute over 'clergy' had hotted up
and infected churches everywhere; the growing authority of the
clergy was alarming many Christians. But those of Clement's
persuasion used Clement's tactics, and adherence to pre-set
moral codes and interpretations of earlier writings already edited
and rendered historically safe was not only demanded, but
enforced. And often for a very good reason; for there were
Christians who had evolved not only a hatred of the clergy, but
also Christians who had evolved for themselves fantastically illiterate theories around the Church's basic doctrines. Conscious of
scriptural manipulation in high places, these Christians tried to
sort out the true from the false and ended up creating an even
greater doctrinal mess of their own.

By 180 such ideas had spawned such wildly diverging
offshoots of standard Christian belief that Irenaeus, Bishop of
Lyons, wrote a five-volume refutation of such deviance – the
writers were from there on called 'heretics' (*hairesis*: 'choice'),

and, for good measure, were linked to Satan. Those guilty of making a choice between one interpretation of the gospel story and another were automatically categorized as having become self-willed and out of control, their safety even among fellow Christians removed at the stroke of a pen. Later, Tertullian brought this absurd situation to a state of dictatorial perfection when he announced that the clergy must not allow their congregations to ask questions, for it is the asking of questions that makes heretics.[12] One question in particular was to be avoided: Where does evil come from? This is the question that must be circumvented for fear of stumbling onto the fact that it reveals the dark side of the Church, the dark side of Christianity, the dark side of Christianity's God. Face this question, and you face the creative darkness which Christianity refuses to acknowledge.

It is, I think, legitimate to identify Tertullian with bringing to perfection that sinister state of mind which eventually invaded Christian thinking; for he went on to make some hair-raising assertions about the nature of truth, assertions justified with statements which reveal a mind utterly closed to all commonsense. Writing that believers must desist from any discussion of Scripture, that all deviation in opinion comes from the Devil, and that Satan has master-minded 'false exegesis', this divinely governed apostolic mind observes that: 'Heretics ought not to be allowed to challenge an appeal to the Scriptures, since we . . . prove that they have nothing to do with the Scriptures. For since they are heretics, they cannot be Christians.'[13] Such reasoning, circular and profoundly silly as it is, quickly became the tenor of so-called inspired Christian reasoning. With dexterity, future Fathers of the Church built intricate travesties of logic on this unassailable foundation, and the stranglehold gained by the clergy on people's lives became the standard form.

RADICAL AND ULTRA-RADICAL CHRISTIANS

Still, there were Christians who rejected this heavy-handed approach without becoming ultra-radical in either their ideas or their behaviour. One such Christian, Valentinus by name, broke quietly with the unquestioning majority and formed an underground group of Christians who, although still a professing part of the standard Church, considered themselves more mature by way of spiritual experience and discernment. Accepting that faith, hope and love were truly the foundation of the Christian life, they added 'understanding' (*gnosis*) to the mix, and developed a doctrine of understanding which invited Christians of standard practice to experience their deeper spiritual levels – shades of the *Gospel of Thomas*. Covert meetings were held, and we learn from Elaine Pagels' fascinating study that Valentinus had learned secret teachings attributed to Paul by a teacher called Theudas. These teachings caused Valentinus to steer a middle course between extreme radicalism and the standard confession of faith, and resulted in an interpretation of Scripture carrying meanings believed to be part of the very early Christian communities – meanings which went 'beyond the literal interpretation of the Scripture to question the gospel's deeper meaning'.[14]

It will be appreciated that educated Christians responded to this kind of thinking, and Pagels records that Tertullian complained that it was often the very best of his membership who deserted the ship of faith for the ship of understanding – a point that should not be overlooked. And so the Church began to subdivide and the Christian community began to fragment in front of the eyes of Tertullian and Irenaeus. Enter Marcus, a doctrinal innovator who was castigated for his alleged seduction of women. He appears to have offered them no more than participation in celebrating the Eucharist – something often denied them in Irenaeus' church.

The reason for such openness towards women was because Valentinus sometimes used the image of divine Father and divine Mother to describe what he believed to be the indescribable Source of all things seen and unseen. Marcus, working from this enlarged vision of God, is recorded by Irenaeus as having allowed women to officiate at church services, and of encouraging them, like Paul, to speak in prophesy; he is even accused of calling down the Holy Spirit on their behalf, and of 'touching them' (blessing them) with his hands. Pagels makes the point that when Irenaeus speaks of Marcus and his followers as 'adulterers', he is in fact using the biblical image of *illicit religious practices*, not accusing them of actual adultery.

But perhaps the most revealing idea that Valentinus inspired is to be found in the *Gospel of Philip*, which offers an alternative explanation to good and evil as cosmic opposites. Discarding this approach, Philip's gospel argues that opposites such as 'good' and 'evil' are actually *interdependent pairs*. Moral law as handed down by the now alarmingly authoritarian Christian Church is the equivalent of eating from the tree of knowledge, the fruit of which delivered not knowledge but a slow death and estrangement from the garden of Eden.[15] Such a view flies in the face of the way in which Gnostic teaching was being interpreted by people such as Irenaeus and Tertullian. These Church Fathers translated *gnosis* as 'hard knowledge', so making Gnosticism into no more than a cerebral creation; but the facts were otherwise. Gnosticism proper was not about intellectual knowledge at all; and neither was it about imagination run riot. At its best, it was about understanding something in terms of deep insight. Such knowledge arose from the depths of the human heart (the unconscious) and signalled, not an intellectual or theological interpretation of God, but an experience of God allied to the discovery that the human self constituted a barrier to spiritual comprehension. Attempting to understand God through the eyes of a self that automatically claimed everything as its own (even God) was deeply problematical. What we had to do was thoroughly examine this so-called self's opinion of itself and note that its claim on everything as its own was, to say the least, misplaced. The idea of the mind being 'my' mind, of the heart being 'my' heart, of God being 'my' God, was an illusion. And so with the Gospels. Just as there were deeper ways of approaching the self, so also there was a deeper way of approaching what these gospels seemed to say about the self in relation to God.

Moral law strictly adhered to was the outcome of minds struggling to get back to God by a self-conscious route. Jesus rejected this self-conscious route and, as a result, deeply angered the upholders of Jewish religious orthodoxy. Like Jesus, the Gnostics believed that each person carried a different set of needs, different levels of comprehension, and different qualities of maturity. To feed everyone on the same strict moral diet was to ignore true need and further distort an already distorted self in need of help. Forcing everything into opposition and demanding *this* choice over *that* choice undermined our ability to act with freedom and love – particularly when we set up one only of those choices as an unquestionable truth. To be told, as Adam was told, that he could eat from *this* tree, but not from *that* tree, clearly suggested a lack of freedom on Adam's part; the intrinsic freedom which truth or real knowledge is supposed to impart; indeed, the very thing the forbidden tree embodied. And this in turn suggested a form of cosmic enslavement which religiously enforced moral law perfectly mirrored. In this sense, the Genesis story could be reversed: God was the Evil One because he denied Adam and Eve comprehension of evil, the Evil One was God because he freely offered that knowledge. Jealous of the fact that these two beings had achieved the knowledge of good and evil, God threw the pair out of the garden and barred their return. Previously ignorant of the existence of evil, the two now recognized that they had been denied this knowledge because it revealed too much about their creator who had imbued them with his own unpredictable nature.

In Gnostic thinking there is a curious reconciliation of God and Satan, of Heaven and Hell, of light and darkness. Satan turns out to be not so much a being ravenously intent on the moral destruction of the human race (a conception of Satan developed at the time of Jesus by the wilderness sectarians, particularly the Essenes), but rather a creative principle, an energy of obstruction and opposition not separate from God, but an integral expression of God's character. *And* ours. As the early history of Satan reveals (in spite of what Genesis appears to be saying), cosmic opposites were unthinkable to the early monotheists of Israel; which rather suggests that the Genesis story is not quite as it ought to be. And there are no cosmic opposites in Valentinus' thinking either; God and Satan constitute one force, one truth, one experience which we break apart due to the perceptual development of the self. There is no Satan in the *Gospel of Philip*, and there is, by Gnostic definition, no Satanic being 'out there' in real life either – God controls everything, even the lower cosmic forces.

The existence of such forces, creative and destructive by turn, are recognized by the Gnostics, but they are thought by advanced Christian Gnostics like Valentinus to inhabit our natures in the form of archetypes, psychic configurations of an anthropomorphic type which are the background of our collective psychology as human beings. Such entities are necessarily projections of the human mind; but they are also arguably 'actual' to the extent that they represent energies of consciousness beyond that of the personal. Human self-consciousness is presumed to be the summit of the evolutionary process; but just as Paul Davies suspects mathematics to be integral to the universe, and not merely an expression of human sensibility, so also could consciousness be integral to matter which is perhaps mathematical at base. This carries us back to de Chardin's notion of consciousness existing in matter from the very beginning, and of Jesus carrying the divine element of self-consciousness potentially resident in matter to its point of fullest expression.

This suggests that the 'little devil' and the 'little angel' which metaphorically sit on our shoulders and whisper diametrically opposed things into our ears are not entirely the result of enculturation or social conditioning, but allied to deeply mysterious elements of consciousness which continually suggest creative 'alternatives' to what we think and do. Here then is the energy base from which angels and demons of more substantial psychic reality can miraculously arise alongside that of dreams and creative reveries. Introduce a distorted religious formula into this mix, and the result will be suitably grotesque. Introduce a pathology into this mix, and almost anything will be possible.

Elaine Pagels is at pains to point out that ethical questions are just as real and as important to these Gnostic Christians as they are to their consensus-loving brothers and sisters; the difference is that they have realized that fear disables our ability to make helpful ethical choices. Connecting this fact to his rejection of cosmic opposites, Philip says: 'Do not fear the flesh, nor love it. If you fear it, it will gain mastery over you; if you love it, it will devour and paralyse you.'[16] This is the dilemma facing all of us, the dilemma of how to balance ourselves mentally between our fears and our loves, our revulsions and our desires, our projections and what actually exists. To live with the constant restriction of fear is to be mastered by life; to live without any kind of restriction is to be overcome by one's own appetites. The secret is simply to avoid extremes; it is extremes of belief and behaviour and theory that bedevil us. Push the moral question too far and we end up killing people for their own good; refuse to properly recognize the moral question and we end up doing exactly the same.

Jesus seems to have understood this; he was not an extremist.

The Satan Jesus talked to in the wilderness was not the Satan of Job's temptation; and neither was he the Satan of later pathological sectarian fear. He was, I believe, simply a human being demonized by the gospel writers for the purpose of deflection. But why? If the gospel writers were trying to please the Romans, then why not say outright that Jesus had rejected Zealot extremism? Wouldn't that have pleased and satisfied their Roman readers? Possibly. But it would also have alerted them to the uncomfortable fact that Jesus had spent what appears to have been a protracted length of time in the company of an enemy of Rome. There had been a secret meeting in the desert between this prominent Nazarene and an important sectarian leader, and this fact, although mitigated by Jesus' refusal to recognize this leader's authority, inadvertently informed the reader that Jesus the Nazarene was known to, and had had complicated dealings with, the militant branch of the desert sectarians. This would not have been a surprise for, as shown by Elaine Pagels, the Nazarenes were viewed by the surviving Jewish community as sectarian heretics who were as responsible as the Zealots for the Roman invasion. To put it mildly, Jesus was much more complicated than he seemed to be, much more complicated than the early Church Fathers wished him to be, and much, much more complicated than the New Testament eventually allowed him to be. This fact, side-stepped by Christian thinkers both then and now, has resulted in an excuse-making policy of allowing anything at all threatening to be conveniently dropped into the demonic dustbin.

CHAPTER EIGHT

The Winsome Doctrine

The Church's belief that its traditional answers are true to reality, that answers found outside of the Church must necessarily be inadequate, and the fact that there are now two distinct Christianities in existence

There is no democracy in Heaven, and if God had his way, there would be no democracy on Earth either. At least that's how it seems in Malachi Martin's scheme of things, in his grand vision of Catholicism rejuvenated. There are only inferiors and superiors, a hierarchy within which self-perfecting individualism (Martin's carefully worded description of the world's alternative to Christianity) is replaced by submission to authority without question. Subordination is the name of the game. There is a mystical union of hearts and wills, an ever-ascending scale of being where unquestioning obedience to authority is accepted as natural and wholesome. Supernaturalisms are the fare of the day, for the whole structure is obviously more than the sum of its parts – God is in control and absolutely anything is possible.

This description of the divine hierarchy is Martin's description of the Jesuit Order as it ought to be, and we are to assume the same structure throughout the Catholic Church when it is functioning as a true extension of the will of God. And Martin views the entire cosmos in the same manner, all the way from 'lifeless stones and earth up through plants, animals, and humans, angels and archangels'.[1] Everything is part of an hierarchic principle of being ending in the Trinity of Father, Son and Holy Spirit. Through the prophets, the Children of Israel were first made aware of God's divine hierarchy, and as the 'Christ', Jesus later instructed his Church in the same multi-levelled system of checks and balances. So everything is in its place by divine fiat. All beings have their place in this pyramid of spiritual authority, and at the interstices of Heaven and Earth stand Christ and the Pope.

Exercising this divinely sanctioned authority, Pope John Paul II recently reasserted the doctrine that Jesus had no brothers and sisters, and that his mother was a virgin before and after Jesus' birth. As reported in *The Australian*, Richard Owen of *The Times* observed that the above statement was made to his regular audience at the Vatican, and added that this clarification of a long-standing historical problem was 'clearly intended to put to rest centuries of speculation that Christ was not Mary's only child'.[2] Well, isn't that a relief! It takes the tension out of the day to know that problems can be removed in such a manner, and that those once thought best able to handle such problems can close up shop and rely wholly on the papa's inspired consciousness. Well, it would if such a claim to inside knowledge was at all sensible, which it is not.

There is a lot at stake in such a question, and John Paul must once again have felt the cool breath of reality on his neck to have made such a feckless pronouncement. Backing away from the disturbing fact that the Gospels speak openly of Jesus' brothers and sisters, John Paul is quoted as having said that the words 'brothers' and 'sisters' are used 'loosely in the Gospels'. Loosely? In the Gospels? Does this mean that the Gospels do not always mean exactly what they say, and that sometimes one has to read between the lines? Is that what 'loosely' means in this context? Or does this interesting word refer only to the numerous passages where Jesus' brothers and sisters are mentioned? And what of His Holiness's other statement that this 'looseness' has resulted from the fact that there is no word for 'cousin' in either Hebrew or Aramaic? Does that solve the problem? Is this something over-looked by scholars? I think not. The Gospels did after all come down to us in Greek, and ancient Greek was not lacking in a word for 'cousin'. This fact cannot be brushed aside. The Gospel writers are presumed to have had first-hand knowledge of Jesus' family situation, so why botch such an important fact? Why allow such ambiguity when the whole heady business of Jesus' divinity and Mary's virginity were at stake? Or were they not at stake at all?

To complicate matters, we are also told by Richard Owen that John Paul II believes that Mary, mother of Jesus, was responsible for saving his life after the assassination attempt in 1981. Why? Because the bullet was fired on the *Feast of Our Lady of Fatima*, and that is considered significant. So convinced was he that this connects the shooting with Mary (Jesuit Father Bowdern's reliance on numbers and feast days seems to be at play here), that the Pope apparently donated the bullet taken from his body to the Fatima shrine. By doing so he confirmed not only that the divine hierarchy was all of a piece, but that Mary had been added to it for good measure. I do not doubt for a moment that John Paul II is perfectly sincere in that belief, but it must be pointed out that by holding such a belief the Pope allows himself to confirm one extrusion of pontifical hot air with another, and by doing so carries the Catholic mind one step further along the path of medieval credulity. Such witlessness is fully evident in what appears to be the unrelated business of Mary's other children; if John Paul's life was saved by Jesus' mother in 1981, then it follows, as night follows day, that she really had been a virgin, was now enthroned in Heaven along with the Father, the Son and the Holy Spirit, and that Jesus could not possibly have had brothers and sisters. *Ergo*, the problem is solved.

For most Catholics, conscious identification with Jesus became the key element in interpreting the will of God; special devotions and feast days became the conduit through which the transformative energy of redemption flowed. And with this redemptive energy came 'insight' and 'revelation', God's confirmation of the hierarchy functioning in his name. In 1670, for instance, at the Paray-le-Monial convent in France, it was revealed to Sister Margaret Mary Alacoque that Jesus' love for humanity was being neglected by the Church's general flock, and that the faithful ought to make reparation on their behalf. Asked by God to make the physical heart of Jesus the centre of a special devotion, this nun of the Visitation Order spread the news, and in 1675 caught the attention of Claude La Colombiere, a young Jesuit who soon confirmed her revelations through similar revelations of his own. Malachi Martin tells us that Claude 'conveyed the divine wishes to his Superiors, and through them to the Roman authorities'.[3]

This is Martin's sleight-of-hand at its best; Claude's and Alacoque's interaction with God take on the quality of an unrecorded telephone conversation, and we are left with the impression that God is in the habit of contacting individuals with specific requests. It's the New Testament all over again; God is the grand puppet-master behind the scenes. Accepting Alacoque's revelations as authentic in the late seventeenth century, Rome is said to have loosed 'a fresh aspect of theological thinking', and

the Jesuits found themselves officially chosen to spread this new
devotion to the community.

Alas, as a result of Modernism in the 20th century, Jesuit
fidelity to this special devotion seems to have evaporated, and
Martin notes that in 1972 Father General Arrupe discovered that
'Jesuits on the whole and in the majority had simply lost interest
in devotion to the Sacred Heart'.[4] Yet no one seems to have
noticed this radical change in the making; it seems to have come
as a shock when the Order most dedicated to the Sacred Heart of
Jesus spurned it as 'childish, primitive, unsophisticated, repellent
[and] unworthy of a modern mind'.[5] Described as 'gross' and
'sensuous' by some, this divinely commissioned devotion was now
seen as more suitable for children and peasants, and as such no
longer applicable to intelligent individuals in the modern age. So
what had happened? Had God changed his mind? Had he decided
to cancel this special devotion through rank and file rejection?
Was devotion to the Sacred Heart of Jesus for one age, but not for
another? Or was it simply that no such commission had ever been
received? Or again, was this astonishing reaction simply the result
of a silent and deadly process working within the Jesuit Order
itself, a process of estrangement from God dressed up in the fancy
workings and wordings of an age diabolically seduced?

In Martin's opinion, the latter, and not the former, was the case,
Father General Arrupe had been fatally flawed in his character
from the very beginning. In the habit of bowing to majority opinion, he had proved himself unable to wield Jesuit authority and
succumbed to the twentieth-century illusion that God was in
favour of a spiritual democracy. Teilhard de Chardin's influence
could be detected in this; he had rejected supernaturalisms as
'monstrous' and advocated 'full self-consciousness' in their stead.
To Martin, this was a travesty of the will of God; God desired that
individuals submit their wills to him through the priestly hierarchy of the Church, not further estrange themselves through
conscious self-aggrandizement. Self-perfecting individualism was
unacceptable as a route to God.

In *Hostage to the Devil*, Martin carefully defines this process of
self-aggrandizement through his study of possessed individuals,
and through the general drift of Western society towards a philosophy of personal meaning replaced by mere usefulness.
Unwittingly under the influence of diabolical forces, Western society is said to have fallen into an unconscious rejection of God's

plan of salvation because of science. For behind the death of meaning lies a set of scientific propositions which, if accepted as 'fact', or even as 'highly probable', automatically annul the idea of God initiating a process of salvation for all human beings. Jesus' death on the cross as a saving act simply melts away in the face of the fact that human beings have 'a remote ancestry during which not merely his body formed but what was called his mind and higher instincts were fashioned'.[6] This is the intellectual Rubicon we are each forced to cross during our lifetime, and the result of accepting the creed of science is a slow but certain diminution of religious belief and feeling – if indeed such a sense of God and his loving plan for all human beings has ever managed to grow in the first place.

Conscious of the gap between Church teaching and scientific theory, Teilhard de Chardin had attempted to construct a bridge between the one and the other, but his formulation had resulted in God becoming part of the cosmos, and Jesus no more than the peak of the evolutionary process. Which was to say that: 'The thrust that would finally bring forth Jesus was an evolutionary accident – a kind of cosmic joke – that started over five billion years ago in helium, hydrogen gases, and amino acids.'[7] Such a view made an utter nonsense of what the Church taught, for it heralded as cosmically automatic the completion of human development without divine revelation. In such a scenario the crucifixion of Jesus was no more than a grotesque scene of physical torture, the life of Jesus an ordinary life, the creation of a universal Church in Jesus' name a political stunt. Useful in the past, perhaps, all this religious double-talk, but not at all applicable to human needs and sensibilities at the end of the twentieth century. The supposed divinity of Jesus was ultimately irreconcilable with evolution, and as such had to be jettisoned on behalf of a vision of the world firmly grounded in scientific fact rather than religious fancy.

Malachi Martin is in no doubt that such reasoning is diabolical at source; not just because it flies in the face of Church doctrine, but because he literally believes it to spring from the dark heart of Satan disguised in the world as dispassionate intellect – there is an inner darkness of which we are unaware. Intellect in itself is not diabolical, but divorced from the truth of the Gospels, and seduced away from the revealed truth of the Church it cannot but fail to comprehend the complete cosmic picture and fall into error. The Devil is real, evil is on the loose,

and our inability to understand and accept this horrifying fact is
at the root of social collapse and personal disintegration. We are
constantly in danger of Satanic attack, oblivious to that fact, and
unwittingly engaged in strengthening Satan's grasp on our world.
Every page of *Hostage to the Devil* is laden with this kind of
thinking, and as a religious tract the book is powerful testimony
to the fact that some leading Catholic intellectuals are unwilling
to throw the diabolical baby out with the doctrinal bath water.

But why a Devil at all? And why evil? Why such rampant opposition to all that is good and wholesome, true and beautiful from
a being said to have been the apex of God's angelic creation? How
did Lucifer manage to fall into rebellion when he was so close to
the divine source in the first instance? That's the puzzler, and no
matter how one looks at it, rationalizes it, theologizes or mythol-
ogizes it, it remains the question which cannot be answered.
Which rather suggests that we are asking the wrong question, for
only questions inadequately formulated result in such an impasse.
So we must find a new question, or approach, and ask exactly
where in the hypothetical cosmic hierarchy of being Lucifer, as a
concept, can be placed. For if evil has its root in a being, in an
entity, and God made that entity, and there is, still, an ideal hierarchy of entities stretching from Heaven to Earth through which
the self-substantiating power of God flows, then any alternative
hierarchy of value that arose must necessarily have arisen by
divine fiat; that is, within the mind of God himself. For his angelic
creation need not be understood, in the first instance, as having
been a separate creation, as 'objects' somehow separated from
God in space and time, but as God expressing himself to himself
within his own divine orbit. Locked within God's orbit, within his
love and beauty and consistency, his angels and archangels were in
fact incapable of evil intention; but they were capable of willing
what their Creator willed, and it seems that he eventually willed
creative disruption.

As a word, 'evil' has taken on the connotation of diabolical
influence, of being somehow the result of a disembodied malev-
olence in the world to which human beings succumb. To be 'evil'
is therefore much more than being 'bad'; it is to be so out of control that control is picked up by forces other than the self. The
self is overcome, subdued, made subservient to the wishes of spirits or demons whose *raison d'être* is the disruption of human life.
And the whole business centres on the human will, on a teasing

of the human will towards decisions which will cause pain and
suffering on an ever-ascending scale of intensity. We do battle, it
seems, not just with other human beings, or with ourselves, but
with invisible powers greedily awaiting a moment of weakness.
That's the storyline, and it has stuck. Why? Because Christianity
has successfully personalized both the holy and the unholy. This,
we are told, is the great Christian contribution to religion, and
not to believe it means that the evil one has got us in his grip.
When not attached to this set of beliefs, to this anciently inspired
vision, the whole modern world is no more than an empty shell
– a shell from which the mysterious sound of the sea has been
cunningly removed.

CRISIS

In his challenging article 'A Western Crisis of Belief', the sociologist John Carroll recognizes (along with Malachi Martin) that
individualism has failed, but that is where agreement ends. Unlike
Martin, this sociologist does not advocate a return to traditional
Christian doctrine, he asks instead for a second Reformation, a
repeat performance of the courage that first broke the stranglehold of a corrupt and corrupting Catholicism. The continuous
gratification of personal needs, wants and desires does not in the
end satisfy the seeking mind, so much is admitted by Carroll; but
neither do tired old doctrines dredged up into the present from the
distant past. Yes, there should be 'an overarching theology or
metaphysics' to hold the whole picture in place; but it should be
'a credible picture of the whole', a Christianity revitalized, not
further marginalized.[8] In contrast to this, Dr David Powys paints
a quite different picture in 'The Unpopular Path of Truth'.
Mentioning John Carroll by name, this Anglican vicar drives us
back into Malachi Martin's arms with the words: 'The Church
must remain true to its calling, not the spiritual fashions of
modern society.'[9] The Church's confused sense of mission should
be replaced with words of truth, he believes, not words of
comfort. The old values should be reinstated; both sin and humanity's obligation to the Divine should be brought to the fore, not the
contradictory spiritual notions of a society seduced by
modernism. And heaven help us if the Church abandons this task,
for not any old belief system will do; it has to supply 'the saving

truths it has from God' whatever the cost. Christians seduced by modern ideas will just have to return to the fold cap in hand. Truthfulness is the key.

Powys' point of divergence with John Carroll seems to be over the nature of the meanings that should be offered to a disillusioned world; he rejects as inadequate meanings 'at odds with orthodox Christian convictions', and asserts that popular spiritual ideas do not help people come to terms with earthly and heavenly realities.[10] Yes, there is almost avid willingness among people to have faith, to seek spiritual things, but the range of beliefs accepted mostly go against the Christian revelation, and as such are intrinsically valueless. Popular spirituality may be very attractive, indeed seductive, but the Church cannot afford to side with such approaches for the sake of saving its own neck. It may be comforting to believe that everything is divine, that people are inherently good, that evil is an illusion, that only the self matters and all religions boil down to the same thing in the end, but that is a travesty of the Gospel message. The reality of sin is overlooked; humanity's obligation to divinity for Christ's redeeming death is sidestepped; Christ's future return abandoned as a promise to be kept.

A second article by John Carroll more than adequately deals with such a charge. In 'Time for a Recovery', Carroll states what everyone knows: the search for meaning has extended *beyond* the Churches. Traditional answers have evaporated and we are obliged to find new ones, not just serve up the old ones with a set jaw and gritted teeth. The age-old questions are real enough, but the age-old answers fall short of satisfying the modern mind. The first Reformation struck when the Catholic Church had lost touch with its own time, and a second Reformation is required for exactly the same reason. Luther and Calvin had the courage to rethink the old doctrines, so making them applicable to modern life, and we have to find the courage to do likewise. Which is to say that Christianity has to pull up its spiritual socks and learn, yet again, how to offer authentic reassurance to an age at the end of its spiritual tether. Humanism has failed in its attempt to replace the religious view with a person-centred equivalent, so it is up to Christianity to surprise itself and supply a vision capable of creatively encompassing the modern world.

But what exactly does that mean, Powys would ask. What does it mean to *creatively encompass the modern world*? Does it mean selling out to Darwinism, the Big Bang theory and artificial intelligence? Does it mean abandoning Jesus' saving power for so-called scientific fact? John Carroll's reply derails the literal quality of such a probable response by pointing out that the more insecure Christianity has become in its own doctrines, the more it has turned to secular issues. Citing the influential German sociologist Max Weber, Carroll reminds us that after the Reformation 'conscience' became the sole mediator between God and individual, and that 'work' was awarded a sacred status. And so there came about a relocating of the sacred, an infusing of the 'everyday' with a sacred glow, and the momentum of this change of attitude is still with us in the form of an *ever deepening connection with the world*. But he is well aware that a Church in flight from theology is in a dangerous state, a vulnerable and unenviable state as it attempts to blend philosophical utilitarianism with scientific Darwinism and abandons its calling. Powys agrees, but not for quite the same reasons, for Carroll the sociologist would have the Church respond to the issues of our time with a new metaphysic, a reworking of the old doctrines into a sturdier, more sensible rebuttal of modernism's soulless claims.

Speaking of the Christian churches and their growing failure to attract and convince, Carroll says that there is no surprise in this 'given that they resolutely avoid rethinking central doctrines in terms that might have some affinity with modern life'.[11] According to Carroll's gospel, this is the platform on which the churches will perish; according to the gospel of David Powys, exactly the opposite is true. Enter Malachi Martin with his theory of the 'winsome doctrine', his belief that dark, malevolent forces are undermining our sacred sensibilities through the factoids of science. Reduced by 'definition' to no more than biological robots with an illusionary sense of self, we are fast generating an overview capable of overpowering our most sacred understandings of self and world.

All three writers are in agreement that such a view will be ultimately disastrous for Western civilization, but Carroll is the only one who comes out batting for a reinterpretation of key Christian doctrines such as Christ's divinity. Taking the metaphysical bull by the horns, he suggests, with some dexterity, that the Gospels contain 'elements close to the view of the Divine as an encompassing energy or consciousness, such as Christ's "I am in my Father, and ye in me, and I in you" '[12]. To my way of thinking, this is a valuable and insightful observation, but I suspect it will not fit too well with the traditionalist's approach, an approach all but incapable of making theological and philosophical adjustment. And that in spite of Professor Douglas Geivett's suggestion in *Evil and the Evidence for God*, that the human mind may be 'a nonmaterial substance or a form of energy that can cause events in the physical world'.[13]

On the subject of theological and philosophical adjustment, it is interesting to read Karen Armstrong's *A History of God* and contemplate the fact that we are presently engaged in a humanist experiment which may or may not work out. Religion has after all been with us since the beginning of civilization, so in historical terms it is quite a new thing to live a life unplugged from religious influence.

Armstrong is aware of what this means; she was brought up Catholic and eventually entered a religious order, only to leave it in search of the very thing she had entered it for – God. Carrying the God of her childhood into adult life without much modification, she tells us that she was later shocked to realize that her life had moved forward on almost all levels, but that her ideas about God had not developed at all. Manufacturing religious experience out of music she then began to notice that the Church's God was hardly ever talked about, and that the Jesus who had taken his place seemed a purely historical figure firmly embedded in his own time. There was of course a sense of God throughout all of this, but he was no more than a taskmaster interested only in her infringement of the rules, or blankly absent when she needed him most. It took years for her to realize that this doctrinally fixed God did not in fact exist, that the real God too had no actual *objective existence*, and that that was the key to the whole affair. So she left the religious life, discarded her taskmaster God and began to 'deliberately create a sense of him' for herself. God could not be discovered in the rational processes, but he could be found in the creative imagination. One generation's ideas about God seldom satisfied another's; so each generation had to create its own image of God and put up with being dubbed 'atheists' by its contemporaries.

All of this is to be found in Armstrong's introduction, and it is a breath of fresh air to read her tight, learned prose, and find oneself smiling for a change. Yes, secular humanism does not seem to be delivering the goods, but neither is Christianity in its present state of doctrinal fixedness. The inner darkness is all but complete, and it is the doctrines of the Christian Church that have helped generate that darkness.

BACK TO THE SIBLINGS

The German historian Uta Ranke-Heinemann has blasted an enormous hole in Catholic thinking. Systematically dismantling the doctrinal edifice of the Church in her bestselling book *Putting Away Childish Things*, she reveals a paternalistic Church unwilling to admit that its early 'teaching stories' have been allowed to harden into never-to-be-questioned dogmas. In a showdown with the Church which is only just getting under way, this first woman Professor of Theology at the University of Essen has been declared ineligible to teach theology and transferred to the history department of the same university.

A student of Rudolf Bultmann's in the 1920s, and a convert to Catholicism in the 1950s, Ranke-Heinemann is of the opinion that a Christian has the right, indeed the intellectual obligation, to say 'No' to fairy-tale doctrines masquerading as eternal truths. Her main point is that Catholic 'truth' is a censored truth, and that 'the God whom we meet at the end of a series of ecclesiastical middlemen is a censored God'.[14] Called on to believe, but not to think, we practise mental gymnastics and studiously avoid the kind of questions we would quite naturally ask under any other set of circumstances. Touching the quick of the situation, she tells us that the Church 'isn't interested in understanding or enlightenment: Every variety of enlightenment strikes it as suspicious, if not worthy of damnation'.[15] Unconcerned with the pain it inflicts on religious intelligence, it punishes for the hurt caused to its own feelings, distrusts doubters and blesses the unquestioning. She adds caustically that 'Jesus lies buried not only in Jerusalem, but also beneath a mountain of kitsch, tall tales, and church phraseology'.[16]

One such tall tale is, of course, the present Pope's argument that Jesus' mother was a virgin both before and after Jesus' birth, and that he had neither brothers nor sisters in the real sense of those words. Made into step-brothers and sisters around 150 by the *Protevangelium of James*, and into cousins by Jerome in or around 400, the problem of Jesus' immediate family members was made to vanish. And for very good reason, for as Ranke-Heinemann observes: 'The whole centre of gravity of Christian faith rests on the fact that Mary conceived and gave birth as a virgin . . . Everything that has been subsequently taught and believed about the deliverance from sin and liberation of the human race through the blood of Jesus Christ . . . is based on this fact.'[17] Hence the title of *Aeiparthenos* (ever-virgin) bestowed on Mary by the Council of Chalcedon in 451. The whole bag of tricks rests on this strange notion. Allow the virgin birth of Jesus to be seriously questioned and the whole edifice of the Christian faith is open to attack. And so John Paul II takes his stand, and the nonsense elements of the story are once again swept under the doctrinal carpet before the faithful have a chance to glimpse their sheer absurdity.

The absurdity starts with a girl of around twelve years of age being led by God into a situation of public disgrace and dishonour. That's how it all started; Mary was in all probability just over twelve when her engagement to Joseph took place. At this time engagement at twelve, or a little older, was common practice; engagements at an older age were considered odd. And if she were engaged and then found to be pregnant? Well, the worst imaginable was possible. Found guilty of adultery at twelve she could have been stoned to death; if older, either strangled or burned. It all depended on the husband; if he was so angry that he took her to court, then the very worst might happen; if not, then only the girl's moral reputation suffered – a penalty by degree depending on the circumstances. It should be remembered that engagement counted as marriage – it was *de jure* marriage. So around the mother of Jesus grew two stories, one miraculous, the other scandalous. The latter was the more probable due to the fact that Joseph agreed to stay with his already pregnant wife. But Mary's child did at least belong to the correct father, and that pointed to 'irregularity' rather than 'adultery'.

It was still a problem of some proportions for the Gospel writers as Mary's factually oriented reply to the archangel Gabriel reveals, for she knew full well that sexual intercourse was required if children were to be conceived, and her reported reply to the angel reflected what she would have said – if she had in fact been visited by an angel, which was not the case. 'How shall this be, since I know no man?' she asks (Luke 1:3–4), her question reflecting not her personal astonishment at the pronouncement of this angel, but

the writer's awareness of the sexual irregularity he has to camou-
flage as he labours at the task of story reconstruction. And what a
reconstruction the Gospels are; they are alive with imagination and
hyperbole. The proof that there is another text struggling to get out
is detectable in the anomalies and contradictions each Gospel
contains, indeed, in their *looseness*. For how strange that Mary will
later accuse her son of being mad, and with the help of his brothers and sisters attempt to rescue him from himself. How strange
that this self-same Mary will not understand her divinely appointed
son when, at the age of twelve, he speaks of his 'heavenly Father';
and how strange that she will apparently forget all about her meeting with Gabriel and fall into the kind of mind-set one associates
with an ordinary mother fearful for a son's sanity.

Or is all of this not nearly as strange as it seems? Is it more the
truth that this mother and son did not get on? That Jesus' kith and
kin did not share in his curiously extended spiritual vision? That
the whole Nazarene party led by Jesus' family was doctrinally separate from the Christian party set up by Paul at Jesus' instigation?
And that Peter, in spite of attempts to reverse his role, was really
at loggerheads with Paul? Is it not historically obvious that the rest
of Jesus' disciples were under James' control, and that it was only
the outbreak of war with the Romans that eventually allowed
Paul's Christian party to win out over the Nazarene Mother
Church? Are not these the historical facts that have been clouded
by mythology and centuries of textual manipulation? And should
not the Christian Churches take responsibility for the whole
extraordinary mess and help initiate the second Christian
Reformation called for by John Carroll?

TWO CHRISTIANITIES

The problem of who is telling the truth about Jesus' death on the
cross, about God's supposed plan of salvation for the world, or
Mary's perpetual virginity, comes into sharp focus in Douglas
Geivett's conservative philosophical study of John Hick's progressive approach to theology and the existence of evil. In *Evil and the
Love of God* (1985), Hick propounds a universal theory of salvation which quite blatantly challenges the Church's major doctrines
of sin, redemption and eternal punishment for the wicked;
whereas Geivett in his weighty response, *Evil and the Evidence for*

God (1993), seeks to prove that Hick's universalism has no place in Christian doctrine, and that his eschatological overview isn't even Christian at base. Yes, Hick does allow for a redemptive process of sorts, a 'soul-making' process of distinctly evolutionary flavour reminiscent of Teilhard de Chardin, but that's about as far as it goes: he does not believe in a God who periodically breaches natural law and reaches down into his creation to augment some divine plan. Geivett, on the other hand, is not so sure; he argues that manipulations of this sort are probable given the nature of God. God is after all concerned about human beings; so it is to be expected that he will communicate with them from time to time – he is in fact *ubiquitously meddlesome*. Although not arguing directly for visitations of the angelic kind, Geivett does argue for the production of 'certain virtues in the life of a believer', and for the fortifying of the mind with 'confidence and peace' during crisis. In other words, God sometimes rewards believers.

As Associate Professor of Philosophy at Biola University in La Miranda, California, Geivett's response to Hick's new and pro-gressive vision of life and afterlife is worth looking at – he argues with flair, is seldom boring, and on many occasions quite enlight-ening. Arguing from the standpoint that God exists, and that he is more probably omnipotent than not, Geivett talks of God's power, intelligence and goodness, equates these traits with a 'person', and asks that we not rule out the possibility of miracles 'involving the manipulation of nature contrary to ordinary regularities'.[18] And firmly to cement this intellectually provocative point in place (angelic visitation and much else may be possible under such an arrangement), he adds: 'For . . . regularities themselves might well depend upon the ongoing participation of God in the operation of "natural" processes.' Such regularities are, of course, the laws governing the cosmos, and Geivett's second point is interesting because it suggests that God might be much nearer to us that we may previously have supposed. The scientific side of his argument stems from an acceptance of the anthropic principle – that the uni-verse has been specifically designed for human life to evolve – and that the incredibly restrictive process of creation necessary to pro-duce and sustain life such as ours following the Big Bang strongly suggests both intelligence and purpose behind the scenes.

Himself an eminent philosopher of religion, Professor Hick also believes in God, but not quite in the same manner as Professor Geivett – Geivett is a stickler for approaching God in the right way. It is not enough to just believe in God; we have carefully to define our theism in relation to the set revelation of Christianity. Now whatever one might think of Geivett's mental perambulations, his God is definitely *there* somewhere; whereas Hick's God is altogether ambiguous in his thereness. Geivett's God is susceptible to 'devotional experiment'; Hick's God seems more like a proposition one either accepts or rejects depending on how ambiguous God happens to be on the day. Geivett's God is benevolent, wishing to make meaningful contact with human beings; Hick's God is altogether hidden, a possible God within or behind the universe as brute fact.

Taking these pictures as they stand, Geivett's God sounds the more attractive of the two. But there is a catch, and it is a big one as far as the modern temperament is concerned: Geivett's God is not averse to condemning human beings to eternal punishment. Why? Because not only do we have to believe that God exists, we also have to desire to be in his presence, and when finally there willingly participate in acts of adoration and worship. So it stands to reason that beings in rebellion against God will be unable to take part in such worship, and that God in his unqualified goodness will congregate them in a domain where the demands of worship and adoration will not be made, namely 'Hell'.

Such reasoning is astonishing. Or as Hick puts it: 'This traditional doctrine of hell is one of the aspects of conservative Christianity that repels.'[19] By saying such a thing, Hick reveals himself to be a Modernist enamoured of what Malachi Martin calls 'the winsome doctrine', for his rejection of hell and punishment sets him up to be viewed by Rigorists like Martin as an exponent of doctrines diabolically reversed. Now, I have no idea how Professor Geivett would finally define such a stance on hell and punishment, but I think Hick accurately describes the gulf between conservative and progressive doctrinal formulas as tension-filled and capable of spawning two distinctly different Christianities. For what is the good of postulating that God has given us free will and intelligence if we are then forced, by dint of a fore-ordained and inflexible plan, to accept a series of logic-defying religious doctrines which make a nonsense of both our intelligence and our free will? What would be the point of such an exercise apart from proving that God can't be bucked?

Well, fine; if that's how God really wants it then there's absolutely nothing we can do about it – except rebel. And that of course is what we are not supposed to do, what we are free to do, but due to the doctrine of hell and eternal punishment thought unlikely to do because of fear. But only if we believe in the old Catholic formula. The Catch-22 is that we find it difficult to stop ourselves from rebelling because we have sufficient free will and intelligence to create other ways of defining God, his purpose, and the reality at large. Geivett may write that 'the reality of hell underwrites the Augustinian conviction that God has not stacked the deck against human freedom', but from where Hick (and many another) stands it is 'morally incredible that a perfectly loving Creator should devise a situation in which millions of men and women suffer eternally'.[20]

Uta Ranke-Heinemann comes to our rescue here when she says that hell 'serves the purpose of cradle-to-grave intimidation'.[21] That is actually the whole situation in a nutshell, an encapsulation of all the learned notions that have accrued around this subject down the centuries. At first a silent kingdom which accepted man and beast indiscriminately, and within which there was no punishment whatsoever, the Judaic underworld (*Sheol*) slowly evolved from Ecclesiates' place of dust and darkness (250 BCE) into Daniel's more hopeful underworld (165 BCE) where resurrection was possible. Influenced by the Greeks and Persians, there was a stirring in *Sheol*, a movement away from the belief that the dead slept forever. Influenced by the death of the Maccabean martyrs, the Jews evolved the idea of 'heaven' (in much the same vein as the German Valhalla), retained the dark and dusty *Sheol* for the rank and file, and created what Ranke-Heinemann refers to as a 'twofold military division . . . between good and evil'.[22] This military division subsequently turned into a moral one and from this there sprang the assumption that 'virtue' and 'morality' are warriors by right. Ranke-Heinemann sums up her introduction to hell and its eventual transformation into a place of torment by saying that 'war and religion have always been a harmonious pair'.[23] The point is well made, I think.

But what of Satan and his angels? Where do they fit in? What does Hick, as a progressive Christian scholar, and traditional Christian scholarship of modern hue, have to say about these dark figures, these denizens of the hell Hick must necessarily reject as a place of punishment? Arguing that Satan and his minions have 'permanent value as a vivid symbol of gratuitous evil perpetrated in society', Hick nevertheless remains doubtful that any appeal can be made 'to the reality of demons to explain the existence of some evils'.[24] This seems to suggest that demons do not actually exist, but can be talked about *as if* they do for religious purposes. On the other hand, Geivett tells us that Augustine attributed 'most natural evil to Satan' (floods, earthquakes and such like), and that Alvin Plantinga, the celebrated philosopher of religion has 'appealed to the logical possibility that what we call natural evil is due to the free action of Satan and his cronies'.[25] Natural evil 'can be attributed to nonhuman free agents of superhuman power', according to Plantinga, but in relation to those who defend the Augustinian position, this is not to assert that such an arrangement is *true*, merely that it is *possible*.[26] On the same page Geivett quotes Richard Swinburne (another eminent philosopher of religion) as saying that the assumption that fallen angels have subjected the world to natural evil 'will do the job . . . and is not *clearly* false'. Not *clearly* false? Not *necessarily* 'true', but 'possible'? I wonder what such statements mean? Are such word arrangements just another way of saying what Hick has already said; or are they a subtle side-stepping of too difficult a set of questions allied to the notion of divine revelation. For that is what it comes down to in the end, the belief that God has 'personally' delivered a revelation to the world in Jesus, and that everything said to be attached to that revelation (the existence of Satan, the perpetual virginity of Mary, or the miracles of Jesus) should be accepted without question; or do such obfuscations indicate deep philosophical unease in the religious camp?

According to Cardinal Newman, human beings became morally imperfect through the use of their free will – they *chose* to disobey rather than obey God. No unease there. Which means that we are not, as Hick suggests, creatures created imperfect so that we might be improved through a process of earthly soul-making, but rather *rebels who have to lay down our arms*. So thought Cardinal Newman, and so thinks Douglas Geivett, it seems. And right behind them is Malachi Martin with an identical overview. So what of Hick's universalist notion that everyone will be perfected in the end, that the process of earthly life is in itself the refining fire which will transform us, and that after death this process will complete itself in a series of other lives not related to the theory of reincarnation? This is Geivett's breakdown of Hick's spiritual system, and I must admit to being as surprised by it as I am by Geivett's willingness to accept the idea of eternal punishment for human beings.

But I am not at all surprised by Geivett's insistence that it is not enough to believe in God, but that what matters is 'how one comes to the conclusion that God exists'.[27] How we approach God is important. If one comes to a belief in God via Christianity's basic argument of 'rebels in need of salvation', then sin, evil and Satan are realities. But if one accepts Hick's notion of everyone making it in the end, then the appeal is not actually to God's saving power over and against sin, evil and Satan, but to the character and quality of human existence with all of its attendant evils intact. Evil then becomes an integral factor in the salvation process (part of God's purpose), not the reason for its existence, and in doing so 'cancels out the prima facie evidence for religious belief'.[28] This is what divides Geivett from Hick, and it is on exactly this subject that we must now dwell if we are to glimpse the mystery of good and evil in conjunction.

ABRAHAM'S DILEMMA

Tradition has it that Abraham's remains lie buried alongside those of his wife Sarah in the Cave of Machpelah, at Hebron, and that in adjacent twin tombs repose his son Isaac and his daughter-in-law Rebecca. Founder of the Jewish religion and father of the Jewish nation, Abraham stands out as the man who was willing to obey his God even when asked to kill his own son. In a curious twist of history and theology this links Abraham with God himself, for as Father to Jesus in Christian theology, God was also willing to sacrifice his son for a sacred purpose.

More to the point, however, are the suggestions of nineteenth-century German scholars that many Old Testament stories should be interpreted as symbols, or metaphors, and not read as historical events. Awarding them the status of myth, these scholars argued for their having been carefully edited and adapted 'to provide historical justification and divine sanction for religious beliefs, practices and rituals of the post-Exilic Israelite establishment'.[29] So writes Paul Johnson in his *History of the Jews*, and he goes on to examine the tendency of these selfsame scholars to undermine the achievements of Mosaic monotheism and reinterpret both the Jewish and Christian revelations as nothing more than 'a determinist sociological development from primitive tribal superstition to sophisticated urban ecclesiology'.[30] Here then is Martin's 'winsome doctrine' with a vengeance.

So what of Abraham and the story of his attempt to sacrifice Isaac? Nothing more than a beat-up for historical and religious purposes? Or do we have to look beyond what Johnson terms the *deformations professionnelles* of nineteenth-century textual historians to the discoveries of modern scientific archaeology and accept that Abraham did exist, and that the story of God's command to sacrifice his son Isaac may have had some basis in reality. The question is: What kind of basis? And what kind of reality? And why am I bothering with this particular story at this particular point? Well, it strikes me that the Abraham/Isaac story may carry within it the rudiments of an approach to the Geivett/Hick problem, and that the findings of the German scholars during the nineteenth century, although overly dismissive, may still be valid for reasons other than those presented at the time. I mean by this that the inner world of a human being can express itself in dream, reverie or vision, and that such expressions can carry symbolically deep comprehensions not yet grasped by the conscious mind. So to speak of symbol and metaphor in relation to these stories is actually valid, although not in the sense of their being nothing more than historico-religious concoctions. But rather because they express the inner world of human beings in the process of moral and ethical transition. I would contend that it is for this reason that these old stories have survived, and that it is up to us to carefully interpret and preserve their archetypal content.

The word 'archetype' derives from *archetypos* in Greek, and breaks down into two parts, *arche* and *typos*. *Arche* means 'foremost' or 'chief', and can be found in its slightly abbreviated form at the beginning of such words as 'archbishop' or 'archangel'. But it is *typos* that is of the greater interest, for it translates as 'a blow or a mark left by a blow, an impress, or mould',[31] and can be detected in such words as 'type' or 'typical' – hence 'archetype' in English. Archetypes are autonomous by nature (*see* chapter 11). They are governed by their own sovereign laws, and although subjective, can reflect themselves onto the screen of external human affairs. Which is to say that archetypes are not only present in our subjective inner world, but are also sometimes detectable in the outer, objective world. Capable of interacting with us through dreams, reveries and visions, archetypes (in the form of internal pressures) drive us hither and thither in search of our own depths, and in moments of psychic distress sometimes penetrate the hard shell of our conscious awareness. Here then is the blow that leaves its mark, the blow from within that leaves a deep impression on our minds.

In primitive psychology the sacrifice of a child symbolized the stopping of time; the child's ritualized death delayed the future. Held magically within the psychic spell of youth offered up to the gods, those making the offering warded off both old age and death. Chronos kills his children because they remind him of his age; Oedipus is exposed on a mountain because it is believed he will kill his father. Agamemnon sacrifices his daughter Iphigenia for political reasons. This opens up the field somewhat and allows us to realize that such acts of ritualized murder were committed on behalf of 'ideas', ideas believed to be of social, economic or religious significance. And so with Abraham, for whom the impulse to murder his son Isaac was felt to spring from God himself, but in a rather peculiar fashion. The text says that God *tempted* him to commit infanticide (Genesis 22:1), and that word allows us to look into the depths of Abraham's mind and heart and feel the presence of an old pagan brutality not yet fully rooted out.

There is virtually no emotion in the story of Abraham's attempt to murder his son Isaac at God's request; but one can feel the emotion bottled up inside the story at every step. The pressure is on from word one, and it does not diminish until Abraham makes his leap of faith, his leap away from old literalisms into the arms of the symbolic. The wood is stacked, Isaac is tied down and the knife is in the air – but the blow is never struck. Why? Because Abraham wakes up to what is going on in his life and makes a choice, and the choice he makes revolutionizes his conscious conception of God. But only because of a three-day journey in silence during which he has had time to think, time to ponder on the meaning of what he is about to do. Yet it is only at the very last minute that these deep ruminations take effect and he spontaneously invents a new way of relating to the circumstances of his life – the way of covenant, or contract with God in place of human sacrifice. For the killing of the ram in place of Isaac is not an off the cuff decision; neither is it something imposed abruptly on him from heaven. It is the transferring of a method of contractual binding from one situation to another. As Paul Johnson points out, 'Abraham, as we know from contemporary archives, came from a legal background where it was mandatory to seal a contract or covenant with an animal sacrifice'.[32]

That is the the clue required properly to understand what is going on here, for it signals not only that the psyche 'holds *within it* the means with which to confront and transform its own blind and brutal forces',[33] it also informs us that our inner world can be radically changed through the blow from within. Abraham sees a way out of his dilemma (the ram caught in the thicket), seizes upon it, and a more human prerogative is asserted. Or, as Westman so accurately puts it in *The Springs of Creativity*: 'The war of opposites ends and the opposites are revealed as harmonious: God and Satan stand together in the sacred precinct; Abraham, the man, stands between them.'[34] That surely is the whole point of this story, the image we should carry from it if we are seriously interested in human freedom.

Our problem is perhaps that we attempt to argue God, as we have argued Jesus, into a state of unblemished and unblemishable purity, an idea of purity governed at every step not by divine revelation as we so smugly suppose, but by our own devastatingly limited understanding of human consciousness and the creative process. The archetypal depths of consciousness create the tensions and pressures which mould and shape us, and these pressures are born out of a capacity to take risks seldom actualized due to conformity of mind and behaviour. We are simply stuck 'timeside' of the equation of life, and have to be literally blasted out of our intellectual and spiritual complacency before anything other than stereotypical beliefs and ideas can emerge. Content with our narrow, verbally hide-bound view of God, universe and self, we imprison our creativity in surface certitudes and deny the possibility that God's dance of life can be anything other that how we describe it. Tempted by God to sacrifice *our* Isaac, we bring the knife down with relish and look around for applause. Which is to say that hell is Isaac knifed to the bone, that Satan smirking in his own private kingdom is Isaac pierced through, and that a God without a dark side is the man Jesus struck through with nails for having had the audacity to defy the orthodoxy of his day.

And so back to Father David Bones in chapter 4, as he struggles with the Devil and realizes, in the last terrifying hours of his spiritual dilemma, that his great strength is his *autonomous will*, his freedom of spirit to *choose*. But alas, this is not as easy as it sounds, for as Malachi Martin writes on David's behalf: 'Now a specific and peculiar agony beset David. He had never known it before. Indeed, afterwards he wondered for a long time how many real choices he had made freely in his life before that night.'[35] When one reads later on that David's choice is to *believe, believe, believe*, then the question as to whether he actually discovered what a real choice is remains open to doubt. For there is little sense of his having made the leap of faith and discovered, in Abraham's terms, the symbolic alternative to murdering Isaac, merely a capitulation to the old, tired literalisms, a giving in to fear as his usurped imagination buckled out of shape.

PART TWO

Darkness Invisible

CHAPTER NINE

The Beating Heart

The historical background to Jesus' life and ministry, his rejection of doctrinal extremism, and the reversal of his role as inaugurator of the End Time

Pertinent and impertinent questions arise automatically when confronted by the curiously distorted relationship between Paul and James, between Paul's Christians and James' Nazarenes. The at-first-glance smooth presentation of affairs in Acts quickly falls apart to reveal fissures in the narrative. Editorially, we are being led astray. There are technical incongruities, contradictions, interpolations and subtle adjustments to the text. And they occur very early on in both Acts and the four Gospels, which brings us to the realization that Paul's heretical Christology was not born overnight, gulped down whole over a period of days or weeks, but slowly and carefully imbibed over a period of years. And this new and startling Christology is straight from Jesus, straight from the great teacher himself, who was physically present, if what we read of the disciples' joy and Paul's astonishment can be taken, for once, at face value. He is in the background as a shadowy figure whose presence and spiritual authority constantly unnerved those about him.

Fantasy? The resuscitation of a discredited theory just for the sake of it? Not in this case; I am absolutely serious. Something quite extraordinary is going on in the New Testament, and it is high time we found out what it is. For considering the fact that Acts has been tampered with in such an obvious manner, and the Epistles too have either been interpolated or written in their entirety by hands other than those claimed for them, it is surely not too difficult a task to consider the possibility of Jesus having been 'written out' of his own script. The Kingdom of God did *not* appear, it was just the Romans as usual. Paul preached the Kingdom's imminent appearance, but later instructed his many converts to go back to their jobs and get on with their lives. The sectarian dream of a physical Kingdom of God on Earth to which the nations would flock did not materialize, and so Jesus the Messiah had to be packed off to heaven so that God would not lose face. Everything would settle down eventually, into theological ambiguity; Jesus' promise was pushed into an ever-receding future, his 'return' in connection with this great event indefinitely postponed.

But not quite for the reasons generally given. What has to be realized is that the appearance of the Kingdom of God and the return of Jesus have probably been linked back to front. Christians today seem to think that Jesus' return from heaven would inaugurate the Kingdom of God on Earth; but the reverse is probably more accurate. His role, I think, was not to be a 'herald' at all, but more of a climactic result once the cosmic dust had settled. It is much more probable that Jesus was waiting for the appearance of the Kingdom to make his grand, preordained entrance, not the Kingdom for him. So in a sense it was God who let everyone down, not Jesus; Jeremiah's day of hoped for 'perfect purity' did not arrive. Of course, it could be argued that Jesus' expectation of the Kingdom's imminent arrival was itself an error – even he could make mistakes. And that in spite of the fact that he was himself God made manifest.

Now, is this too difficult to contemplate as a theoretical scenario? Or is it difficult only because it crosses the taboo line and destroys our fragile conception of the first century as somehow miraculous? The Kingdom of God did not arrive, so Jesus, after his natural death, was turned into a heavenly-lodged spectator constantly on the cosmic telephone. Could that be it? Could it be that many Christian scholars wilfully ignore certain elements of historical reality because they are deeply afraid of the consequences? Admit that the physics of the planet were no different in the first century from what they are today, and that supernaturalisms of the sort bandied about in the New Testament simply do not occur, and one is left with a belief vacuum of threatening proportions. Yes, things happen in life that none of us can explain, but there is an extraordinary stability to the world we live in, and that fact is much, much more puzzling than any supposed disruption of natural law. Simply put, the Kingdom of God did not materialize as hoped because that is not how God (whatever we think God might be) works. End of story. End of the nonsense. End of the dream.

Carsten Thiede and Matthew D'Ancona offer a sensible alternative to blind acceptance or bland rejection of New Testament supernaturalisms; they ask us to consider the possibility of the miraculous element being *figurative*, that is, not literal but metaphorical. But if the miracles are metaphorical, then the Ascension too is metaphorical, and as such there is every reason to suspect that Jesus really was there in the flesh, as he himself stated. So we are confronted by an unexpected literalism, and are driven to realize that such metaphors may conceal historical realities. From this vantage point we are then in a position to ask the prime question: why metaphorical at all? Why the inability to properly articulate or determine what was going on in this man's life? Why the window dressing? What was he up to? What was it like to be in his presence? What had he discovered that made him so very different from everyone else?

These are the questions we need to ask, to bother about, worry about, attend to, not flipperty-flapperty questions like whether he walked on water or raised the dead. He did not do any of these things; but he quite obviously did do and say things that made the impressionable people around him think he probably could. *That* is the point, and *that* is what we need to appreciate as we draw closer and closer to this powerful individual. We are not dealing with a magician or a charlatan or a god; we are dealing with an archetype on legs, a human personality resonating almost dangerously with the numinous. Driven by realizations about which we can only guess, Jesus systematically challenged Jewish orthodoxy and sectarian aspirations. Neither held the ultimate answers he was after; neither were capable of appreciating the new and revolutionary relationship with God he himself was exhibiting in his personal life: he was his own man.

THE APOCALYPTIC AND THE PROPHETIC

The impression one gets of Jesus in the New Testament is of a man at odds with the religious community. Yes, he is a Jew, and he is mindful of things Jewish; but he is also a rebel, although not of the spear-throwing variety. He is no Zealot, just an individual irked by religious red tape. In fact he comes across as a kind of prophet, but also more than a prophet. He is not at all like John the Baptist, or Elijah, or Jeremiah; rather, he is an Isaiah-type, a thinker. But when he overturns the moneychangers' tables in the Temple his temper is that of Elijah; and when he weeps over Jerusalem, he is Jeremiah. He opens his ministry with John the Baptist's call to repentance, but does not himself seem to have baptized (except perhaps secretly, as a letter by Clement of Alexandria suggests – *see* p 184) from there on. Standing for individual conscience, for commonsense and a reinterpretation of the Mosaic Law as it applied to everyday life, he progressively angered the religious authorities until they could take no more. Closing in on him, they brought him to trial for heresy and handed him over to the Romans for punishment.

Jesus was born into an apocalyptic era, and he responded to it like any other Jew. But his response was different, peculiar to himself; he sidestepped Jewish nationalism, Jewish traditionalism, Jewish adventurism and came down on the side of a personal covenant with God. Yes, the Torah was necessary, but only as a moral and ethical back-up system; the bulk of the Law was now obsolete as far as he was concerned. It was the spirit of the Law that mattered, not its combination of letters. Faith in God was what mattered. Repentance, not Temple sacrifice, was the answer.

So what was the root of Jesus' theology? Paul Johnson points to heterodox Judaism and the Hellenization of Galilee. I think that is correct. The theology espoused by Jesus was definitely heterodox in flavour (Nazarene/Nasara); his background in pagan Galilee was certainly responsible for his lack of religious pretension. His full teachings, as delivered to, and developed by Paul, were humane and universalistic. Suitable for diaspora Jews and Gentile converts, these teachings were probably directly influenced by diaspora thinking through the Jewish teacher Hillel. If he was a pupil of Hillel's, which is thought possible by many scholars, Jesus would have learned to handle exactly the kind of aphorisms he eventually came out with; it is recognized that he did in fact use at least one of Hillel's pithy remarks. Paul, on the other hand, borrowed freely from known Greek writers, used Greek allusions (running the race, etc.), and was obviously quite at home in Gentile company. Johnson notes that Jesus' father's name, Joseph, was Hebrew, but his mother's name, Mary, was a Greek version of Miriam. And two of Jesus' brothers, Judah and Simon, had Hebrew names; whereas his other two brothers, James and Joses, did not. Translation problems? An oversight? A meaningful slip-up? Who knows. Perhaps just a reflection of the cultural mix which was, by the time of Jesus, a mix already threatened by forces of conservatism so strong that they eventually destroyed the Jewish nation.

When Herod the Great died, stability died with him; the tyrant's hands had held a tight rein. One-time allies of Rome against the Greeks, the Jews now found themselves governed directly by Rome. During his event-filled reign, Herod had done everything possible to separate religion and state, the diaspora Jews playing an important roll in his plans. So when in 37 BCE the Sanhedrin tried to make Mosaic Law operative in secular affairs, Herod had 46 of its members executed. His plan was simple: he wanted to internationalize Jerusalem and make it the tourist capital of the Middle East. Rebuilding the Temple at his own expense, he supported the Olympic Games and inaugurated a miniature welfare state for diaspora Jews; a system of help for the sick, the poor, widows and orphans later adopted to good effect by the Christians in Rome. In 4 BCE, just before his death, he had a golden eagle set up over the main entrance to the Temple; an act which sparked revolt from Torah students and resulted in them being arrested and burned alive. When he died there came a sigh of relief from those communities interested in traditional values – a sigh which quickly turned into a roar. From there on the Rigorists periodically tested themselves against the tide of Greek culture and Roman arrogance, their intransigence erupting into violence on five occasions. In 66 CE (the fourth occasion) the Romans finally flattened Judea. In 135 they felt compelled to repeat the process.

The reason was Jewish literacy. Extremist groups devoured apocalyptic literature and believed themselves in possession of mysteries pertaining to the future of the Jewish nation. Convinced that there was going to be a great battle on Earth between good and evil, between the Children of Light and the Children of Darkness, they mentally prepared themselves for that terrible day, caused it, and suffered the consequences. The world fell in; the Jewish nation was scattered to the four winds. This ought to act as a salutary warning to present-day Christians awaiting a similar confrontation – beware of self-fulfilling prophesies.

The more broad-minded diaspora Jews must have looked on with dismay; but what else could one do with fanatics but exterminate them? It was the fanatics that were the problem; they were incapable of seeing the larger picture. It was the Zealots who had infuriated the Romans; and the Sicarii ('dagger men') had terrorized their collaborating countrymen and killed them silently in crowded public places. Founded by Judah the Galilean in 6 CE, this ultra- violent terrorist fringe had plagued both Romans and the Jewish élite with their protests and uprisings. And they were everywhere, in every party; even among the wilderness isolationists. The isolationist Essenes and the separatist Pharisees were, on the whole, pacifists by nature, but there were wild elements in both parties who craved a purity of almost mystical proportions. These were the Children of the Light, the self-appointed judges of the Jewish nation.

The Jerusalem Nazarenes belonged to the fringe of this millenarian milieu, but may well have had a militantly active branch; Jesus' visit from 'Satan' while in the wilderness strongly suggests as much. His overturning of the money-changers' tables in the Temple shows him to have had a purist streak. Paul Johnson makes interesting reading when we come to this aspect of Jesus' life; he argues effectively for Jesus having had a sectarian view of the Temple, a view which rendered the Temple a source of evil. Predicting its destruction, he 'treated the Temple authorities and the whole central system of Judaic administration with silent contempt'.[1] The Temple was an obstacle to purity, Jesus believed, and as such was better down than up. Perhaps this explains his supposed prophesy about its destruction – not so much a prophesy, more of a metaphor suggesting rejection, or a pragmatic projection, perhaps. But this Jesus was not a fanatic in anyone's terms; the beating heart of his theology-cum-philosophy was not violence, it was liberation.

Jesus was a rebel; he was not a terrorist. He was open and expansive in his teachings, not closed-off and pernickety. But he did speak in parables, and parables by their very nature conceal other levels of meaning. And he could often be oblique in what he said, hinting at, but not directly articulating his innermost thoughts. He was, in fact, enigmatic on many issues, preferring not to reveal his opinion. But clear on others, very clear, and sometimes passionate in his judgements. A man for all seasons, human and approachable. Not so the Zealots and Sicarii and the millenarian wilderness isolationists with their military camps and lookout towers. They were absolutely sure of what they believed, this range of purists whose Rigorist approach to the Law stemmed from the Shammai school (50 BCE to 30 CE) and its unbending ideas of spiritual and physical cleanliness; a school of thought at which Jesus directed his venom whenever and wherever it appeared.

This anger, this hatred, was all legitimately founded on a history of arrogant attack by reformist Jewish intellectuals who wished to merge the Jewish religion with Greek sensibility, and at the same time deprovincialize the Scriptures. Rallying to Greek culture like moths to a flame, upper-class, secularly educated Jews tried forcefully to reform the Torah, and the result was chaos. Johnson's view is that the reformers did not want to abolish the Law, rather, just 'purge it of those elements which forbade participation in Greek culture'. But not for nothing had the Maccabean nationalists fought and died. With what Johnson describes as a 'display of militant rationalism', the high priest Menelaus attempted to abolish the Mosaic Law in 167 BCE, and in retaliation for the publication of a decree making secular law the main arbiter of dispute, the pious Jews, the *hasidim*, came out against him in force. So the first martyrologies were written, and zeal for the law intensified.

Paul Johnson captures the subtlety of the situation when he says: 'With their failure, the reformers discredited the notion of reform itself.'[2] That is an important point; the reformers' heavy-handedness led to ferocious mobs of religious extremists on the streets of Jerusalem, mobs infectious in their discontent. Later, under Alexander Jannaeus as High Priest, 6000 pious Jews would be slaughtered, so causing a revolt of the Rigorists which lasted six years. Fifty thousand Jews died as a result, and from out of the ashes of this revolt sprang the Pharisees separatist religious party.

Unlike Jesus, the Rigorists could see no middle ground; they were quite unconcerned with the fact that poor Jews, the *am ha-arez*, were living shocking lives and being hounded at every turn. It was no concern of theirs that such people could not keep clean and so obey the laws of purity; it was not their concern that they could not obey the dietary laws because they had to eat whatever came their way. Stolidly oblivious to everything and everyone because their unquestioning acceptance of Scripture left them no room to be creatively compassionate, they denounced and harangued and protested until a total impasse was set up between Rigorist and reformist attitudes. From the second century BCE onwards, the obsession with apocalyptic themes grew and hardened, each generation trying to work out if it would be in *their* time that God's warrior Messiah would appear. When would

God wind up the whole ugly affair and inaugurate his kingdom on Earth? Unlike the Pharisees, who believed in an afterlife, the Rigorists were more interested in an earthly kingdom, and an earthly kingdom meant war with the Children of Darkness.

Behind this reasoning resonated the idea that the House of David would be restored to power, so displacing the Herodians. Isaiah, the thinking man's prophet, had prophesied the appearance of a great ruler dispensing justice, and this figure, allied to the idea of a warrior Messiah and a Suffering Servant merged into the expectation of a miraculously restored dynastic king of archetypal power and bearing. When spliced with the prophetic books of Daniel and Enoch, there emerged the dream of the end of days and the Four Last Things – Death, Judgement, Hell and Heaven.[3] The apocalyptic package was complete; all it needed was a taker. Confusion of interpretation was rife on this issue right up until the time of Jesus, but most Jews eventually decided that their Messiah would be a military leader, and that his kingdom would be a wholly physical affair. The existing order would change spiritually, that was taken for granted, but as an affair perceived to take place on Earth there would also be changes on the more mundane level of government and taxes.

LOVE AND HATE

The history of early Judaism is a history of splits and counter-splits, of groups merging and separating for reasons cultural, political and eschatological. The early Hasidim Rigorists (precursors of the Essenes) separated from the later profane political aims of the Maccabean-Hasmonean kings in or around 141 BCE, and the Essenes (dissident priests of the house of Zadok) separated themselves from the Temple priesthood for identical reasons. Holding on to the unrealized messianic hopes of the Hasidim as if they were just about to be realized, the Qumran Essenes set up a pattern of expectation (in spite of ongoing failure) which both the Nazarene and Christian communities later doggedly upheld. Continuing to cherish the hope of God's intervention in human affairs, the Essenes recalculated the date of expected messianic fulfilment and reset the apocalyptic clock. Only the scholarly Pharisees disagreed. Separating themselves from Essene expectations, they formed a democratic religious party and were viewed as 'apostate' by the Qumran isolationists. Similarly at odds with the whole apocalyptic scenario, the educated, cosmopolitan Jewish élite intensified its reformist policy, and the more Israel ceased to reflect its ancient heritage, the more convinced the Rigorists and Isolationists became that God was about to strike.

So, too, John the Baptist. Taking his message of instant repentance to the whole of Israel, John broke away from Essene isolationism and offered the apocalyptic vision of the sectarians to the whole Jewish nation. In *The Dead Sea Community*, an early but still highly pertinent study of the Qumran Essenes by Professor Kurt Schubert, the author perfectly captures the sense of continuing divergence from Qumranite ideals when he says: 'If John the Baptist had already broken through the sectarian character of Qumran Essene Judaism and turned to all Israel with his message, Jesus and his circle were even more broadminded. There is actually not a trace of the sectarian narrowness and group snobbery of the Qumran people in Jesus.'[4]

Schubert's opinion is that Jesus was related to the Qumran Essenes by common milieu (he could not have escaped being influenced by them), but that his teachings were of a completely different calibre. With John, the split in visionary opinion with the Essenes had become visible; with Jesus that split turned into a party of direct opposition. It was not the liberal Pharisees that Jesus attacked as his ministry progressed, it was specifically the narrow-mindedness of the Qumran sectarians. Hammering relentlessly at their extreme views, Jesus revealed himself to be a serious religious reformer and messianic candidate. Himself a believer in the imminent appearance of the Kingdom of God, Jesus nevertheless chose a route to that Kingdom exactly opposite in kind to that of the Essenes. Faith in God would replace obedience to Law; Law would be relegated to the level of a moral and ethical back-up system secondary in importance to openness of heart. But faith in God with a double twist, for when everything came out in the theological wash, Paul's idea of 'faith in God' turned out to be centred in Jesus himself. A new and troubling theology was on the loose, and even the Pharisees were horrified at its implications.

Kurt Schubert's study of the Dead Sea Community's origins and teachings reveal that this Rigorist community also carried the notion of 'faith' in relation to their Teacher of Righteousness. Unnamed, and difficult to date, this Teacher demanded faith in his judgements and pronouncements; a faith, it must be presumed, eventually stretched to its limit as his prophetic utterances about the future of Israel came to naught. Certainly not a 'justifying faith' in the Pauline sense; more a faith in the Teacher's message which not all of the Qumran community need have shared. And so it can be said that Paul's view was probably a conscious reversal of what this particular community believed, and this in turn suggests a connection between the two communities at a fundamental level. In this sense, it is not similarity of doctrine that bound them together, but rather finely geared dissimilarities which, by their mirror-like construction, now suggest prior connection in hope and belief. And so Jesus singled out the Qumran Essenes for castigation, and the Children of Light turned their hatred on this upstart who treated the Law with such contempt.

The gulf between Jesus and the Qumran Essenes was immense. Jesus preached forgiveness for one's enemies; the Qumran Essenes preached hatred for one's enemies. Hatred and vengeance were the backbone of Essene eschatology; the war to come would be a war of vengeance on those who had rejected what they believed. The Qumran texts confirm this perception of things, and in Matthew 5:43–4 Jesus spells it out pretty clearly when he says: 'Ye have heard that it hath been said, Thou shalt love thy neighbour, and hate thine enemy. But I say unto you, Love your enemies, bless them that curse you, do good to them that hate you, and pray for them that despitefully use you, and persecute you.' Referring to this text, Kurt Schubert tells us that there is no such injunction in either the Old Testament or in the literature of Jewish tradition; only in the Qumran texts is one instructed to hate one's enemies. In fact there is hardly one Dead Sea Scroll in which the injunction to hate one's enemies does not appear. Jesus' reversal of this injunction therefore shows him to have been consciously targeting the Qumran Essenes. Withdrawing themselves from what they termed 'men of corruption' (the world in general), the Qumran Essenes would not even accept food or drink from an outsider. Jesus, on the other hand, visited the homes of Pharisees, sat and talked with 'publicans and sinners', chatted to women (even Samarian women), broke the Sabbath laws and not only drank fermented wine, but on one occasion is said to have used his 'powers' (at his mother's instigation) to supply a vast quantity of it for the pleasure of others. (And for his own pleasure, if the term 'wine-bibber' has any meaning.) All in all, not a stuffy-minded individual in anyone's terms; in fact the kind of leader the *am ha-arez* (economically poor) had been waiting for since Ezra's dour entrance into Jerusalem.

And that brings us to a major point, for when Jesus speaks of the 'poor in Spirit' being blessed (in the Sermon on the Mount), he is in fact again referring directly to the Essenes, not to the economically poor. In the Qumran texts the Essene community is referred to as 'the poor of the Spirit', 'the poor of grace', and as 'poor servants of thy redemption'. On this occasion the context is the prophet Isaiah's description of the poor as those who are 'of contrite Spirit, and trembleth at my word'.[5] It is to these 'voluntary poor' that Jesus is referring; and the fact that he does so shows him to have been in sympathy with Essene values when they properly served their spiritual purpose. It is interesting to note that the early Nazarene-cum-Christian communities practised 'poverty' in exactly this sense. So were they copying Essene practice? Or perhaps not so much copying as extending that practice to allow the economically poor access to the same spiritual and economic benefits as the educated and the well-to-do? Such an attitude is implicit in Jesus' teachings, and it goes hand in hand with his dismissal of narrow-mindedness, bigotry and exclusivist ideas.

Paul Johnson touches the quick of this when he says that the Apostle Paul 'drew upon an emotion deep in Judaism, deep in the ancient religion of Yahweh . . . the idea that God would overthrow the established order of the world, making the poor rich and the weak strong, prefer the innocent to the wise and elevate the lowly and humble'.[6] The keynote was spiritual revolution, a whole new way of perceiving oneself and of approaching God. This of course was exactly what the ordinary people had been waiting to hear, and in hearing it they responded with understandable enthusiasm and excitement. Here was a teacher, an educated man, a Nazarene leader (and potential Davidic king?) from Galilee who at last understood their plight. And he was his own man; he had the courage, the brains and the wit to stand up against the religious authorities and beat them at their own game. Unpretentious to a fault, he had slammed the nitpicking restrictions of the holier-than-thou Essenes and opened up a whole new way of thinking about God. It wasn't just the money-changers' tables in the Temple he had overturned; it was just about everything in his path.

THE INCARNATE CHRIST

Recognizing that it is not the circumstances of Jesus' crucifixion and burial that matter, but the obstinate belief in his resurrection afterwards, Johnson homes in on the prime factor underpinning Christian belief: Jesus survived the cross, and that fact alone is what sparked off both the Christian movement and its Nazarene equivalent.

Christians have long since recognized the importance of the resurrection to their belief system, and I believe them to be correct in this, albeit not to the extent that I think Jesus underwent actual death. No, what we are dealing with here is a piece of ancient theology which the Roman Church formalized into a doctrine of world salvation. And on one level, legitimately so; for by the time of Jesus that theology had undergone considerable development and was pointing to a substrate of human experience, growth and maturity capable of carrying an individual beyond the confines of normal human experience. I believe Jesus and Paul were wide awake to the implications of their shared theology, and Paul Johnson seems to be in agreement when he says: 'What Jesus challenged, and Paul specifically denied, was the fundamental salvation-process of Judaism: the election, the covenant, the Law. They were inoperative, superseded, finished. A complex theological process can be summed up simply: Jesus invented Christianity, and Paul preached it.'[7] Now that is a startling statement; it reinterprets much of New Testament opinion. For it suggests that Paul was the only one who really understood what Jesus had been saying during his short ministry. The disciples under Jesus' brother James were still quite orthodox in their Judaism in spite of being sectarians; whereas Paul the Rigorist turned into a Torah-denying disciple of Jesus from the moment of his conversion. How strange. This was a radical change of mind, and it did not fit with what the Nazarene Jerusalem community held to be the 'truth' in relation to Jesus' life, ministry, crucifixion, burial and resurrection. It was almost as if there were two Jesuses backed by two quite different theological programmes.

I have no desire to put words into Paul Johnson's mouth, but I think it implicit in his statement about Jesus inventing Christianity and Paul preaching it, that if the Apostle Paul was the only one who really understood Jesus, and accurately purveyed his theological intentions, then these two personalities may well have met and discussed the whole panorama of ideas this erudite thinker eventually presented to the world. Why? Because he is the *only* follower of Jesus to peddle such a range of ideas; the disciples under James were still functioning as orthodox Jews, albeit with a sectarian bias. Johnson is of the opinion that Paul had the training to understand Jesus' theology, and in line with this he says, 'once he was convinced that the resurrection was a fact and Jesus' claims to be the Christ true' (how else could he be sure of this unless he had met Jesus in the flesh?), then he began to explain that theology to others. I agree. Paul was utterly convinced that Jesus was physically alive; and he was also convinced that this physical Jesus had undergone some kind of spiritual metamorphosis. Imbibing the meaning of this transformation of Jesus' psyche over a three-year period, he then launched out into his own remarkable, individualistic ministry. Yes, Paul was convinced of Jesus' resurrection, but not on the basis of some self-created illusion, or delusion. This man had not been interacting with a phantom Jesus in his mind; he had met up with a flesh and blood Jesus who shocked him into changing sides. I do not think there's any other explanation for his new-found certainty, and supernaturalisms of the sort suggested in Acts are just too far-fetched to contemplate seriously.

Then comes Johnson's observation that Jesus and Paul had their theological roots in *Palestinian* Judaism, not in concepts belonging to the Hellenistic diaspora. This too is an important point: their mutual theology was not pagan in origin, it did not have a Greek base, or a Graeco-Jewish reformist base; it was without doubt heterodox-Jewish in origin. In this sense, ancient Nazarene beliefs from the *Essa* camp perfectly fit the bill. Making 'the Christ' (the archetypal ground of being) incarnate (express itself) in Jesus, Paul, at Jesus' own instigation, probably reintroduced the ancient appreciation of *Essa* (Jesus) as a divine being, and in so doing released the archetypal energy of what appeared to be a new religious concept into the community at large. No longer just the Messiah of Israel, Jesus now took on the additional corona of man *transformed*; or, more accurate still, man *transfigured*.

CHAPTER TEN

The Nazarene Community

The problem of Christian scholars mistaking the Nazarenes for Christians, the mystery of Paul's trip to Arabia, and the further mystery of there being two Gospels of Jesus

In their fascinating book *The Hiram Key*, (hereafter referred to as *Hiram*) Christopher Knight and Robert Lomas pinpoint the Nazarene community as vitally important to our understanding of Christian origins; in fact they go as far as to suggest that the great library of Alexandria was burned to the ground by Christians because it contained so much information about these Nazarenes. But wasn't the original Nazarene community Christian? Why would Christians destroy evidence of their own origins? The answer Knight and Lomas give to this question is a deadly one: 'The Romanised Church destroyed any evidence that portrayed its saviour as a mortal rather than a god.'[1] So what are they suggesting? Well, they are suggesting, indeed *stating* that the Church at Rome's view of Jesus the Nazarene was very different from that of the Jerusalem Church which it eventually replaced. For as we saw earlier, that is what happened, the Jerusalem Church, the Mother Church, was replaced by the Church at Rome after the destruction of the Jewish state by the Romans in 70. Hence the visit of the *desposyni*, the blood relatives of Jesus, to Sylvester I in 318. They wanted their Church, their authority and their status as the original and not yet defunct Church of the Apostles back. What they really wanted was the church *at* Rome to submit itself to the authority of the Jerusalem Church. This was of course quite impossible, for by this time what the Roman Church believed about Jesus was dramatically different from what the Jerusalem Church held to be original and true. In any case, the Jerusalem Church was now no longer in Jerusalem, it was scattered throughout Palestine, Syria and Mesopotamia.

The early Jerusalem Church was run by the Nazarenes, some-times spelt 'Nazareanes' or 'Nazoreans'. And as the research of Knight and Lomas shows, in present-day Arabic the word used to designate a Christian is *Nasrani*, which translates interestingly as 'ordinary little fishes'.[2] The authors of *Hiram* then observe that this term, although possibly related to the notion of Christians as 'fishers of men', is more likely connected to the ancient association of priest and fish; not so much the fish as an object, but the fact that fish are only to be found in water. It is the 'water' that is significant, not the fish, and this in spite of the fact that the ancient Greek word for fish was *i-ch-th-u-s*, so forming the initials of the phrase *Iesous Christos theou uios sorter* – 'Jesus Christ, Son of God, Saviour'. The basic connection was that Jesus was closely linked with John the Baptist at the beginning of his ministry, and John's ministry was one of baptism. As the Nazarenes are believed to have turned into the baptism-based Mandean sect many centuries later (a sect which survives to this day in southern Iraq), and the Mandeans too are associated historically with John the Baptist, then the Nazarenes were probable supporters of the view that repentance and baptism went together. In itself, this is no great discovery, but what *is*, is that the present-day Mandeans of Iraq consider Jesus the Nazarene to have been a rebel or heretic who betrayed Nazarene secret doctrine and falsified religious truth.

Of course the other water-fixated sect at the time of Jesus was the Essene brotherhood, a sect numbering around 4000 with its desert headquarters at Qumran. Much has been written about these Essenes, and scholars are now quite willing to admit that Jesus probably interacted with them. According to Dr Hugh Schonfield, the Mandean-Nazarenes were probably affiliated with the Essenes and other groups practising ritual ablution, for he speaks of there being a direct link between the Mandean *Sidra d'Yaha* (Book of John the Baptist) and the Aramaic *Genesis Apocryphon* discovered among the Dead Sea Scrolls. Schonfield also reminds us that Paul, after his conversion, is taken by Ananias (a devout man of the Law) to 'see' and 'hear' the Just One. Then, like any typical Essene-Nazarene, Ananias urges Paul to 'wash away his sins by baptism'. Thus there is little doubt that Ananias was a Nazarene, and his offer to introduce Paul to the Just One suggests a meeting with Jesus' brother James, who was known as

James the Just. Then again, the meeting may have been with the revered Essene Teacher of Righteousness; for they were after all in Damascus, and Qumran, the headquarters of the Essene covenantors, was not far away. Or perhaps the Just One and the Teacher of Righteousness were one and the same person.

In the first chapter of *Jesus and the Dead Sea Scrolls*, J H Charlesworth tells us that the Qumran community housed around 200 souls, and that the rest of the sect were to be found scattered throughout Galilee, Palestine and Judea. There were Essenes everywhere. They were in nearly every township and they were certainly in Jerusalem.[3] The writers of *Hiram* go one better than Charlesworth and directly link the Qumran Essenes with the Nazarenes; in fact they postulate that they were one and the same sect, and that Jesus' brother James was indeed the famed Essene Teacher of Righteousness. This interpretation of events is upheld by the notable Dead Sea Scrolls scholars Robert Eisenman and Michael Wise, and it seems to be an opinion shared by Philip Davies, Professor of Biblical Studies at the University of Sheffield. In a review of *The Hiram Key*, Professor Davies courageously states: 'Academic orthodoxies should always be challenged, and I would recommend this book to anyone who wants to believe that there are more threads to history than we yet know.' Obliquely put, but none the less important as a statement.[4]

The attempt by many Christian scholars to completely separate Jesus from the Essenes is understandable, but not permissible in the light of modern research. Knight and Lomas refer to such attempts as a protection of the 'specialness' of Jesus, and J H Charlesworth agrees. The idea that Jesus was unique, indeed a divine being, is protected as a notion by keeping Jesus and the Essenes well apart. Such a ploy, in Charlesworth's opinion, is non-historical, dogmatic and apologetic. Deny that Jesus most probably interacted with the Essenes and you undermine his historicity.[5] The Essenes were everywhere; Jesus would have had to go out of his way to avoid them.

But that does not make Jesus or the Nazarene sect to which he belonged Essene by nature and doctrine, in spite of the fact that the Nazarenes do seem to have shared doctrinal ideas with the Essenes. But what of Jesus? There was little of the Essene way of life or mentality about him; in fact he was diametrically opposed to just about everything the Essenes stood for. He drank wine and had female company. He broke the strict rules of the Sabbath,

and by his behaviour encouraged others to do the same. This was
no Essene. Yet he was a Nazarene, and the Nazarenes were very,
very strict when it came to such things. Jesus' brother James was
so strict that he even upheld Nazarite doctrine, and the Nazarites
were second to none when it came to obeying the Law of Moses.
And he also affiliated with the Ebionites (the Poor Ones), and they
were similarly strict. So what about Jesus? How did this rebel fit
into the Nazarene camp?

The facts are that Jesus did not fit into the Nazarene camp; yet
he was a Nazarene, his family, as Hugh Schonfield points out,
constituting a veritable dynasty of Nazarene leaders. And it is at
exactly this point that the Mandean notion of Jesus being not only
a 'rebel', but a 'heretic' who betrayed Nazarene secret doctrine,
begins to make sense. For, as can be surmised from the Gospels,
Jesus and his brother James had very little contact with one
another; and it is made plain that even Jesus' mother thought his
behaviour and ideas quite mad. A probable disciple of John the
Baptist, Jesus took over this prophet's circle of followers after his
imprisonment and slowly transformed them into quite a different
kind of group. Start his ministry with the words 'Repent, for the
kingdom of heaven is at hand'[6] he may have done, but by the end
this sectarian cry of warning had been dramatically altered.

J H Charlesworth flatly rejects Eisenman's theory that the
Dead Sea Scrolls should be placed in the Herodian period, and he
is equally scathing of the Australian *Dead Sea Scrolls* scholar,
Barbara Thiering, who contends that Jesus survived the cross. In
relation to Thiering, he emphasizes the point by quoting Father
Terry Purcell's condemnation of the Australian Broadcasting
Commission for screening a documentary critical of Christian
beliefs by Thiering on Palm Sunday. Purcell was of the opinion
that it was 'absurd' for the ABC to have shown something that
'debunks the whole of Christianity and shows Christianity as a
sham'.[7] Why absurd? If Thiering's researches are even close to
what really happened, then what better time than Palm Sunday
to make her views known? Are Christians so intellectually delicate that they cannot face even the possibility that their quite
extraordinary explanation of New Testament events is mistaken?
And anyway, it was never at any time Barbara Thiering's intention to 'show Christianity as a sham'. Having read her work
quite carefully, I detect nothing more than a questing spirit and
well-stocked head.

Christian apologists have created an extraordinary theological smokescreen to explain the inexplicable nature of their spiritual vision, and the reason the job has been so difficult is because their premise is basically faulty. This point is perhaps made best by Burton Mack, Professor of New Testament at Clairemont School of Theology, when he says: 'Christians have never been comfortable with the notion of myth or willing to see their own myths as the product of human imagination and intellectual labour.'[8] Knight and Lomas are equally direct: 'The inescapable conclusion is that Christianity . . . deludes itself by keeping its thinking supremely muddled.'[9]

It could be argued that the very facts that push Jesus the Nazarene outside of both the Nazarene and Essene camps have been used by Christian apologists to place him above and beyond history and time altogether. But a proper historical context for Jesus as rebel and heretic is now possible, a context usurped to (illegitimately) underpin the utterly strange notion that Jesus was somehow God squeezed into a human body. Now if Father Purcell would like something truly absurd to get his teeth into, then I suggest he ignore the ABC's programming schedules and deal with that extraordinary claim, a claim not made for Jesus by the original Jerusalem Church, and only later made to appear as an accepted fact by the church *at* Rome. Enmeshed in Paul's theology, which the Jerusalem Church flatly rejected, this new seat of disconnected apostolic authority began to methodically elaborate on what it believed to be the central theme of Paul's teachings – Jesus Christ as an overt incarnation of God – and the whole sorry exercise of logic manipulation, story escalation and theological fabrication was on track for its long and well-documented future of terror and legitimized violence. And all because the Roman Church failed to do what Jesus did out there in the wilderness – reject the temptation of glory, power, riches and authority. This point was not lost on Feodor Dostoevsky; he suggested that the Church of Rome embraced what Jesus turned down, that it willingly took to its breast the counsel of Matthew's Satanic tempter.

THE MYTH MAKER

The Apostle Paul is of course the key to the whole extraordinary affair; he seems to have single-handedly invented Christianity as we now understand it, and heavily influenced the theological direction of the Roman Church in spite of initial rejection. As recorded in the New Testament, he was at first shunned by the church *at* Rome due to the fact that it was run by the Nazarenes; that is, it was sectarian-Jewish in composition and not at all the Gentile-dominated Church it would later become. In his sturdy and rewarding study of the New Testament period, Will Durant pinpoints Paul's problems in Rome when he says: 'His attitude offended . . . the Christian community that he found in Rome. These converts, chiefly Jews, preferred the Christianity that had been brought to them from Jerusalem; they practised circumcision, and were hardly distinguished by Rome from the orthodox Jews.'[10] Yes, 'Jesus' was being preached by these Jews, but not at all in the manner of Paul. The name 'Christian' (*Khristianoi* – followers of the Messiah or Anointed One) was not used by the Nazarenes, but in scorn of Paul's converts (Jews and Gentile women) by fellow pagans at Antioch.

The facts are that the Nazarenes at Jerusalem distrusted Paul; and not just because of his past, but because of what he had been up to since his conversion. Talk with the Just One he may have done, but his behaviour since then had left the Nazarenes unmoved. So much so, that when he did finally appear in Jerusalem, James the Just, leader of the Nazarene community, demanded that he purify himself in the Temple to prove that he was still a dutiful Jew. Little did Paul realize as he walked into the Temple precincts that this simple act of purification would result in his arrest by the Roman authorities for inciting a riot – Jewish orthodoxy felt his very presence there to be an insult.

The Nazarene sectaries to which Peter belonged were still part of the Jewish community; they had abandoned neither the Law nor the Temple, and preached what Paul considered 'another Jesus'. Paul becomes really ferocious about it all in his Epistle to the Galatians. He marvels that his converts have been redirected to believe in another gospel during his absence. But not quite 'another', he then admits – just a troubling perversion of what he himself preaches. The truth of the matter, however, was the exact reverse; it was he, not this other party who was guilty of changing the character of the original gospel – the Nazarene Gospel of Jesus as the Messiah of Israel which he, Paul, had transformed into the hypnotic 'Christ of faith'. He does not brook argument, saying angrily: 'But though we, or an angel from heaven, preach any other gospel unto you than that which we have preached unto you, let him be accursed.'[11] Strong words. Not even a 'fallen' angel is cited, just any old angel. But it is not really angels he fears, it is men. 'If any man preach another gospel unto you . . .' After his arrest, Paul admits before the High Priest and his elders that what he preaches is in fact a new religion, 'heresy', in their terms; but he will also claim to believe in the Law of Moses, a claim which will be rejected as patently untrue.

Will Durant sums up Paul's doctrinal situation succinctly: 'Paul created a theology of which none but the vaguest warrants can be found in the words of Christ: that every man born of woman inherits the guilt of Adam, and can be saved from eternal damnation only by the atoning death of the Son of God.'[12] A 'mystery' indeed. Jesus is no longer the Jewish Messiah, the Messiah of Israel, the Archetypal Adam and Light Adam of the wilderness sectarians; he is now the Logos whose death will deliver the whole world from sin and damnation. The 'Christ' of grandiose metaphysical speculation is on the loose, and the rather dull version of Jesus' accomplishments as held by the Nazarenes will not be able to compete. The Law of Moses is defunct; even the idea of being a Jew is obsolete. Stirring stuff, but anathema to those who held Judaism to be God's final revelation to the nations.

In *The Myth Maker*, published in 1986, Hyam Maccoby argues that Jesus' brother James and the Apostle Peter were life-long adherents of Pharisaic Judaism. Paul, on the other hand, is denied a Pharisaic background, is said to have come from a Gentile milieu, and to be the creator of a new religion centred on Jesus as a divine saviour. And then Maccoby pulls out the stops and accuses Paul of having created his concept of Jesus out of ideas taken from Hellenistic religion, Gnosticism and the mystery cults. Finally, he argues for Paul having played a devious and adventurous political game with the Jerusalem Church, who eventually disowned him. Reviewing Maccoby's book, Hugh Schonfield said, 'I believe that Hyam Maccoby's views on the Apostle Paul are worthy of careful consideration.' Not without reason was Schonfield taken with Maccoby's studies, for Schonfield too had said much the same thing about Paul in his own best-selling books on Christianity and its origins.

A Fellow of Leo Baeck College, London, Maccoby's special field of study is Judaism and Christianity; and the flyleaf of his penetrating study on Paul reveals that he has also been engaged in a research programme for the Hebrew University, Jerusalem, on the origins of Christian anti-Semitism. In respect for his scholarship and integrity, Maccoby was invited in 1980 to give the Cardinal Bea Memorial Lecture in Westminster Cathedral. A Talmudic scholar of long standing, his book on Paul's background and teachings is drawn from the earliest accounts, that of the Ebionite community as reported by Epiphanius, and as mentioned earlier, the Ebionites were closely aligned with, if not actually identical to, the Nazarenes.

One of Maccoby's prime observations is that the four Gospels were written *after* Paul's letters; the letters are believed to have been written around 50–60, the Gospels in the period 70–110. This means that Paul's theological notions were known to the writers of the Gospels, and that they directly influenced their perception of Jesus' personality and purpose. Yet at the same time the Gospels reflect traditions and writings prior to Paul's theological input, and these earlier sources remain detectable in the Gospels in spite of the efforts of Paulinist editors. There is a real Jesus in the Gospels, but he has been overlaid with Pauline-type interpretations to such an extent that, as noted earlier, his every act and word is read in a divine context. The ordinary man has vanished; the Son of God is in permanent residence. Paul's heretical views are no longer heretical; they have been taken up by the now predominantly Gentile Church at Rome and used to further displace the original Nazarene Church at Jerusalem.

Ebionite writings were suppressed by the Roman Church because they asserted that Jesus was an ordinary human being; that he had not abrogated Jewish Law as taught by Paul; and that Paul was not born a Jew, but was the son of Gentiles converted to the Jewish faith. Termed 'heretical' for such views, the Ebionites were persecuted and dismissed. Hyam Maccoby is not amused by this fact; he states flatly that the Ebionites 'were the same group that had earlier been called the Nazarenes', and that they were in fact much more likely to possess accurate knowledge about Jesus and James and Paul than their persecutors. In this light, he utterly rejects what he terms the 'scurrilous' propaganda-based dismissal of Ebionite claims by Christian scholars both ancient and modern.

Whatever their sectarian proclivities, the Nazarenes were fundamentally Jews observant of the Torah. They continued to go to the Temple as James' purification demand of Paul shows; and their acceptance of Temple worship clearly signified an acceptance of the Temple priesthood. Dynastic leaders they might spawn, but these leaders were not seen as, or considered themselves to be, an alternative priesthood to that of the Temple. Only later, under the influence of Paul, would a separate priesthood emerge; a priest-hood whose vestments were patterned on both Jewish and pagan models. Followed by sacraments which replaced the sacraments of the Temple, and by churches which displaced the Temple as the centre of sacramental activity, Paul's new religion separated itself from the Nazarenes and everything Jewish. Meet outside of syna-gogue and Temple the Nazarenes certainly did, but their getting together in such a fashion did not constitute the founding of a separate church.

The principal observation made by Maccoby at this point is that in spite of Jesus having chosen Peter as leader of this Church to be, it is in fact Jesus' brother James, the Just, who immediately takes over leadership of the Nazarenes after the crucifixion. Peter is there, but he is not in control. Why? Because he is not a blood relative; he is not of 'royal' blood. The leadership of the Nazarenes was not priestly, it was kingly. Jesus' intention had never been to found a church; it had been to claim a throne. The nature of the so-called Jerusalem Church was not ecclesiastical, but monarchi-cal. Hence the continuation of Jesus' descendants as leaders of the Nazarene community, descendants who were to be persecuted for centuries by the Romans as pretenders to the throne of David. And on the question of Jesus' supposed divinity, Peter himself makes plain how Jesus was perceived by the Nazarenes when he addresses the Jews after Pentecost. He says: 'I speak of Jesus of Nazareth, *a man singled out by God* and made known to you' (emphasis added). Maccoby remarks that nothing said then, or later, was inconsistent with Jewish attitudes. To Peter, Jesus was not God come down to Earth; he was not the Son of God; he was the Messiah, Israel's kingly claimant preparing to inaugurate God's new Kingdom on Earth.

THE RESURRECTED JESUS

The hopes of Christianity are pinned, not so much on the histori-cal Jesus as preserved in the Gospels, but on the post-resurrection Jesus whose claims, through Paul, were written into the Gospels by writers schooled in Pauline theology. But is this really the whole story? Is Paul wholly responsible for the divinization of Jesus in the New Testament? Might it not be more accurate to say that what now passes as Pauline theology has itself undergone considerable manipulation since the early days of the predominantly Gentile Church at Rome? For is it not the case that Paul's letters have been tampered with; indeed, that some of them were not written by Paul at all? Most scholars admit this to be so; but so far I have not come across anyone who interprets this fact as significant in itself. Paul's undoubtedly curious notions about Jesus were appropriated by others, and many of the views said to be his belong to those who eventually adopted and developed his sometimes erratically written texts.

The give-away in this complicated situation is the fact that Paul does not break with the Nazarene community in Jerusalem; in fact he does everything possible to keep the tie intact. Why bother? Why not cut all ties with these tiresome Nazarenes and found a Church to his own liking? This is after all what happened after his death; a completely new Church is established in Rome. But not by Paul. Paul is rejected by the Nazarenes in Rome and left to fret about his treatment in letters. But in 64 the Nazarene Church of Rome – if indeed it can be legitimately called a 'church' at this point – was decimated by Nero. Elaine Pagels estimates that Paul probably died in Rome ten years before this event, an event which saw the members of that Church burned alive as human torches in Nero's own garden. Now the term 'Christian' is used of these unfortunates, but they are more likely to have been Nazarene sectarians faithful to the Torah – Nazarenes with a Gentile following of 'God-fearers' already present.

Maccoby's approach to all of this is to say that Paul could not bear to cut ties with the authority of the Jerusalem Nazarenes; to have detached himself would have been to 'sink into the forlorn status of being a Gentile again'.[13] That makes a lot of sense. But the deviousness he then accuses Paul of is perhaps a little too strong. Yes, Paul was devious, there is no doubt about that; but he also believed passionately in his version of the Jesus story, and his passion for the resurrected Jesus should not be overlooked. Through regular interaction with what appears to be a phantom Jesus, Paul sets out to transform Judaism, and to my way of thinking his extraordinary zeal, patience, forbearance and dedication suggest not deviousness, but starry-eyed religious conviction based on what he perceived as irrefutable evidence for Jesus' survival of the cross. Paul's Jesus is alive and well and waiting to step back into the arena of history at the appropriate moment. Paul believed that this was going to happen with every fibre of his being; and to understand this man's actions we have to keep that fact ever before us. And there's something about the way Jesus is referred to in Acts that shifts the weight from phantom being to that of a physically present Messiah. The impression one gets is of clandestine meetings with Paul as Jesus moves from safe house to safe house. Once again Dr Thiering's *pesher*-driven overview of an alive, post-crucifixion Jesus slips into view.

The book of Acts has been thoroughly edited, but not so thoroughly that the real story it contains cannot be detected. The real story *is* there but has been manipulated into a form which reduces to a minimum the seriousness of the confrontation between Paul, James and the other apostles. Even more important, however, is the creation of a Gnostic-type Jesus, a phantom Jesus with whom Paul regularly communicates. There is little scholarly doubt that Paul was influenced by Gnostic thinking, but to exactly what extent is still under debate. And so with the New Testament as a whole; it too had a layer of Gnostic thinking spliced into its variegated texts prior to final manipulation and not removed because this layer proved useful to the writer-editors as they disguised what actually happened to Jesus after the resurrection. Jesus was flesh and blood after the resurrection, yet at the same time *not* flesh and blood. He could eat food but he could also walk through walls. The promised Kingdom of God had failed to appear, so ideas and events had to be carefully rearranged to obscure what had actually happened, and the Gnostic layer proved very useful for a Jesus who could not show his face.

For it must be remembered that the Nazarenes too were waiting for Jesus' return, and they were not at all starry eyed; they were hard-headed, Torah-loving sectarian Jews with a secular arm preparing to take on the Roman Empire. As Maccoby himself observes: 'Even though this movement had been politically quiescent for some years, waiting for the return of Jesus, there was known to be one wing of the party which was more activist, and wished to pursue Jesus' aims even in his temporary absence.'[14] The aims of Jesus? Temporary absence? There is obviously another understanding of Jesus' 'aims' in relation to the Nazarenes; which is to say that our mental picture of Jesus has been tampered with to a considerable degree. There is also quite obviously another

understanding of Jesus' absence after the resurrection in relation
to that militant wing of Nazarenes. These fighters were not waiting for a miracle, they were belatedly waiting either for a signal or
for Jesus to change his mind. It was probably a high-ranking
representative of this secular arm of the Nazarenes that Jesus met
with in the wilderness at the very beginning of his ministry.

THE KINGDOM OF GOD

The Nazarene community did not accept Paul's interpretation of
Jesus as a divine being, or Saviour (except in the Messianic sense);
and in line with this did not accept the idea that his being in existence somehow annulled the Law of Moses. They rejected such a
notion outright. And it should be kept in mind that the people
doing the rejecting were the disciples of that very Jesus now in
charge of the Jerusalem community – the disciples who
abandoned Jesus at his arrest. Called 'Nazarenes' because they
constituted an arm of the sectarian wilderness tradition, this
community preached Jesus the Jewish Messiah along orthodox
lines, and eventually paid for it with their lives. For although in
one sense orthodox, they were in another sense heterodox, and
this leaves us with a paradox which no Christian scholar has ever
satisfactorily addressed or explained!

The Jerusalem Nazarenes were by no means all love and light
and heavenly sentiment; they had strong political aims which have
been excised from the New Testament as if by magic. They were
what Maccoby calls 'nuisances' to the High Priest of the Temple in
spite of their orthodoxy. And it is the High Priest, as Maccoby
shows, who relentlessly persecutes Paul, not only because he is a
convert to the Nazarene cause, but also a one-time law
enforcement officer guilty of joining the very Nazarenes he had
been officially hired to hunt down on Rome's behalf. Paul was a
known deserter from the High Priest's own camp, and it is this fact
that irritatingly complicates things for Paul when he is recognized
and attacked in the Temple. For when he first turns up in Jerusalem
to face these strong-minded Nazarene Apostles he is no longer a
practising Nazarene respectful of the Torah, he is a curiously
hybrid creature carrying doctrinal ideas which both the Nazarenes
and orthodox Jewry considered to be heresy. The political situation
had changed somewhat in relation to the Nazarenes, settled

somewhat, but not all that much; these orthodox Nazarenes were still viewed with suspicion and distrust by the Temple priesthood. And this is why James asks Paul to purify himself. Asks? Perhaps that is the wrong word. Perhaps 'forces' would be the better choice. For by doing so, James hopes to kill two sacrificial birds with one stone. He hopes to allay priesthood fears of renewed Nazarene intransigence towards the Romans; and he knows that by having Paul associate with ultra-strict Nazarite practice he has him over a theological barrel on the subject of atonement.

Paul had been preaching all over Asia Minor that Jesus' supposed death on the cross was for the 'atonement of sin', that this ordeal had been consciously suffered by Jesus for that very reason, and that his resurrection afterwards proved beyond doubt that God had ordained the whole business. Jesus was alive and ready to appear the moment God began to work the miracle of inaugurating the Kingdom of God on earth. This is what they were waiting for. They were not waiting for Jesus to arrive back from heaven; they were waiting for God to make his move – only then would Jesus appear. And he would appear in the flesh. For the Kingdom of God was a physical kingdom, a kingdom on Earth which all nations would eventually recognize and willingly enter.

The whole controversy between regular Jews and their sectarian counterparts was over the Jewish nation's level of purity and how it could be strengthened. Roman occupation was not just one nation lording it over another; it was proof positive that Satan had 'infiltrated and taken over God's own people, turning them into allies of the Evil One'. So writes Elaine Pagels, and at the same time she offers us alternative names for Satan, that of 'Mastema' and 'Prince of Darkness'. Purity was all that mattered. Jews who did not attend properly to the purity rituals were assisting Satan, who in turn was assisting Rome to retain its grip on Israel's throat. It was a vicious circle; it was a cosmic war between angels and demons, between God and Satan. Accommodate the Romans, appease them in any way whatsoever, and you were guilty of treason; a treason exhibited by Paul the moment he admitted to being a Roman citizen.

Maccoby suspects that the passage in Acts telling us that Paul had been a Roman citizen from birth is only there to hide the fact that he had bought this prized possession not long before; it was his insurance policy against Jewish attack for known doctrinal irregularities. It was almost certainly bought with a large portion of the money contributed to him by Jew and Gentile God-fearers for the Jerusalem Church during his missionary travels. He had brought the money to Jerusalem to sweeten the Nazarene Council's attitude; but the whole situation had disintegrated into farce when James demanded that he purify himself in the Temple. Virtually on trial for heresy, he had submitted to James' will and found himself embroiled in a riot. Forced through fear to admit that he was a Roman citizen, a citizen of the very nation the Nazarene sectarians hated with their whole being, Paul's claim to be a Pharisee of the Pharisees, a Hebrew of the Hebrews, was blown to smithereens.

PAUL AND JAMES

Hyam Maccoby's approach to the question of Paul's probable dishonesty is to say: 'Paul would not consider it dishonest to use funds collected for the "Jerusalem Church" . . . because this was not just a matter of personal advantage, but of high policy, affecting the whole future of Christianity.'[15] He goes on to suggest that for Paul, everything would have hinged on whether the Jerusalem Church responded to his point of view; if they did not, then submission to their leadership as 'the official centre of the Jesus movement' would have been impossible. I think this is an accurate reading of the situation; but it leaves us with a serious question mark over the quality of Paul's deviousness. As such an act suggests, he was certainly devious, but his deviousness was on behalf of his 'vision', and this reveals a man driven by ideas which he considered of the utmost importance. The energy he expends on his missionary journeys, the beatings he takes, the dangers he endures all suggest a mind utterly convinced of some great truth. So what was going on? Maccoby constructs a picture of Jesus much along the lines of his brother James, a Jesus who would not have condoned Paul's interpretation of things; but the later Mandean-Nazarene accusation that Jesus was a 'rebel' and a 'heretic' who betrayed Nazarene secret doctrine should not be forgotten.

What secret doctrine? The Jerusalem Nazarenes were basically orthodox Jews of sectarian persuasion who wanted the whole Jewish nation to take the Torah seriously; everyone was aware of what they thought, of what they believed. So what could Jesus, as a Nazarene, have known about his own sect that those inside the sect did not want anyone outside to know about? And, more importantly, to whom did he betray these mysterious secrets?

That Jesus possessed 'secrets' is attested to in a letter by Clement of Alexandria. He writes: 'Mark . . . wrote [an account of] the Lord's doings, not, however, declaring all, nor yet hinting at the secret [ones], but selecting those he thought most useful for increasing the faith of those who were being instructed.' This letter, discovered by Professor Morton Smith, is considered genuine because of Clement's obvious embarrassment when trying to explain to someone that certain secret teachings of Jesus did actually exist, but that they were being used by a group called the Carpocratians for scurrilous purposes. The letter goes on to say: '[Thus] he composed a more spiritual Gospel for the use of those who were being perfected. Nevertheless, he yet did not divulge the things not to be uttered, nor did he write down the hierophantic teachings of the Lord.' Interesting. But of even more interest is Clement's passionate plea that such teachings should be denied authenticity on oath, for '. . . not all true [things] are to be said to all men'.

Clement of Alexandria has been accused of being a Gnostic, and there is certainly good evidence for his having held at least some Gnostic ideas; but as can be seen from this letter, he is astutely aware of how damaging to orthodox Christianity the secret Gospel of Mark might be if its existence is made known. Yes, it exists, and it is authentic; but in the wrong hands its images and meanings could be used adversely. So he concludes that fools should be answered from their own folly, and that '. . . the light of the truth should be hidden from those who are mentally blind'.

Jesus was considered mad by his own family; his mother attempts to rescue him from himself early on in his ministry, but is curtly dismissed. And Jesus' own brother, James, is not even a disciple. Or is all of this a blind to dissociate Jesus from his Nazarene background, an erasure of history to pluck him out of his Jewish-sectarian milieu? The answer is Yes. He is robbed of Nazarene connections and made to stand, to a certain extent, against the Law of Moses; but not everything is fabrication or clever editing. This Jesus *is* a rebel, he *is* on a collision course with the Temple priesthood, he *is* at variance with family expectations, and he *is* strangely hypnotic. Something is going on over and above the textual tampering, something so strange that it will reverberate into the community and grow rather than diminish with the passage of time. The editors of the Gospels certainly erad- icated any sign of Nazarene influence on Jesus, but they could not wholly eradicate the Nazarenes from Acts; to have done so would have left too great a hole in the text. And so they altered the text to make Paul acceptable to the Nazarene community. Well, almost; but not quite. They were clumsy, inept, too sure of them- selves. At first glance the surface story of Acts seems to hold, but at second and third glance the whole edifice breaks apart to reveal conflict, dissension and violence.

Many of the supposed 'facts' stated in the book of Acts are fabrications; and none more so than Paul's journey to Jerusalem immediately after his conversion to submit himself to James' apostolic authority. It did not happen. In his Galatian Epistle (considered genuine) Paul clearly spells out what really happened, and it flatly contradicts the story in Acts. For just as Paul rails against those who are perverting his version of the Gospel, he also rails against those who say his first act was to go up to Jerusalem. 'Immediately,' he says, winding up to a surprise announcement, 'I conferred not with flesh and blood: Neither went I up to Jerusalem to them which were apostles before me; but I went into Arabia, and returned again unto Damascus. Then after three years I went up to Jerusalem to see Peter, and abode with him fifteen days. But other of the apostles I saw none, save James the Lord's brother.'[16] Not Jerusalem but Arabia? Then back to Damascus? Three years?

The book of Acts has a different story to tell; not an overt lie, I might add, but certainly an interesting abridgement of the facts. And very, very complicated. Paul, then called Saul (or Paul, depending on the circumstances), becomes a Nazarene disciple of Jesus, is baptized and instructed in Nazarene teaching ('there fell from his eyes as it had been scales'), immediately preaches that Jesus is the Son of God in the Damascus synagogues to the consternation of Torah-loving Jews, and then flees the city at night because, as it says, the Jews wanted to kill him. This is to say that the orthodox Jews of Damascus did not like what they were hear- ing; they were amazed that this persecutor of Nazarenes should have changed sides and was now preaching that Jesus was Israel's long-awaited Messiah. For they knew of this man; they were aware of his reputation and his status as an official arresting offi- cer of Nazarenes associated with the Temple High Priest. They

knew he was a torturer and a killer. Imagine, then, their amazement when this hired thug turns up in the synagogues of
Damascus preaching that Jesus is not only Israel's Messiah, but
also an inexplicable physical manifestation of Israel's God.

Later, much later, perhaps weeks or months later, a group of
these Jews suddenly decide to kill Paul, and from there on the
story becomes progressively more bizarre. For why should they
want to kill him? Hasn't he merely preached what the Nazarenes
were already preaching? So why haven't the orthodox Jews of
Damascus clamped down on these Nazarenes? Paul is after all
preaching *their* doctrines, *their* version of Jesus, *their* heresy of
Jesus as a divine being. Or is he? Could it be that Paul did not
actually start preaching in that way until much, much later?
Perhaps, even, three years later? And is it not strange that these
Nazarenes are being hunted down on foreign territory by hench-
men of the High Priest, when in Jerusalem itself, right under the
nose of the High Priest, the Apostolic leaders of the whole
Nazarene community seem to be going about their business as
usual. No, there is something very wrong with this story; it is
quite obviously a fabrication, created out of a truncated set of
actual events.

There is little doubt that the story of Paul as it comes across in
Acts was written partly by Jerusalem-sensitive Nazarenes, and
that their relationship to the Nazarenes at Damascus was not necessarily a straightforward one. Historically, these Damascus
Nazarenes are a worry; they have regular contact with a 'visionary Jesus' (the Jerusalem Nazarenes have no such contact), and are
either Gnostics in disguise, or another branch of the Nazarene sect
at odds with those who partly edited Acts. If the latter, then it's my
guess that their Jesus is not in the least visionary; he is there in
Damascus with them, in a safe house, and people like Ananias are
his conduit to the real world. This might explain the rather odd
fact that the later Mandean sect refers to itself as 'Nazarene', yet
at the same time rejects Jesus as a rebel who betrayed and
distorted sacred religious truth. How odd that two sects bearing
the same name, and with the same basic history, should view Jesus
so differently. Or is this the direct result of there having been two
branches of the same sect, one upholding an orthodox, the other
a heterodox Jesus? Nazarenes they both certainly were, but the
Mandean-Nazarenes probably reflected the split camp problem
over Jesus' status as an individual. And as this problem has been

made to disappear in the New Testament through editorial interference, then the question is: What else has been made to vanish
for the sake of later continuity?

In relation to the Nazarenes, there are two Jesuses in the New
Testament, and the more interesting one is the one who survived
the cross. For as Paul's conversion experience shows, Jesus was
not wholly a prisoner; he moved around quite a bit. And when
Paul was finally set to work preaching this *other* gospel about
Jesus, he periodically turned up to supply Paul with information.
Preposterous? Perhaps, perhaps not. Perhaps we just have to recognize that as far as the New Testament is concerned, we are being
hoodwinked at almost every step, and that the simple Gospel story
of Jesus' resurrection obscures a physical event of utterly mundane
character. Ritually significant without a doubt, and certainly masterful as an operation, but really no more than a Houdini act, an
illusion, a conjuring trick which paid off handsomely. Jesus was
alive, and Paul was so stunned by that fact that he instantly
changed sides.

PAUL AND THE PHANTOM JESUS

Biblical scholars are well aware that the New Testament has been
tampered with, that it has been carefully edited and interpolated
to satisfy the needs and desires of various first-century groups.
Not to realize that this is so is perfectly understandable. To
deny that this is so for reasons of faith and conviction is
perfectly understandable. To claim that it is not so and simultaneously claim membership of the scholarly community is not
only objectionable, it is a non sequitur. Scholarship which does
not fundamentally question the make-up of the New Testament
is not scholarship at all, it is apologetics. My reason for pointing
this out is two-fold: (1) the baleful cry set up by Christians when
someone publishes a book critical of Christianity is an unfortunate distraction from serious exegesis; and (2) the unconscious
fear of serious scholars to cross taboo lines set up by such
Christians is equally problematic.

One such taboo area is of course Jesus' survival of the cross, not
as the risen Lord of all eternity due to 'Resurrection', but as Israel's
rejected Messiah due to 'resuscitation'. Personally, I am not in the
least concerned with how this might have been accomplished, I am

only concerned with the fact that it probably did happen. First-century 'certainty' concerning Jesus' resurrection does not strike me as psychological escapism; it strikes me as real astonishment at a real event: Jesus survived, and it was this fact that both galvanized the Nazarene community and reversed Paul's fanaticism. The whole resurrection story hums with intrigue, and Gnostic influence has not altogether dimmed the obvious physicality of the 'risen' Jesus. He might appear as if by magic through walls, but when he does he is flesh and blood. He eats; he drinks; he can be touched; he can keep appointments; he can give advice; he travels; and he knows exactly what is going on.

The belatedly hired Apostle Paul would not have changed sides unless shocked to his core; which makes it highly probable that he was confronted by a living Jesus and reduced to a state of mental paralysis. Hysterically blind, he is led into Damascus, spends three days in seclusion without food, and is visited by Ananias who, it should be remembered, has just had a talk with Jesus about the fact that Paul is very, very dangerous. Ananias isn't enamoured with the idea of going to see Paul (he knows all about him), but is pacified when Jesus tells him that Paul is a chosen vessel ear-marked for a ministry among the Gentiles. Chosen? And then Ananias complicates the whole story by mentioning to Jesus that he has heard of Paul's persecution of Nazarenes in Jerusalem. What persecutions? According to Acts, James, Peter and Paul will quite soon be wandering in and out of Jerusalem at will without being persecuted by anyone. This suggests either that the political climate has suddenly changed, or that Paul was the only person doing the persecuting (highly unlikely), or that a much, much longer period of time elapses after Paul's conversion than is implied in this text. Paul's Galatian Epistle confirms that this is so, and at the same time reveals what so intrigued the philosopher Alfred North Whitehead, that is, Paul's visit to Arabia.

Gnostic influence on this story could be argued, and probably sustained; but the appearance of a phantom Jesus to Paul and Ananias could equally be the result of later Church editors remov-ing any signs of Jesus' physical presence for theological reasons – reasons resulting from Paul's own curiously developed ideas about Jesus adopted and rearranged to create the illusion of apostolic continuity between Jerusalem and Rome. A two-pronged insur-ance policy is set up with Paul as one prong and Peter as the other; and that in spite of the fact that Peter is at loggerheads with Paul over obedience to the Torah. It is a complete whitewash to make Peter succumb 'through a vision' to Paul's doctrine of the uncircumcision; the whole business is a blatant fiction. And Paul cannot be allowed to vanish off to Arabia and appear in Jerusalem three years later; he has to be seen to submit himself almost immediately to the Nazarene Apostles so that the Jerusalem Church's apostolic authority can be seen to flow unhindered to the future Roman Church. Paul's initial rejection by the Jerusalem-run Church of Rome will be overlooked in favour of the fast-growing post-64 Church run by Gentile 'God-fearers'. Yes, Paul's actual contribution to this fellowship of predominantly Gentile Christians eager for martyrdom will be real enough, but after his death his ideas, teetering as they are on the brink of heresy, will be made to topple over into radical pagan literalisms.

Why *did* Paul go to Arabia? Why does he not write about his stay there? Every move save this is recorded. Silence reigns over this ever so important journey. Something is being held back, covered up, yet at the same time pointed to for reasons historically peculiar. Paul wants us to realize that *his* Jesus, *his* Gospel, *his* vision of the risen Christ should not be confused with either orthodox Nazarene opinion or orthodox Judaism; *his* Jesus has an extra dimension which allows for the development of a more radical messianic theology. And where does it come from? It comes from Arabia, just as Dr Hugh Schonfield suspected way back in the 1960s. As he states in *The Passover Plot*, it was 'probably while in the borders of Arabia, Paul acquired the inspiration from which he developed his concept of the heavenly Messiah who had incarnated in the earthly Jesus'.[17] An astute observation, and one I think was suspected by A N Whitehead.

A convert to orthodox Nazarene beliefs Paul may appear to be, but when he returns from Arabia his Jesus has undergone a character transformation. Yes, there is an 'alive' Jesus in his life as he so clearly states; but there is also a Jesus of the theological imagination which progressively tips this real Jesus towards divinity. As the research of Professor Kamal Salibi has shown – but for which he has received little recognition or applause – the Nazarene sect had its ancient roots in western Arabia. And so Paul's choice of Arabia strongly suggests that he was made aware of Nazarene origins immediately after his conversion. Known historically as the 'Nasara', the Nazarenes (for political and religious reasons) were the original sectarian drop-outs. As such they could be traced back to the fourth century BCE where they were known to have split into rival factions. Their mutual founder, leader and teacher, Essa by name, was viewed as a prophet by one side, but believed to be divine, or semi-divine, by the other. So it was interesting to note that the name Essa, when translated from Arabic into Aramaic and then Greek, came out as *Iesous*, which equals 'Jesus', and that it was around *this* Jesus that Paul quickly constructed his theologically profound, but inherently heretical Christology on his return to Damascus.

After Paul's death, the Roman Church (probably as a result of documents in Paul's possession) further developed this mysterious figure into the wonder-working Jesus of the Gospels, and like a shadow given substance, *this* Jesus was made to walk on water, walk through walls and raise the dead. And it was without doubt this same Jesus that the Council of Nicea eventually nominated in 325 as God incarnate in human flesh. Here then are the 'secret doctrines' that the later Mandean-Nazarenes accused Jesus of betraying; the doctrines that Paul progressively pushed to the edge of heresy; the doctrines of which Jesus' brother James heartily disapproved; the doctrines that the Christian Church developed and used as a weapon against the Nazarenes and later the whole Jewish nation. The title 'heretic' was liberally distributed, and the purveyors of this title remained blissfully ignorant of the fact that it is they who were the *actual* heretics.

CHAPTER ELEVEN

In the Name of '*IS*'?

The name 'Jesus', its sacred significance in relation to the Nazarenes and the Christians, and the conquering, revealing, sacrificing, dying and reappearing Jesus-archetype in Jewish history

The name 'Jesus' contains within it a reference to a time centuries before Jesus' birth and also harbours clues in relation to the idea of Jesus as a divine being. In relation to this, Carsten Peter Thiede and Matthew D'Ancona's highly controversial book *The Jesus Papyrus* is worth looking at. Arguing clearly and cogently for Matthew's Gospel being much earlier in date than the 80s of the first century, these researchers have turned New Testament studies on their head. From a detailed study of three tiny fragments of papyrus locked up in an Oxford college showcase, Thiede conjectures that these virtually ignored fragments of papyrus were probably written no more than 40 years after the crucifixion. It is therefore conceivable that this papyrus was handled by 'one of the "five hundred brothers and sisters" whom Paul says saw the resurrected Jesus'. This is the claim on their book's cover, and it is an important one. For if correct, then Matthew's Gospel reflects early first-century perceptions of Jesus and, as I argued in chapter 7 when analysing the wilderness temptation story, the verbal dressing of Jesus' interaction with Satan suggests an attempt to obscure a much earlier scenario – one of political rather than scribal content.

Keeping all of this in mind, it is interesting to note that the writer of Matthew's Gospel sometimes abbreviates Jesus' name, so creating what Thiede terms a *nomen sacrum*, or 'holy name'. This is done by taking the first and last letters of Jesus' name in Greek, which is *Iesous*, and rendering it as *IS*. Fascinated as I was to stumble on this strange system of abbreviation, and convincing as Thiede's explanation for this curiosity seemed to be, I could not help wondering if there was perhaps another explanation, not so much an alternative as a parallel explanation harking back to a much earlier period in the history of the Nazarenes. This is in spite of the fact that Thiede and his colleague also cite a more ordinary example of a *nomen sacrum* using the same system in relation to the Greek word *kyrie*, meaning 'Lord'. Taking the 'K' and the 'E' from *kyrie*, Matthew renders it as *KE*. This is a very convincing explanation, and seems to rule out any possible alternative. So it is with trepidation that I suggest that *IS* may also refer to a holy name of much greater antiquity, namely, that of the Jewish-Arabian prophet Essa, founder and leader of the Nazarene sect in approximately 400 BCE. Otherwise I find it difficult to understand why Matthew would want to abbreviate Jesus' Greek name to the equivalent of 'JS' in English, and why the abbreviation of what was at that time a very common Jewish name should be construed as carrying a sacred overtone.

As I noted in chapter 10, the name Essa, written in Arabic either as 'Isa' or 'Issa', but pronounced 'Essa' in both Arabic and 1st-century Coptic Egyptian, belonged to the founder teacher of the western Arabian Nazarene sect then known as the 'Nasara'. So in developing a *nomen sacrum* for the Gospel Jesus, would it not make more sense if this abbreviation of a common Jewish name referred not to the Gospel Jesus as such, but to the founder of the sect to which Jesus belonged? *Essa* transliterates as *Iesous* (Jesus) when passed from Arabic into Aramaic and then Greek, and this fact, in conjunction with the *nomen sacrum* appearing only in Jesus' Greek name (*Iesous*), suggests a connection with things Nazarene. For is it not odd that on almost every occasion that Jesus is referred to in the Gospels as being *of* Nazareth, the word 'Nazareth' ought to read 'Nazarene'? This subterfuge strongly suggests that Jesus' close affiliation with the Nazarenes has been deleted, and this in turn suggests that as a group, the beliefs of the Nazarene sect played a much more important role in Jesus' life than the Gospels are willing to convey.

To use the first and last letters of Jesus' name in Greek as a code to signify that this Jesus was more important than all the other Jesuses around is perfectly plausible. But I would argue that such a curious abbreviation signals much, much more. The Gospel Jesus may well have been perceived by his followers as in some sense sacred, but I think the key to understanding what this meant lies not in Jesus himself, but in what he represented as a Nazarene dynastic leader. Which is to say that his name was not arbitrarily given, but that it reflected the origins of the sect to which he belonged. And so it can be said that the name 'Jesus', when abbreviated, was not only a code-name for this particular Jesus, but also a power name belonging to the sect's distant past. For it should be remembered that Jesus gave his name to his disciples to use as a power name when healing the sick, and when exorcising demons, and it is probable that he too used his own name for similar purposes. There is of course no record of this, but that is not surprising when one considers the political implications of such a statement, and that Jesus has been intentionally shorn of all political significance in the Gospels.

In relation to Jesus, I think the *nomen sacrum* refers not to Jesus himself, but to the fact that he carried this ancient name by way of blood relationship; he was, in other words, part of a dynasty or caliphate, as suggested by Dr Hugh Schonfield back in the 1960s. This might also explain why Paul immediately headed for Arabia and not Jerusalem; he had been dispatched for a purpose, either to retrieve documents (the now lost *Gospel of the Nazarenes*, perhaps), or to undergo initiation into the heterodox Arabian branch of the Nazarene sect. This is not as strange as it may sound; something doctrinally odd is at the back of Paul's Christology; and the possibility of Jesus carrying an ancient and holy name signifying 'sacredness' is perfectly plausible. When Paul returned from that journey he was an utterly changed man; and so also was the Jesus he preached. Unrecognizable as the man he once was, Paul the lightning-struck convert did not preach the Jesus known to the Nazarenes of Jerusalem (the historical Jesus), but the Jesus of the Hijaz mountains of western Arabia superimposed on the Jesus of the gospels. Here then, as I suggest in my earlier work *Jesus the Heretic*, is the phantom Jesus of the New Testament, the Jesus so accurately intuited by scholars never to have existed in real life. And yet as real as real can be in relation to that ancient Arabian Jesus carrying the theological trappings of a man who, somehow, became divine.

NOMINA SACRA/NOMINA DIVINA

Imagine my mounting interest when I came across further reference to the use of 'holy names' hidden in the Gospels, that such systems of abbreviation were a 'striking feature', and that Thiede and D'Ancona interpreted these shortened versions of Jesus' Greek name as a conscious attempt to 'emulate the Jewish custom of abbreviating the name of God'. I was stopped in my tracks when I read that, for I knew instinctively what was coming, and it exactly matched what I had already suggested in relation to the god/man Essa. For these authors proposed that abbreviations such as *IS* in the New Testament 'implied a dramatic theological claim about the nature and role of Jesus', and this meant that the early Christian community saw Jesus as 'divine', so undermining the idea of a developed Christology having been added to the Gospels near the end of the first century.

But as I was about to discover from the work of Professor Stephen Hoeller, a similar connotation of divinity was attached to Jesus' name in Hebrew. Hebrew too could be shown to carry a set of meanings pertinent to the notion of divinity in relation to Jesus. For Hoeller's studies in comparative religion revealed a curious dual carriageway of meanings in the name 'Jesus' as it appeared in Hebrew, and this made the name of God (*Yahveh*) and the name of Jesus (*Yehoshva*) expressive of one another. In Hebrew, the four-lettered name of God came out as *Yod, Heh, Vav, Heh*; the name of Jesus as *Yod, Heh, [Shin], Vav, Heh*. The addition of the holy letter *shin* in Jesus' name could therefore be interpreted as a completion or rectification of the name of God, and this reflected an evolved form of thinking found not only in the canonical Gospels, but also in the so-called apocryphal, or Gnostic Gospels.[1]

In his intriguing book *Jesus the Magician*, Professor Morton Smith suggests that magical deification may have been unusually prominent in Jewish tradition.[2] In this context, Jesus' name was indeed a power name, such as a magician might own or use. Jesus was accused of being a magician, of being in league with dark forces. And, as I have previously noted, he gives his disciples the authority (the power) to heal the sick and cast out devils in his *name*. Living as itinerant exorcists, Jesus' disciples find that they too can control what are conceived of as demons if they use Jesus' name. Mark's Gospel records that King Herod heard of Jesus because his 'name was spread abroad'. (Mark 6:14) There is the added factor of his having the habit of forgiving sins. Taking over John the Baptist's group of followers, Jesus seems to have reinter-preted John's message of forgiveness through repentance and the new rite of baptism and replaced it with what Morton Smith describes as 'trust in his power'. So the scribes are offended, and accuse Jesus of claiming 'divine power'. Credited by the populace to possess this divine power, it was not too big a step for Jesus to fulfil expectations and function as a species of divine being. Particularly if he believed himself to embody, through his name, the spirit of Essa, the divinely attributed founder-teacher of the Nazarene sect.

Thiede and D'Ancona then speculate that the abbreviating of Jesus' Greek name must have been 'developed and introduced by one of the two Christian communities which possessed such authority, the Jerusalem Church or the Church at Antioch where the followers of Jesus were first called Christians'. Suddenly, I was back on familiar territory, and I was in disagreement. Yes, Jesus had been viewed as divine by the early Christian Church, and this view (as confirmed by Stephen Hoeller) was reflected in texts other than those eventually declared canonical, but I could not agree that the use of a coded abbreviation could have been introduced by the Jerusalem Church in conjunction with the Church at Antioch. When I read this claim, I immediately doubled back to a previous statement about the two communities. Yes, there it was again, the supposition that the Nazarene sectarian community in Jerusalem (the Jerusalem 'Church', so-called) under Jesus' brother James could have sanctioned the idea of Jesus being divine. *That* was a head-scratcher. Had Christian theology so blurred the historical canvas that such an utterly impossible notion was being accepted without critical hesitation? I went back further, and came across our old friend the *Birkat ha-minim*, the prayer/curse authorized by the Academy at Jamnia against the heretics and hotheads who had caused Rome to attack the Jewish state.

> May apostates have no hope and may the kingdom of impertinence be uprooted in our day. May the *Nozrim* and *Minim* [the Christians] disappear in the twinkling of an eye. May they be removed from the book of the living and not be inscribed among the just. Bless you, Lord, you who cast down the proud.[3]

What fascinated me about this was not the prayer in itself, but the historical oversight in relation to the word *Nosrim*, for Thiede had translated this term as 'the Christians', and in doing so had obscured the fact that *Nosrim*, as Professor Pagels so clearly states when citing the same curse, refers to the Nazarenes. The very fact that this prayer separates *Nosrim* from *Minim*, and the word *Minum* is a blanket term for 'heretics', rather suggests the use of a double, not a single, category of rejection. Yes, the term *Minim* refers to the Christians with their notion of a 'divine' Messiah; but the term *Nozrim* refers specifically to the well-known Nazarene sect by that time held equally responsible with the Zealots for the destruction of Jerusalem and everything Jewish. In this context, Hyam Maccoby also remarks that the name used for Jesus' followers was *notzerim*, and sees this word as similar to Nazarene. So not so much a translation of these two ever-so-different words, I realized, more an interpretation due to preconceived ideas about the nature of the early Jerusalem community.

The problem, as usual, was the use of 'Christian' as a blanket term for the Jerusalem and Antiochene community, plus the persistent and incomprehensible inclusion of James the Just in this mix, as if these communities were fundamentally one and the same. They were not. James upheld the Torah and everything it contained; Paul payed lip service to the Torah when it suited him. James believed that his brother Jesus was the Messiah of Israel; Paul had other ideas. Yes, there were two communities, and yes they both preached 'Jesus', but to lump them together and call them 'the Christians' is less than accurate. The Jerusalem Nararenes certainly sustained the orthodox Jewish community's attitude of inclusion for Gentiles, and may well have altered the rules somewhat to accommodate Paul's early mission, but when they discovered the true nature of his Christology that relationship was severed. The games played with Peter as he shuttles backwards and forwards between these two communities would be laughable but for the seriousness of the results.

As I have shown in the previous chapter, the name 'Christian' wasn't used by the Nazarenes at all, but only in scorn of Paul's converts (Jews and predominantly Gentile women) by fellow pagans at Antioch, and from then on of the Pauline community alone. The name 'Christian' was a later development and had nothing whatsoever to do with the Nazarenes. The Jerusalem community was Nazarene (*Nozrim, Nazrim* or *Notzerim*), indeed virtually Nazarite in its observance of the Torah; the Antioch Christian community, composed of converted Jews and Gentile 'God-fearers', was virtually anti-Torah and under the sway of ideas considered heretical by both orthodox Nazarenes and Jewish orthodoxy. And yet, as Hyam Maccoby has shown, there were Christian sects specifically called 'Nazarenes'. Rather than confuse the issue, this fact actually clarifies it; it bolsters the contention that Paul's Nazarenes were not quite the same as those in Jerusalem. It was probably a Nazarene faction who schooled Paul in the notion of Jesus' being in some sense divine. Again Maccoby comes to our rescue: 'We also read of Nazarenes who believed in the Torah, but also believed in the virgin birth of Jesus and in his divine nature.'[4] This has to be the Nazarene sect Paul stayed with for three years; the sect who sent him to Arabia to complete his religious education; the sect who still worshipped the mystic Essa (Jesus), and who would evolve with their Jewish and Gentile converts into the Christians of New Testament fame. For as the Koran reveals, Essa was born of a virgin, was considered divine, and his followers were an heretical branch of the *Nasara*, the Nazarenes of the Arabian Hijaz. Professor Ranke-Heinemann, like most other scholars, sees the Koranic Jesus as no more than a garbled version of canonical or apocryphal gospel accounts; whereas Professor Salibi (a specialist in Arabic and Hebrew) sees the Koranic Jesus as original and ancient. Speaking of the Christian interpretation, Salibi says simply that it cannot be otherwise for theological reasons.

HISTORICAL CONFUSION

The complexity of this situation is touched upon by Thiede and D'Ancona themselves when writing of the persecution of Rome's Christians by Nero in 64. A strange situation erupted as Nero first accused and then arrested many of these followers of Jesus for starting the great fire of Rome. The authors inform us that 'there were divisions among Roman Christians over questions of attitude and interpretation. Christians denounced and betrayed other Christians when the persecution started.'[5] There were apparently 'disagreements', 'divisions' and 'jealousy' between Christians, and the whole mess led to the arrest and execution of both Peter and Paul. Interesting. But of even greater interest is a paragraph further down the same page where we read: 'All our sources suggest that Christians and Jewish Christians were by now clearly distinguished from the Jews. In the early years, Jewish Christians and Jews were often confused by outsiders.'[6] Indeed they were. But what a potpourri this all is and not, per- haps, as historically tidy as we are led to believe. Yes, the Romans eventually worked out who was who and persecuted only those who offended their sensibilities, but the persecuted were more likely to have been Nazarene sectarians than Paul's Gentile Christians. The Romans may have worked out who was who, but modern scholars seem to be having problems doing the same thing. 'The authorities,' writes D'Ancona, 'sought out and punished the Christians and only the Christians; Jews were not affected. A wall between the two communities was erected in the largest city of the empire and the dialogue was not resumed.'[7]

True. But I sense a twist in the text here, a twist which makes Nazarenes into Jews, and by doing so makes the wall between Nazarene sectarians and Christians disappear. Yes, both Jews and Nazarenes become heretical Christians must have suffered and died as a result of Nero's pointing finger, but for my money it was the Nazarene community preaching Jesus the Messiah who probably took the brunt of Nero's savagery. Peter de Rosa places the situation in its context when he says: 'Christians were taken by the Romans to be a Jewish sect.'[8] And the historian Will Durant agrees; he describes these so-called Christians as 'hardly distinguished by Rome from the orthodox Jews'.[9] It is pretty certain then that what is being described is not a persecution of Paul's Christians as such, but more a persecution of James' Nazarene community mistakenly called 'Christians' by later Christian writers.

And so we come to the in-fighting between Nazarene and Christian; an in-fighting that had them reaching for each other's throats. We are told that they denounced and betrayed one another. Denounced and betrayed? And done because of divisions over attitude and interpretation. Divisions of attitude and interpretation over what? Alas, we are not told. Tacitus and Clement of Rome do not spell out the reasons, and so the whole problem of what was actually going on slips away into the mist of later Christian exegesis. But not entirely; the major clue is the rather obvious one that in July '65 war broke out between the Romans and the Jews; a war which went on for five years and resulted in the siege and destruction of Jerusalem by Titus in 70. Just like that, a war between the Romans and the Jews. Well, not quite, Jewish sectarian hatred of the Romans had been gathering for years, and when the dam finally burst Rome responded with her usual swiftness.

Similarly in Rome herself, I would imagine, but not all in the one evening and probably not without some kind of warning. And so chaos reigned in the Nazarene/Christian communities over what had attracted Nero's attention, and the doctrinal squabbling which erupted served Nero's purpose all the more. A large part of Rome ended up in ashes, and the Nazarenes, who were Jews yet different from Jews, and oddly similar to the Christians, yet not Christians, probably became Nero's scapegoats. Doctrinally separated they certainly were, but as these two groups burned side by side in the Emperor's garden their screams must have become one indistinguishable cacophony of pain.

THE AGREEMENT

Paul came to Jerusalem to face the leaders of the Nazarene community not immediately but, according to his Galatian letter, three years after his conversion, spent fifteen days with Peter, and did not return for a further fourteen. So proof of doctrinal continuity between the two communities is, in anyone's terms, scant. Yes, Peter is said to have interacted with Paul and his converts, and probably did so; but the blatantly obvious apologetics of the book of Acts make a nonsense of his ever having agreed with Paul's dismissal of the Torah. The historian Will Durant comments dryly that Peter and Paul laboured as rivals to win converts in Rome, and that about sums up the situation: they were spreading, I would imagine, almost diametrically opposed notions of Jesus by that time. A waverer Peter may have been; traitor to the Jewish faith he was not. Hyam Maccoby makes it abundantly clear in his riveting study of Paul, Peter and the so-called Jerusalem 'Church', that Peter never renounced his Nazarene-Jewish beliefs – there are numerous technicalities of Jewish law at work within the text of Acts which disallow such an idea. This means that Paul's notion of salvation by faith in Jesus as the Mystic Christ did not replace Peter's belief in, and his adherence to, the Torah. Which makes Peter's account of a vision in which a voice instructs him to eat unclean meat a rather obvious Christian addition to the text, and a clumsy one at that. And unlike Paul's call to the Jews, Peter's call for them to be 'baptized' is not a call to a new religion, but a call for them to join the Nazarene sectarians and adopt a religious stance against Rome.

The Jerusalem Nazarenes were lovers of the Torah. Jesus' brother James continued to be held in high respect by orthodox

Jewry right up until his death in 62, and during this period the
Nazarenes boosted their numbers to approximately 8000 through
the inclusion of orthodox Jews (and Essenes?) into their party.[10]
What has to be understood is that, prior to the Roman invasion of
Judea, the Nazarene community dominated Paul's scattering
of churches in authority; it was only after the invasion that this
community waned both in numbers and in power and the Jews
ostracized both the Nazarenes and the Christians as heretics and
trouble-makers. What is mistakenly termed 'Judaic Christianity'
survived, as Durant shows, for a further five centuries in the form
of the Ebionim ('the poor'), and this group, reminiscent of the
Qumran Essenes in many ways, continued to practise community
sharing and the full Jewish Law.

The agreement Paul came to with the leaders of the Jerusalem
community over the Gentiles was soon broken. Showing an
almost complete disregard for the Torah, Paul angered orthodox
Jews everywhere, and as a result eventually incurred the wrath of
the Nazarenes, who sent leading disciples to Antioch in an attempt
to reverse such a dangerous trend. And so back to Jerusalem Paul
was forced to go, to explain himself before the Jerusalem Council,
and it was reluctantly agreed that pagan proselytes should not be
forced to accept the full Law of Moses, but made to obey only the
injunctions against immorality and the eating of strangled or
sacrificial animals. A compromise. And promises of financial
support from Antioch to help ease the tension. So Paul returned to
Antioch, resumed his subversive preaching against the Torah, and
was again reported to Jerusalem for going too far. It is one thing
to advocate reduced observance of the Torah for Gentile God-
fearers, but it is quite another to tell orthodox Jews that they
should abandon the Torah altogether and replace it with the
divine Jesus. At that moment Peter arrived, proceeded to eat with
Paul's Gentiles because he thought that the food before him had
been prepared in accordance with the Law (a technicality highlighted by Maccoby), then discovered that it had not; Paul had not
kept his part of the agreement with the Jerusalem Council. Forced
to abandon the table for that reason, and that reason alone, Peter
showed himself to be a true Nazarene and a good Jew. Later, Paul
told the story of how he challenged Peter to his face over this
event, but his description of that event was almost entirely imaginary. Other incidents followed, at Corinth, and these incidents
filtered back to James and caused Paul to again journey back to

Jerusalem where he was reminded that 'thousands' of Torah-loving Jews had now been added to the Nazarene party. Advised to undergo purification in the Temple to prove that he too observed the Law, he submitted and caused a riot. Accused by the High Priest and some elders of having preached a 'new religion', his devious dealings with the Nazarenes were at last brought out into the open.

Up until that moment, the impression one gets is that observance of the Law is the only factor separating Paul's Christians from the Jerusalem Nazarenes; and that only because of the massive influx of Jews to the Nazarene party. With further adjustment of attitude to the Torah on both sides (allowing for the fact that many Jews would have refused to consider any such adjustment) everything would have been alright. Yes, the Jews were a bit of a problem. All they had was the Torah. Paul, on the other hand, had Jesus, and Jesus was *the Christ*. For in spite of how things seem in the early stages of Acts, Paul wasn't just preaching cessation of the Law; and neither was he preaching Jesus the Jewish Messiah; he was preaching Jesus as Son of God and Saviour of the whole world, thus doing away with the heart of Jewish atonement doctrine. That is what all the fuss was about; he was single-handedly dismantling Judaism. But perhaps not always as obviously as one might think; for his willingness to take part in the Temple purification rite was in direct contradiction to Jesus' power to save, and this highlights both the deviousness detected in Paul by Hyam Maccoby, and the fact that Paul's teachings reflected a view of Jesus which straddled traditions. As he travelled around, Paul may have played at being a Jew to Jews and a Greek to Greeks, but he was never a theological crook, at least not consciously so. But he was eventually beaten at his own game by James, the Lord's brother, who asked him to prove himself an obedient Jew and enter the Temple with some Nazarites. He had met his match. Walking into the Temple, he walked into a doctrinal trap.

THE TRUE PROPHET

In relation to Jesus, orthodox Nazarenes seem to have interpreted their beliefs in accordance with Judaism, not apart from Judaism. It is true that they were sectarians with a vision of things integrally different from Judaism, but their execution of those differences was within the strict framework of the Law. As wilderness sectarians, they strove to perfect the Law in their lives, not to obliterate it like Paul. In *A Separate God*, the respected French scholar Simone Petrement observes that the Jewish community in Jerusalem 'did not believe one could be saved simply by grace and faith, setting themselves against Paul on this point';[11] it seems that they were more inclined to view Jesus as an ordinary man adopted by God because of his holiness, not as divine in origin. Rigorously monotheistic, they rejected Paul's notion of Jesus' divinity, which rather suggests that something very odd was going on in Paul's Christian community. To complicate the issue further, it is quite probable that Jesus was responsible for what was going on; but only in the sense of his being the carrier of what was probably an ancient Jewish-Arabian tradition. The abbreviation of Jesus' Greek name to *IS* certainly suggests an early first-century belief in his sacredness or divinity by the Gospel writers; but this too seems to reflect a much earlier period, and another Jesus altogether. For as we saw earlier, a cult centred on the name 'Jesus' seems to have existed in relation to a branch of the Nazarene sect as early as 400 BCE, and the chances are that it was this heterodox branch of the Nazarenes which quickly blossomed into the 'Christian' community led by Paul, thus explaining the rapid growth of the community, its organizational ability and its highly evolved doctrinal ideas. It is a point of wonder among some scholars, but the early Christian community's capacity for organization and doctrinal sophistication is easily explained if it existed previously under a different name.

Professor Hoeller speaks of a 'Joshua connection', and in doing so refers to the curious fact that the name 'Joshua' embodies what he terms 'the first archetypal prefiguration of the messianic principle: a conqueror, a lawgiver, a concealer, and preserver of the true Gnosis, or secret doctrine'.[12] Identifying three Joshuas, Hoeller names them as Joshua, son of Nun (a word meaning 'fish', the traditional symbol of Christ), the Essene Teacher of Righteousness and the Jesus of the Gospels. Perceiving these three figures as 'organically connected', he defines them as conquering, revealing, sacrificing, dying and reappearing images. Then, as one would expect, he points out that the Essenes were conscious of their Teacher's archetypal connections with spiritual figures from the past, and in doing so adds the names 'Joseph' and 'Asaph' to the list. Joseph the patriarch and Asaph the Levite embody, we are told, 'the archetypal qualities appearing as the *suffering holy one and the inspired seer and miracle worker*'.[13] So far so good. And then Hoeller expands on the name 'Asaph', showing that in ancient Islamic records there was a teacher called Jo-Asaph (Joseph), and that the Ahmadiyya movement (an influential Moslem sect) believed that Jo-Asaph was identical with Jesus, and that he survived his crucifixion.[14] But it is Hoeller's summation of all of this that interests me, for his detailed overview finally states that 'the figure of the Christian Saviour is the last and greatest of a series of archetypal images manifesting in Jewish tradition'.[15]

It is therefore interesting to note, as Ahmed Osman does in his book *The House of the Messiah*, that 'Paul frequently perplexes us by apparently throwing Christ's activity back into the Old Testament'.[16] Osman, a teacher of Arabic, is in fact referring to the perplexity of A T Hanson, Professor of Theology at the University of Hull, and goes on to show that Hanson did not consider Paul to be saying that these texts were fulfilled in Christ, but rather 'this is what Christ says'. Now that is an interesting statement, for it suggests that the Jesus Paul was talking to in his so-called visions was well aware of the traditions backgrounding his own teachings. And so to Osman the idea of Jesus having been present with the Israelites in the wilderness is no surprise, for as Paul inadvertently reveals, they too had had the Gospel of Jesus preached to them without success. So Jesus (Joshua) succeeds Moses as the leader of the Israelites, and Moses speaks of him as a Prophet of God (Deut 18:15). Fine. But this is not the Gospel Jesus somehow appearing in the past as some literalist interpreters of these passages would like to think; it is *another* Jesus altogether, a cult figure whose name reflected the name of God, and whose teachings seem to have paralleled those of the Gospel Jesus.

So we return to Simone Petrement, for in relation to the Jerusalem community, this scholar remarks on the sect's speculation on 'successive appearances of the "true prophet" '. Putting this statement into context, she then says: 'Whereas the incarnations of the "true prophet" in the Jewish-Christian myth have very little to do with the New Testament; they rather tend to exalt the great figures of Judaism and to underline the continuity between the Old Testament and the New.'[17] Hoeller's description of these figures as 'archetypal images manifesting in Jewish tradition' pulls these different identities into proper focus, for what we are quite obviously dealing with is not the literal incarnation of one being or identity age by age, but the conscious donning of an archetypal mantle in the tradition of Elisha and Elijah.

In the light of what is now known of Nazarene origins, it is distinctly possible that the Jesus Paul preached and worshipped was a composite figure, an amalgamation of the Gospel Jesus, the Arabian Jesus Essa, and other Jesus-type figures in Jewish history. Hence the reason for Jesus' Greek name concealing the letters *IS*, a probable allusion to the Jewish-Arabian founder-teacher of the Nazarene sect. Now such information is of interest in itself, but there is the added factor of the 'resurrection' to consider, which, when viewed in the light of a possible Arabian connection, is a connection strongly suggestive of a 'divinity cult' of considerable antiquity. Jesus' survival after his crucifixion then takes on ritualistic significance. For the Jesus of Paul's theological imagination is a saviour figure reminiscent of other saviour figures, and as such Jesus' crucifixion, burial and resurrection can be viewed as events concealing, like his name, divine content.

Yet he is at the same time an ordinary man, the abbreviation of his name reflecting not actual divinity (a view which Thiede's findings will no doubt further encourage), but a concept of man become a God which was well-known in that part of the world. For it has to be said that just because the Christian disciples of Jesus may have thought him divine does not mean that he *was* divine; it just means that something very odd was going on in the Christian camp. Either that, or some important factor in relation to the idea of Jesus' divinity has been lost to us. Obscured perhaps by later theological development, the specialness of Jesus to these heterodox Nazarenes has probably undergone an unwarranted transformation. The very fact that the Nazarenes spawned, at a very early date, a heterodox branch centred on a God/man must surely cause hesitation, if not a re-evaluation of the whole Gospel story.

Well aware of the impact their detailed and absorbing study will have on Christian thinking, Thiede and D'Ancona offer a note of caution in the last chapter of *The Jesus Papyrus*. In relation to the first-century mind, they ask us to remember that the 'peasants and townsmen believed in demons, miracles and charismatic healing. They saw the numinous, the divine and the supernatural at work in their daily lives; the "open door" to heaven of Revelation 4 was always ajar. Reality was permanently subject to moments of petty transfiguration when the difference between the natural and the supernatural would appear blurred.'[18] Blurred indeed; and no less so than first-century history itself when viewed through the eyes of twentieth-century believers in Christ's divinity. The spell is still operative; reality is still vulnerable to archetypal pressure.

The authors then argue for the Gospels being perceived as a 'mixture of myth and empirical information' (subjective truth and historical fact), and ask that such a juxtaposition of the 'figurative' and the 'literal' be understood as perfectly natural to the Gospel writers. Oswald Spengler captures this point perfectly in *The Decline of the West* when he says: 'This is what thrills us . . . the collision of facts with truths, of two worlds that will never understand one another, and his [Jesus'] entire incomprehension of what was happening about him.'[19] Two worlds in collision – the so-called subjective, and the so-called objective. Thiede and D'Ancona add that it is a matter of personal faith whether one accepts the story of the Gospels at face value, but point out that the authors of these unusual books 'considered them of overwhelming and perhaps even terrifying significance'.[20] I like that; it clearly identifies the sense of urgency in the Gospels, the sense of men and women confronted by a great mystery: a mystery which changed lives. That fact cannot be denied. And then comes what is probably their most pertinent insight, an insight which differentiates between what is 'true' and what is 'authentic'. They tell us that scientists cannot say whether the Gospels are true or untrue, but they can make judgements about their 'authenticity' on the basis of empirical observation. Which allows – if fundamental authenticity *can* be shown – for a convergence of the Jesus of history and the Christ of faith. Once again I found myself nodding in agreement, but even as I nodded I sensed danger; the danger of a Jesus only recently rescued from the too bright backing lights of Christian exegesis thrust back into the limelight as wholly God. Fine for some; but a right old bother for anyone trying to make historical and psychological sense out of Jesus' life.

PROMOTION/DEMOTION

In this chapter we have seen Jesus promoted to the level of divinity, and then as quickly demoted to the level of an ordinary man carrying a 'tradition of divinity'. Viewed as divine because of this tradition, or, more accurately, as an ordinary man *become* divine (not quite the same thing as straight divinity), Jesus takes on a double aspect to his personality and general mentality. For if viewed as 'special' *in this way*, then as carrier of that specialness Jesus too must have viewed himself as special, and lived that specialness out in everything he did and said. Here then is the numinous aspect of Jesus' behaviour and thinking: he too believed something extraordinary to have happened in his life, in his consciousness, and he radiated this extraordinary 'something' wherever he went. There was a sense in which he *was* Essa, Joshua, Joseph or Jo-Asaph. His life was given over to an idea, and that idea eventually changed his life into an archetypal fact. Meaning what? Meaning that the discipline of holding such an idea in place minute by minute, hour by hour, day by day, eventually transformed him into a truly awe-inspiring presence.

Again we must turn to Oswald Spengler to capture fully the flavour of this mighty dream Jesus was caught up in: the dream of Messiahship which came upon him suddenly as a terrible realization. 'But there was a moment in his life,' writes Spengler, 'when an inkling, and then high certainty, came over him – "Thou art thyself It!" '.[21] Unable at first to accept such an astonishing claim for himself, Jesus eventually gave in to the presence of the archetype, and in doing so set in motion a mystery which enveloped not only himself, and his disciples, but the whole Jewish nation. The world was an illusion 'that might at any moment without warning vanish into nothingness'. So writes Spengler, and in penning those words he offers us a momentary glimpse into the creative darkness of Jesus' consciousness; an archetypal darkness within which the past merges with the present. To grasp what Spengler is getting at here is to grasp the meaning of the New Testament, the lost meaning of Jesus' divinity brought dangerously close to a theological truism in Paul's ever-expanding Christology.

Carl Jung's description of an 'archetype' is worth quoting at this point, for it coalesces perfectly with what we have discovered about Jesus in historical terms, and with what Oswald Spengler surmised about Jesus in psychological terms. Being a primordial image, an archetype is by way of definition 'a figure – be it demon, a human being, or a process – that constantly recurs in the course of history and appears whenever creative fantasy is freely expressed'.[22] Using this precise quote Professor Hoeller, in his study of Jung and the lost gospels of Qumran and Nag

Hammadi, confirms Spengler's sense of the archetypal by telling us that archetypes are autonomous, that they are governed by their own sovereign laws, and that although subjective, they manage to reflect themselves onto the screen of external human affairs. Archetypes are therefore present not only in the inner subjective world of the human psyche, they are also detectable in the arena of human history.[23] But as Jung came to realize, an archetypal image *is not the thing in itself*, merely an expression of a mysterious something belonging to an inaccessible level of psychic reality, and capable of interacting with us through dreams, reveries, visions and artistic creations. Here then is the dream-like force driving Jesus out of Galilee, the visionary force directing his feet towards Jerusalem, the irresistible creative force causing his words to lodge in the minds of those confronted by him. And so Thiede and D'Ancona use the word 'numinous' in relation to the mentality of that historical period, for it accurately indicates another reality, a reality only occasionally sensed in our time; the awe-inspiring reality and presence of divinity in everyday life.

At first close to Jesus, his Baptist-oriented disciples eventually fell away and scattered, only to be galvanized back into life when he survived his crucifixion and appeared to them *in the flesh*. Like Paul, they were shocked to the core, frightened out of their wits, made as little children by this spectre who proved his physicality in a number of ways. I'm not a spirit, he told them. I'm flesh and blood; and don't you forget it. And they didn't – not ever. Jesus' physical resurrection became the key to their future Gospel, their story of how he surprised everyone and made even his reluctant brother James recognize his Messiahship, but only in orthodox terms. Jesus and James did not see eye to eye on everything, and would soon separate over Jesus' claim that he was now in some sense 'divine'. For James did not fully comprehend what had happened to his brother; but Paul did. James could not forget the fact that they had had a common father, Joseph, and a common mother, Mary. And he could not forget that Jesus' dynastic leadership of the Nazarenes was still in question because of the irregularities of his birth – many Nazarenes viewed Jesus as illegitimate. Paul, on the other hand, sensed the leap that had taken place in Jesus' mind, and responded wholeheartedly to the archetypal intensity of this remarkable man.

But not James. James would not buy the story that this brother of his had been mentally and spiritually transformed to such an extent; and that in spite of the fact that he recognized him as Israel's legitimate Messiah. No, he would not accept that Jesus should be made into a God/man; neither would he accept Paul's theological justification for such a move. Perfectly aware of ancient Nazarene traditions, and of the early split in Nazarene ranks, he held to his orthodox views and kept Paul at arm's length. Jesus, too, for that matter; for there is only one meeting between these brothers on record, and it is an informational blank. It was too dangerous, he must have felt, too close to past mistakes, too close to what these Gentile converts of Paul's expected from their spiritual leaders to ever be properly understood. Yes, the orthodox Nazarene idea of the Messiah was in itself a deeply spiritual vision different from that of the Jews, a majestic insight into how God bridged the gap between himself and his human creation, but to push this vision of messianic endowment as far as Paul had pushed it was to invite not just orthodox Jewish disapproval, it was to invite the accusation of full-blown heresy. Whatever happened, that had to be avoided.

Hyam Maccoby interprets the situation thus: 'The belief that Jesus had been resurrected was indeed the mark of the movement after Jesus' death. Without this belief, the movement would simply have ceased to exist.'[24] I agree. But perhaps the word 'death' is too strong. For when speaking to the Jews at Pentecost, Peter says: 'I speak of Jesus of Nazareth, *a man singled out by God* and made known to you.' [emphasis added] A man? And then Peter too speaks of Jesus having been 'killed'; but perhaps only because he doesn't really understand what has taken place. Shocked as they all were by Jesus' appearance in the upper room, the question of how he had managed to survive death would not have arisen for Peter in any practical sense. His Messiah was alive, *ergo* God had brought him back from the dead. It was that simple. And what a flutter it must have caused in the chest. Alive. ALIVE! Unique because of their mutual belief that Jesus was alive, the orthodox and heterodox Nazarene parties must have felt unstoppable as they went about their daily business. Jesus was alive and in Damascus, and the Kingdom of God was just around the corner. What a shock the Romans were going to get when that kingdom materialized and Jesus stood forth as God's chosen Son.

THE DAY OF RECKONING

But for the Roman invasion of Judea, James' orthodox view of Jesus would probably have prevailed – Paul's visits to Jerusalem at long intervals show that he was ultimately subservient to the Jerusalem Nazarene Council, and as his letters reveal, his 'churches' were in varying stages of spiritual disintegration. The Nazarene sectarians grew rapidly into a major religious party with many orthodox Jewish connections, causing Paul's 'Christian' movement to struggle for survival. But in the end it was all for naught, sectarian idiocy stirred the Roman beast into action, and the Jewish nation tumbled into a bloody abyss. Jerusalem fell, and with it the reputation of the Nazarenes and the Christians. Forced to abandon Jerusalem in 70, the Nazarenes were barred from the synagogue as heretics and dispersed to Caesarea and other cities. And so too the Christians; for although carrying a different name, they were in fact Nazarenes by origin, albeit it of a heretical variety. And so arose the *birkat ha-minim* ('benediction of the heretics'), the double-barrelled prayer against the Nazarenes and the Christians, the two sectarian bodies with the same archetypally driven leader.

But it did not last for long, this exclusion from Jerusalem of the Christians, for as Thiede and D'Ancona record, 'the city's Christians who had not participated in the revolt against the Romans were soon allowed to return, settling once more on the south-western hill, today's Mount Zion'.[25] Now that is very odd, for weren't they already earmarked as having burned down most of the Roman capital in or around 65? Did the Romans have such a short memory that the by now well-known name did not ring alarm bells? Or is this the final proof that it wasn't the 'Christians' who suffered the brunt of Nero's madness at all, but the Nazarene community not yet displaced by Paul's *ecclesia* in Rome? And as these Nazarenes were to go on to create a dynastic succession based on Jesus' blood relations, a succession of heirs (*desposyni*) preserved by name down to 132, should it not be self-evident that the claims made by this same group as late as 318 before Sylvester I cannot any longer be ignored by Christian scholars?

The original Jesus community survived and, according to Hugh Schonfield, was still in existence in northern and eastern Palestine until the fifth century. To suggest, therefore, as is common among Christian scholars, that this original community was quickly reabsorbed into Judaism is to make a mockery of history. Hyam Maccoby too rejects this tendency of scholars to make the Nazarenes 'slip back into Judaism', for it does not fit with New Testament evidence, and is clearly born from the need to make uncomfortable facts vanish. Yes, Jesus seems to have been on Paul's side, and Paul's Christology was certainly very different from that of James' Nazarene party, but the extraordinary belief system eventually developed around Jesus by Rome's exalted Christian leaders was perhaps as different from Paul's belief system as Paul's was from that of the Nazarenes. For it is not only the Nazarenes who have been made to fit into a pattern that did not actually exist, Paul too has been made to creatively fit a pattern not entirely of his own making. By exactly what margin this is the case is still to be decided, but no one seriously interested in Paul's theological-cum-social constructions can surely ignore the two faces of Paul as presented in the New Testament. Maccoby would argue for Jesus being of a Jamesian persuasion, and would, I think, consider the later Roman Church a natural extension of Paul's theological vision. I would argue for Paul's theology and historically suspect interaction with the Nazarene community (in both Jerusalem and Rome) being used by what remained of the Christian community, and eventually reconstituted by a usurping ecclesiastical hierarchy desperate to legitimize its growing power among the scattered Christian communities.

So it was not so much all Paul's fault then, but certainly born out of his basic theology, a theology based not on imagination, but on the verifiable facts of a Jewish-Arabian mysticism devoted to the God/man Essa. Totally integrated and elaborated upon by the end of the second century, and by the fourth part of a picture thought perfect in continuity. There was no problem then for Pope Sylvester to dismiss these rough Nazarenes when they turned up, these 'poor ones' claiming the right of apostolic succession from Jesus through James. For with the Emperor Constantine at his elbow, and the Roman army virtually at his command, Sylvester could see no good reason to rock the barque of Christ as it set sail for what he believed would be a glorious future.

CHAPTER TWELVE

With Our Mother's Milk

The calibration of our minds towards accepting conscious sleep as natural, and the fact that many of the Gnostic sects sprang from the same Nazarene background

Christian heretics of the early centuries are not discussed very much; rather, they are simply dismissed as deviants who do not require any explanation. There was, it is believed, a single community of believers called 'Christians' in the beginning and the heretics were those who held alternative notions about Christ and had to be banished from that community. It was that simple. There was a single doctrine of Jesus as the Christ of God, and in unbroken succession we are recipients of that doctrine because the Church has kept her eye steadily on the central truth of Jesus' divinity and mission. You either accept or reject the fact of Jesus' divine mission, and on the basis of your decision end up in Heaven or Hell. End of story. End result of 2000 years of faithfulness to a set of ideas considered to be the revealed truth.

That is the basic Christian argument, and it is utter nonsense. For there never ever was a simple community with one set of beliefs; there were dozens of communities, and those eventually deemed heretic were those who lost out in the power struggle between ideas. It should not be presumed that those who won this struggle were correct, and the others wrong (for that is exactly what I meant by 'dismissed as deviants'); this is an attitude deeply entrenched in the Christian psyche. Passed on to the unsuspecting faithful as if self-evident when it is in fact nothing of the kind, this attitude is roundly rejected by scholars but accepted by clergymen as the regulating will of God. But it was not until the fourth century that this 'regulating will of God' got under way at the hands of Athanasius, Bishop of Alexandria, who in his 39th Festal Letter let it be known that only certain books were to be considered divinely inspired, and therefore canonical. As from that moment the lines of demarcation were drawn, the books not on the list being deemed either apocryphal or heretical and proclaimed anathema. The scene was now set for conflict, those who had considered themselves good Christians on Monday discovering to their amazement on Tuesday that they were now classified as heretics. The dividing line was in place, the sheep and the goats were about to be separated with a vengeance. And all because Athanasius was 'influenced by the need and advantage of the Church', a statement of simple truth laden with dire implications for the future.

The effect of Athanasius' 39th Festal Letter on the broad sweep of Christian communities was one of fear – those in possession of the aforementioned apocryphal writings (previously termed 'gospels') had to get rid of them; it was either that or own up to holding a view of Jesus at variance with this powerful faction. It was not as if Athanasius had not experienced the same thing himself – a mere 11 years earlier he had been forced to hide in Upper Egypt as a result of a doctrinal shift among those of his own group. So it can be said that ideas about Jesus and his status had been quite fluid up until this point, but from the moment this churchman produced his list of inspired books, the atmosphere changed. For it was no longer a matter of arguing over this or that approach, it was now a matter of being declared 'already dead' (cut off from Salvation) by the ruling faction if you persisted in your use of writings considered subversive. In *Fragments of a Faith Forgotten*, G R S Mead puts his finger on the pulse of the whole thing when he says that the Scriptures eventually turned into a literary fetish deprived of reason, and that 'inspiration had ceased in the infancy of the Faith'.[1] The 'textual God' had again appeared, and he was about to stamp his disapproval on everyone and everything out of alignment with his pet group.

When he published his book in 1960, G R S Mead wrote of Christianity's origins 'being imbibed with our mothers' milk', and of it being an integral part of the consciousness of the Western world. Stamped upon, and interwoven with, our earliest memories, the sheer solemnity of Christian doctrine finds its way into our heart of hearts; that is, it affects us deeply without our realizing it. And even if unconcerned with its ideas and beliefs on the surface of consciousness, we may still be strongly influenced by those ideas and beliefs at the unconscious level. For some, this results in an unquestioning attitude towards Christianity, a curious inability to shrug off the superstition that somehow, against all reason, Christianity is probably correct in its pronouncements in spite of much evidence to the contrary. For others, it is a nagging doubt about their rejection of Christianity. Which suggests that anyone born within the confines of Christendom has a struggle on their hands if they wish to shake off the claim that Jesus was literally God in a human body, and that the Christian Church was in the mind of God before the world came into being. Did I say struggle? Sorry. I meant to say 'battle'. For as Mead points out, Christianity is something we have grown used to, it is a part of us at the cultural level, and as such is backed by the stupendous power of inertia which force of custom carries.[2] Hence death-bed conversions and the sudden leap that some people make from unbelief to belief. We've been got at, and our principal spiritual battle is waking up to that fact.

THE GNOSTICS

What better place to start than in the first century among the many Christian communities trying to develop their ideas through direct experience of God and self. That is where it was all happening; no wonder Athanasius was so worried. There were Christian communities out there with the most extraordinary ideas – ideas which undermined the Roman Church's authority and treated it as no more than another branch of the faith. A branch! Imagine! And that was not all. Some of these so-called Christians believed that Christianity was a system of lost knowledge that could be translated into a world philosophy. The soul could be known in the same way as the body, and in the end Christianity as an exact science of the soul could be made satisfying to even the most exacting intellect. Designated as the 'first-born of Satan' for their intransigence against the ruling élite, many of these communities were forced underground, and the result was an ever-deepening subversion which spread its tentacles in all directions.

Given the blanket name of 'Gnostics' because of their insistence that *gnosis* (knowledge) was integral to spiritual wisdom, these intrepid explorers of the inner reality reached conclusions about God, self and world which the Church felt compelled to reject. And they were eventually in a position to make their rejection stick, for by the fourth century previously victimized Christian bishops were in control of Rome's legal arm, and any group considered heretical were defined as criminals and persecuted as such. So the narrow orthodoxies of the Church became the norm, and Christian teaching was reduced, as Professor Stephan Hoeller puts it, to the lowest common denominator. The Roman 'branch', because of good fortune (Constantine's beneficence), had taken over and was now able to dictate both the content and direction of the Faith. The Faith was now 'Roman', and would soon be 'Catholic', that is, universally accepted, because of power-politics being played to the nth degree. Accused by the Roman Church of having created doctrines allied, not to Christ, but to the thinking of Plato, Pythagoras, Aristotle, Orpheus and Heraclitus, the Gnostic communities were categorized as corrupt in their basic vision and dismissed as a universal danger. And this in spite of the fact that the Gnostic writings make no direct allusion to these philosophers at any time.[3]

Successful in terms of it being the centrally positioned controlling Christian faction in the Roman Empire, the church at Rome worked to accommodate its rapidly growing flock by simplifying its message of the Christ; the result was, as Hoeller so accurately states, a reduction to the lowest common denominator of what had previously been a faith carrying considerable subtlety. Retreating to the monasteries, some Gnostics adapted as best they could to the mental restrictions placed upon them; others withdrew and formed secret congregations, nurturing, in Mead's words 'a hidden life of great activity'.[4] Private libraries of banned books were legion, and 'schools' or 'workshops' were formed where a veritable science of the sacred was developed. The Church was appalled. These Gnostics seemed to be in every thicket, their teachings ever more dangerous to, and distant from, orthodoxy, and nowhere more so than in Egypt, at Alexandria, where the greatest public library in the pagan world was housed. Thus the Alexandrian library was probably the principal source of information on past religious systems for Gnostically inclined Christian scholars, and this may well have been the reason for its destruction by fire at more orthodox hands. Then there were the mystics, those inner travellers to whom the staid doctrines of the ruling Church were merely echoes of things deeper and richer. And not just an undisciplined rabble of esotericists, as the Church would still like us to believe, more often than not they were highly disciplined and skilled groups of individuals dedicated to a purpose which the Roman Church had already lost sight of – spiritual liberation, a liberation of the spirit alligned with Jesus' own suppressed teachings. Yes, there were rogues and vagabonds and charlatans among the Gnostics, and some of them may even have been quite mad, but no more so than many of the orthodox churchmen of the day. They too had an unorthodox element, and could be said without contradiction to have perfected the art of being odd long before the close of the fourth century.

But I would like here to concentrate on one particular community, namely the Mandeans, for it is among this curious congregation of individuals that one detects the remnants of the old Nazarene Church so impudently ejected from Rome by Pope Sylvester I in 318. Stephan Hoeller unravels the basic historical complexities surrounding this group when he refers to the Mandeans as 'non-Christians', and notes that they 'constitute a vital, previously missing link connecting the gnostizing late flowering of the Essenes with the classical Gnosis'.[5] That sums up the whole situation pretty well, I think, and allows us to explore the issue of the Mandeans and their origins from a respectably speculative base. For as it insinuated in the literature regarding this group, there is every reason to believe that the Mandeans were either an offshoot of the Nazarenes, or that the Nazarenes were themselves part of a larger grouping originally termed 'Mandean'. Dr Hugh Schonfield calls the Nazarenes 'Mandean-Nazarenes', so making them one and the same. This accords with the now growing notion of the Ebionites and even the Nazarites as being integral to the Nazarene party.

The principal clue to their identity lies in their reverence for John the Baptist, and their bitter rejection of the idea of divinity being applied to Jesus by the church at Rome. Referred to by the French scholar Simone Petrement as 'Gnostics', the Mandeans are linked again and again with the Nazarenes and described as an unresolved historical problem. Unresolved indeed – Petrement has it that the Mandeans are 'a mixture of Jewish-Christianity and Gnosticism'.[6] The plot thickens, for these Jewish Christians seemingly viewed Christianity as an 'enemy', saying outright that it should not be believed in. Yet they are called Jewish Christians, and that seems to connect them with Christianity. So what is going on? Is it possible that scholars are overlooking the obvious, that the Jewish Christian Church was not Christian at all, but rather Nazarene?

Simone Petrement's answer is Yes, eventually, but with qualification. She agrees that both the Jewish Christians and the Mandeans called themselves 'Nazarenes', and she notes that

Mandean Gnosticism closely resembled Christian Gnosticism in its heterodox evaluation of Jesus, but she then moves off into the influence of Christian Gnosticism in Syria and Egypt and thinks the 'Christian' influence on the Mandeans may have come from there. While that is of course quite possible, my bet is that these 'Christian' Mandeans have simply been badly labelled, and that it is the labelling that has bedevilled scholars ever since. The distancing effect of the Mandeans from the Christian Church noted by scholars is therefore not some late phenomenon, but in my view integral to their character and belief system right from the start – they are quite possibly all that remained of the original Nazarene Church of Jerusalem.

But Petrement is not finished there, she then states that it is more defensible to say that Mandeanism has a Christian rather than a Jewish origin,[7] and finally reveals that she thinks that this is so because the original Mandeans were probably the Jewish Christians who left Jerusalem before the siege of the city by the Romans in 70. This, however, leaves the word 'Christian' tacked on to the Nazarene-Mandeans, yet at the same time separates these Nazarenes from their fundamentally Jewish, heterodox orientation, and makes them into Christian apologists allied to Paul, which they certainly never were. So the point of confusion is the word 'Christian', for in spite of being applied to the Nazarenes by just about everyone, this term did not apply to these Torah-loving Jews of Arabian, sectarian descent. Remove the hyphen from 'Jewish-Christian' and the puzzle is not only solved, it is also resolved. Petrement is quite aware that this is the case, for in the early pages of her massive work on the origins of Gnosticism she states plainly, in relation to these Nazarenes, that 'in the early centuries of our time, there was a Judeo-Christianity that was not Christianity at all but simply a branch of it, which was soon considered heretical'.[8] Why? Because in spite of venerating Christ, they 'did not consider him absolutely divine or consubstantially united with the one God'.[9]

THE MANDEAN-NAZARENES

The controversial Biblical scholar, Dr Barbara Thiering, does not pull her punches on the question of whether Jesus survived the crucifixion or not; she states unequivocally that Jesus did not die on the cross, and is of the opinion that he remained the leader of his party for almost 40 years after that gruelling event. In deep seclusion for both political and ascetic reasons, Jesus is said to have met regularly with Peter and Paul to guide them in doctrinal policy changes, and these changes led finally to the separation of the Christian party from the Jewish Nazarene party led by Jesus' brother James. Now Thiering's claims are highly unusual in terms of Biblical scholarship, and her methodology is still under question, but the very fact that she can seriously make such claims and hope eventually to prove her methodology sound, suggests that New Testament studies may yet deliver up surprises in relation to Jesus' life, crucifixion and resurrection. The whole story has not been told and the discovery and translation of documents and Gospel fragments may finally reveal unexpected levels of complexity.

No more so than with the Mandeans, who carry within their doctrines and history vital clues as to how Jesus was seen by his contemporaries. For as Jean Doresse revealed in his 1958 study of the Egyptian Gnostics, the Mandeans eventually denounced Jesus as a 'teacher of falsehoods',[10] and this coalesces perfectly with what we learned in chapter 10 from Christopher Knight and Robert Lomas of Jesus being both a 'heretic' and a 'betrayer of secret doctrine'. These authors observed that present-day Mandean-Nazarenes in southern Iraq trace their heritage back not to Jesus, but to John the Baptist, and that these people 'take their name from the word "Manda" which means "secret doctrine" '.[11] Identifying these Mandeans as being of 'direct descent from the original Church of Jerusalem', Knight and Lomas then link the name Nazarene with the phonetically similar 'Naassenes' – whose doctrines also sprang from Jesus' brother James – and observe that they had a strong distaste for anything sexual, and an equally strong preference for cleansing by water.

This carries us back both to the restrictive mind-set of the Qumranite Essenes and to Stephan Hoeller's introductory statement that the Mandean-Nazarenes were non-Christians constituting 'a vital, previously missing link connecting the gnos-tizing late flowering of the Essenes with the classical gnosis'.[12] Suddenly, the whole picture begins to blossom with meaning, the Nazarene Jerusalem Church being seen to have been much, much more complicated in its origins and eventual effect than previously supposed, or admitted.

This, of course, leaves us with the conundrum of how the Mandeans could be simultaneously worshippers of Jesus, yet consider him a heretic and betrayer of their secrets. These are diametrically opposed views, and cannot be reconciled, surely. The fact is, they can be, for as 'Mandean' is another name for the Nazarenes as a baptizing sect, and the Nazarenes were composed of both orthodox and heterodox branches, the anomaly is resolved. It was the Damascus Nazarenes (possibly a branch of the Essenes) who schooled Paul in his new perception of Jesus, and were later dubbed 'Christians' at Antioch, and it was the Jerusalem Nazarenes of Jewish (Pharisaic) alliance who opposed Paul's new vision with their Torah-abiding conception of Jesus as the Messiah of Israel. Doresse confirms that the Naassene claim to have received their doctrines by way of Jesus' brother James is correct,[13] and states that other groups such as the 'Peratae' the 'Sethians' and even the 'Ophites' were basically the same heresy under other names. Dividing into a number of sects which remained fundamentally united in thought and teaching, the Naassenes, however, reflected not the heterodox teachings of the Christian Nazarenes as developed under the guidance of Paul, but rather orthodox Nazarene belief with, perhaps, its Arabian doctrinal background developed as a form of gnosticism after James' death.

The case seems to be that in spite of being devout followers of the Torah, which Paul's Christian-Nazarenes were not, the Jerusalem Nazarenes were at the same time unorthodox at base. This is what separated the Jerusalem Nazarenes from Judaism proper; they were called 'Nazarenes' for that very reason – they were a highly influential Jewish sect harbouring many ideas at variance with Judaism in spite of their orthodox veneer. And so we have a 'Mandean' conglomerate of baptizing sects, and the Naassene choice of their name reveals what lay at the base of it all, for this Hebrew name translates as 'serpent', and this corresponds unequivocally, as we shall see, to the idea of deciphering and finding out in the old Sumerian-cum-Genesis sense of that word. Here then is the root of the *gnosis*, the underlying theme of knowledge and comprehension made available to the high Gnostic initiates, and it has nothing whatsoever to do with intellectualisms. In fact, it could not be further away from the idea of 'knowledge' in the conscious sense, for it reflects not 'head knowledge' (as the Christian Fathers so erroneously supposed) but a methodology or discipline through which an enlarged perception of self and the world could be had.

THE MYSTERIOUS RACE OF PERFECT MEN

The initiates of Gnosticism were not the muddled idiots the early Church Fathers took them to be; they were skilled scientists of the soul armed with an exact vocabulary. By 'soul' I do not mean some curious substance or spiritual geometry hidden within the human breast, but the potential that we each possess in relation to our personal growth and maturity *in combination with others*, whatever their level of development might happen to be. *That* is the bottom line of Gnosticism when it functioned properly, and the attempt by the Church to distract attention away from this movement and make a laughing stock of it through jibes and false accusations is another of the crimes Roman Christianity still has to answer for.

It can of course be argued that there were mitigating circumstances – much of Gnostic imagery and symbolism was so obscure as to be utterly unintelligible to anyone looking in from the outside. Doresse echoes the problem when he says of the Naassene-Ophites that their cult of the serpent cannot be explained,[14] for in the topsy-turvy world of Gnosticism the evil serpent of Genesis ought to be reversed and exalted as the 'revealer of *gnosis* to Adam', so making him into a saviour figure; in fact this does not happen. Doresse is puzzled. But he would perhaps not have been so puzzled had he had access to Julian Jaynes' study of the bicameral mind. With Jaynes' insights at his disposal, I think he would have immediately realized that the *gnosis* of Genesis is entirely different from this the second *gnosis* – the *gnosis* of the return to the bicameral space via the subjective 'I' which first arose. So the Genesis serpent retains something of its evil reputation for the Naassene-Ophites, for it was after all the advent of the subjective 'I' which first created the mental barrier separating the speaking God from the listening heart. By this phrase I mean the reactive space, or chamber, within which the subjective 'I' eventually evolved, that extraordinarily versatile space which allowed human beings to function without the knowledge of a personal existence such as we now have. To put that another way, it was as if they didn't awake when the car journey was over.

The language of the Naassene-Nazarenes is still obscure, but it is no longer unintelligible. Jean Doresse gives us the basic code being used is as follows: the human brain is 'Eden'; the membranes enveloping the brain are the 'heavens'; and the head is 'Paradise'. Epiphanius makes similar observations in connection with the Ophite-Nazarenes. He observes that there is a river with branches flowing out of Eden (the brain), and these branches he identifies with the human senses. The eye is the river Phison; the ear is the river Geon; and the breath is the river Tigris. Doresse's footnotes also reveal that 'the land of bondage' (Egypt) in the Biblical Genesis equals the *evil of matter*; so when it is said that the Gnostic master Mani 'left Egypt', it simply means that he died. Here then is the underlying meaning of Gnostic teachings made clear, the verbal code used by these early psychologists brought to the surface for our scrutiny and admiration. And at the base of it all a vision of reconciliation, a vision of opposites reversed and in union, a vision in the 'heavens' (high up inside the head) of a coiled serpent which speaks not of evil, but of energy. So when in their obscure teachings these sectarians speak of Christ 'mastering the serpent',[15] they do not mean that he mastered evil, but that he brought the serpent as *energy* (the energy of the biosystem in relation to consciousness) under control. That, basically, is the key to the whole edifice of Gnosticism, and without that key we are left with Christianity as it has now become.

It is interesting to note that the human senses play an important role in relation to Gnostic enlightenment. Perfected man is not concerned with beliefs about anything in particular, he is an experimentalist who has realized that sense perceptions are responsible for an anomaly in human consciousness – namely sleep. But not the sleep of the night, rather the sleep of the day, the sleep of perceptually identifying with the world to such an extent that we forget to remember ourselves and become veritable automatons for much of the time. Caught in *physis* (matter), as the Gnostics were so fond of saying, we function in a not dissimilar fashion to our pre-conscious ancestors (we are unaware), but do have the ability to wake up to ourselves from time to time. 'Wake up to yourself' we say to others (and to ourselves), and in using such an arrangement of words reveal an unconscious knowledge of our shared predicament. We are asleep on the face of reality, hypnotized by its demands, somnambulistically ensconced in thought, speech and deed to such an extent that our ability to will an authentic act is all but non-existent. Or, as the Gnostic Jesus says: 'Know what is before thy face, and what is hidden from you will be revealed to you.'[16] So what is hidden? The Kingdom of God, of course. It is there right in front of our eyes, but we cannot detect its presence.

In Gnostic terms, human beings are slaves chained to the world, beings who continually suffer because their senses have been usurped through attachment to the world. Only in this sense is matter 'evil'; it is not evil in its own right. And so in one of the Gnostic texts we read that Jesus, in relation to a stage of Salvation, reverses the rotation of the world to counteract its effect. It is the *effect* of the world that is being battled against, not the world itself.[17] But there is a barrier between the worlds, and to penetrate beyond it, this seemingly impassable barrier, it is necessary to first realize that this exists, and then consciously attempt to dismantle it.

Doresse writes of this in exact terms: 'This "gnosis" moreover, is to be not so much a "knowing" as a remembering; it is to awaken the neophyte, to recall him to his original nature.'[18] This suggests that the Gnostics saw our original primordial nature as superior to matter, that is, not under the sway of 'perception' locked into matter; but that is perhaps too hasty an interpretation. Yes, these Gnostics were certainly enamoured by the possibility of linking up again with the original energy of consciousness, but they clearly understood the dangers involved – their story of Christ mastering the serpent confirms this. It was not just a matter of returning to the primordial state, the state before consciousness emerged, it was a matter of balancing conscious and unconscious energies so that both were operative at the same time. Getting perceptually locked in matter was our first awakening, our 'Genesis', our primary experience of ourselves *as* selves over against the world as objective event. Our second awakening was the attempt to break the chains of perceptual slavery to matter, to the world of distraction and engagement, and initiate a sustained condition of conscious awareness over against the self as subjective event. We had escaped once, now we had to escape all over again.

The subjective 'I' was seen to be fast asleep amidst all of its grand conscious activity, and only through extraordinary effort could it find the will to surface, as a conscious self, for any length of time. Oddly enough, this resistance was not due to the 'I' warding off the idea of transcendence (it rather liked the *idea* of transcendence); it was due rather to the utterly banal fact that it could not resist dipping back into the mesmerizing stream of conscious engagement. Whether internally or externally, the demand to function without cognizance of self was simply too great. And on top of all this was the added factor of having to suffer consciously as it witnessed not only its inability to remain awake, but also its inability to relate to others. Weighed down by the burden of the conditions it placed on others, it more often than not closed down the process of its own transcendence through fear and shame. Fearful of what was being revealed, and ashamed of its own inability to attain what every human being on the planet already believed themselves to have attained, it fell or fled or slipped back into its narrowly focused stream of attention. In Gnostic terms, this was the nature of the battle we were each engaged in, and it was a battle so subtle in form, so invisible because of its high visibility that we mostly lived and died without ever realizing that there was a problem

The Jungian analyst Erich Neumann captures the intricacies of the situation when he says that consciousness 'is a *late product* of the womb of the unconscious'[19] (emphasis added). Just how late may have surprised Neumann. He also notes that this process is going on in our daily lives, in the act of falling asleep and awakening from sleep, and talks of us re-experiencing the emergence of consciousness from unconsciousness during the early stages of childhood. For it is in childhood that the process of falling asleep and awakening takes on special significance, and that significance is allied to the fact that the child is not yet properly conscious, but still embedded in primordial unconsciousness even when awake. In a world all of its own, the child, through its parents, engages in the struggle to attain the kind of consciousness possessed by its parents, and in due course succeeds because of them. This ascent towards consciousness, says Neumann, 'is the "unnatural" thing in nature . . . and constitutes the history of man's conscious development'.[20]

And so it has always been, right from the very beginning when the first conscious stirrings occurred – there was a battle to be engaged in. So the problem is nostalgia. We are nostalgic for our primordial beginning. We intuit it to have been a paradisiacal state greater than our present conscious state, and if we are religious, we are tempted to make a return journey in search of it. What we do not realize is that we are then in great danger of losing everything gained since human beings first emerged from the blind security of creation's womb. The outcome of this dangerous stage in conscious development is termed 'uroboric incest' by Neumann, and refers to such things as 'the *unio mystica* of the saint to the drunkard's cravings for unconsciousness and the death-romanticism of the Germanic races'.[21] Such a desire signals self-abandonment, surrender and regression; it is, in other words, infantile. Thus said Neumann in 1949, and his observation that the infantile ego is responsible for this tendency towards self-abandonment holds good today – we are, in other words, ever in danger of regression and surrender to forces inimical to consciousness.

THE DILEMMA OF THE NAZARENES

To not properly recognize the existence of the Nazarenes, or their role in early Christianity, is to be under the influence of a distorted history. The Nazarenes are fundamental to the story of Christianity, and ignoring them changes nothing. And if they are not ignored, but called by other names and made to disappear into the historical morass by a sleight of the theological imagination, then there is still a problem by way of the tearing effect they have on the fabric of historical analysis. So when Christian scholars say that the Nazarenes, as a group, reverted into the fold of Judaism, and are therefore of no historical consequence, they are in fact manipulating history to suit themselves. For these Nazarene sectarians neither left nor joined with Judaism again, they simply continued to run parallel to this great religious tradition as they had done from the very beginning. Sectarians for the very reason that they harboured ideas and doctrines at variance with Judaism, yet deeply attached to Judaism by way of devotion to the Torah, the Nazarenes attracted many thousands of Jews into their ranks and became a religious force to be reckoned with. Described by Hugh Schonfield as having a leadership functioning not unlike the Sanhedrin, this Jewish scholar goes on to describe the Nazarene Elders as 'the *de facto* government of Israel loyal to the Messiah and exercising the same kind of powers'.[22] No ordinary group these Nazarenes; they were a power group carrying, if only in their own imagination, considerable authority.

But there were at the same time the other Nazarenes, led by Paul, and they were quite different again in teaching and doctrine. As Schonfield shows, the Jews could not tolerate the fact that

there were 'two rival authorities among the Nazoreans, two pre-
sentations of Jesus as the Messiah, two inspirations, two
gospels'.[23] This was the state of play during those early years, and
Schonfield's statement reinforces my contention that there were in
fact rival Nazarene factions. Paul was forced, on more than one
occasion, to attend the Nazarene Council when it met in
Jerusalem under James' auspices, so making James' Nazarenes an
authority that could not be ignored. Schonfield then makes the
same observation as Hyam Maccoby – Paul had no intention of
starting a new religion. He wanted his Christian-Nazarenes to be
recognized as *part of Israel*. The problem was that Paul's
Christians repudiated the Jewish Torah, and that made it impossible for them to remain within Judaism. This fact, in combination
with the problem of the Christian statement that Jesus was in
some sense 'divine', astonished Jewish orthodoxy and intensified
the split between the rival Nazarene groups.

This suggests that such a statement of doctrine was not made at
the beginning of Paul's ministry, and that he kept his elevated theology of the Christ, and his full rejection of the Torah, under wraps
for some time. If he had not done so, the split with James' Nazarene
party would have been immediate. And if, as I contend, Jesus was
alive and well and there, somewhere, in the Pauline camp, then that
rivalry would have been even more intense. For Jesus was, it should
be remembered, James' elder brother, and whether James liked it or
not, that made Jesus, as the Messiah returned from the dead, the
legitimate leader of both groups. So it is with an inflated confidence
that Paul first appears before James (a confidence which has long
since mystified scholars), for is he not an Apostle created by Jesus
himself, and is not James bound by blood and station to seriously
consider and listen to his declarations? And James did listen, he did
attempt to accommodate Paul's requests, and this strongly suggests
that Jesus was alive; for only he (and the Nazarene leadership in
Jerusalem) had the authority to confer such a title on anyone.

Hugh Schonfield adds the finishing touches to this situation
when he notes that Paul 'claimed an intimacy with the mind of
Jesus greater than that of those who had companied with him on
earth and had been chosen by him'.[24] Now Schonfield did not
believe that Jesus was alive in the sense that I suggest, but it is
interesting to note that this Jewish scholar did believe Jesus to
have survived his crucifixion, and to have inadvertently died of the
spear wound delivered while on the cross. This is to say that he

saw Jesus' death as a mistake, as a plan gone wrong, as an extraordinary act of courage and spiritual bravado which almost came off. With regard to James and Jesus' disciples, he describes Paul as having been 'a presumptuous upstart' in their eyes. For Paul quite obviously considered his authority greater than that of the Jerusalem Elders.

So why go along with Paul's claim to apostleship? Why humour him? Why accommodate him unless there was good reason to believe that his credentials were authentic? That is the question that has not been answered and to suggest that James only humoured Paul because he saw the possibility of making money out of the Gentiles is insufficient to explain the long and tortuous negotiations that ensued. No, Paul's Jesus was not visionary, he was flesh and blood and capable of exerting pressure on the factions as he waited for God to fulfil his side of the bargain. And there is a further piece of evidence to support this idea, for if Jesus had died on the cross, then James and Jesus' disciples would have ceased to believe in him as the Messiah. He had to survive for the Nazarenes to survive, for whatever their complexion politically or religiously, they looked to him as the *final* messianic arbiter of Israel's fate, and to be 'final' he had to live on in concrete terms. Dreams and visions by a few worthies would not have been enough; only someone they could touch and argue with would have convinced these tough-minded men to continue in the face of such opposition.

That there was another gospel doing its rounds is mentioned by Paul, a gospel of the 'circumcision' opposed to his gospel of the 'uncircumcision', and it is this Jewish gospel to which we must now turn our attention, for it is in fact not Jewish at all. In spite of its quite obvious Jewish trimmings, the Nazarene gospel of Jesus as the Messiah of Israel was in fact heretical in Jewish eyes, for this self-same Jesus had been rejected by the Jewish nation and crucified by the Romans as a political subversive. These were the ugly facts of history, and they could not be conjured away. Jesus was a failed Jewish Messiah, an apostate Messiah, a Messiah of Galilean imagination who had flouted the very law James' Nazarenes upheld, and this fact made the Nazarenes suspect in Jewish eyes in spite of the Jerusalem contingent's obvious devotion to the Torah. And there was more, for like John the Baptist, Jesus had broken with the ancient religious code of Judaism and made the individual more important than the collective, and there were even Nazarenes who said that his crucifixion had been an atonement for Israel in its own right. This was the heart of the matter, for such views made the Torah obsolete by definition, and on top of it all was the little matter of militant Nazarenes angering the Romans and endangering Israel's whole future. On the whole, a bothersome bunch these Nazarenes, and the branch called 'Christian' was proving itself the most recalcitrant of all.

So is it surprising that after the fall of Jerusalem to the Romans in the year 70 the Jews should later earmark the whole Nazarene conglomerate as responsible for the debacle that took place? And is it surprising that the Jews should compose a curse to be read in the synagogue so that Nazarenes in general, and Christian Nazarenes in particular, could be winkled out and expelled? The *birkat ha-minim* curse (composed approximately 80 CE) admirably sums up the whole situation, for it links these Nazarenes with the idea of 'apostasy', and in doing so accuses them not only of assisting in Israel's destruction because of their militancy, but of having abandoned the vows and principles of the Jewish religion. The prayer-curse against the Nazarenes is quite explicit – it wants these Nazarenes to disappear, it wants them removed from the book of the living. Strong sentiments. A total rejection of everything the Nazarenes stood for in spite of their orthodoxy in Jerusalem, and indicative of the fact that their surface orthodoxy obscured beliefs not in accordance with Jewish religious practice. And that in spite of James the Just's impeccable orthodoxy, which suggests that we are not being told the whole story in relationship to these Nazarenes. So who were they? What were they up to? And why did they end up carrying the blame for just about everything that went wrong for Israel? Apart from the Zealots, no other group was so stigmatized, and the attempt to gather these Nazarene factions under one banner and make them all 'Christian' in outlook is at best a mistake, and at worst an attempt at concealment.

THE FRAGMENTATION OF THE NAZARENES

The apparent fragmentation of the Nazarenes into Ebionites, Mandeans, Naassenes and others, suggests a group of some internal complexity either regrouping for purposes of survival, or perhaps reflecting particular aspects of doctrine and belief.

Or both. And as it is known that Jesus' brother James was an Ebionite leader, and that the term 'Mandean' probably applied to the whole Nazarene conglomerate, then the appearance of so many Nazarene branches post-70 becomes less problematic.

For instance, the word 'Ebionite' simply means 'the poor', and seems to have constituted a branch of the Nazarenes specifically interested in diet. Being strict vegetarians, the Ebionites can be said to have deviated from the main Nazarene body and to have taken on a separate identity as a result. But although separate in this sense, they were in every other sense still part of the Nazarene fold. Schonfield is adamant on this point, being of the opinion that the Ebionites cannot be regarded as a separate denomination to the Nazarenes for the very reason of their belief that Jesus was born in a normal manner, and their categorical rejection of Paul's divine Christ. Such thinking, he argues, sets them firmly in the orthodox Nazarene camp.[25] Epiphanius, Bishop of Salamis in the fourth century, states that the Jewish Christians (Nazarenes) wrote an anti-Pauline book called the Acts of the Apostles, and that the Ebionites used a book by the same name. Oddly enough, James the Just is mentioned in this book as being against the Temple, and is said to have rejected Temple sacrifices and the fire on the altar. Now as James was a leader of the Ebionite community due to his own dietary habits, this expansion on his beliefs cannot but be of interest, and the added factor of James being of singular importance to *all* of the Nazarene groups should not be overlooked.

Neither can the fact recorded by Epiphanius that the Nazarenes possessed Hebrew versions of the Gospels of Matthew and John, and the Acts of the Apostles. As these books were not translations of the canonical gospels, were anti-Pauline, and presented a picture of Jesus at variance with 'Christian' tradition, the existence of gospels and travel tales predating the canonical gospels and Acts has to be considered possible. It is interesting to note in this respect that the Jewish gospel parody – the *Toldoth Jesu* – was based not on the canonical gospels, but on the Nazarene-Ebionite texts;[26] this rather suggests the Nazarene gospels to have been the original gospels in Jewish eyes. In conjunction with this, the word 'Mandean' stands out as important in its own right, for as we saw earlier, *manda* means 'secret knowledge', and this suggests that the Nazarene conglomerate considered themselves to be in possession of knowledge beyond Judaism's theological grasp. Having their own gospels, their own travel tales of the Apostles, and a body of doctrine considered so important as to be kept secret, these Nazarenes begin to emerge from the mists of Gnostic speculation as not at all staid in the manner reflected by their founder, James the Just.

Referring to the general run of texts used by the Gnostic sects, Jean Doresse mentions as 'noteworthy' the fact that these heretical 'Churches', despite their surface differences, used the same myths and the same writings.[27] This suggests that there was an underlying continuity of thought allied to Jesus which, although at variance with the canonical Gospels, and difficult to interpret due to complexity of image and symbol, was nevertheless coherent at base. And when one realizes that these seemingly incomprehensible images and symbols are stand-ins for the human brain, the inner landscape of consciousness and sense-perceptions allied to a system of 'transformation', the whole strange scheme shared by so many sects begins to take on a quite different aura – these Gnostics were not as silly as they sounded, merely ultra-cautious in the face of a growing persecution. Doresse puts it thus: 'The sects knew how to hide from their enemies a great deal of their mysteries.'[28] He is not at all sure that many of the Church's accusation against the Gnostics have any foundation, for he notes that the same sects seen through different eyes can be described in a completely different light.

On this score it is important to realize that the Gnostics were written about mostly by their Christian enemies, and that these Christians had very good reasons to discredit teachings linked to Jesus' brother James and their Nazarene precursors. Doresse eventually gives in to his suspicions and says, 'Was Gnosticism really such a shapeless conglomeration of different religions, disparate philosophies, of astrology and magic as is here painted for us, perhaps in forced colours?'[29] Forced colours indeed. And he has good reason for his suspicions, for, odd as it may sound, even those Gnostic sects with no apparent Nazarene connection held James the Just in high regard. I wonder why.

THE REGROUPING OF THE NAZARENES

Speaking of the Naassenes and the Ophites, Simone Petrement wonders if their claim to be Gnostics meant that they saw that name as the name of their sect; or whether, as is more likely, they saw the name 'Gnostic' as meaning Christian. Irenaeus makes an interesting slip in this regard when he speaks of heretics as 'Gnostics falsely so-called', so making orthodox Christians 'Gnostic' by definition.[30] With her usual clarity, Petrement sums up the situation by saying that Gnostic heretics probably used the term 'Gnostic' in all innocence, and that their use of this term did not mean that they saw themselves as a sect within Christianity. This French scholar also notes that sects claiming to be Gnostic are of relatively late date, probably around the middle of the second century. As such, they reflect an adopted state in reaction to a Church who used the term 'Gnostic' by way of derision.

The Church, in its estimation, had the true *gnosis*; the Gnostics did not and were given the name 'Gnostic' by way of sarcasm. In relation to names in general, the facts of the situation seem to have been as follows: Names such as 'Ophite', 'Naassene' or 'Peratae' were not designatory in any real sense; they were merely labels stuck on to certain otherwise unnamed groups with particular doctrinal proclivities discovered in their writings. Petrement makes this plain when she says of Irenaeus that he did not really know who the Ophites were, and that he simply created this name out of their writings because he could not identify their principal teacher, or master. Mead concurs. Ophitism, he says, 'is a general term among the heresiologists for almost everything they cannot ascribe to a certain teacher'.[31]

Oddly enough, the meaning given to Ophites by the Church Fathers is 'serpent worshippers', and this links them directly with the Naassenes, whose name also means 'serpent'. But not in quite the same sense, for it is one thing to have the word 'serpent' *in* your name, it is quite another to be nominated 'a serpent worshipper'. Mead explains the situation by pointing out that such an accusation was merely a term of abuse – the early Fathers of the Roman Church were not above twisting the truth of a situation to their own benefit. And it *was* to their benefit to deride Christians who just happened to believe that Jesus was an ordinary man born of ordinary parents. For whatever else they said about Jesus, and whatever the nature of the doctrines they created out of experimentation, that seems to have been the basic belief of these so-called Gnostic Christians. And it was this Nazarene-oriented rejection of Rome's divine Jesus that eventually made these groups anathema in Rome's eyes. Hence the background fact that the Ebionites, Ophites, Naassenes, Mandeans and Peratae are *all* Nazarene affiliated – in other words, they are coexisting offshoots of the Jerusalem Church attempting to challenge the Roman Church on its progressive elevation of Jesus to the heretical status of God incarnate. Even the title 'Peratae' is a mock-up, to use the appropriate term, for it means 'son' or 'word', so revealing itself as a conceptual extract and not an actual name.[32] Schonfield sums up the whole crazy debacle with the following statement:

> Catholic Christianity had good reason to seek to discredit the Nazoreans and to brand them as heretical. For one thing it was fatal to the doctrine of the deity of Jesus that his own Apostles and the Christian membership of his family had held that he was no more than man, and had been anointed by the Spirit of God at his baptism, thus becoming the Messiah (the Christ). The true apostolic tradition had to be fiercely denied and controverted; but in the late second century when a movement arose urging the Church to return to what came to be called the Adoptionist view, that Christ had been received into sonship of God when he was baptised in terms of Psalm ii. 6–7, its advocates could still point out that this view had been held 'by all the first Christians and by the Apostles themselves'. The evidence available establishes that they were right.[33]

As a result of the war with Rome, the Nazarenes fled Jerusalem and migrated to Pella in the year 66. Schonfield thinks it likely that at least some of the leaders escaped, and adds that the Nazarenes were numerous in other parts of the country, so allowing for a regrouping. But many must have died in Jerusalem, caught in the swell and turmoil of a city besieged. By the year 70 all the main characters in this extraordinary play of forces were dead. James, Peter and Paul were dead, as were most, if not all of the original disciples. Jesus, too, was probably dead. Governed by the family of Jesus, the Nazarene party went through a period of disintegration and factionalism, but eventually regrouped. The Roman Church had its own troubles, undergoing a long and arduous period of persecution at the hands of its Roman masters. Evading capture, members of Jesus' family elected Simeon, his first cousin, as head of the Nazarene administration, and this set the pace for a dynasty of Hebrew leaders carrying the traditions and beliefs of the original Nazarenes into the future.

According to Schonfield, the Nazarenes congregated in the outlying areas of Galilee, Auranitis and Gaulanitis, and managed not only to survive, but also to proselytize these areas successfully and bring many Jews into the Nazarene fold. Holding doggedly to the belief that Jesus was the true Messiah of Israel, these Nazarenes underwent the persecutions of the Emperor Domitian, and during the Bar Kochba revolt refused this new Messiah recognition. Cut off from the Christians, and suffering from what Schonfield refers to as 'eccentricities' due to being influenced by Baptists, Essenes, Samaritans and others, the Nazarenes nevertheless managed to sustain a central system of government. Known as the Heirs the family of Jesus was later written of by Hegesippus as 'those who take the lead of the whole Church as witnesses, even the kindred of the Lord, and when profound peace was established throughout the Church they continued to the time of Trajan Caesar'.

On having recorded this statement, Schonfield laments the fact that so little is known about these Nazarenes and their leaders due to a loss of records, adding that he suspects such a loss of documentation to have been due to wilful destruction and suppression. He then notes that both Eusebius and Epiphanius acknowledge the Nazarenes to have survived persecution and gained large numbers of Jewish converts, which implies that the Nazarene groups considered in this chapter were, as already suggested, more homogeneous than as presented by the heretic-hunting Church Fathers, and this is confirmed by Malachi Martin's reference to these self-same Nazarenes appearing before Pope Sylvester I in 318.

So the whole situation can be summed up thus: the scattered Christian community with all its differences and anomalies eventually succumbed to the new faith as presented by the Roman faction, and from then on the Nazarene Mother Church, itself fractured into many related groups, was deemed heretical because it viewed Jesus as an ordinary man chosen by God to carry the title of 'Messiah' ('son of God' in symbolic terms), not 'Christ' in the theological sense of God literally made manifest in human flesh. Powerless to fight the Roman Church because of its military strength, the Nazarenes did the next best thing, they went underground and blamed Paul for all their woes. In a sense they were right to do so, for Paul eventually drove the Jesus myth right to the edge of blasphemy, and after his death the embryonic

Roman Church toppled his theology of the Christ into the abyss of imagination run riot. And Peter is the other unfortunate, for he is made to change sides and become the connecting apostolic link affording the Roman Church a continuity with the Nazarenes that never actually existed in real terms. All in all, this is a pretty depressing tale, and no less depressing today when one sees the teeming millions still emotionally subservient to a faith whose credentials are at heart forgeries.

Is it any wonder then that Western spirituality has failed to bring about that intrinsic change in the human spirit so long hoped for? Is it any wonder that our civilization has raped and plundered the whole globe in the name of Christ? And is it any wonder that we are now faced with a multi-faceted Church rent by conflict, hatred, sexual abuse, misogyny and general small-mindedness? If it were not so pathetic, the Church's bravado in the face of ever-encroaching proofs as to her real nature would be laughable, but so much suffering and stupidity has resulted from her theological makebelieve that laughter is not appropriate. Imbibed with our mother's milk, the manipulated story of Jesus has been used to calibrate our mentalities to an alarming extent and, as suggested at the beginning of this chapter, our principal spiritual battle is waking up to that fact. Backed, as Mead said in 1960, by the 'stupendous power of inertia, the force of custom, against which but few have the strength to struggle', our task is to become properly conscious of our conscious existence, not merely spectators locked fast in conscious dream. *That*, I believe, was Jesus' ultimate message, but it has become scrambled beyond all recognition.

CHAPTER THIRTEEN

The Personal God

Human consciousness, the development of the self and the central nervous system's organization of the archetypes

Why a personal God? Why the move away from polytheism with its major gods and goddesses to an eventual proliferation of minor gods and goddesses to the idea of one big God who can be related to personally? What happened to make this happen? And where does Jesus fit into this puzzle? Why did he make the move towards a personal God and shrug off the distancing aspect of Judaism and the Law? Why the Jewish fascination with Law; and from where and for what reason an *empty* Holy of Holies in the Jerusalem Temple? Why an empty room at the heart of Judaism?

THE ORIGINS OF OUR SPIRITUAL HISTORY

In *The History of the Devil*, the French author Gerald Messadie speaks of Mesopotamia as the place where the West's spiritual history was forged.[1] Few scholars would disagree with him. So why such a resistance from many Christian scholars to properly recognize the infiltration of religious ideas from ancient Mesopotamia into Judaism and Christianity? Why the tendency to either ignore such connections, or belittle them as mere background noise to the main event of Christianity's birth in the first century CE? An historian turned philosopher who has written controversial studies of the life of Jesus, Messadie says that travellers to Mesopotamia today would find it hard to believe that the grand empires of Sumer, Assyria and Babylon had been fashioned from these flatlands. They might also be astonished to learn that the concept of Satan, or the Devil, most probably started in Persia six centuries before Jesus appeared on the scene. But I think they would be even more astonished to learn that it was in Mesopotamia that religious consciousness probably underwent its most remarkable transformation – a transformation in substance without which Judaism and Christianity could not have arisen.

The uncomfortable truth that Christian scholars had to contend with as the world opened up in the mid-nineteenth century was that their civilization had its roots in the cultures of the Near East, and that Greece and Rome, like Syria and Anatolia before them, had merely acted as conduits for religious ideas and experiences belonging to a third millennium empire called Akkad – a civilization which itself reflected the even earlier civilization of Sumer. What a shock that was; it immediately began to undermine the idea of divine revelation without a precursor; for it quickly became evident that Christianity's claim of historical and theological uniqueness was, to say the least, overblown. Yes, Jesus had certainly taken a personal direction when speaking of Israel's God, and this was without doubt a change in direction from orthodox Judaism's insistence that Law was all that mattered, but there was much in Christianity and Judaism that resonated with earlier religious ideas, and this resonating of concepts and religious experience was more than a fluke, more than a chance similarity due to proximity of cultural and language – Christianity was (and still is) merely a stage in the evolution of religious consciousness, and perhaps a retrogression rather than a progression when its long and violent history is examined in detail. The more astonishing change in religious consciousness had erupted in Mesopotamia during the third millennium, and it is to the great civilizations of Mesopotamia that we now must turn in our attempt to understand the transition of human consciousness from one level to another.

THE STILL SMALL VOICE

In his quite extraordinary book *The Origin of Consciousness and the Breakdown of the Bicameral Mind*, the psychologist Julian Jaynes cites some figures on auditory and visual hallucinations recorded during the last century in England. Using only normal people in good health in these studies, it was shown that out of 7,717 men, and 7,599 women, hallucinations were experienced in 7.8 and 12 per cent of these groups respectively. Oddly enough, twice as many visual hallucinations as auditory were recorded, and such experiences were most frequent between 20 and 29 years of age. Jaynes points out that this is the exact age at which schizophrenia generally appears. As to why such an old study was used, the reason given is that treatments such as Thorazine (chemotherapy) now eliminate hallucinations altogether. Questioning the use of such treatments, Jaynes notes that patients experiencing hallucinations are generally friendly and more positive towards others than non-hallucinating patients.[2]

For our purposes, however, his most important observation is that 'Hallucinations *must* have some innate structure in the nervous system.'[3] Even schizophrenics 'profoundly' deaf since birth can apparently experience auditory hallucinations, and these can range from the voice of God to that of angels, devils, enemies or dead relatives. Voices can also come from woods or fields, walls, cellars or roofs of houses, from Heaven or Hell, from parts of the body or even from bits of clothing. Such voices threaten, admonish, command, instruct, mock, sneer or curse, and can even be experienced as 'foreign bodies' welling up in the mouth. And in what Jaynes calls 'twilight states', scenes of a distinctly religious nature can be hallucinated in broad daylight – the heavens can stand open and a God can speak to the patient. And it doesn't much matter that it is only the patient who hears or sees in this manner, for they consider themselves 'singled out by divine forces', and feel compelled to obey these 'elemental auditory powers' without question.

Julian Jaynes' basic thesis is that schizophrenic hallucinations are of a similar order of experience to that of communication with the gods in antiquity. That is his main tack, and it is a useful theoretical structure to have at hand when considering both Old and New Testament auditory-cum-visionary phenomena. A study of modern schizophrenia throws much light on the inner voices and visions experienced in Biblical times, and Jaynes seriously suggests that the whole of third millennium Mesopotamian society was naturally schizophrenic or 'bicameral', that is, two-chambered, or double-minded in their experience of the self. Which is to say that their experience of the 'self' was not at all like ours, but more in the form of a non-conscious, non-subjective self governed by a dominant self which seemed to be a separate entity of divine dimension. The authority of such a voice (or voices) was absolute; it was an authority which could not be argued with. And schizophrenics today consider their voices objectively real in spite of life's general experiences. Capable of gaining a measure of control of their voices after long experience, they are however generally held in a position of unquestioning submission.

To help us get to grips with this startling thesis of schizophrenia having been a general condition of third millennium society, Jaynes puts forward the observations that when listening to someone talk there is a sense in which we momentarily become the other person; that is, we let the other person become part of us for a few brief seconds – we let them 'in' by allowing what is being said to completely usurp our attention. A second or two later we are again attending to our own thoughts as primary, but during those moments of real listening we become secondary to the primacy of the other. Which is to say that we momentarily suspend our identities, that we hold our psychic breath and allow the other to breathe for us. Conversation during which a willing suspension of identity does not periodically take place in the other produces frustration and the sense of the other not communicating properly. Only by making such a move can we truly understand what the other is talking about, for to understand the other means to *under*stand, or stand 'just below' the other, to 'give way' to the other with respect to conscious attention.[4]

Spatial distance also plays an important role in our influencing of the other, or in their influencing of us. There are culturally established distances for general communication, and these are only broken under special circumstances. Stand too close to someone during a conversation, and you will see them back off to a safe distance. Jaynes makes the point that when someone is too close there is the sense of their trying to control your thoughts; when too far away, of their 'not controlling them enough for you to understand . . . comfortably'.[5] The latter part of that statement carries a much greater punch than many psychologists might suppose. Conversing with someone at a proximity under what we generally allow either means we are in the presence of a lover or an enemy. Hence face to face threatening during which one person gains authority over another. And again there is an unusual insight from Jaynes when he points out that our constant judging of the other, our constant criticizing and pigeonholing of the other in our heads is simply our attempt to regulate the other's influence over us. Perhaps too our bouts of inattention when another is speaking, when in spite of quality of content we decide to hold the other at arm's length by refusing to *under*stand them. Imagine then the loss of control when the 'other' is a disembodied voice inside one's own head which cannot be kept at a safe distance. What to do then? Unhindered by boundaries, this voice cannot be drawn away from or reduced in authority through criticism. It is all-prevailing and encompassing; it is a voice as omniscient and omnipotent as the old voice of the gods, and cannot be disobeyed.

But surely that is to misunderstand the word 'voice' in relation to these early societies? Isn't the word 'voice' merely a way of speaking based on a way of describing an imaginative relationship with the gods of antiquity? Isn't it no more than a metaphor when used by these ancient peoples? Perhaps not. Julian Jaynes presents a convincing case for such voices having been an integral part of everyday life in all ancient societies; which is to say that the voices spoken of in the old texts were heard in a literal manner. If a man or woman said that a god had spoken to them, they were not playing some imaginative game, they were reporting an experience which no one doubted because they too heard similar voices on a regular basis. Jaynes' point is that individuals then were not individuals in our sense of that word; they were non-subjective. Non-subjective? How could such a thing be? How could someone who had built a society, related to others and had children not have a subjective self? Jaynes' answer is surprisingly simple: through a split-brain process (parallel processing?) still with us to a limited extent in normal individuals, and fully visible in those experiencing strong schizophrenic episodes. Pushed about like a robot by internal voices which were part of his own psyche not yet integrated into a neuronal whole, early man functioned without a personal ego.

The questions this raises are twofold: What does it feel like to function without a personal ego? And, can such a state be described or defined? The answer to question two is 'Yes'; but it requires a certain ingenuity of mind to imagine ones way into question one. For what one has to do is imagine a situation within which ego is not operative, but consciousness can be clearly seen to function without impairment. Jaynes chooses the driving of a car to illustrate the point, and his observations perfectly capture the oddity of a mind simultaneously conscious and unconscious. For when driving a car we often slip into what is commonly referred to as 'automatic pilot', and during this phase somehow manage to avoid other cars, not mount the pavement, apply brake and clutch when required, and arrive at our destination unscathed. Enthralled by personal thoughts, or by a conversation with a passenger which carries us into deep subjective involvement, we *unconsciously* drive our car and arrive where we wish to go with little actual memory of how we managed to do so. Jaynes refers to this unconscious state as being in 'a totally interacting reciprocity of stimulation . . . while my consciousness is . . . off on other topics'.[6] Subtract that consciousness altogether, and a nonsubjective or egoless human being is caught in the searchlight of our conscious scrutiny. Jaynes tells us that 'the world would happen to him and his actions would be inextricably part of that happening with no consciousness whatever'.[7] So if confronted by a blocked road, or a flat tyre, such an individual would not react as we would react, he would be forced to wait for his inner voice to speak a solution from stored-up 'wisdom' – which is not at all the same thing as saying that his memory came on line. In this sense the divinity would convey the necessary information so that the man might extricate himself from the situation.

Describing the gods and goddesses as 'organisations of the central nervous system',[8] Jaynes says that they gave orders, advised and led in a similar fashion to the ego/superego relationship postulated by Freud. Truly hallucinatory in origin, the gods had a separate existence inside the individual, and as societies grew in complexity the individual incorporated and organized the voices of his superiors into an internal pantheon of authority figures whose voices could also be heard *within* the individual. The king obeyed the dead king as a god, heard his voice within himself, and when he too died, became the admonishing and advising voice of the king who followed. The lowly labourer did not hear the voice of the dead king (that would have led to anarchy); but he did hear the voices of his immediate superiors, and had the dictates of the higher gods relayed to him through a priesthood. Every household had its own shrine containing idols or figurines, and these were the personal gods of the ordinary people, little gods who could be importuned to speak with gods more elevated in the divine hierarchy. The old texts stated that a man lived in the shadow of his personal god, and Jaynes tells us that personal names usually reflected this close relationship between human and divine.

With the breakdown of this dependent mental state, and the first flickerings of subjectivity proper, the priesthood would have blossomed into a complex hierarchy where prayers (one-way talking) would have taken the place of actual dialogue with the gods, and this in turn would have resulted in the construction of intermediaries such as angels and demons. Perhaps this is why angels looked just like men (the wings were added later) in spite of being able to enter the presence of divinity – they had simply retained bicameral ability – and why demons encompassed the notion of breakdown and anarchy. For there must have been a long transition period when individuals already subjectively inclined were identified by their bicameral brothers and sisters as 'different', and such individuals may have been looked upon as evil because of their ability to practise deceit, the deceit of hiding, on a long-term basis, the fact that they were now *thinking their own thoughts*. But when almost everyone had reached this stage of subjectivity, the stragglers would in turn have taken on a special aura, for were they not the only remaining ones capable of speaking directly to the gods? The whole notion of Satan/Devil/Lucifer being the 'father of lies' begins to make sense in this context.

But first chaos and breakdown. For when the hallucinated voices eventually weakened and all but disappeared, the individual must have found it difficult to make up his or her mind about anything. But that they did eventually make up their minds is obvious, and that they knew something dramatic had happened within themselves is on record. Jaynes uses the *Iliad* as an example of human beings functioning without ego, but notes that at the end of this great poem Hector and Agenor *talk to themselves*. Nothing terribly unusual in that for us, but to these two characters a unique event, an event of such astonishment that they both use exactly the same words to describe the experience. Jaynes records their words: 'But wherefore does my life say this to me?' Indeed, for which cause or reason had the words materialized? There was no divine context. The words had appeared as if from nowhere and there was no indication that a god, goddess or interiorized superior was in control. Such words would have seemed to come from nowhere, out of sheer emptiness, to have formed in the mouth without prior existence and be curiously without conviction.

That must have astonished the speaker. Which raises the question: did these changelings experience incipient subjectivity in the same way as we sometimes experience inspiration? Could it be that they found their own voice sounding within them as odd as we find the voice of inspiration which occasionally breaks into audible clarity? For we do hear that voice from time to time; we do sometimes actually hear another voice articulating the sentences or ideas we are about to speak *before we speak them.* Perhaps the hangover of this is our incessant need to talk to ourselves, why we slip so easily into our inner world of dialogue and disappear from sight. Left only with Elijah's 'still small voice' to nudge at us during creative reverie, we stumble from one conscious decision to another. How odd. How odd we look, all of us, as we mumble our way through our lives. And how difficult for those who just happen to be wired up a little differently, who actually have the curious ability to hear, and sometimes see, pathologically confused remnants of the old divinities.

THE PROCESS OF BREAKDOWN

Julian Jaynes draws our attention to the Sumerian epic poem *Atrahasis*, for it contains a vital sense of breakdown in communication between the gods and human society.

> The people become numerous . . .
> The god was depressed by their uproar
> Enlil heard their noise,
> He exclaimed to the great gods
> The noise of mankind has become burdensome . . .[9]

The problem was that as society became more complex, so did the decisions that had to be made. And the sheer number of decisions that had to be made was equally daunting. So the deities proliferated to handle the vast flow of new contexts (Gerald Messadie speaks of 4000 gods), and advanced polytheism became the way out of a problem which in turn created its own problems. Literally swarming with gods and goddesses and internalized authority figures to handle the ever-growing trade in decision-making, there arose the need for some other organizing principle to control the mental traffic of village life become city life. Termed the Intermediate Period by scholars – who insist that outside force did not cause the recorded breakdown in social cohesion – authority frayed to breaking point, broke, and initiated a period of chaos. Jaynes speaks of a built-in periodicity in bicameral theocratic collapse allied to loss of hallucinatory control. That feels right; and it also helps explain the constant desire of later theocracies to return to earlier forms of worship, the desire to re-enter a Rigorist-type relationship with the gods based on revelation alone.

The extra organizing principle that arose seems to have been writing, the ability to create grocery lists and so contain the problem of what went where to whom and why. There were no banks. Jaynes tells us that the word translated as 'money' is incorrect – no money has ever been found from these early periods. He even rejects the word 'rent', replaces it with 'tithing', and talks of wine being 'exchanged' rather than 'purchased'. Imposing modern categories of thought on what was basically a bartering system, modern scholars have inadvertently distorted our picture of the distant past and allowed us to assume the existence of civilizations not unlike our own in mentality.

So says this Princeton psychologist, and the more one reads of this extended period with Jaynes' overview in mind, the more it seems that this precocious thinker may be correct. Writing things down seems to indicate a reduction in auditory hallucination, a change-over from the god's voice to a personal voice in rudimentary form, from the certainty of divine communication to the vagaries of human speech and the ever-growing interpretative necessity of written language. So two things were happening simultaneously: the taking of control away from the bicameral mind due to the pressure of a civilization grown too large, and the breakdown of the bicameral mind towards the subjective state which may in itself have been driven by evolutionary pressure. Hence Richard Friedman's disappearing God of the early Old Testament period; God had simply served his purpose and been replaced by the self-serving 'I' of the individual. Banished into the hinterland of consciousness, this disappearing God would show his face from time to time, but only a Moses or a Jacob would have the capacity to hear and see him.

But these divinities who had once inhabited the human brain were not out for the count. They were still distantly there. Near. Still subjectively sensed and worshipped from afar through a growing corpus of texts trying to describe the way it had once been. They were far away yet still near. Really close, yet spoken of through the distance of language in the head and in writing. And every so often there occurred an individual with the bicameral gift of hearing and seeing the God at first hand, of knowing what the God wanted, of being able to speak the God's words

and guide a village or a whole society as it manoeuvred subjectively through the deep and treacherous waters of intellection
and subjective desire. There was a sense of deep awe as such individuals straddled the mental divide and revealed the corrective
steps for a society gone wrong, for a king who had forgotten the
needs of his people, for a priesthood reduced to guesswork. But
sometimes there was a distorting voice, a garbled mixture of
bicameral gift and subjective imagination – authority without
substance. And sometimes no gift at all, just a cunning simulation
of powers bestowed.

But before this stage of breakdown and replacement there was
the need for little personal gods to talk to the big impersonal gods
who were fast receding into the heavens due to social overload.
Functioning as an adjunct of language evolution within the individual, the gods articulated to the individual what the individual
already knew but *did not know he knew until told*, and the result
was a system of personal volition identified always as 'other' until
subjectivity proper (the next step in an evolutionary process allied
to the spread of language) began to form. Jaynes is careful not to
make the arising of consciousness a biological necessity; instead,
he places the emphasis on the growth of language as a spoken and
written medium carrying survival value. It is language which initiates the slow change from bicamerality to personal subjectivity,
and it is the use of language which will eventually slam the door
on bicamerality altogether.

It would be only too easy to move into a discussion of what
consciousness is at this point, but that would take us away from
our theme of the personal god, and it is on this that I wish to
concentrate. Yet we cannot move too far away from such a
question, because it is integral to our understanding of what
happened to human beings during the third millennium.
Conscious of being conscious they seem not to have been, but
conscious by way of *reacting* to their environment and to one
another they certainly were. This fact clears the ground for
Jaynes' approach to how consciousness functioned in relation to
the 'I', and it does not seem to have functioned in the way we
generally think it functioned. Jaynes says simply that we are
'continually reacting to things in ways that have no phenomenal
component in consciousness whatever',[10] and this fact speaks of
our only being conscious *of being conscious* from time to time.
That, in a nutshell, is the problem we have to comprehend. If we

do not recognize that there is a problem, then we have simply not cottoned on to the explosive nature of what Jaynes is highlighting – we are behaving mostly in an unconscious manner during our waking hours as psychiatry has recognized for a long, long time. We are awake, but we are not conscious. We are engaged in conversation, but we are not necessarily conscious. We are reacting subtly to all sorts of stimuli, but we are not necessarily conscious. We are reading the words on this page, but we are not . . . Ah, now we are; and that is Jaynes' point exactly.

So what if we never bother to wake up and *remember* that we are conscious human beings, that we have the ability to shift focus and become conscious of being conscious? What then? Would it make any difference? Would we be able to detect that we had forgotten to be conscious of being conscious? The answer is No. We would not know. We would be quite *un*conscious of the fact that we were functioning perfectly well without a vestige of consciousness registering on us as an existential fact. And it is this rather startling fact that has to be appreciated before we can assimilate what was going on in Mesopotamia all those millennia ago. Jaynes postulates that there was no subjective recognition of a personal space, no 'I' to punctuate the days and years, no sense of self to break the internal trance of obedience to the god. They were living inside a cocoon of mind from which there was no escape. This is hard to imagine and to accept until we consider that we spend much of our time in a similar (but not identical) state, a state of suspended subjectivity, a state of reactivity which can last for hours or even days without us *waking up* to that fact. As Malachi Martin says of Father David Bones' state of consciousness, his 'autonomous will' wasn't used much; he just went along with the flow.

The point of this discussion is that the little gods not only helped produce a sense of connection with the big gods, they also inadvertently strengthened the sense of separation from the larger gods and at the same time highlighted the idea of the personal, the small, the intimate. It was a two-way traffic of influences which must have eventually helped rupture the once cosy bicameral connection and produce, in combination with the god's words as commands committed to paper, the first inklings of decision-making without divine assistance. For as Jaynes points out, written commands could be ignored, whereas injunctions straight from the 'god within' could not. Which suggests that the voices began to break

down and fall silent, that the gods began to withdraw as the clam-
our of large, complex societies increased, and that the advent of
writing developed on the gods' behalf was in fact the principal reason for the gods' final disappearing act. Relying more and more on
the god's words transferred to static written forms, to the god's
words repeated endlessly out of the original context, the individual
could, in a rudimentary fashion, sort of forget to remember to obey.
And in the growing, stuttering silence which developed within the
individual as the voice of the gods petered out, the first of many
recalcitrant thoughts began to take shape – thoughts which at first
utterly astonished the thinker.

In their well-researched and stimulating book *The Hiram Key*,
Christopher Knight and Robert Lomas confirm Jaynes' basic observations when they note that the relationship between the Sumerians
and their gods declined noticeably during the eighteenth century
BCE. It was at this point that the personal gods (who were generally
nameless) took on particular importance as 'guardians' of the individual, and were felt to be specifically related to the individual who
conversed with them. Such gods were inherited from within the
family, from the father, and as such lay behind the generally
misunderstood statement 'he worshipped the god of his fathers'.
The term 'father' in this sense did not refer to the nation, but to the
family of the individual, and expressed both identity and birthright.
Looked after by his personal god, an individual could however be
deserted by that god for not paying close enough attention to his
god's requirements, or for directly disobeying his personal god in
some fashion.[11] The great gods were already fading from everyday
life, and the personal gods were all that was left to keep the individual in his or her place. The great gods were still named and
called upon, but the voices which had once been hallucinated from
them no longer functioned. They were now just pieces of stone,
empty-eyed giants whose mouths were equally empty. And so a
power vacuum formed, and into that curious psychic emptiness
flew not only the angelic guardians, but also the dark powers and
shadows of individual subjectivity made doubly concrete.

It is interesting to note that subjectively conscious human
beings were at their most cruel when attempting to enforce the
secondhand, written words of their now silent gods. The whole
society had hung together when the god's voice was distinct, and
it had even managed a semblance of unity when the voices
became intermittent; but when the terrible silence struck there

was nothing to fall back on but the violence generally used against other societies and their gods. So the great codes of human behaviour appeared, the codes of Hammurabi and Moses, and with them the rise of aristocratically based priesthoods with the power to enforce ruthlessly whatever they claimed the god had said. The gods may have fallen silent, but the priesthoods in each society were all aclamour with their divined pronouncements and demands. No longer the certainty of directly inspired words and concepts, more a process of intuition, or guessing, a foreseeing or predicting or conjecturing which quickly deteriorated into a self-serving nightmare where external law replaced inner contract.

· The predictament of third-millennium man was that he eventually shed his slave-like bicameral relationship with the gods and found himself stranded on the human side of the consciousness continuum – he became subjectively isolated and began to trade ideas with himself. Alone where he had once been in a relationship, he did everything in his power to re-establish that relationship, but instead inadvertently distanced himself further still from the very gods he wished to draw close to, so setting up an ever-strengthening conscious barrier. And so the little household gods proliferated, and man's sense of his own existence in relation to such personal forces began in turn to personalize and strengthen his rudimentary sense of self, and when the process was complete he stepped out into the possibility of a life without any gods whatsoever. So the gods receded, and in all but name, statue and written text vanished from sight and hearing. But they were in fact still there, lurking in the shadows of consciousness as nudgings from another realm, and would sometimes unexpectedly break through the now strongly evolved subjective barrier in reverie or dream to reinstate their divine claim on the individual.

Our predicament, by way of comparison, is that we have completely lost sight of our bicameral beginnings, have had to wait until the appearance of a Jaynes to make similar observations by others academically respectable, and are now unconscious prisoners of subjective consciousness in much the same manner as we were once prisoners of objectively perceived divinity. Prisoners of a low-grade reality because it has never quite dawned on us that the reality we deal with on a minute by minute basis is lacking a prime ingredient – a sense of self – we function mostly without any sense of self, relate artificially (even when emotionally charged) to others caught in exactly the same trap of reactive consciousness, and the result is a world of misunderstanding and truncated reasoning. We are not present. We are fundamentally absent. We are on a mental holiday from our own space. We are no better than zombies. No. Not quite as bad as that; but damned near it. We do have the ability to wake up, and from time to time do so, but have the habit of again re-entering the zombie-like state so quickly that we do not properly detect that we have been awake and fall immediately back into the sleep of self-forgetfulness. If not concerned with philosophical questions, we imagine a continuity of self in time and space which in fact is without substance in existential terms, and only hazily sense that this is the root of our problems. We do not *under*stand one another, and seldom bring an authentic sense of our own innate existence to the innumerable social contracts we so robotically engage in.

On the other hand we categorically deny the existence of a self on any level, and in doing so become a menace not only to ourselves, and others, but also to the world we so outrageously inhabit as non-habited beings. Like the behaviourist who not so long ago could deny the existence of consciousness with a straight face, but never ever doubted his own, we can also deny ourselves a 'self' and inadvertently fall into the trap of a self-fulfilling prophesy. Forgetting to remember that we tend to forget ourselves most of the time, we succumb to our own private system of alienation and confirm our own worst fears.

THE HEBREWS

The earliest sections of the Old Testament are most probably borrowings from earlier centuries, and from a variety of countries, and did not necessarily take place in the time order given, or even entail the people named. The nomadic Hebrews, or Khabiru (also sometimes termed Hapiru, Habiru or Abiru), are known to have borrowed heroic stories, songs and sermons from others for their own use, and out of these literary artefacts constructed the beginnings of a linear history for themselves. This is not to say that they did not possess story-histories of their own, simply that they had an eye for a good yarn, a longing to understand their own origins in the larger context of prehistory, and an eventual historical purpose which helped transform nomadic wanderings into something a little more structured and attractive.

The Genesis story of the Garden of Eden, for instance, is Sumerian in origin, and many of the cities mentioned in Genesis (Ur, Larsa and Haram) belonged to that early civilization. Before the time of the Hebrew kings the people were overseen by 'judges'; this is seen in the fact that the ancient Sumerians were deeply concerned with 'justice', not merely with rules and regulations as the later Babylonians were. The Jewish New Year is a period of evaluation when human behaviour is weighed, and it is probably no coincidence that the Sumerians had a deity who annually judged the people, and that Abraham, the acclaimed father of the Jewish nation, came from the Sumerian city of Ur where the ancient stories would have been well known.

But perhaps the most telling overlap between these cultures is the Genesis story of creation and the unearthing of an artefact in Mesopotamia depicting an almost identical storyline. The image unearthed was of a serpent entwined on a tree bearing some kind of fruit, and the Mesopotamian texts speak of someone called 'Adapa' being granted knowledge, but *not eternal life* by the god Enki. By itself, such a find would be enough to make one suspect cross-fertilization of concepts, but when we discover that the Hebrew for 'serpent' is *nahash*, and that the root of this word, NHSH, means not only 'snake' but also to 'decipher or find out', and that Enki was the Sumerian god of knowledge, then the whole puzzle of Genesis begins to fall into place. For depicted along with serpent, tree and fruit is the moon's crescent, and this symbol apparently stood for none other than the god Enki.[12] This does rather suggest that the Genesis story has been rearranged to suit some other purpose, and that the idea of knowledge gained at the expense of eternal life is a distorted and truncated version of human beings *waking up* or *consciously emerging* from the god's presence never to return. No longer a slave of the god's all-encompassing will, Adapa-cum-Adam became a person in his own right, a subjectively conscious individual to whom re-entry back into the god's space would have to be accomplished by other means.

Writing of the Genesis period, Paul Johnson notes the anomaly of an unvisualized God always being presented as a person. Curious. And this God who is a 'person' makes moral decisions, so presenting man with moral categories. Johnson says that this differentiated the Jews from the nations around them, who worshipped all sorts of things. And so the Jews are portrayed right from the very beginning as knowing right from wrong in an intrinsic fashion. The universe is fundamentally moral because God is moral, and this moral God eventually shows his hand by attempting to destroy the whole human race with a great flood because he likes neither their attitude nor their behaviour. And so we have the story of Noah and his ark, and the rest is Jewish history at its best.

Well, not quite. In 1965 the British Museum discovered two tablets referring to the flood in a deposit at Ur, Abraham's city of origin, and in this much earlier written record we again have a God regretting that he has made the human race, and resolving to destroy it with an avalanche of water. But it is not to be, for once again the god Enki appears and the humans are warned. Knowledge indeed. And twice purveyed to human beings by a god *separate from* the god who first banishes them, and then tries to exterminate them. Something odd is going on here. But what? Might it be that the god of knowledge, Enki, is in fact human consciousness subjectively at work within itself, and that the god of destruction is nothing more than the fears of the people projected on to the undoubtedly dramatic upheavals then taking place in nature? Our problem now is that we imagine people in the distant past to have been just like ourselves; that is, similar, if not identical, to ourselves re our mental processes. But it would seem that they were quite different; their mental state may first have been totally subjective. Later Jewish texts made Noah a righteous man, so creating a moral context for the story, but in the original tale the survivor is a priest-king called Ziusudra, King of the south Babylonian city of Shuruppak, and reigning in 2900 BCE.

What interests me about the Jewish account of the creation is that their unvisualized God is presented as a person. Why? Who is this invisible God who goes walking in the Garden of Eden in the cool of the day? And how can Adam and Eve hope to hide from this their creator? He shouts to them, and they hear his voice, and 'come out of hiding' to speak with him about what has happened to them. How odd. And how odd that they should suddenly realize that they are naked, whereas before they were oblivious to their nakedness. One minute unconscious of their state, the next minute conscious of it. One minute working for God, then all of a sudden possessed of knowledge which in some fashion made them not unlike gods themselves. And dangerous

too now that they had knowledge, for they could now differentiate between good and evil like God himself, and as such might
decide to go all the way and become immortal by partaking of
God's own special diet – the fruit of the tree of life. Curious. And
even more curious that all of this is a mishmash of folklore
and mythology and history laced now with morality and made
into the reason that human beings first lost contact with their
God. Disobedience is the keyword. Guilt is the result. Punishment
is the reward. And what a punishment. Exiled into a hard-edged
reality where they have to survive by their own efforts, by their
own intelligence, by their new power to decipher and find out.
And before that terrible moment of exile struck, the image of them
trying to explain and justify their actions to a God who was there
yet curiously not there, a God with whom they had a close
personal relationship, a God who had taken to leaving them to
their own devices knowing the dangers.

I think all of the above is self-explanatory within the context of
Julian Jaynes' thesis of the bicameral mind; it is very apparent as
one reads the text. And it does not take too much imagination to
realize that the God Adam walks and talks with is actually himself
as a split persona – he is simply talking to himself *as if* to another.
And Eve as the weak link in the chain is no more than a telling
glimpse into who woke up first – the tree of the knowledge of
good and evil is exactly what it says it is, it is a new capacity
of mind. But the whole story has been literalized; it is now long
after the event of bicameral breakdown, and the writer/compiler
of this ancient Jewish text is simply trying to make sense out of
something that no longer makes sense. But he recognizes the
borrowed text's importance, realizes that he is dealing with an
ancient conception of creation predating Hebrew existence, and
with the sureness of a good theologian creates a moral context to
explain the story's curious contents.

By the time of writing the Hebrew God was one God, he was
undivided, and that in spite of the fact that Genesis has God say:
'Behold, the man is become as one of *us*, to know good and evil.'[13]
(emphasis added) Us? Is there a Sumerian pantheon of divinities
lurking in the background here? But not for long; the Hebrew
conception of God as one God will evolve quickly and single this
people out as different from their neighbours. Well, not quite. They
will certainly evolve the notion of one great God, but it will take
many, many centuries to make that God the one and only God of

Israel. And this is where the problem lies, for as Paul Johnson points out in his history of this people, the Jews eventually saw everything in their past as providentially designed, and moral in context. Every step taken was either towards God or away from God, so making the times away from God an intrinsic part of their journey with God. That, however, is theology, it is not history. The whole history of the Israelites is the history of a people at odds with itself, and with its conception of God. The Israelite God shows himself to be peevish, jealous and insensitive. He is just a big kid with too much power. He is a bully in need of a good psychiatrist.

The Very Reverend Tom Wright (Dean of Lichfield) would reject my statement that much of Jewish history is theology in disguise. He would argue that such an arrangement *is* history, and his argument is based on the belief that there is no split between God, history and logic. If we believe in any kind of God at all, then that God must be there *in* history in some form at all times.

This is problematical; it hinges on the idea of a conscious God, a God who in some sense or other is a 'person', and as such drags us back into the kind of mental space harboured by Jesus' disciples, and used by the early Christian Church to excuse its worst excesses. It is, in other words, an epistemological dead end, and it is equally deadly in terms of extracting ourselves from the religious conflicts of the twentieth century. What is going on around us, and *in* us, has to be our touchstone; we simply cannot afford the luxury of perceiving God as an overblown human neighbour whose characteristics are mirror-reflections of our own in a state of ultimate perfection. If God is 'conscious' in any sense similar to ourselves, and 'moral' in some vastly extended human manner, then He does indeed constitute the menace many have suspected Him of being. For when all is said and done, such a God is no God at all, He is a fantasy of the human imagination which must necessarily fail in His humanly fabricated purpose because of constant aberration this end of the space–time continuum. If Christianity is presently the highest reflection of God on Earth, the only true measure of what God is and means, then we are surely in trouble.

THE TEXTUAL GOD

Jesus personalized the God of Israel and made him his 'father', so becoming a 'son of God' by definition. He entered into a new relationship with Israel's God, and in doing so set in motion a spiritual sensibility which reintroduced his followers to their hidden, bicameral aspect. But there was a complication. It was no longer a matter of simply returning to the old relationship with the God within, for subjective consciousness with its strong analog 'I' could not be dismantled, merely circumvented from time to time. And anyway, the whole idea of God had undergone a transformation; he was now a textual God, a God of the written word who could only be glimpsed by way of prayer and the Law. Only through the Torah could God be known. Or as the Gospel of John puts it: 'In the beginning was the Word, and the Word was with God, and the Word was God.'[14] It was now the recorded history of Israel and her Laws which constituted contact with God, the voice of the prophets having fallen silent long before. And so what a stir when John the Baptist turned up with his message of repentance for the individual. Who had ever heard of such a thing? The individual? Wasn't God's will only done when the 'nation' turned towards him? Wasn't it a collective effort that God expected?

The Baptist's message of repentance changed the whole focus of Jewish religious life, and after John's arrest Jesus took over and developed the idea of personal repentance further still. For in his spiritual vision personal repentance heralded a drawing close to God in a new way, and as a result of this shift in religious psychology God was intuited to reciprocate. The only problem with this was that the God who reciprocated for the early Christians was not the God who had walked with Adam in the cool of the day, it was the textual God of the Torah who came on line. Gigantic in conception due to having swallowed all the other gods of antiquity, God as the Word was too much for the subjective 'I' to handle in a personal sense; he short-circuited human psychology and the result was a scrambled-egg version of Judaism, and of much else. Trying to digest the textual God of Judaism drawn near, the early Christians inadvertently released within themselves something of the old bicameral relationship with the self, but in the end this activity of the mind intertwined with the heart broke down into the recorded charismatic chaos of Paul's enthusiastic congregations. Contact with what lay beyond the subjective 'I' had been made, but it was being forced through a theological filter which inadvertently distorted its shape and meaning. Recognizing that there was a problem with the early

Christian (Nazarene) Church on more than one level, the later Church curtailed such activity and channelled it through a return to reliance on Scripture. The Word was back in place with a vengeance, and to keep it all 'human', to keep it simultaneously personal and transcendent, the messenger was eventually transformed into the message by way of interpretive gloss. Jesus was now the Word made flesh. The problem was solved.

But the problem was not solved; it would reappear. Century after century the problem of Jesus being made into the Word, into God, into the message of good tidings for all human beings began to reveal itself as no more than an interpretive mistake. But it was too late to change. Too late to do anything about it once the Church had become a powerful institution utterly dependent for its status and credibility on that mistake. A Catch-22 not only with the capacity to disorient the participants, but progressively dangerous in its overall effect as societies grew ever more complex. And so grew the necessity to resort to the sword, to killing, to murder, to segregation and genocide so that God's blueprint for human salvation could remain steadily operative. The textual God was on the loose, and there was no arguing with him. His voice could not actually be heard, but his past commands could be heard loud and clear in the mouths of his priesthood. Forget the process of history, the process of science and medicine, the process of philosophy and mathematics. Forget the natural process of human development and relationship. It was all just a matter of belief, a matter of focus and faith and human folly brought to heel. God was in control *even* when everything was out of control, just as the Jews had continued to be his chosen people when estranged from his presence through outright idolatry. There was no escape. No escape in life, and no escape in death. Submission to the 'God of the texts' was the answer, the answer we each had to recognize and act upon before the blackness of death caught us in its irreversible clutches. The God of the texts. The God who had lost his voice and could now only be heard by way of priestly guesswork.

CHAPTER FOURTEEN

The Transfiguration

Passion and reason in the service of a ritualistic dream – a dream of perfect freedom for the human spirit

Marcello Craveri rejects the traditionally accepted Mount Tabor as an unsuitable location for the Transfiguration of Jesus due to its distance from Caesarea Philippi, the city visited by Jesus and his disciples prior to the event. He points instead to the majestic 8,500 feet high Mount Hermon as a more likely spot due to its close proximity to that city. While noting that both mythologists and rationalists have tried to explain this extraordinary story of shining light and physical transformation, he rather lamely suggests that one of the three disciples accompanying Jesus may have had a dream which he later related to the others. Michael Grant is similarly not convinced by the storyline of the Transfiguration. Describing the appearance of Moses and Elijah to Peter, James and John as 'conjured up' by the Gospel writers, he adds for good measure that the story 'contains elements that look like deliberate inventions'.[1]

In contrast to these authors, John Ferguson follows a slightly unconventional line of Christian reasoning and refers to the Transfiguration of Jesus as a 'mystic's ecstasy'. He also speaks of the disciples' experience of a brilliant light as a phenomenon well-known in mystical experience.[2] Holding to the pragmatic line, Craveri visualizes Jesus walking ahead of the disciples on some high ledge and being struck by a brilliant ray of sunlight. *Ergo*, the description of his being transfigured by a blinding light from Heaven is thrust into a more sensible context. No mysticism here. Yes, something important happened, but it was not the manifestation of divine power. The transfiguring moment for Jesus lay not in his prayers but in his decision fully to inaugurate the Messianic Age by undergoing ritual crucifixion at Jerusalem. That was the key to the whole affair.

Referring to the appearance of Moses and Elijah, Craveri speculates that the appearance of these two Old Testament figures probably signifies the arrival of two Essene monks to encourage Jesus in his pre-planned mission.[3] Essenes? Now this way of reading the text will be automatically rejected by Christians, but it may not be as unlikely as it sounds. Luke's Gospel states that there 'talked with him two men, which were Moses and Elias: Who appeared in glory, and spake of his decease which he should accomplish in Jerusalem'.[4] Two men? Accomplish? As the Dead Sea Scrolls scholar Barbara Thiering tells us that high-ranking Essenes carried, for ritual purposes, the names of archangels and prophets, Craveri's theory of an outsider influence has to be taken seriously. For as is now realized on a broad front, our mental portrait of Jesus has been deeply influenced by two thousand years of theological interpretation. As with the meeting between Jesus and Satan in the wilderness, these two men symbolizing both the Law and the Prophets are more likely to have been chosen advisers than hallucinations, literary inventions or Moses and Elijah visiting Earth from some other dimension. And so too with the men in white robes (referred to as men or angels in different Gospels) seen later at the tomb. Jesus, it seems, was not wholly dependent on his immediate quota of disciples – there were others working with him toward the completion of a Messianic plan. On this basis an alternative meaning can be given to Luke's report on Jesus' countenance being 'altered' as he prayed[5] – it could be said that he was anticipating (as he would again later in Gethsemane) what was in store for him at Jerusalem, but on this occasion experienced euphoria instead of fear and despair.

But perhaps more pertinent observations come from the historian Karen Armstrong. She notes that Jesus was in possession of certain 'powers' (*dunamis*), and that he promised these self-same powers to his disciples. But only if they had 'faith'. Faith? Faith in what? Faith in God of course. Jesus was not asking them to believe in theological propositions; he was asking them to 'cultivate an inner attitude of surrender and openness to God'.[6] There was not anything he, Jesus, could do, that they would not be able to do if they matched his level of faith and reliance on God – the powers of the Spirit were for everyone. Western Christians later interpreted the Transfiguration as God's power physically manifested in Jesus, and in line with Jesus' teachings accepted that a robust faith could produce the same powers in believers. Believers? Believers in what? Believers in Jesus as the Son of God come down to Earth to save all human beings in all ages from eternal damnation. This is to say that the proposition had changed from faith in God to faith in Jesus, and that faith in Jesus necessitated unerring belief in a rapidly growing theology built around Jesus as God incarnate in human flesh. The teachings of Jesus had been turned on their head.

Not without good reason, however, for in what he said and did Jesus seemed to reveal God's hidden love and concern for human beings, and observers eventually concluded that God had been literally glimpsed in Jesus. Speaking with the authority of a Moses, or an Elijah, this Nazarene had healed the sick and made demons subservient to his will. More importantly, he had accomplished a remarkable deed in Jerusalem, and it was this deed which marked him out as special. Transfigured in his innermost being, he had turned towards Jerusalem, and with a steely resolve consciously submitted himself to trial and crucifixion. Why? To complete Israel's centuries-old act of atonement. The ritual of crucifixion followed by a miraculous resurrection would usher in an entirely new covenant with Israel's God.

In Byzantine theology as developed by Maximus the Confessor (580–662 CE), human beings could unite with God. Karen Armstrong notes that this was a quite different approach from the Latins, to whom God 'was an optional extra, an alien, external reality tacked on to the human condition'.[7] The Western tradition is described by Armstrong as 'eccentric' because of its concern with sin and atonement, rather than with the human condition transfigured in the same sense that Jesus was transfigured – to conceive of God in such an eccentric fashion is to run the risk of making God into an idolatrous object *out there* somewhere. The Eastern Church, on the other hand, did not conceive of transfiguration as an 'invasion by a supernatural reality', but as 'an enhancement of powers that were natural to humanity'.[8] But it was necessary for us to open up to God for this natural condition to erupt – we had to surrender to God without reserve. Only then would there be triggered off that transformation and eventual transfiguration of heart, mind and body which Jesus, as an ordinary son of Israel elevated to Messiahship, had eventually experienced.

Now this is a long way away from saying that the disciples saw no more than Jesus lit up by the sun's rays and thought him transfigured; it is in fact to accept the story at face value and suggest, as John Ferguson has done, that Jesus probably did undergo some kind of deep spiritual experience on Mount Hermon. I concur. Something very powerful is going on in this story, and the temptation to sidestep it and see it as a normal event elevated through sleight-of-hand is perhaps to do it a grave injustice. This is not to suggest that the two men who appeared were in fact who they are said to have been – sectarian visitation is the more likely scenario. But as to Jesus having undergone some kind of epiphany as he contemplated what lay ahead of him, that is quite believable. And it is also probable that the surrendering of his will to the will of God was of such intensity that it produced psychic phenomena. Engaged in what seems to have been a ritualistic encounter with advisers sent to strengthen his resolve, Jesus may well have entered a deep state of contemplation.

Yet it is down to earth in many respects, this strange, light-filled story. The disciples are obviously extraneous to the event, mere spectators overawed by what is going on – a fact which should not be overlooked. Peter blurts out something about building tabernacles to Jesus and his two visitors, and the rather stupefied tenor of the statement puts these disciples outside of those who are in the know. So this is not so much a general conversation between Jesus and these sectarians as a set piece of theatre driven by the Scriptures and fuelled by deep emotion. It was a plan carefully executed down to the last detail; a plan which would even include the lending of a donkey to Jesus when he arrived at Jerusalem, and the hiring of a room by a helper not of his immediate group. Facts such as these cannot be easily explained; they have to be accepted for what they are – clear indications that Jesus was the central pivot in a politico-religious movement. Transfigured in body and mind he may well have been, but the very intensity of spirit which triggered off such an experience was allied to a purpose distinctly political as well as deeply religious. At the end of the day he was not only Israel's priestly Messiah, he was also Israel's Messianic King.

THE HUMANITY OF JESUS

To appreciate what happened to Jesus on Mount Hermon, we must first fully appreciate that Jesus was in every respect a human being. There was no doubt in anyone's mind that this was the case. He had grown up like any other child in Palestine. He was flesh and blood. If he cut himself, he bled. He could get angry, thirsty, hungry or tired. He was fully human in every respect; and in spite of rumour, his birth had been like any other birth. Both his mother and father were known to the disciples, and the family of Jesus was proud of the physical lineage which connected Jesus to the Davidic Kings through his father's line. This is to reiterate what we all know but keep on forgetting – that Jesus was a human being in every sense.

In fact he was so human that the New Testament cannot avoid recording that fact, and on one occasion reveals this human being at the end of his psychological tether. Sweating drops of blood in the Garden of Gethsemane as he contemplates the horrors of crucifixion, he shows himself not only capable of fear and despair, but in a few words places himself in a sensible context in relation to Israel's God. This is not God praying to himself, or an inexplicable bit of God talking to some other bit; it is a man fully conscious of his own inadequacy bending his will to what he believes to be a divine purpose. In this sense, the term 'Son of man' is not some clever allusion to veiled divinity, it is exactly what it seems to be, a reference to the fact that Jesus was *of* humanity in the fullest possible sense. And the term 'Son of God' should not be wrenched out of its original Jewish context and made into a literalism – such a title pointed only to his nearness to God, to the indisputable fact that he had surrendered more of his will to God than others of his generation. In his challenging book *Jesus and the Tide of Time*, John Ferguson quotes Bethune-Baker: 'It was not that the Son of God came down from Heaven, but that the Son of man ascended up on high.'[9] That, I think, perfectly captures the situation. Jesus was not God reaching down to man, but man reaching up to God. Perhaps this is the lost meaning of the Ascension story – he managed, finally, to make his will totally subservient to the will of God.

And what a will he had. No ordinary will here. No buckling at the knees through superstition or fear to the religious mumbo-jumbo of his day – a stark rejection of Judaism's sillier aspects and a constant searching for that perfect balance of love and determination to know the will of God at first hand. In this sense an autonomous will, a will and mind perceptually unshackled from ingrained religious patterns. Not just for the sake of being

different. Not just a rebel. Not just an anarchist. A man of sensibility and passion whose capacity to reason was in the service of
a grand dream – a dream of perfect freedom for the human spirit.
His was not a dream of perfection. No, what he was after was a
stripping away of stuffiness, not a thicker application of it to
human affairs. He had seen through the sectarian game and
wanted no part in any madcap adventure against the Romans. It
was not the Pharisees he was against, it was the nationalists that
drove him to a spitting anger. Yes, the Temple was in need of a
good cleansing, but it was these narrow-minded sectarians with
their interminable restrictions on thought and behaviour that
were the real problem – they thought they were going to initiate
the Kingdom of God on Earth, but what they were in fact about
to initiate was the greatest disaster in Israel's history.

The experience on Mount Hermon was a turning point for
Jesus. Before leaving Casaerea Philippi he seems to have experienced uncertainty of intention, hence his question to Peter:
'Whom do men say that I am?' It is almost as if he needs reassurance. But when that reassurance comes, he is unnerved;
Messiahship is suddenly too much to contemplate – he tells his
disciples to keep their mouths shut. Locked away in the safety of
his mind the idea of being Israel's Messiah was a manageable concept; but voiced aloud it took on the tenor of a mind deranged by
unseemly spiritual ambition. How could anyone claim such a
thing and hope to be taken seriously? It was one thing silently to
contemplate such a possibility; it was quite another to articulate it
for others to hear. Yet that was his conviction, and there was no
avoiding the consequences. He was Israel's Messiah; he was certain of that now. And others were just as certain. His disciples had
suspected it ever since the arrest of John the Baptist, and as his
meetings with the breakaway sectarians became more and more
frequent, any doubts his disciples may have had were cast aside.

But to imagine for one moment that Jesus thought of himself as
God incarnate in human flesh is to push his experience of himself
and God far too far – and that in spite of indications in the New
Testament that his name carried a divine connotation. Son of God
he certainly was, but not God's son in the literal sense. The whole
of Israel was God's *firstborn* son (Exodus 4:22), the adopted son
of God, and Jesus too, because of his obedience to God beyond
the restrictions of man-made religion, was also an adopted son of
God in this limited sense. He was the Messiah, and as the Messiah

was automatically termed 'Son of God' by way of messianic, archetypal definition.

This fact is clearly seen in Matthew 16:16 where Peter, in response to Jesus' question, says 'You are the Messiah, the Son of God.' And again in Matthew 26:63 when the high priest challenges Jesus with the words: 'I adjure thee by the living God, that thou tell us whether thou be the Messiah, the Son of God.' On both occasions the word 'Christ' is used in Matthew's Gospel, but this is merely the Greek word for 'Messiah', and has no connotation other than that. What is of importance here is the secondary title 'Son of God' tacked on to 'Messiah'. That is the give away. The eventual accusation of blasphemy directed at Jesus by the High Priest was not because he claimed to be God's son, it was because he claimed to be the *Messiah of Israel*, a claim soundly rejected by Israel's religious leaders in relation to this Nazarene leader. Yes, one man would eventually die for the people, but in religious parlance this meant only that Jesus would be sacrificed in order to nip sectarian dreams in the bud. Totally innocent of harbouring insurgent values, Jesus became the nation's scapegoat through dint of circumstance and association alone. This is to say that he was not somehow God dying for the sins of the people, but rather a man facing an excruciating ordeal as part of sectarian imaginings. To the religious authorities of the day he was no more than a bothersome Galilean who had to be got out of the way; to his sectarian followers and personal disciples he was the Messiah, the long-awaited archetypal Son of God.

CONTRADICTIONS AND CONTRASTS

The highly informal quality of Jesus' approach to religious observance is striking, particularly when it is weighed against the intensity of his spiritual life. How could he balance the two when such intensity was generally backed by Rigorist opinions and nationalistic tendencies? How could he stop himself from closing off instead of opening up when his whole background was infused with doctrinal fixity? Yet open up he continually did, find the balance he managed to do – and that in spite of the fact that he was a sectarian leader schooled in the aspiration of a Galilean sect with a long and complicated history. Holding views plainly at odds with orthodox Judaism, austere Essenism and the strict Pharisee-aligned

Nazarenism of his brother James, Jesus created a hybrid religious philosophy which in the early days angered his family and eventually split the Nazarene party in two. And it may even be feasible to suggest that he had a considerable following of dissident Essenes at his disposal. As it is thought likely that substantial numbers of Essenes helped swell the ranks of James' Nazarene party, it does not strain the imagination to suggest that Jesus too must have attracted liberal-minded Essenes into his camp.

Christian scholars will baulk at such a suggestion, but the tendency to keep the Essenes away from Jesus at all costs is now recognized by consensus scholars as untenable. In fact the Herodian party, which is a shadowy presence in the background of the Gospels, is thought to have been the Essenes by another name; and it is also thought likely that Jesus' stinging criticism of the Pharisees was in fact aimed at this very group. The basic story of Jesus has been tampered with, its focus changed, and an uncritical acceptance of that story as it now stands in the New Testament betrays a gullibility based on fear and superstition. If we are to move on in our understanding of Jesus, in our appreciation of his mentality and purpose, we have to learn to accommodate the uncomfortable fact that Jesus was a fallible human being, a Jewish sectarian in possession of a grand vision which failed. The Kingdom of God did not appear. The Roman Empire did not vanish in a puff of smoke. The nation of Israel was not heralded throughout the Gentile world as God's chosen people. There was only the carnage of total war, the destruction of everything ever hoped for, the realization that rabid nationalism and eschatological dreaming was in the end worth nothing at all. Ideological fixity, however handled, must always disappoint.

From the information available about Jesus in the New Testament, and from the studies of thinkers on both sides of the scholarly divide, it seems probable that this Nazarene was bound ideologically, and for purposes ultimately obscure, to the idea of undergoing the trauma of crucifixion. It was not by chance that he underwent arrest and trial – his arrest was stage-managed to the last detail. It was not by chance that he survived these horrors and continued to direct operations from the sidelines. But perhaps he was not quite the same man after the event as before it. For as the years passed and the expected Kingdom of God showed no sign of materializing, he must finally have accepted and assimilated his mistake. The plan had failed. The attempts of men to manipulate

God had failed. Nationalism had unravelled Israel, and a split Nazarenism had further muddied the waters. So the Zealots and the Nazarenes and the Christians were cursed and banned from the synagogues, and the Jews, scattered to the four winds, began to consolidate wherever possible. All was confusion, a scrambling to adjust doctrinal notions, a splitting of groups already splintered and a falling away of Paul's Christians in the east prior to the Roman invasion of Judea. Afterwards, with Paul and Peter and Jesus dead, there was a polarization of opinion about Jesus among those who still considered him important. Accepted still as the legitimate Messiah of Israel by the Nazarenes and Ebionites, this remarkable man's status was heightened by the Christians at Rome until he eventually matched the sun God, Sol Invictus. Later rejected by the Mandean-Nazarenes as a betrayer of secrets, he was progressively spiritualized by Gnostic Christians until the whole emphasis was laid on inner knowledge rather than stale doctrine. The Kingdom was about to take on an inner, rather than an outer reality.

But as he knelt in the Garden of Gethsemane and poured out his heart to God, there was no notion of any of this in Jesus' mind, nor of the grand fiasco he was involved in. Without doubt he was a godly man capable of intense self-scrutiny; a sophisticated man with a set of complex beliefs allied to culture and religious training; an insightful man capable of breaking out and away from the narrow fundamentalism of his day; and a courageous man willing to confront prejudice and religious xenophobia wherever he found it. But when all is said and done, he was a man caught up in the grand imaginings of a religious sect which, due to a twist of history, was to finally subjugate the Roman Empire and don her mantle. Jesus' personal relationship to God was bent in a blasphemous direction by those who later adapted Paul's complex theological notions to their own purpose. There was little understanding of what lay at the heart of Jesus' message as the juggernaut of Roman Christianity gathered momentum, as the first layers of theological speculation hardened into dogma. The Galilean Messiah was transmuted into a paragon of virtue, into God himself; his family's sectarian beliefs were transposed from orthodoxy to heterodoxy with a stroke of the pen. History was turned on its ear and religious sensibility corkscrewed. Intellectual honesty was made into an elaborate game of subterfuge and Jesus the Galilean, the Nazarene, the man to whom self-deception was abhorrent, was transformed into the greatest deception of all time. Yet he was unaware that any of this would happen as he knelt in the Garden of Gethsemane. Like the rest of us, he was a man of his time influenced by the failings of his time.

In the apocryphal Acts of Peter so beloved of the Gnostics, Peter speaks in guarded tones of what he witnessed on Mount Hermon. In fact he is so careful that all he can say is *Talem eum vidi qualem capere potui* ('I saw him in such a form as I was able to take in').[10] Writing of this incident, and of those very words, Henry Corbin terms such an experience 'theophanic' (the visible manifestation of God to man), and goes on to give further examples of people seeing forms of God *appropriate to their capacity*. Carrying this concept further, Corbin speaks of perception possessing 'a personal character', and of the field of vision as defined by the 'dimension of being . . . common to this or that group'.[11] In the same way, Origen, the great Alexandrian Father, spoke of those who witnessed the Transfiguration of Jesus as experiencing it 'according as each man was worthy'.

In relation to this, I would like to suggest that there are three ways in which we can approach the story of the Transfiguration: (1) as a completely natural event during which Jesus was caught in a stream of sunlight and thought to have been Transfigured by supernatural means; (2) as a literal event during which he emanated divine light from his body because he was intrinsically divine; and (3) as a moment of deep contemplation during which he was Transfigured as a result of reaching out towards his God. This last is my choice. Why? Because, as Karen Armstrong so succinctly says in relation to this story, 'Jesus' glorified humanity showed us the deified human condition to which we could all aspire.'[12] *That*, to my way of thinking, is the more sensible approach – and that in spite of the fact that Malachi Martin would see it as the 'winsome doctrine' again raising its ugly head. Yes, we can see the Transfiguration of Jesus in different ways, and the way in which we see it determines our capacity for freedom.

BACK TO THE KINGDOM OF GOD

It seems strange that a man as intelligent as Jesus did not realize that the Jewish dream of a physical Kingdom of God on Earth was a utopian hope incapable of fulfilment. But as Hugh Schonfield

has shown in *The Passover Plot*, Jesus was a man of his time relying on a blueprint of Messiahship gleaned from the prophetic
books. Splicing past history onto the present (the persecution of
the Teacher of Righteousness and much else), the contents of these
strange documents were made to live again. And so the fortunes
of the Elect were mapped, and the Scriptures made to divulge the
exact character and course of his mission. However we explain
away the non-appearance of the Kingdom of God, the facts are
that Jesus believed in it, the multiple sectarian groups believed in
it, and orthodox Jewry believed in it. Jesus even taught his disciples a prayer to that effect, and was obviously convinced that a
spiritual transformation of the physical world was part of the
Messianic sequence. In the twinkling of an eye all would be
changed. The lion would lie down with the lamb. Weapons would
be reshaped into useful tools. Israel's heroic dead would be raised
up. But only if he, Jesus, enacted the drama of the Suffering
Servant. The whole Messianic package was a drama which had to
be played out in the real world.

So too for the wilderness sectarians. Patterning their daily
behaviour on what they thought was a fair representation of how
this Kingdom would function, they lived austere, Law-driven lives
devoted to interminable rituals of cleanliness. Atonement was of
the people on behalf of the people through prayer and rituals
meticulously enacted by a priestly élite. Orthodox Jews, on the
other hand, were less strict in their observance of the Law and
relied on animal sacrifice to wash away the sins of the nation. So
ingrained was the practice of ritual slaughter that it continued in
the Temple right up until 70. By way of contrast, Jesus seems to
have rejected Temple practice, abhorred Qumranite exclusiveness,
and advocated an open-ended attitude to the Law which broke
with Jewish Orthodoxy and strict Nazarene policy. Offering an
almost casual forgiveness for sins, this upstart of a Messiah
methodically 'carried out certain actions calculated to have
particular effect'. So says Schonfield; and warming to his subject
he adds, 'it is as if he [Jesus] was a chemist in a laboratory
confidently following a formula set down in an authoritative
textbook'.[13] The question is: Which textbook? How to break away
from the rituals of cleanliness and purity to such an extent and
still expect the Kingdom of God to materialize? Or was it just by
way of reaction to Essene rigour that Jesus ended up making
human beings more important than rote observance? Might it be

that Jesus' interaction with Essene thought was at base a reaction against ideas he himself had once held?

In *History and Eschatology*, Rudolf Bultman sets the context for Rigorist beliefs by noting that Israel's Old Covenant with God was grounded in a historical event (Moses and the Law), whereas the New Covenant between God and the Christians was grounded in the concept of history's end. For the Christians, the game of history had completed itself in the incarnation, crucifixion, resurrection and glorification of the 'Christ'. All that was left was a sweeping-up operation before the Messiah reappeared in triumph. Theologically, Christians were not part of history, they were an eschatological event in their own right – they *were* the end-time. The new aeon was imminent. The Kingdom of God was just around the corner. God was about to wind up the whole messy business of human society and inaugurate a theocratic state with the New Israel (the Christians) in charge. But it did not happen. The Son of Man did not appear in clouds of glory. History continued and Christianity fell back into it like a stone into a pond.

However, all this was only after a period of euphoria and certainty during which Christians and orthodox Nazarenes fully expected God to make his move. Bultman observes that the expectation that the end-time had been reached runs through most of the New Testament. In Paul's opinion 'the night is far spent, the day is at hand' (Rom. 13:12). For Peter 'The end of all things is at hand' (I Peter 4:7) And the writer of Revelation is equally sure that 'The time is near' (Rev. 1:3; 22:10). Israel's history had reached its goal; it was about to be consummated in a time of troubles. And so Christianity slowly became a new religion – it had no option – and Paul's intricate theology of Messiahship and the end-time began to corkscrew in the face of unfulfilled promises. Laying the emphasis more and more on the nature of the Messiah, and less and less on the expectation of a world about to end because of that Messiah's obedience to the will of God, Paul's Jesus began to inflate towards theological disaster – that is, Jesus the messenger ended up as the message.

Buried in this fiasco of a turn-around by Paul was a perception of things that not only centred on Jesus but belonged to Jesus, and that were in all likelihood passed on by Jesus to Paul during their regular meetings. How else can we explain Paul's grasp of the fact that life is about real situations rather than doctrine? As Bultman points out in relation to Paul, 'the demands of God are summed up in the commandment of love, that is, in a commandment which does not consist in formulated statements'.[14] Does that sound familiar? It was life that mattered. It was encounters with one's fellow human beings that mattered. Love did not grow out of doctrine; it grew out of people interacting. Now such a notion had not appeared in Paul's mind by magic, it appeared because of his close association with the man who had introduced such ideas to an astonished Israel. *That* is his declaration. The Nazarene party under Jesus' brother James was still boxed in by orthodox notions, the separatist Pharisees were similarly closed off, and the Rigorist isolationism of the Qumranite Essenes remained intact. When dealing with the daily grind of life and relationships, Paul's teachings so closely reflected Jesus' teachings that we can only marvel at the idea of these two men never having met – an opinion held by scholars in spite of the fact that Paul presents himself to the Nazarene Council as a 'Jesus-appointed' Apostle.

So what of Jesus? What of his disappointment as the years went by and there was no sign of the Kingdom? What did he think of it all as he waited for God to act and nothing happened? What did he think as old age came upon him and he saw the threat of Roman invasion grow ever more certain? What then of his glorious reappearance on the scene as God's chosen vessel? For as has been suggested elsewhere, he could not make his move until God made his move, and time was running out. It was not a matter of Jesus presenting himself and the Kingdom materializing; it was a matter of the Kingdom materializing and Jesus stepping forward. Jesus was not God initiating his own wishes; he was an ordinary man awaiting the good pleasure of his heavenly Father. Well, perhaps not 'ordinary' in the usual sense of that word; but certainly a man of his time governed by the thinking of his time. No way out of that one. Jesus' expectations were the expectations of those around him. At a time in Israel's history when everyone was under eschatological pressure, he had responded on behalf of his people, fulfilled the conditions of Messiahship and inadvertently transformed himself in the process. Or, to again quote Karen Armstrong's description of Jesus after his experience on Mount Hermon, his 'glorified humanity showed us the deified human condition to which we could all aspire'.[15] Hence Paul's fascination with Jesus, his conviction that this man was in some sense divine.

Paul was convinced that Jesus' life and teachings heralded a perfect freedom; but he seems not to have anticipated the appearance of a Church using the name of Christ to enslave rather than set free. Jesus the man of flesh and blood and untoward opinions was eventually turned into a phantom, into a mirage upholding the Roman Church's every wish, and as a mirage in its own right, that Church offered its apparently substantial services to a world in need. John Baldock, author of *The Alternative Gospel*, puts it best: 'There can be little doubt that in turning Jesus himself into the message the Church has led the Westernised world into a spiritual desert, in which it [the Church] is more of a mirage than the oasis it holds itself to be.'[16] Turning Jesus into a spiritual head-locking device, this organization of self-appointed authority figures began systematically to fit this device to all and sundry, and the result was entrapment in doctrinal imaginings of ever sturdier formation. Jesus was God. His mother had undergone an immaculate conception and remained a virgin after giving birth to God in the shape of a human being. This being, Jesus, could walk on water and make withered limbs reappear as if by magic. He could make the blind see, raise the dead and detect fish under water. In fact there was absolutely nothing he could not do – he was the most powerful being ever to have appeared on earth. And you had better believe it, for if you did not, then you would burn in hell for all eternity.

THE OUTER AND THE INNER

Such was the tenor of the early centuries of Christianity's growth towards might and power, and things have not changed much. Jesus is still being peddled as God squeezed into a human body, and Mary is now Queen of Heaven as well as Virgin Mother of God on Earth. The head-locking device is still worn by believers, and the fight to retain the Church's traditional values and attitudes is a fight engaged in every day by those who interpret the modern world as bound by Satan and firmly in the grip of his grotesque minions. There is a Heaven and there is a Hell, there is bliss and there is damnation, and those who say something different are not only deluded, but unwittingly in the pay of diabolical forces. However the world may appear on the surface, *that* is the underlying reality, and churchmen who go along with the 'winsome doctrine' are anathema before God.

This is of course to say that *anyone* who questions Christianity's traditional doctrines is heading for the flames.

I, the author of this book, am heading for the flames. As are you, the reader, if you have ceased to believe in the old fashioned way. In fact it is better never to have believed, never to have heard the name of Jesus than to have heard it and dismissed it; or worse still, have fallen away from it into apathy or wilful rejection. Or, as Paul put it, once you have heard the Jesus story you have no cloak for your sin. In spite of it being the twentieth century, this kind of thinking remains evident at the highest levels of Catholic Christianity. And many Anglicans and Presbyterians are quite in accord with such an approach. Evangelicals and Fundamentalists of all hues are well-known for their stand on these issues, and there's many a fence-sitter in each of those categories who, when under pressure, tends to back the highly vocal conservative minority for fear of undermining Christianity as an institution. Now not all Christians are so reticent, but the Catholic hierarchy is bound to the old doctrines for reasons of continuity, and simple believers, 'disinformed, deformed, and infantilised by two thousand years of the Church's fairy-tale preaching' cannot, as the theologian/historian Uta Ranke-Heinemann states, bear the insights that are available to them.

Conservatives consider all the basic doctrines of early Christianity sacrosanct. But if there is a particular doctrine held dear by such stalwarts of the Faith, then it is the doctrine of Christ's atoning death on the cross. Without that doctrine Christianity is as nothing. So what a pity that it makes no sense at all, this business of a Jewish man in his mid-thirties functioning as a human sacrifice – it is as blatantly inadequate a vision today as it was when Jesus himself mistakenly attempted to make it the cornerstone of his Messianic vision. Yes, mistaken; he was a human being and he made mistakes just like the rest of us. The only difference between him and the rest of us being that he believed himself to be the Messiah of Israel, God's archetypal Son chosen by angelic forces, so that the mistakes, when they came, tended to be of some proportion. And the mistakes of the Church which picked up on his basic mistake and made it the cornerstone of their reasoning have been similarly impressive, but only because they misunderstood what he was up to – they thought he was trying to save the whole world by himself, when he was in fact attempting to single-handedly initiate the close-down sequence of his age.

It was Jesus' hope to cancel Israel's debt of sin and wayward-ness before God through a ritualistic act, and also to offer the

Gentile world shelter in Israel's about-to-be-revealed theocracy. That is what he was attempting to do. As an operation planned and executed with military precision it seemed incapable of failing. But fail it did. It failed utterly to impress Israel's God, and that in spite of the fact that it had taken every ounce of courage and faith this remarkable man possessed. The age continued; time was not annulled. The Romans came instead of the Kingdom and Israel was beaten into the ground. So what went wrong? Why did this God-centred man fail in his extraordinary mission? Well, there's really only one answer to such a question, and it isn't very nice – religious naivety. As a man of his times Jesus was heavily influenced by sectarian ideas, and it was these ideas that let him down. Yet in every other way he was well ahead of his time. He was a reformer. He challenged the accepted religious practices of Jewish orthodoxy and severely denounced the extremes of sectarian narrow-mindedness. He healed when he was not supposed to heal. He forgave sins and invited censure. He broke the laws of the Sabbath and spoke of that holy day being made for the people, not the people for it. He had untoward views on just about every level of religious thought, and he hated the tendency of the Temple priesthood to turn Judaism's sacrificial procedures into a gigantic commercial transaction. He was, in effect, the new broom that sweeps clean, but he miscalculated – God, he discovered, is, when all is said and done, inscrutable.

AN INHUMAN THEOLOGY

Elaine Pagels and Uta Ranke-Heinemann have each contributed much of importance to the subject of Jesus, and to the problem of the cross. Pagels has opened our eyes to the importance of Christian Gnosticism, and Ranke-Heinemann has challenged us with her dismantling of Christian doctrine. Reminding us that Christianity during the first few centuries was an 'illegal sect whose members increasingly reflected the diverse interests of an ever more complex population',[17] Pagels notes that after the Church's elevation to the level of imperial institution in the fourth century, Christian teaching changed from being a celebration of human freedom to one where universal bondage to sin became the central, preoccupying focus. In her turn, Uta Ranke-Heinemann attacks the Catholic Church's preoccupation with suffering and points to its inhuman theology of the cross as the root of this spiritual malady.

Now the very fact that early Christianity was not preoccupied with sin and suffering suggests a view of the cross and its purpose not quite the same as that held by the later Church. So what happened? Where did the optimism go? The joy? The exuberance? The freedom? Why, and how, did the theology of the cross change? Ranke-Heinemann is aware of its baleful effect on human affairs. She writes of a theology which 'built substructures under and superstructures over' Jesus' crucifixion, and speaks of a 'frozen theology' and a 'petrified dogmatic edifice'. Quoting the Viennese historian Fredrich Heer, she reveals that both Goethe and Schiller saw Christians as 'cruel enemies of life, as venerators of the cross, unhinged by the spasms of penitence'.[18] Her own opinion is that the theology of the cross has probably not assisted human beings towards humane action, but actually helped promote our inhumanity to each another down the centuries. Her book, *Putting Away Childish Things*, ends on this sobering note, and Pagels is not far behind with a similar condemnation. In *Adam, Eve and the Serpent*, she talks of the Christian view of freedom changing when Christianity became the religion of the emperors. And then she pinpoints the cause of it all – Augustine. It is Augustine who read into the message of Jesus, Paul and the Genesis story his 'theory of original sin.'[19] Becoming the dominant influence in Western Christianity, Augustine's rank pessimism about human nature was to infiltrate and destroy the 'freedoms' enjoyed earlier by Paul's churches – the rule of law was back in place.

And yet Karen Armstrong can write in *The First Christian* that Paul's Christianity 'became a religion far more concerned with sin, with eternal life, with mystical dying in the death of Jesus and the attainment of freedom from the fetters of sin and death'.[20] So was Augustine really to blame? Or do we have a scrambled view of Paul's teachings because an Augustine-type view of things was later added to the Epistles? There are definitely two Pauls in the New Testament, and one of them is undoubtedly a fake. How else can we explain the Epistles bearing Paul's name that were never written by him? Paul number one is bright, hopeful, respects women and sounds like Jesus (as one would expect); Paul number two is darkly obsessed with sin and dislikes women. Paul number one is relaxed about the Law; Paul number two virtually reinvents the Law. So what is going on? Has someone been tampering with Paul's image; or is it simply that Paul lost sight of his original vision and turned conservative? That is a possibility. It might just be that with the failure of Jesus' expectations concerning the Kingdom, he began to rationalize previous hopes into a new shape. Karen Armstrong notes that he eventually takes Christianity right out of the world altogether,[21] and that could suggests a shift in perception.

What is going on here can perhaps be detected in the fact that the Gospels reflect Pauline opinion – the question is: which Paul? Armstrong notes that Jesus' Sermon on the Mount is not concerned with earthly necessities; but that may only reflect additions made to Paul's thinking. If this is the case, then the Jesus who seems utterly disinterested in earthly things may also be a fake, a figure moulded in hindsight by Christians so ensconced *in* time that escape *out of* time became their obsession. The Kingdom on Earth had not arrived, so the emphasis was placed on a heavenly Kingdom, and finally on Heaven alone. Jesus' mistake has now vanished without trace; it has been transposed onto a new ethereal key which many rank and file Christians will refine through exhaustive experiment – Gnosticism is up and running.

The problem, so it seems, was that the Church at Rome turned into an earthly, imperial institution selling a heavenly kingdom modelled on an earthly kingdom while at the same time consolidating an earthly kingdom for themselves. If you see what I mean. And so the Gnostic Christians (rank and file Christians with little interest in hierarchies) became sandwiched between what the Church had to sell, and what she wanted to be – a glorious earthly reflection of a heavenly ideal. Allow these Gnostic Christians too much freedom and they would undermine the earthly authority of those selling that heavenly ideal.

The point is this: Jesus did not ascend into this heavenly ideal after his resurrection, he stayed on Earth and hung around waiting for the Kingdom to abruptly happen – it did not happen and he eventually died and was buried like everyone else. But he made his mark in spite of this, in fact he single-handedly revolutionized religious thinking and set in motion a search which carried Nazarenes and Christians into the depths of their own hearts and minds. The Zealots, backed by sectarian fanaticism, were to bait the Romans until they were forced to respond, but with the destruction of Jerusalem and the breakdown of the fabric of

Jewish life these hardliners were jettisoned by many sectarians in favour of the inner journey. The Kingdom was now 'within', had in many respects always been there, and it would now grow downwards into the human psyche with astonishing results. Creating highly complex symbolic schemes to disguise what was going on, Christian Gnostics would explore the inner world with a contagious enthusiasm, and Nazarene-affiliated groups would follow a similar pattern. Hence the curious fact that so many of the Jewish sectarian groups can be traced back to the Nazarenes (Ebionites, Ophites, Mandeans) and the equally curious fact that these Nazarenes expound a Jesus story utterly different from the by now well-established Church at Rome. But so too is the Jesus story of the Gnostic Christians different, and as they are probably all that is left of Paul's scattered flock, the anomalous nature of the situation becomes self-evident.

Rank and file Christians for whom the transfiguration of the self eventually took precedence over the sufferings of the cross were dubbed 'Gnostic' by the Roman Church, and as it is likely that all Christians carried this title, the inference to be drawn is that 'knowledge' in the sense of deep spiritual experience had been part of an earlier programme now made subservient to dry dogma. As an insult, the term Gnostic is therefore a reverse flip – it denotes a Church which has lost sight of its own spiritual base. Intransigent to a fault, this hierarchy of self-appointed authority figures inadvertently draws attention to the fact that the kind of *gnosis* they accuse rank and file Christians of exercising is in fact the very type of *gnosis* they themselves are promoting – a rational *gnosis* allied to fixed doctrinal notions.

THE TRUE CHURCH

In *The Gnostic Gospels* Elaine Pagels prises open the Gnostic world and confronts us with a mentality quite other than the one expected. Revealing what she terms 'the other side of the coin', she draws our attention to the fact that not only did orthodox Christianity denounce the Gnostics, the Gnostics denounced the orthodox as 'unknowingly empty, not knowing who they are, like dumb animals'.[22] Accusing orthodox Christians of having built an 'imitation church', these Gnostics then elaborate fully on their grievances and voice the opinion that the Church at Rome has enslaved its flock through fear and forced it to obey earthly representatives. The Roman Church is also referred to as a counterfeit Church that claims exclusive legitimacy, and those who lead it are described as blind because they speak of things about which they know nothing. This is their principal failing, and out of their arrogance springs the notion of doctrines which cannot be questioned by anyone. Oppressing their flock, the hierarchy of this Church is described as slandering the truth and preaching a false Christ.

Elaine Pagels captures the essence of the problem when she tells us that by the end of the second century orthodoxy had established objective criteria for church membership. She writes: 'Whoever confessed the Creed, accepted the ritual of baptism, participated in worship, and obeyed the clergy was accepted as a fellow Christian.'[23] The beating heart of the Christian faith had been lost, and into the vacuum created had poured man-made doctrines backed by emotional investment. And so there arose confusion in many a Christian's mind as to who was telling the truth about Jesus, and with the help of a central authority complete with ever-extending powers, the Roman Church eventually managed to foist their doctrinal creations on the Christian mind. That is the basic story, and it is hotly refuted to this day by a Church hierarchy which refuses to consider the claims of these Gnostics as viable on any level. But the truth will out – modern scholarship has blown the lid off this particular pot, and feeble attempts by Church-oriented scholars to put that lid back on again have failed. Gnostic Christians set up qualitative criteria and looked for evidence of spiritual maturity in those claiming to be Christian. In contrast to this approach, the bishops did away with qualitative criteria and attempted to unify the scattered churches through standardization of doctrine. It was no longer what you experienced in your own depths that mattered; all that matter was what you believed with your mind. And do not try to have the best of both worlds; if you belonged to an orthodox church and were foolish enough to hold a cult meal or baptize someone without the bishop being present, then not only had you separated yourself from the legitimate Church, you had also separated yourself from God.[24]

So the gospels of the Gnostics were banned, and along with the suppression of these curious writings went the suppression of those who understood their message. Full of symbols and veiled language concerning interior processes, these gospels were either hidden by initiates so that their insights might survive, or destroyed by those who found those insights incomprehensible and threatening. Classified by Irenaeus as apostate, and therefore worse than pagans, the Gnostic Christians were described as evil seducers and hounded from pillar to post. And what was the reason for this harassment? Because they claimed, in their Christian maturity, to be able to discriminate for themselves between what was true and what was false. They did not need to be told what to believe, they said. They did not require the advice of 'waterless canals' (the bishops); and neither did they need doctrines which bound the mind to fixed paths of thought. Their Christianity was founded not on beliefs, but on relationship, their behaviour not on the dictates of authority figures, but on the presence of God in their midst. The rule of faith had displaced conscience and made the arbitrary notions of men sacrosanct. How could anyone awake to the Spirit of Truth accept such nonsense as God-directed?

As we have already seen, it was the educated Christians who divorced themselves from the Roman Church. Tertullian complained that it was the cream of his membership who deserted the ship of faith for the ship of understanding. And as discussed earlier, the word 'understanding' should not be interpreted as referring to a desire for knowledge in the intellectual sense – that is a false accusation made against the Gnostic Christians by their doctrinally hidebound bishops. *Gnosis* was not 'hard knowledge', it was deep insight into the things of the spirit. The human mind was backgrounded by archetypal energies, and the release of those energies automatically cleared perception of its dependence on external forms. This was the heart of their secret Gospel, and it was also the heart of Jesus' Gospel.

This carries us back to the fact that Jesus was himself a non-conformist in religious terms. So it is no surprise that those who took his basic teachings seriously were also nonconformists, that they could stand neither the restrictions nor the claustrophobia of religious narrow-mindedness. And that is exactly how the Church ended up, as a narrow-minded, short-sighted and altogether pompous institution. It has not changed much. Oh yes, it has modernized its image to some extent, but only because it had no option – the world was streaking away from it and its foolishness was becoming self-evident. Now Paul may have considered the cleverness of the world foolishness, and the foolishness of

Christian belief a mark of intelligence, but if he had lived for a few hundred years he would have rapidly changed his tune. For in spite of the evidence in the Epistles of Paul to the contrary, I do not think he believed what the Roman Church ended up believing; in fact I think he would have been affronted by Catholic doctrine as it eventually evolved. Paul has been blamed over and over again for writing the Roman Church a blank cheque, but a careful comparison of the Epistles suggests doctrinal skulduggery from the very beginning. There is a phantom Jesus in the Gospels, and there is a phantom Paul in the Epistles, and we would do well to carefully study their separate profiles.

CHAPTER FIFTEEN

The Paragon Dismantled

The attempt to defuse the mythology of Jesus being literally God, the theology of hyperbole used to stop him from becoming properly human, and the redefinition of transcendence

In chapter 14 we considered the humanity of Jesus and concluded that he had been a man like any other. He was subject to anger, pain, thirst, weariness, sadness, fear and death. And he was capable of making mistakes; which is to say that his knowledge was human knowledge, his belief system a reflection of the culture and time into which he was born. He had no knowledge of modern physics. He was not aware of viruses or germs or the possibility of antiseptics, knew nothing of the combustion engine, and could not have told you that Mars followed an elliptical orbit. All in all, a diminution of what has been said about him by others. But not a dismissal. Not easily dismissed, this highly unusual man whose unique sense of God separated him from his religious peers. He was unusual, yes, unique certainly, but not by any stretch of the imagination either perfect or all-knowing in the sense eventually suggested by Catholic thinkers.

Until recently, such thinkers were telling us that Jesus had access to four levels of knowledge, and that this knowledge precluded the possibility of his being ignorant in any way whatsoever. The four levels were as follows: divine knowledge, beatific knowledge, infused knowledge and human knowledge. Straightforward enough for the convinced Catholic mind to digest, this quadruple injection of knowledge into the earthly Jesus, but mind-bendingly awkward to anyone with even the vaguest sense of logic. Divine knowledge was his because he was God in person (an idea which automatically annulled his being fully human at a stroke); beatific knowledge was his because as perfect man he possessed the capacity to intercept himself as God in a face-to-face seeing (a muddled idea in anyone's terms); infused knowledge was his because the angels had been so infused and he had made the angels (sheer sophistry); and ordinary human knowledge was his in plenitude because as God there was nothing a human being could know that he did not already know (an utterly silly idea which removed the necessity for even considering the other three).

Now if there was ever a window into the absurdity of Christian doctrine, this is it, for it is only when confronted by such obviously fabricated categories that we have a chance to intercept Christian folly at its most blatant. For the Jesus who emerges from this mishmash of *non sequiturs* is a paradox not by reason of being divine, but by way of human ingenuity and credulity pushed to their limit. We are being hoodwinked by language prostituted to the purpose of logical fallacy. We are being distracted from the possibility of a real spiritual life through the machinations of minds given over to fairy tales. Alright, so Teilhard de Chardin admitted that a humble believer in the catechism was more likely to lead a life of real charity than he was, but that does not mean that such believers are to be read as better than Teilhard. All it means is that they are secure in their ignorance, and that their security of mind and heart helps society to remain secure in turn. Fine. But it should be realized that holding to such a belief system has very little to do with being 'spiritual' – it is just crowd control by another name. De Chardin was well aware of what was going on in such hearts and minds, that is why he refused to give in and said that his sophisticated faith was the only type of faith he could tolerate. And it is also why he thought this sophisticated faith of his exactly the kind of faith needed by these simple believers, for he knew by experience that the catechism's simple-minded summary of Christianity was not enough for a hungry soul to survive on.

And that is the crux of the matter, the decisive point which must in the end govern our response to de Chardin's remark, for either God has created a truth far too difficult for the bulk of human beings to take in, or human beings have created a truth far too simple to do God's truth justice. But there is a catch in all of this, and the catch is that God's truth is in fact very simple, whereas man's truth has been complicated beyond belief. Now I mean that in the literal sense, not the metaphorical. I mean that Western Christian religious practice is backed by doctrines so complicated, so obscure and so idiotic that belief in them takes every ounce of credulity a believer can muster. Which is to suggest that credulity has reached truly sophisticated levels of expression, and that innocence is being betrayed by a false simplicity. There is no sensible exegesis by theologians of New Testament texts to show that a Jesus having perfect knowledge does not accord with Scripture. There is no real attempt to explain Luke's statement that Jesus grew in wisdom (2:52); Mark's that Jesus, along with the angels, did not know the day or the hour of the earth's ending (13:32); or Matthew's suggestion that Jesus thought God's kingdom would come during the life time of his hearers (10:23). How to explain such incongruities?

Mouthing the Creed does not guarantee a spiritual life, and prayer to a God capable of inventing and sustaining Christian orthodoxy must, by its very nature, be an exercise in futility. For imagine what such a God must be like. He must be like the clergy he is supposed to delight in. He must be like the Curia in Rome, all law and order, tradition and political nous; and he must, in some sense, be like all the papas who have occupied St Peter's throne. He must be like John XXII, who spent 63 per cent of his resources on war; like Innocent III, who inaugurated the Albigensian Crusade, or, say, like Boniface VIII, posthumously nominated by the French as a heretic. And there is even a sense in which he must be like Malachi Martin whose dark, despairing and depressing vision would have us all end up burning in hell for eternity. Either that, or he is not like these individuals at all, and is perhaps so removed from such a hidebound hierarchy that if he appeared on Earth and presented himself to them they would be incapable of recognizing him.

Now to suggest such a thing is not at all odd, daring, mischievous or misrepresentative – it is simply unavoidable. Why? Because in historical terms Christianity has squandered its inheritance and forfeited the right to pronounce on anything other than, say, the stock market. And this is not to overlook the Church's good works and good intentions; it is to remind her, in her own words, that good intentions are the paving stones to hell, and that good works are in themselves not enough when it comes to measuring the authenticity of a life. A life is more than doing or saying the right thing, it is being awake to the fact that we are, mostly, not awake, but fast asleep in the face of reality. Fast asleep and proud of it. Eyes closed tight and proud of it. Minds closed down and proud of it. That is our state of being, and the Church has contributed more than her fair share to our condition; in fact it could be said without fear of contradiction that she has single-handedly initiated that condition through a prolonged programme of indoctrination.

The problem has been, from the very beginning, that the Christ figure the Church is founded on was just a man like any other man; albeit a man with his eyes wide open. That, in real terms, was the only difference between Jesus and those he had to deal with. But just as it is occasionally possible to wake up inside a dream and know that we are dreaming, yet not be able to escape from the structure of our dream, so too was Jesus caught inside the structure of his time and culture – we have to dream our dreams through to the end. Ultimately there is no escape from the dream of existence. Pray intensely, indeed transcend himself Jesus may well have done, but when he opened his eyes he was still in first-century Palestine, not twentieth-century Britain or America. And if he had managed to awaken in twentieth-century Palestine? Well, what a shock – nothing would have changed much. The Rigorist would still have been holding forth, the liberals doing likewise. The killing and the butchering and the torture would not have stopped. And that in spite of his having been here, in spite of 2000 years having passed during which his Grand Return from Heaven was at first expected imminently. Heaven itself was ravaged by war a long, long time before. The promise of peace on Earth and good will towards all men as tinselly as a cheap Christmas decoration. Lies all of it, but what an attractive untruth.

And all part of God's plan for the human race, this fiasco of a religion with its constant mistranslation of his wishes. The killing and the torture and the lies all due to human weakness in spite of the Holy Spirit's instructions and the claim of one man to be God's virtual mouthpiece in the world. In spite of the horror, the carnage, the bloodlust, God ruling the world with clear-cut decrees through his priesthood, through the man Jesus, from Heaven, who was not actually a man at all but God perfectly imitating a man for purposes theologically oblique. Confusion built on confusion as this God's dark purposed matured in an equally dark world and the human heart underwent a breaking and a tearing. Mountains of theology. Vast tracks of intricately worded commentary on what God wanted, or did not want. Self-assured clerics bustling, like black crows, across the world's surface to herd the damned into God's earthly kingdom. And all done with the best of intentions, one has to presume, with the belief that 'belief' was all that mattered. So what a catastrophe when it is shown that 'belief' is not only not enough, but tantamount to having done nothing at all with one's spiritual talents. Or, to rearrange the problem and put it into an ex-priest's words: 'Once the "Christian" mind forsakes the human Jesus who lived on our Earth, then it breaks the connection between his work and us, and ultimately destroys all reason we have for hope.'[1]

The writer of these words was Peter Kelly, a committed Catholic, ex-priest and author of *Searching for Truth*, a book which attempts to reconcile contemporary critical biblical scholarship and Church history with spiritual belief. So says the flyleaf, and the book bravely tries to live up to its description, Kelly placing an appreciation of Jesus' physicality high on his agenda of spiritual realizations. For if Christianity is our chosen paradigm, and we lose sight of Jesus' humanity, then we have lost spiritual focus. This is to suggest that Jesus' humanity, his physicality, his flesh and blood reality is something we must come to understand as connecting us to spiritual truth. But Peter Kelly goes on to talk of Jesus' resurrection body as 'transformed' in substance – that is, as different from, say, the bodies of Lazarus or Jairus' daughter when brought back from the dead by Jesus, and as he seems to accept that Jesus could suddenly walk through walls due to his resurrection experience, and even appear in more than one location simultaneously (bi-location), his view of Jesus reflects traditional overtones in spite of his insistence that the pre-resurrection body of Jesus was fully human. From being fully human, Jesus again takes on paragon status.

Now this shows a certain naivety of approach, for if one accepts the miracle aspect of Jesus' ministry in a literal vein, then one automatically blurs his humanity with a divine aspect. And as the divine aspect inevitably overpowers the human aspect, one is left with a hybrid Jesus to whom the body was no more than a disguise. Once again the resurrected body of Jesus is pushed beyond space and time, his previous existence as a man, as a human being, turned into an unrepeatable theological trick. So what to do? How to rescue the man Jesus from out of his God image? And to what end this rescuing of his humanity? Why bother if Jesus the man is later going to give way to the unimaginable?

THE PROFOUNDEST MYSTERY

The arguments for and against Jesus being described as a 'this' or a 'that' are handled well by Peter Kelly; he makes a real effort to assess the stages of thought involved, but in the end falls back on 'mystery' and leaves one with the paragon intact. Well, not quite. The paragon has now undergone modification and taken on a curious air, an air of mystery not altogether aligned with the mystery we are used to. Yes, we're back to square one, but the journey has not left Jesus unscathed; he is not quite as he was, and many a Christian reading Kelly's examination of the issues involved might be shocked to detect a lessening of traditional values. And again that is not quite the case, for many ideas held by Christians about Jesus are not strictly traditional at all, but folksy in the sense that they reflect different historical stages of thought about Jesus. It is in this sense that Kelly deconstructs and rebuilds Jesus' image.

The first adjustment he offers is couched thus:

> The statement that Jesus is God is false if it is taken as 'real iden-tification'; that is, if it is taken to mean that in his being, his substance, his physical existence, his flesh and blood, his essential reality, in what he is in his own self . . . he is other than a man. Jesus is not God in the sense that he is a man; that is, 'is' has a different meaning in the two assertions.[2]

This is a flying start, one would think, but Kelly's next statement annuls the first and adds a note of confusion, a confusion which rapidly deepens due to the superimposition of Christianity's principal prejudice – that Jesus was God's chosen vehicle to the exclusion of all others. As a man Jesus is not God, but in some inexplicable sense he is God because 'in him alone, and in him completely, was God's self-communication made to man; and in him alone was (and is) God's full and irrevocable giving of himself, God's sending of his spirit to the world'.[3] If given the chance, the Dean of Lichfield (Tom Wright) could not have done a better job of this, methinks; it is a perfect example of what a friend once described as epistemological panic. And there is no warrant for it in Scripture either – unless one is willing to return Jesus to his Jewish fold and see him through Jewish eyes. But to do so is to step out of the Christian dream of superiority and land oneself in the twilight zone of archetypal happenings, and as it is this very zone that has been borrowed by Christianity and turned into a fleshly conundrum concerning deity, it is an inadvisable move if one wishes to retain the illusion of Jesus as a Christian, rather than a Jewish Messiah.

Quoting R C Rayner, Peter Kelly then refers to Jesus as 'the profoundest mystery', and with a further twist of language tells us that the sense in which Jesus *is* God 'rests not on such real identification but on an entirely singular unity of separate realities, between which an infinite distance always exists, a unity met nowhere else'. Nowhere else indeed. Such a statement is meaningless and is a 'profound mystery' due to its lack of meaning. True it may be that one can be trained to think in such a fashion, but the premise on which such training rests is itself a dream without substance, an interpretation of Jewish archetypal thinking rendered blasphemous through literalization. And he has a problem, too, with his history, for when talking of the Christians, even before they were called Christians,[4] he construes James' community to be identical to Paul's community, and commits James and his followers to believing that Jesus was literally God, something the Nazarenes did not at any time believe, and are known to have vehemently refuted for centuries. And no wonder, for when talking of Jesus' unity with God Kelly tells us that 'We can no more known what that is than we can know what God is.' A stunning argument in anyone's terms, and followed by an equally stunning summation: 'We do not know therefore what positively it means in itself to say, "Jesus is God"; but in a true sense he is.'[5]

But there is more. Describing God as the ultimate meaning of the universe, Peter Kelly makes Jesus the disclosure of that meaning, and in doing so equates Jesus with God in the sense of his having been a perfect conduit for the will of God. Now this is a legitimate way of attaching Jesus to God, but Kelly cannot resist pushing the metaphor too far and the result is a subtle literalization of Jesus back into being God in some sense not properly disclosed. This is the tenor of everything Kelly writes about Jesus, and although it is a serious attempt to wrestle Jesus away from the pagan-type literalizations indulged in by many Christians, we are nevertheless left with an utterly incomprehensible Jesus whose humanity, personality, character and very identity are constantly in jeopardy. With nothing but verbal dexterity at his disposal, Kelly continues to bend Jesus' temperament away from the human, and the result is an inhuman Jesus ever teetering on the edge of theological disaster. Yet still fully human according to Kelly, in the sense that Jesus was the Second Person of the Trinity, another obfuscation of dizzying proportions. And qualified with the words 'so long as it is rightly understood that "God took flesh in him" '; which is not to be interpreted as meaning that God literally became man – such a view is 'fraught with perils of serious misunderstanding'.[6] A search for the truth? Surely. But a search carried out blindfolded in spite of the book's flyleaf stating that Peter Kelly is 'at odds with the Church's official self-designation as expressed in ecclesiastical documents'.

But let us be fair, Peter Kelly is in very good company when it comes to such reasoning; he is following a well thought-out line of theology developed by the Jesuit theologian Karl Rahner. For Rahner is of the opinion that Christians 'cannot leap over fifteen hundred years of Classical Christology or push it aside as if it were a matter of indifference'.[7] He is adamant. This cannot be done if there is 'an enduring Gospel of Jesus Christ as the One who gives us an ultimate trust and an ultimate hope for the eternal significance and final validity of our existence'.[8] Why? Because 'for almost two thousand years Christianity has acknowledged this Christology and lived according to it'.[9] There is a steady tradition of interpreting Jesus as God reflected in the world, and that tradition cannot be thrown aside just because historical study has complicated Jesus' nature, status and calling. The Church's present Christology has meaning for today; it is still comprehensible in spite of changes to the boundaries of knowledge. So says Rahner, and his carefully worded prose informs us that 'cheap' and 'hasty' rejections of Classical Christology will not do.

But he is nevertheless aware that all is not well in the Christological camp; there are problems to be overcome, historical preconditions and premises which make it more difficult to accept the old idea-formulations. However, such difficulties, real as they might be, should not be allowed to generate a new Christology divorced from the original blue-print – any new vision must be intrinsically related to the history of the Christian faith. There is, as C S Lewis suggested, a *basic* Christianity, and we ought to stay connected and true to this basic vision – the 'fashionable' ought to be penetrated to reveal its paltry limitations. The old Christological arguments may sound a bit strange to modern, educated ears, and the route resulting from them appear 'long and winding', but these old ways of seeing and interpreting Christ's worth are still binding and beneficial. Why? Because they force us to meet God at a radical level, and in a unique manner. Jesus was objectively a man; but he was also the unsurpassable Word of God. And so we can talk 'paradoxically', 'analogously' or 'dialectically' about Jesus and God without fear of being thought old fashioned.[10]

How convenient.

In *Those Incredible Christians*, Dr Hugh Schonfield replies to such a claim thus: 'Christian thinking, instinctively as it would seem, shapes itself to a pattern involving the apprehension of God through the personality of a man. There is still a primordial fear of an Otherness beyond the grasp of human definition and explanation.'[11] I like that as a statement; it captures the essence of the problem – God as *alien other*. The tendency of the human mind is either to doubt or deny the existence of God because it draws the mind too near to the darkness of ultimate *other*, and our tendency to veer away from ultimate *other* has resulted in mechanisms of fear reduction, in comforting stories, in an imagined descent of God as *other* into time and space for our individual benefit. Comforting indeed, but riddled with problems at the epistemological level; and paradoxical beyond all sensible systems of belief when translated into Christological formula. Forced to meet God at what Rahner calls the 'radical level' (the interstices of *otherness* and the human), Jesus the man becomes for us the Christ of God, and in that moment the hostile *otherness* of existence is cancelled out in love. Schonfield terms this envisioned relationship between God and man 'attractive', likens it to the relationship between father and child, but in the end shows himself unconvinced that the alien *otherness* of God can be so easily contained. 'After all,' he says, 'we have not so far succeeded in accepting Otherness as congenial even within the limited framework of our own species.'[12] And he had good reason for thinking along such lines, for in relation to Christian rejection of his Jewish-oriented scholarship with its insider comprehension of Jesus, his status and his times, he noted that the much-vaunted love of Christians for their fellow man was conspicuously absent in his case.

The point is well made by Schonfield in relation to our fear of an otherness 'beyond the grasp of human definition and explanation'. Any hint of ultimate otherness and we ricochet back towards the comfort zone of New Testament myth and marvel, or towards a vacuous denial that the boundary of Being scares us more than we care to admit. And if bound to the Christian myth, then locked into the human rather than the Divine because the Divine, by definition, has been recast in human mould. So in a sense we are bereft of the Divine because the Divine has been rendered comfortably human in Jesus, the radical point of contact between the two being loaded, not towards the incomprehensible darkness of God, but towards the light-filled explanations of men. Not then a radical point of contact with God, this Jesus, this sectarian Jew of the first century, more a point of departure, a point of severance from the depths of being construed as a connection.

But not for Karl Rahner. To this theologian 'Jesus was crucified and is risen into the incomprehensible darkness of God',[13] so creating a way into God not previously open to human beings. The gap between God and man has been cancelled out, the alien otherness of God breached by the love of God declared through Jesus as the Word of God. But Rahner's complex statements harbour the unspoken assumption that classical Christology accurately reflects not only first century notions about Jesus, but also the will of God before the foundation of the world. This is to suggest, as Peter Kelly also suggests, that the quite separate communities of James and Paul believed the same thing, and that they each held identical views as to Jesus' nature and identity. But as is now well known, they did no such thing. And to talk of an 'enduring Gospel of Jesus Christ' as if these communities were one and the same, is to gloss over the facts of history and rely instead on the over-developed imagination of Church Councils. Yes, notions similar in kind to classical Christology did exist in first century Palestine, but they were at root Jewish-cum-Nazarene conceptions of the Messiah as Archetypal Man and even at their most theologically daring did not topple over into the overt belief that Jesus was God. A divine being, yes, according to Kamal Salibi's study of the heretical branch of the ancient *Nasara*, but not literally God in any shape or form. And for the early Apostolic community under James, it was a safe enough vision for thousands of orthodox Jews to join Nazarene ranks prior to the Roman invasion – a substantial proof in itself that such an heretical notion was not being bandied about by the Jerusalem community. So yes, let's penetrate the fashionable and reveal its paltry limitations; but while we're at it, let's also penetrate the theologically inflated Christology developed by the fourth-century Roman Church and attempt to right 1,500 years of classical misinterpretation.

The problem in doing this, for Christians, is of course the idea that Jesus the Nazarene had no spiritual equal – he is felt to have been spiritually unique. That is where the problem lies. And it is there, in this idea of uniqueness and unsurpassability that we find the old classical root allowing Jesus to be somehow God in the flesh continuing in new form. Yes, there has been modification to the idea of Jesus being God to the extent that the physical Jesus is no longer conceived of as God *literally* in the flesh; but the notion continues through paradox, analogy and dialectical argument that Jesus was, as Peter Kelly puts it (quoting Gunther Bornkamm), '*the* Word of God to the world; Jesus himself, prior to and in all his works *the* work of God in the world; Jesus himself prior to and in all the stories the decisive and final history of God in the world'.[14] This is of course pure hyperbole, it is exaggeration, it is inflation, and it is full of danger.

As Karl Rahner is compelled to admit when speaking in a similar manner, such language reflects a long and winding road that does not seem connected to the simple Gospel of the New Testament. He is right. It is not connected. The connection is purely imaginative. It is enthusiasm gone berserk. It is the old classical Christology with its tendency to mingle the divine and the human again on the loose. And Rahner is well aware of the dangers, for at the end of his chapter on old and new Christologies he names the name of the game by saying: 'But every concept of the incarnation which views Jesus' humanity, either overtly or implicitly, merely as the guise God takes upon himself in order to signalise his speaking presence, is and remains a heresy.'[15] And he goes further. In classical Christology the 'is' in Jesus *is* God, 'does not mean *identity* between subject and predicate . . . it only means a unity and link'.[16] And what does this boil down to? It boils down to Jesus having a 'unique relationship' with God. But like Peter Kelly, this idea of a 'unique relationship' between Jesus and God does not stop Rahner from making the baseless assertion that because of this relationship Jesus is therefore 'the unsupersedable Word of God for us . . . which involves God himself, bringing him into our history'.[17] The jump in logic at this point is remarkable, unfounded, and gratuitous. Once again the *fact* of Jesus' humanity is thrown aside in a statement which power-glides him away from, rather than towards, humanity. From there on in it is all downhill as Rahner and Peter Kelly attempt to have the best of both worlds and end up with a hybrid Jesus whose flesh and blood humanity is whittled away sentence by sentence on behalf of an epistemological game. And why do these writers feel so compelled? Because, 'the Christian faith . . . is inconceivable without at least an ultimate continuity of genuine historical tradition'.[18] So says Rahner, and so he reveals the sheer artificiality of the situation.

As mentioned in the Epilogue of my earlier book, *Jesus the Heretic*, the rank of *Insan Kamil* (Complete Man) is given to Jesus by Muslim mystical writers, and this term seems to signify a unique and sustained level of consciousness. Now this is a very different approach from that of Christian writers, for whom the word 'complete', in relation to Jesus, is replaced by the word 'perfect', and connotes a sinless condition. And as the Muslim idea of completeness constitutes a rank as well as a condition of consciousness, the difference between the approaches looms large. There is no suggestion whatsoever of divinity in the title *Insan Kamil*; such an individual may have reached a level of moral perfection, but this does not preclude him from having been morally ordinary at an earlier period of his life. Or, as Karl Rahner puts it in a slightly different context, 'Jesus also believed, hoped, searched and was tempted'.[19] This statement substantiates the classical Christological position on Jesus as 'true and perfect man', for there is no doubt that he found himself in possession of a perfect human nature in the sense of his being *perfectly ordinary as a human being*, not in the sense of his nature being, from the start, perfect. In this sense it is again Rahner who comes to our rescue, for he states that Jesus was subservient to 'the sombre facts of historical existence with its limits, dependency and baseness', and adds for good measure that there could be 'no true and full humanity' in relation to Jesus unless this were the case.[20]

But speak like this as they will, writers such as Rahner and Kelly do not actually mean what they say, for in the next breath both thinkers elevate Jesus beyond any such influence, and the result is a Jesus so utterly removed from human limitation that their very coining of the words is no more than a joke – a joke at our intellectual and spiritual expense. Their so carefully constructed sentences and meanings crash like Erich von Daniken's chariots, and the result is not, as they seem to think, God as man in any real sense, but rather man managing, through theological trickery, to divinize himself by proxy through Jesus. In this sense, Jesus is turned into an inappropriate myth; and even if a myth which was once appropriate, not to be considered indefinitely significant, surely. For as Don Cupitt states in his telling essay 'The Christ of Christendom', 'the suggestion that the classical doctrine of the incarnation belongs, not to the essence of Christianity, but only to a certain period in Church history, now ended, will certainly startle many people. Nevertheless, I believe it is true.'[21] The historical facts speak for themselves, and no amount of verbal chicanery can alter these facts.

THE ESSENCE OF CHRISTIANITY

Classical Christology has humanized deity – God is now perceived, however tentatively, as an elderly, bearded man; or, bizarrely, as a human hand emerging from a cloud. Which is to say that a human image, of sorts, has come between us and God, and try as we might, we cannot rid ourselves of this image. It is rather like Malachi Martin suggesting that possessed people cannot stop cursing God in their heart of hearts – we, so it seems, cannot stop ourselves from sensing God as a human being. He is up there somewhere, he is male, and Jesus in some incomprehensible manner is this God, yet simultaneously not this God. Jesus is God, God is Jesus, and Jesus, as it just so happens, is also a human being.

But the essence of Jesus' teachings was not that he himself was God, but that God was open to approach. Jesus' message was that God could be approached as *father* – there was a way to enter the dark, alien otherness of God and survive. But not in some personal, Daddy-in-the-sky sense – this was not a literal fact, it was a poetic truth which had to be understood as such.[22] Rote prayers and the niceties of the Law were useful mechanisms, but when all was said and done the essence of the religious life was not dogma, or belief, or mechanical supplication of the ego through the ego, but surrender to God. Surrender was the essence of the spiritual life, not mental constructs about God and his purposes. There was a darkness at the heart of consciousness, at the heart of matter, at the heart of what mattered, and this darkness had to be stepped into come what may. Death was part of this darkness, but it was better not to wait for the darkness to overtake one, but willingly to enter the darkness while alive and strong. This was the challenge facing all of us, and as we learned to draw near to this darkness and bear the terrible pressure of its presence, or the presence of its absence, everything changed.

The tendency for many Christian thinkers, however, is to attempt what Karl Rahner demands and hold on to the Church's ancient Christology while juggling incomprehensibly with Jesus as a man of flesh and blood. That is, Christians learn to hold both views simultaneously and simply ignore the fact that these diametrically opposed conceptions of Jesus cannot be amalgamated. Or they pretend that they can be amalgamated through the construction of word-bridges utterly devoid of meaning – bridges for which meaning can only be claimed due to a collapsing of categories. In her 1977 essay, 'A Cloud of Witnesses', Frances Young, a lecturer in New Testament studies, admits that there are 'two stories . . . which cannot be fitted together in a literal way';[23] but she does not, as a result, feel the need to make these stories fit together by some non-literal method. No, Young's approach, although similar to Rahner's and Kelly's at first glance, is in fact the more honest attempt, for she is able to say that God was in Christ reconciling the world to himself, but feels no compulsion to spell out such an idea in terms of a literal incarnation. Two stories, yes, but she admits that the unique focus she chooses when perceiving Jesus as a reconciling force is not due to some unplumbable mystery, but simply the result of her consciously choosing to do so. It is a fully conscious, intelligent decision bereft of obscure, superstitious nudgings – this woman is not engaged in an epistemological conjuring act. The myth of Christ is still evocative of 'truth', not because of a single event in history, but because of repeated events of forgiveness throughout history. There is, ultimately, no obvious reason why forgiveness, as a conscious act in relation to suffering, should exist in our world at all, and the fact that it does is more surprising than any single event in any single century. To truly forgive someone is to exhibit a quality of consciousness quite beyond explanation.

But what of God in all of this? If Jesus is not God, then who or what is God? If Jesus is not the Second Person of the Trinity, then how do we describe or approach God? Frances Young captures our dilemma when she says that to talk of God introduces an 'unknown, or only dimly known, quantity into the situation'. From there on what we say and think 'enters the realm of analogies which are only half-adequate'.[24] This in turn leads to the realization that all statements about God must by necessity be expressed in 'here and now' terms, in the language of inadequacy. Shorn of literalisms, however, God regains the safety of mystery and recedes from conceptual view; for in a sense he was never really there at all, merely believed to have been there through some intricate theological footwork. With Jesus dismantled, however, he again takes on darkness as his mantle and ceases to *be* in any concrete sense; that is, the illusion that we have captured God inside an idea or image evaporates. And so we are back, not to square one as many a theologian might think or fear, but to that ever-renewable point in history where God is stripped of projections. Hard it may be for the Christian Churches to accept such a challenge, heretical it may seem to those whose spiritual focus is lodged, by default, in flesh and blood, but for those who manage to shrug off Jesus' inflated persona, a relief beyond description.

THE CRUNCH POINT

The crunch point in Christological thought is to be found in a basic disagreement between Karl Rahner and Frances Young. Rahner is of the opinion that a person who acknowledges Jesus cannot do so individualistically, but only through the faith of the Church. It is the Church that has passed the Gospel of Jesus on to him, and it is the proclamation and theology of that Church which must stand as guide and mentor in the Christological debate. Young, on the other hand, argues that genuine faith in Jesus takes many different forms. Yes, there are those who continue to believe what they were taught as children, but there are also those who make the faith their own through obedience to their gut-centre. This exactly describes what the radical Gnostic Christians did – they turned towards the incomprehensible darkness of God and jettisoned the light of mere men. But as seen earlier, Rahner will not allow 1,500 years of classical Christology to be pushed aside – the traditional Gospel of Jesus is an enduring Gospel and should not be abandoned. Young counteracts with the observation that a faith reduced to a set of definitions and propositions is a distortion, and adds that 'attempts to produce creeds are inevitably divisive or compromising'.[25] She then notes that Eusebius of Caesarea signed the Nicene Creed in 325 for the sake of Church unity, but that he was not at all happy about it. Rahner refutes such an approach and demands that we make classical Christology binding on ourselves. Why? Because it is only through Jesus that we can find 'an ultimate trust and an ultimate hope for the eternal significance and final validity of our existence'.[26] Really? To my mind such a statement is, to say the least, overblown.

Frances Young's rebuttal of such thinking is worth looking at closely. In a single paragraph she sinks the notion of Jesus as the only way to God by noting that certain credal definitions create heresy. Now this is not how Rahner would define the situation. He would argue, I think, that credal definitions 'highlight' rather than 'create' heresy. There is a fundamental set of truths, these truths have been defined and guarded by Christians down the centuries, and any weakening of their substance divorces present-day Christianity from its ancient roots. Young counterattacks with a question: 'How far ought we to discriminate between orthodoxy and heresy?'[27] Meaning what? Meaning simply that a fanatical adherence to what one believes to be unchangeable truth is divisive and dangerous. To believe that we have the truth all wrapped up and neatly packaged is spiritual arrogance. And so Young directs us away from arrogantly dogmatic claims towards claims which are healing and constructive, and in doing so sets the pace for a complete re-evaluation of the Creed – a re-evaluation closely tied to the fact that classical Christology was culturally inspired. For when all is said and done, the Jesus of classical Christology is not based on the actual figure of Jesus, but on a figure created out of the promises of God as found in the Old Testament. There were many different promises, and Young notes that 'different promises were valued by different people, and expectations revolved around different speculative figures constructed out of the promises'.[28]

In Jesus' case, however, all of these speculative figures seem to have collapsed into one, and the result was God's promises viewed as *embodied* in Jesus. In this sense, 'embodied' does not mean 'incarnated', it merely means as applied to Jesus by others. Identified as all of these speculative figures, Jesus first emerged in the Christian mind as such an embodiment, and only later evolved into a literal incarnation of divinity by way of out of context speculation. Showered with high-sounding titles which he at no time claimed for himself, the Jesus of the New Testament's 'Son of Man' self-designation was ignored – particularly when, as in Mark's Gospel (8:38), he seems to be referring to someone else. Frances Young allows for there having been some continuity between the Church's view of Jesus, and Jesus' view of his own mission, but she is doubtful that the two views were in any sense identical.[29] The Church preached 'Jesus'; Jesus preached the Kingdom of God.

More important still, however, is Young's observation that in the Pauline writings the idea of a pre-existing Jesus-type figure began to develop. Described as having existed from the very moment of creation, this figure was conceived of as having been *sent* from God. But as Young is quick to point out, Paul nowhere identifies this figure with God, and makes plain that the relationship of this figure to God is one of 'delegated authority' and 'perfect obedience'. And then she spells it all out in a rush: 'Indeed, he is the archetypal man and the archetypal Son of God, [the man] who will bear the image of the man of heaven.'[30] The 'man *of* heaven' is not Jesus; he is the archetype with which Jesus has consciously identified. The wisdom-language, the language of 'hypostasis' developed by the Jews, will be pressed into service by the Christians, and the result will be the heresy of the Nicene conclusion. Translating 'Jewish Wisdom-language into the Logos-concept of contemporary philosophy,'[31] Christians will invest a delicate theological idea with flesh and blood, and the result will be a phantom Jesus of ever-growing proportions. And the proof that this figure is a phantom is to be detected in the fact that this figure eventually overpowers God and makes him disappear, not into darkness and mystery, but into mental oblivion – the human has successfully usurped the Divine while claiming to do exactly the opposite.

Yet the New Testament evaluation of Jesus cannot be entirely out of character according to Frances Young – there must have been something about Jesus to have elicited such a positive response from his disciples. Something powerful was going on in this man, and this 'something' caused his followers to believe that God had been disclosed to them in a unique manner. But as Young is quick to point out, does it really matter how we perceive this disclosure? Must there only be one way of talking about Jesus? Surely not. For as God is but dimly known to the human mind, how then can we say with certainty that we fully understand this disclosure of God in a human life? Jesus was not understood then, and he is not understood now. Nothing has changed. Everyone has a different opinion of him, and these opinions form a multiplicity of Christologies which deepen rather than weaken the case for his importance.

THE FINAL PICTURE

In his book *Who was Jesus?* the Very Reverend Dr Tom Wright, Dean of Lichfield, picks up on the Christological problem and states that the term 'Son of God' has no connection whatsoever with the idea of Virgin Birth, that it was a title for Israel and the true Messiah, and that it was Paul who took this title and transformed it *against* Jewish interpretation into a 'fresh understanding of Jesus'.[32] And then comes an illuminating remark: 'He [Paul] clearly held the view that, as well as being a fully human being, Jesus was also, in some sense, on God's side of the equation as well.'[33] On God's side of the equation? What exactly does that mean? Does it have any a meaning beyond that of the obvious? Does it somehow go beyond the idea of Jesus being on God's side to that of Jesus being so lodged on God's side that he was somehow understood to be God? Is that Wright's insinuation? Apparently not. He goes on to say: 'But "Son of God" didn't get the full meaning that it now has within Christianity until much later.'[34] How much later? Around the fourth century perhaps?

Dr Schonfield's scholarship is a little more forthright; he tells us that: 'Catholic Christianity had good reason to seek to discredit the Nazarenes and to brand them as heretical. For one thing it was fatal to the doctrine of the deity of Jesus that his own Apostles and the Christian members of his own family had held that he was no more than man.'[35] That is straightforward enough, I think; and coming from a highly regarded Jewish scholar with a lifelong interest in Christianity, cannot be ignored. But it is when speaking of the juxtaposition of Nazarene Christianity, Pauline Christianity and orthodox Catholic Christianity that Schonfield really makes his mark and reveals what has been glossed over by countless Christian scholars. With regard to the Nazarenes he says: 'This Christianity in its teaching about Jesus continued in the tradition it had directly inherited, and could justifiably regard Pauline and Catholic Christianity as heretical. It was not, as its opponents alleged, Jewish Christianity which debased the person of Jesus, but the Church in general which was misled into deifying him.'[36] I think that states quite clearly what had taken place by the end of the 1st century, and I think it throws the idea of Jesus being 'lodged on God's side' into a less woolly context.

The Dean of Lichfield states that the most persistent mistake over the last two hundred years has been the use of 'Christ', which simply means 'Messiah', 'as though it was a divine title'.[37] To understand what is going on we have to realize that 'if Jesus thought of himself as the Messiah, this is a completely different matter to the possibility . . . that he might have believed that

Israel's God was active in and through him in a unique way'.[38] The possibility? Might? I thought it was all fixed up that that was *exactly* how he thought of himself. Apparently not, for later Wright lets us in on a little secret: Jesus simply picked up on the mood of the times, on the 'massive expectation – *and applied it to himself*'.[39] The italics are Wright's, not mine. This did not mean, of course, 'that he was an egoist, or that he imagined himself to be playing at being "God" in some high-and-mighty sense'.[40] Fine. But what to do when the Dean, at the beginning of his fascinating and courageous analysis of Christianity, clearly misuses early Jewish thinking on *Shekinah* (the presence of God), and calls Jesus 'the true *Shekinah*', so changing what was understood by Jewish scholars as a 'reflection' of God into a literalism, a physical entity identified with Jesus. Is this permissible? I think not; and that in spite of some nifty footwork around the Essenes (who are not supposed to have anything to do with anything), a plea to see Jesus as the *place* where Israel was to meet her God, and a reference to the Torah (God's Law) as an 'entity' in existence before the world was made.[41] Fine. Okay. But as *Shekinah* was interpreted by Jewish thinkers as the 'reality or basis behind all being revealed to human beings as an experience', and was not in any sense a licence to make a human being into God, it appears that yet another Christian thinker is to be found wanting. The Pharisaic mystics identified *Shekinah* or Glory with 'Wisdom' (the ineffable *female* emanation of God), the son with peace – hence 'Prince of Peace' as applied to Jesus. The personification of Wisdom in Judaism was female, not male; it was *Sophia*. And so we have the attempt by some feminist Christians to retrieve Sophia as a female image of God.

The problem that arises here is that most Protestant theologians know very little about Sophia outside of obscure Gnostic evocations of this figure, and to most Catholic thinkers, Sophia has been associated with Mary because the Wisdom texts (prior to Vatican II) were read on Marian feasts. In his excellent article, 'The Wisdom of God: Sophia and Christian Theology', Leo Lefebure points to the fact that the Gospel of John 'uses the language of Sophia to describe the Word (Logos)'. From there on in everything said of the Logos belongs to Sophia 'except for the identification of the Logos as God. The substitution of the masculine "Logos" for the feminine "Sophia" may have been inspired by the maleness of Jesus.'[42] So says Lefebure, and his use of the word 'substitution' clarifies the situation enormously, for as Frances Young notes, the problem of Jesus' relationship to God the Father was solved through 'the translation of Jewish Wisdom-language into the Logos-concept'. Athanasius may have argued that as the Son is the offspring from the Father's substance, then he is both *Sophia* (Wisdom) and Word (*Logos*), but this interpretation is based on a series of theological blunders and does not capture the original delicacy of Pharisaic and sectarian-Nazarene-cum-Gnostic insight. The Gnostic approach was to say that Sophia or Wisdom was no longer acknowledged by the male creator God (the human ego-personality projected), that it lorded it over the creation and that the 'mother' had to wait for recognition. It would appear that we are still waiting. For reasons both multifarious and nefarious, Sophia has fallen into general neglect in the West, and this has lead to a feminist interest in Gnostic forms by way of a backlash. As always, when psyche is denied expression, human nous eventually finds a way to right the balance.

Wright's thinking on this matter is necessarily orthodox, and as a result distorts early Jewish speculations about Sophia; it pushes a point of view rejected to this day by Judaism, and underscores the move made by the later Church towards long-range theological error. In relation to Jesus as the *Logos* the ifs, buts and maybes in his text show such a conception to be an utterly impossible vision either to substantiate or make clear when the chips are down, and taking refuge behind 'paradox' and 'ambiguity' is simply not good enough, not when what you are actually talking about is his *confusion*. And so we have to question the stand of a Karl Rahner, a Peter Kelly or a Tom Wright when they help perpetuate the old systems of thought in a new guise, and through the open enquiry of a Frances Young and a Hugh Schonfield attempt to pull Jesus back into living focus. For in its attempt to cancel the problem of how a transcendent God could relate to the physical world, Christianity created a quasi-divine being out of Jewish-sectarian thinking, and the result was a theological impasse followed by endless suffering. Through inadequate argument and distorted interpretation of Scripture, the early Fathers promoted a Jesus who never actually existed, and it is only fear bred of long-term theological misunderstanding that stops many of us from admitting that that is the case.

Epilogue

As I complete this book, a group of 50 New Testament schol-ars in the USA have decided that Judas did not betray Jesus for 30 pieces of silver – the story is a deception: it did not happen. A surprising pronouncement, one would think. But not at all. This same group has also given its verdict on the Nativity, the Resurrection and the Sermon on the Mount, and all three stories have been declared unauthentic. Called the Jesus Seminar, this group of thinkers has made a mark for itself through a process of cool debunking which many will find offensive, and just as many will find highly satisfying. For the debate is in fact polarized as to what happened in Jesus' life, and to what he owed his spiritual authority. Was he in some sense God struggling to make himself known to us? Or have we been misled in thinking this due to clev-erly written and edited fictions? And so, in *Time* magazine for April 1996, David van Biema can write that 'Christological chat-ter pervades even the Internet, and dozens of other volumes on the search for Jesus are either just published or in the works'. There is now a publishing industry built around the question of who, or what, Jesus was, and opinions of multiple hue and quality are everywhere to be found.

In this fascinating article, the views of 'radical exegetes', 'spir-ited conservatives' and 'traditionalists' are aired for the benefit of the general populace, and this is no bad thing, for as the writer observes, most churchgoers were, until recently, oblivious to the tangles scholars have got themselves into over the question of whether the Gospels can be trusted. But it was not the Jesus Seminar's debunking of virtually everything in the Gospels that interested me, rather the words 'Christological chatter' as used by David van Biema. For those words sum up the nature of the debate. Chatter indeed. A veritable avalanche of opinions pulling the public mind this way and that. But to what end? For chatter is just chatter, when all is said and done, and the outcome of chatter is, well, nothing at all in terms of a spiritual life. Yet the chatter is important on one level at least, it helps clear away some of the sillier aspects of Christological thinking and leaves us with a cleared pitch. That is important. It is necessary for us to clear our minds of theological *clutter* and attempt to home in on the underlying principles of spirituality offered by the New Testament. Jesus did not 'chatter' about the weaker aspects of Jewish-sectarian theology, he challenged such weakness by offering a crisp set of living alternatives to both it and a tired orthodoxy.

Jesus was not a theologian, more an impertinent religious teacher who attempted to break the stranglehold of the old religious guard on the public mind. He was no fool; and he was no one's fool. Now, we may never fully understand the relationship of Jesus to his brother James, the Nazarene party or to Paul and his Christians, but the very fact that both parties stuck by their claim that he was in some sense special as a human being, and later developed separate Christologies to help explain the impact of his life and teachings strongly suggests a real Jesus, not some patchwork quilt of a man created out of words alone. The Jesus Seminar can divide Jesus by two as often as they like, debunk virtually everything said by him as revisionist hyperbole, but I think something is amiss in such an approach. Why? Because I sense that Christianity has, at its core, a message which will eventually surprise everyone, even itself, and this fact suggests that it did at one time have clear access to that core. There is no doubt whatsoever that Jesus was not God in disguise, but he was certainly a man of advanced spiritual talents, and his capacity to sidestep political and religious narrow-mindedness and offer a dynamic spiritual alternative marks him out as highly significant.

Yet he was limited in his thinking; he was not perfect. He could detect the Kingdom of God already on Earth in the sense of a heightened perception of reality, but continued to believe that God would initiate an actual Kingdom on Earth governed by the Archetypal Man of Heaven. Or, as the Very Reverend Tom Wright is quoted by Biema as saying, 'the Gospels provide sufficient evidence to deduce not just a wandering sage who was crucified for reasons unclear, but a prophet who announced a coming Kingdom of God'. According to Wright, the Enlightenment's belief that it knows what Jesus was, and can therefore say that Christianity is obviously a mistake, is reductionist nonsense. You have to stick with the history, not jettison it. I agree. Where I do not agree with Wright is in his mixing of history with theology;

the result is constructionist nonsense. And dangerous nonsense at that. For a God who intervenes in history must end up embroiled in history, and such a God cannot but end up taking sides. Argue as one might for a righteous God who wants to see righteousness flower on Earth instead of evil, the notion of a God who secretly pokes about in people's minds to that end is simply too limited a conception to have any validity. No, I do not think God influences history in any direct sense, but I do think history influences how we perceive God, and I consider that the more telling perception. God may not stave off the horrors of a concentration camp, but we can if we wake up and take responsibility for our lives. Or to put it another way, 'In history, a man proclaimed the possibility of transcending history; and we, in history also, can verify his claim in practice.'¹ So says Don Cupitt, and I think him correct in this assessment. In the final analysis it is we who must move beyond history, not God who must embed himself within it. And this means, in turn, moving beyond the Jesus of history as well as the Jesus of faith.

But there is a price to pay for attempting to transcend history. The psychologist Carl Jung understood this fact better than most, and in *Modern Man in Search of a Soul* he describes both the process and its workings with characteristic precision. In fact he is so precise that he admits straight away that the process of transcending history must, by necessity, remain vague. Why? Because it has to do with something universal, and as such 'exceeds the grasp of any single human being'.² But it can be described, in part, and the description carries us not into the future, but deeply into the present. It is in the present that history is transcended. If we wish to transcend history, or the past, then we must so fully enter the present, the immediate present, that both past and future are cancelled out. But this is no easy task, for such a journey carries us to the very edge of the world. Meaning what? Meaning that we have to become conscious to a superlative degree. Or, as Jung so carefully explains, 'to be wholly of the present means to be fully conscious of one's existence . . . it requires the most intensive and extensive consciousness'.³

Don Cupitt's suggestion that we can verify Jesus' experience of transcending history *in practice* contains a powerful insight into the spiritual process. For unless I am very much mistaken, Cupitt is not suggesting a by proxy transcendence of history *through* Jesus, but an individual attempt to transcend history and the world *in the same fashion* as Jesus. But as Jung points out, this is no easy task; it takes everything we've got to successfully negotiate our way from being locked in history to being free of its bonds. There is a price to pay, and the price of such freedom is the safety and security of being submerged in a common unconsciousness. To be alive in the present is not enough – everyone is so alive. What we have to attempt is an aliveness to the present in the sense of being properly conscious of our own personal existence moment by moment. Nothing is easier to simulate, of course, than an awareness of the present – particularly when asked – but the sustaining of that awareness is an entirely different matter. Awake one minute, we are fast asleep the next and have no knowledge of the transition. It is as if we are alive, and then inexplicably dead, and then just as inexplicably alive again. As if we are for ever being resurrected, but cannot resist the dark comforts of the tomb.

The point I am aiming at is this. Jesus seems to have successfully resisted unconsciousness and become superlatively aware and awake; but this is not to say that he was either perfect, sinless, or all-knowing. He was, in every respect, a man like any other man; but he does seem to have transcended the petty history of his time and locked his eye on an interaction with God which others found either threatening or liberating. Suffering a minimum of unconsciousness, he strove to perfect a relationship with God which finally cast him in the role of outsider, or stranger, and those who follow his example and attempt to step out of the historical process are similarly so-called. And again it is Jung who captures the heart of the matter: 'The man whom we can with justice call "modern" is solitary. He is so of necessity and at all times, for every step towards a fuller consciousness of the present removes him further from his original *participation mystique* with the mass of men.'⁴ Which means that he has literally to tear himself loose from the unconscious mob whose values, hopes, aspirations and ambitions are of this world, and of this world alone. Coming to the edge of that world, to the edge of the dark abyss which constitutes the self in its search for meaning, he places his trust beyond the self and steps out into the unknown. That this is what Jesus did is self-evident. What is not self-evident is what this means in relation to the many Christologies erected around his personality and identity.

In a basic sense, Jesus was a 'modern' man at the cutting edge of his time, and like any man or woman who attempts to hold their awareness steady, was confronted by the necessity to be creative. Breaking with tradition, he atoned for his rejection of the past by an originality of thought and action which amazed and then angered his religious peers. Subject to his culture and time in the general sense, he nevertheless broke with that culture and defied his times through an evaluation of religious practice which marked him out as a reformer and visionary. Skilled in debate, he stood up to the religiously conservative minds of his day and demanded that they re-think their relationship to God. But to describe him thus is to do no more than scrape the surface of what was going on in his life, for this man seems to have been engaged in much more than social reform. The flurry of opinions around him at the time, and later, signal an unusual consciousness, and if even a small percentage of the statements attributed to him in the so-called Apocryphal Gospels are accurate, then he was the bearer of a message somewhat different from the one generally attributed to him.

This fact brings us back to Don Cupitt's statement that we can verify for ourselves Jesus' experience of transcending history. It is, therefore, not a matter of staring endlessly and adoringly at the messenger; it is a matter of turning ourselves into the messenger in the sense of taking on the task that he took on – the task of consciously waking up to the fact that we are predominantly unconscious of our unconscious state, that we are driven predominantly by our emotions. For in concrete terms that is what to transcend history means; it means to be conscious of being conscious as we go about our daily business. But not in some crippling self- conscious sense, rather in the sense of attaching our awareness of self to our awareness of the *other*. Not one *or* the other, but both. The world as *other* plus ourselves. Human beings as *other* plus ourselves. God as *other* plus ourselves. For that seems to be our problem, we are either locked into the *self* side of things, or into the *other* side of things, and as we all know from experience, never the twain shall meet. There is a gap, a gulf, an abyss between these polarities, and only a cancelling of that apparently unbridgeable space can produce meaningful relationship. Universal indeed, this experience, and at its most intense an experience which ultimately exceeds the grasp of any single individual.

As conceived by the early Church Fathers, and as elaborated upon by theologians then and since, Jesus the Nazarene was metaphysically unique in his demands; that is, he expected his disciples

to live lives of extraordinary holiness. They were to turn the other
cheek when struck, go not one mile but two on behalf of the
other, give away their clothes and forgive the *other* seventy times
seven. Strong stuff. In fact more demanding, in practical terms,
than anything the sectaries ever dreamt up, and not at all the kind
of reaction shown by later Christians at Rome, even to one
another. And as he seems to have spent a lot of his time lambast-
ing the religiously narrow-minded, a conundrum in terms of what
was actually what in his overview of moral behaviour. Why, on
the one hand, make such demands, and on the other break the
Law of Moses over and over again? How can we balance such
moral and ethical contradictions? Well, the answer to this question lies, I think, in the nature of the moral demands made by
Jesus on his disciples. Simply put, they were over the top, and that
fact alone suggests that they were not actually moral demands at
all, but a mental discipline of some kind. And this is in no way to
belittle Jesus' moral stature, it is to focus in on Cupitt's contention
that he was engaged in a process of transcendence, a process
which he undoubtedly shared with his followers. And the purpose
of this process? Well, I suspect it had only one purpose – conscious
suffering. He was, in other words, teaching his disciples to
consciously bear the pain of their ever-so-human natures.

But it would disappear, this teaching; it would be transformed
into dry moral injunction bereft of skill, intention and subtlety. Left
with the Law in a new guise, the Christians would soon realize that
they did not have the power to generate the kind of holiness
demanded by Jesus, and with the help of a distorted picture of this
Messiah and his intentions, fall eventually into the trap of generating an emotionally driven attachment to this extraordinary man.
How soon this happened is difficult to determine, but that it eventually became the standard response to Jesus is quite beyond doubt.
In awe of his memory, and of those who had journeyed throughout
Palestine and Judea with him, the second- and third-century
Christians of Rome systematically reconstructed Jesus out of their
need (they were undergoing heavy persecution during those
centuries), and in the end succumbed to their own flights of imagination. Awarded power, prestige and authority in the fourth century
by Constantine, they further embellished Jesus by turning him into
a Roman Emperor by proxy to suit their new circumstances.

And yet behind this adorned and inflated figure resonated a real
Jesus, a human being with imagination who stirred the imagination

of his followers to such an extent that a cult of divinity began to take shape in his name. Perhaps he was not completely without fault this Jesus who, after his crucifixion and impressive return from what appeared to be death, began to speak of himself in terms not altogether modest. Or are we being led astray when at the end of Matthew's Gospel we hear Jesus say: 'All power is given unto me in heaven and in earth.'? Is this Jesus a later construct, a Jesus already backed by a developed theology of divinity? Or is he simply speaking in the coded language of the Man of Heaven, the language of the Messianic archetype later construed to mean; what in Jewish-cum-sectarian terms it could not and should not mean? I suspect the latter, and in saying so again find myself supporting Peter Thiede's contention that the Gospels are in fact much older than presently considered feasible.

Frances Young reminds us that titles such as Messiah, Son of Man, Son of God, Lord and Logos belonged to Jesus' culture and time – they existed long before the early Christians took them up, and could be found in 'non-Christian documents and with non-Christian interpretations'.[5] This is important; it throws Jesus' shadow backwards, not forwards, so to speak. He was, as already stated, a man of his times and culture, and the titles later given to him by Christians belonged to the political, social, nationalistic, prophetic, religious, apocalyptic and supernatural elements embedded in that culture. Which is to suggest that his titles are not even coherent, for they come from sources often 'distinct', and on occasions even 'incompatible' due to being 'associated with particular kinds of title and particular ways of interpreting scriptural promises'.[6] And as if this were not enough, Greek thinkers then added their contribution to this interpretative porridge, and the result was the beginnings of that peculiar Christology where Jesus was confused with God, and the idea of 'salvation' through Jesus began to form and take root.

But only in an intellectual sense. The idea that Jesus was somehow God was based not on revelation, but on a linguistic attempt to produce a foolproof theory of Jesus' divinity unspoiled by human characteristics, yet at the same time fully human and morally perfect. That was the Catch-22. Fully human, yet morally perfect. Which meant that Jesus had come into the world perfect, lived a perfect life, and ascended back to Heaven without that perfection ever being found wanting. Hardly the life of a mediator, for as Young notes, 'if the Logos is inherently perfect and incapable of change, progress or suffering, he is no more able to mediate than the transcendent God himself'.[7] In some sense, Jesus has to have suffered on the cross for the curious archetypal ritual he was engaged in to have had efficacy, and if that is the case, then he must also have consciously suffered from the knowledge that he was, like everyone else, inadequate on the moral level. Only God is good, he said on one occasion, and he did not mean by that that he was perfect because he was God – to think along such lines is ludicrous. No, Jesus was not morally perfect, or sinless; but he was awake to that fact in a unique and powerful manner, and in spite of a smoothed-out New Testament story line, one can still detect the underlying discipline of his thinking.

And it is in relation to the idea of Jesus' moral perfection that the greatest theological mistakes have been made. Confronted at every turn in Christian scholarship with an interpretation of Jesus' moral status which, to my mind, has no New Testament backing whatsoever, we are each and every one of us forced into a false state of acceptance or rejection. For how can we argue coherently for a re-thinking of doctrinal shapes, if hanging around at the back of one's mind is the utterly absurd notion that this man never did anything wrong in his life? How can we talk sensibly about anything at all with that as the background to one's thinking? A perfect Jesus. A moral paragon. Or, more accurately, a moral pest who angers and inflames. History tells us so. Of all the major religions to appear on this planet, Christianity has proved itself to be the most violent, the one most conducive to confrontation and conflict. And this is not to overlook the hundreds of thousands of good Christians who have laboured lovingly, age by age, on behalf of humanity since the first century; it is simply to face the fact that these often extraordinary individuals were as they were, not because of the Church, but in spite of it. For while they laboured among the sick, the illiterate and the broken hearted, their doctrinally hidebound Church was eventually torturing and murdering individuals and whole communities on a scale equal to the ravages of the Third Reich at its worst. Talk if you will, if you dare, about God using such a Church in spite of its massive failings, but do not expect intelligent men and women to any longer accept such a view as having any real meaning.

Which brings us back to the term 'transcendence' as used by Don Cupitt, for when attached to Jung's extended idea of transcendence as a 'stepping out of history', rather than in the more limited Christian sense of a 'history-transcending truth', we find ourselves facing the uncomfortable fact that the Christian notion of transcendence is looped back into a deformed Christology, and as such is itself deformed into the belief that 'belief' in that Christology equals an act of transcendence in its own right. As a subject, transcendence is of course multi-levelled and highly complex, but it must be pretty obvious by now that the human transcendence of history is not allied to beliefs about anything, but to a quite literal transformation in perception which allows the perceiver to experience at first-hand the objective world as God's world. In this sense, the Kingdom of God is staring us in the face, but we are so embroiled in our emotionally governed psyches, so usurped by our interminable inner dialogues, so depleted in our creative energies, that we seldom give that world a second glance. And all because we have been robbed of our spiritual heritage, left spiritually destitute by a faith dying in its own epistemological debris. So it is up to us to do something about it. It is up to us to change direction and face the fact that we have lost all sense of God, all sense of the creative darkness, all sense of the process of transcendence which can carry us far beyond the limitations of history or faith. For as suggested at the beginning of this book, faith has nothing whatsoever to do with belief, it has to do with trust, our ability to face the creative darkness, and hold steady.

Notes

PROLOGUE

  1 Noel, Gerard, *The Anatomy of the Catholic Church*, p 64
  2 Brasher, Joseph S, *Popes Through the Ages*, p 514
  3 Jung, C G, *Aion*, p 109
  4 Schonfield, Hugh, *Those Incredible Christians*, p 120
  5 Rosa, Peter de, *Vicars of Christ*, p 82

1 THE CHALLENGE

  1 Noel, Gerard, *The Anatomy of the Catholic Church*, p 33
  2 Ibid, p 34
  3 Rosa, Peter de, *Vicars of Christ*, p 6
  4 Baigent, Michael, Richard Leigh and Henry Lincoln, *The Holy Blood and The Holy Grail*, p 20
  5 Post, Laurens van der, *Jung and the Story of Our Time*, p 89
  6 Rosa, Peter de, *Vicars of Christ*, p 375
  7 Brennan, J H, *Occult Reich* p 70
  8 Ibid, p 69
  9 Cohn, Norman, *Europe's Inner Demons*, p 61
10 Ibid, p 60
11 Ibid
12 Hodson, Geoffrey, *The Kingdom of the Gods*, p 171
13 Friedman, Richard Elliott, *The Disappearance of God*, p 279

2 LES FLEURS DU MAL

  1 Hastings, Macdonald, *Jesuit Child*, p 120
  2 Martin, Malachi, *The Jesuits*, p 158
  3 Ibid, p 156
  4 Ibid, p 157
  5 Martin, Malachi, *Hostage to the Devil*, p 160
  6 Ibid, p 12

7 Ibid, p 93
8 Ibid, p 94
9 Ibid, p 163
10 Martin, Malachi, *The Decline and Fall of the Roman Church*, p 47
11 Ibid, p 42
12 Schonfield, Hugh, *The Passover Plot*, p 243
13 Ibid, p 245
14 Schonfield, Hugh, *Those Incredible Christians*, p 151
15 Ranke-Heinemann, Uta, *Putting Away Childish Things*, p 173
16 Ibid
17 Ibid, quote taken from back cover.
18 Martin, Malachi, *The Decline and Fall of the Roman Church*, p 44
19 Ibid
20 Ibid, p 47
21 Rosa, Peter de, *Vicars of Christ*, p 33
22 Ibid, p 19
23 Ranke-Heinemann, Uta, *Putting Away Childish Things*, p 213
24 Rosa, Peter de, *Vicars of Christ*, p 60
25 Ibid, p 81
26 Ibid, p 82
27 Martin, Malachi, *The Decline and Fall of the Roman Church*, p 50
28 Ibid, p 42
29 Ibid
30 Schonfield, Hugh, *Those Incredible Christians*, p 120
31 Hastings, Macdonald, *Jesuit Child*, p 230
32 Martin, Malachi, *The Decline and Fall of the Roman Church*, p 47
33 Vogt, Joseph, *The Decline of Rome*, p 104
34 Martin, Malachi, *The Decline and Fall of the Roman Church*, p 156
35 Ranke-Heinemann, Uta, *Putting Away Childish Things*, p 206

3 THE HISTORICAL WHITEWASH

1 Baker, Roger, *Binding the Devil*, p 57
2 Schonfield, Hugh, *Those Incredible Christians*, p 160
3 Ibid, p 144
4 Rosa, Peter de, *Vicars of Christ*, p 31
5 Schonfield, Hugh, *Those Incredible Christians*, p 145
6 Ibid
7 Ibid
8 Revelation 11:15
9 Schonfield, Hugh, *Those Incredible Christians*, p 150
10 Ibid, p 152
11 Ibid, p 163

12 Ibid, p 155
13 Scott, Sir Walter, *Demonology and Witchcraft*
14 Boettner, Loraine, *Roman Catholicism*, p 121
15 Rosa, Peter de, *Vicars of Christ*, p 19
16 Boettner, Loraine, *Roman Catholicism*, p 120
17 Ibid, p 123
18 Ibid, p 119
19 Martin, Malachi, *The Jesuits*, p 175

4 THE DARK RENAISSANCE

1 Purcell, Mary, *The First Jesuit, St Ignatius Loyola*, p 316
2 Ibid, p 317
3 Martin, Malachi, *The Jesuits*, p 185
4 *Encyclopaedia Britannica*, vol 19, p 128
5 Martin, Malachi, *The Jesuits*, p 181
6 Ibid, p 179
7 Ibid, p 180
8 Rosa, Peter de, *Vicars of Christ*, p 226
9 Ibid, p 228
10 Aquinas, Thomas, *Summa Theologia*, vol iv, p 90
11 Boettner, Loraine, *Roman Catholicism*, p 426
12 Martin, Malachi, *The Decline and Fall of the Roman Church*, p 51
13 Ibid, p 44
14 Durant, Will, *The Age of Faith*, p 78
15 Ibid
16 Smith, Prof P in *Encyclopaedia Britannica*, vol 19, p 124
17 Ibid, p 125

5 THE FATAL THREAD IN MODERNISM

1 de Chardin, Teilhard, *Let me Explain* p 159
2 Martin, Malachi, *The Jesuits*, p 288
3 Martin, Malachi, *Hostage to the Devil*, p 93
4 Ibid, p 98
5 Ibid
6 Ibid, p 94
7 Ibid, p 148
8 Martin, Malachi, *The Jesuits*, p 88
9 de Chardin, Teilhard, *Let Me Explain*, p 51
10 Ibid, p 45

11 Ibid, p 41
12 Martin, Malachi, *Hostage to the Devil*, p 107
13 Ibid
14 Ibid, p 114
15 Ibid, p 129
16 Ibid, p 130
17 Ibid, p 131

6 A VEIL ACROSS THE FACE OF TRUTH

1 Martin, Malachi, *Hostage to the Devil*, p 262
2 Ibid, p 257
3 Allen, Thomas, *Possessed*, p xv
4 Martin, Malachi, *The Jesuits*, p 392
5 Ibid, p 37
6 Allen, Thomas, *Possessed*, p 209
7 Ibid, p 188
8 Ibid, p 207
9 Ibid, p 214
10 Ibid, p 215
11 Ibid, p 203
12 Ibid, p 215

7 SATAN AND JESUS

1 Craveri, Marcello, *The Life of Jesus*, p 85
2 Luke 4:6
3 Craveri, Marcello, *The Life of Jesus* p 83
4 Pagels, Elaine, *The Origin of Satan*, p 81
5 Schubert, Kurt, *The Dead Sea Community*, p 132
6 Pagels, Elaine, *The Origin of Satan*, p 69
7 Ibid, p 70
8 Luke 22:3
9 Pagels, Elaine, *The Origin of Satan*, p 124
10 Ranke-Heinemann, Uta, *Putting Away Childish Things*, p 227
11 Ibid
12 Pagels, Elaine, *The Origin of Satan*, p 164
13 Ibid, p 165
14 Ibid, p 167
15 Ibid, p 171
16 Ibid, p 172

8 THE WINSOME DOCTRINE

1 Martin, Malachi, *The Jesuits*, p 188
2 Owen, Richard, *The Weekend Australian*, August 31, 1996
3 Martin, Malachi, *The Jesuits*, pp 208–09
4 Ibid, p 222
5 Ibid, p 223
6 Martin, Malachi, *Hostage to the Devil*, p 95
7 Ibid
8 *The Age*, 20 June, 1996
9 Ibid, 6 June 1996
10 Ibid
11 Carroll, John, 'Time for Recovery', *The Age*, 21 June, 1996
12 Ibid
13 Geivett, Douglas R, *Evil and the Evidence for God*, p 110
14 Ranke-Heinemann, Uta, *Putting Away Childish Things*, p 1
15 Ibid, p 2
16 Ibid, p 3
17 Ibid, p 38
18 Geivett, Douglas R, *Evil and the Evidence for God*, p 125
19 Ibid, p 236 (per Hick's invited response in Geivett's book)
20 Ibid
21 Ranke-Heinemann, Uta, *Putting Away Childish Things*, p 228
22 Ibid, p 231
23 Ibid
24 Geivett, Douglas R, *Evil and the Evidence for God*, p 42 (per Hick's invited response in Geivett's book)
25 Ibid, p 186
26 Ibid
27 Ibid, p 80
28 Ibid
29 Johnson, Paul, *A History of the Jews*, pp 4–5
30 Ibid
31 Westman, H, *The Springs of Creativity*, p 32
32 Johnson, Paul, *A History of the Jews*, p 18
33 Westman, H, *The Springs of Creativity*, p 112
34 Ibid, p 115
35 Martin, Malachi, *Hostage to the Devil*, p 161

9 THE BEATING HEART

1 Johnson, Paul, *A History of the Jews*, p 127
2 Ibid, p 105

3 Ibid, p 124
4 Schubert, Kurt, *The Dead Sea Community*, p 146
5 Isaiah 66:2
6 Johnson, Paul, *A History of the Jews*, p 132
7 Ibid, p 131

10 THE NAZARENE COMMUNITY

1 Knight, Christopher, and Lomas, Robert, *The Hiram Key*, p 66
2 Ibid, p 73
3 Charlesworth, James H (ed), *Jesus and the Dead Sea Scrolls*, p 6
4 Knight, Christopher, and Lomas, Robert, *The Hiram Key*, p 55
5 Charlesworth, James H (ed), *Jesus and the Dead Sea Scrolls*, p 5
6 Matthew 4:17
7 Charlesworth, James H (ed), *Jesus and the Dead Sea Scrolls*, p 5
8 Mack, Burton L, *The Lost Gospel*, p 207
9 Knight, Christopher, and Lomas, Robert, *The Hiram Key*, p 64
10 Durant, Will, *Caesar and Christ*, p 587
11 Galatians 1:8
12 Durant, Will, *Caesar and Christ*, p 588
13 Maccoby, Hyam, *The Myth Maker*, p 152
14 Ibid, p 164
15 Ibid, p 162
16 Galatians 1:16–19
17 Schonfield, Hugh, *The Passover Plot*, p 225

11 IN THE NAME OF 'IS'?

1 Hoeller, Stephan, *Jung and the Lost Gospels*, p 52
2 Smith, Morton, *Jesus the Magician*, p 114
3 Thiede, Carsten P, and D'Ancona, Matthew, *The Jesus Papyrus*, p 73
4 Maccoby, Hyam, *The Myth Maker*, p 176
5 Thiede, Carsten P and D'Ancona, Matthew, *The Jesus Papyrus*, p 72
6 Ibid
7 Ibid
8 Rosa, Peter de, *Vicars of Christ*, p 44
9 Durant, Will, *Caesar and Christ*, p 587
10 Ibid, p 576
11 Petrement, Simone, *A Separate God*, p 472
12 Hoeller, Stephan, *Jung and the Lost Gospels*, p 51
13 Ibid, p 53
14 Ibid

15 Ibid, p 55
16 Osman, Ahmed, *The House of the Messiah*, p 54
17 Petrement, Simone, *A Separate God*, p 473
18 Thiede, Carsten P, and D'Ancona, Matthew, *The Jesus Papyrus*, p 149
19 Spengler, Oswald, *The Decline of the West*, vol 2, p 215
20 Thiede, Carsten P, and D'Ancona, Matthew, *The Jesus Papyrus*, p 148
21 Spengler, Oswald, *The Decline of the West*, vol 2 p 215
22 Jung, C G, *The Spirit in Man, Art and Literature*, vol 15, para 27
23 Hoeller, Stephan, *Jung and the Lost Gospels*, p 58
24 Maccoby, Hyam, *The Myth Maker*, p 125
25 Thiede, Carsten P, and D'Ancona, Matthew, *The Jesus Papyrus*, p 72

12 WITH OUR MOTHER'S MILK

1 Mead, G R S, *Fragments of a Faith Forgotten*, p 14
 2 Ibid p 29
 3 Doresse, Jean, *The Secret Books of the Egyptian Gnostics*, p 263
 4 Mead, G R S, *Fragments of a Faith Forgotten*, p 96
 5 Hoeller, Stephan, *Jung and the Lost Gospels*, p 93
 6 Petrement, Simone, *A Separate God*, p 229
 7 Ibid, p 230
 8 Ibid, p 36
 9 Ibid
10 Doresse, Jean, *The Secret Books of the Egyptian Gnostics*, p 315
11 Knight, Christopher, and Lomas, Robert, *The Hiram Key*, p 75
12 Hoeller, Stephan, *Jung and the Lost Gospels*, p 93
13 Doresse, Jean, *The Secret Books of the Egyptian Gnostics*, p 48
14 Ibid, p 261
15 Ibid, p 50
16 Ibid, p 228
17 Ibid, p 111
18 Ibid, p 113
19 Neumann, Erich, *The Origins and History of Consciousness*, p 18
20 Ibid, p 16
21 Ibid, p 17
22 Schonfield, Hugh, *Those Incredible Christians*, p 73
23 Ibid, p 64
24 Ibid, p 63
25 Ibid, p 152
26 Ibid, pp 154–5
27 Doresse, Jean, *The Secret Books of the Egyptian Gnostics*, p 36

28 Ibid, p 61
29 Ibid, p 62
30 Petrement, Simone, *A Separate God*, p 356
31 Mead, G R S, *Fragments of a Faith Forgotten*, p 158
32 Petrement, Simone, *A Separate God*, p 116
33 Schonfield, Hugh, *Those Incredible Christians*, p 117

13 THE PERSONAL GOD

 1 Messadie, Gerald, *The History of the Devil*, p 91
 2 Jaynes, Julian, *The Origins of Consciousness and the Breakdown of the Bicameral Mind*, p 88
 3 Ibid, p 91
 4 Ibid, p 199
 5 Ibid, p 97
 6 Ibid, p 85
 7 Ibid
 8 Ibid, p 74
 9 Ibid, p 195
10 Ibid, p 22
11 Knight, Christopher and Lomas, Robert, *The Hiram Key*, p 88
12 Sitchen, Zecharia, *The 12th Planet*, p 371
13 Genesis 3:22.
14 John 1:1

14 THE TRANSFIGURATION

 1 Grant, Michael, *Jesus*, p 105
 2 Ferguson, John, *Jesus in the Tide of Time*, p 46
 3 Craveri, Marcello, *The Life of Jesus*, p 237
 4 Luke 9:30–31
 5 Ibid, 9:29
 6 Armstrong, Karen, *A History of God*, p 99
 7 Ibid, p 151
 8 Ibid
 9 Ferguson, John, *Jesus in the Tide of Time*, p 73
10 *Eranos*, Bollingen Series xxx, 5, *Man and Transformation*, papers edited by Joseph Campbell (1964) p 69
11 Ibid, pp 70–1
12 Armstrong, Karen, *A History of God*, p 151
13 Schonfield, Hugh, *The Passover Plot*, pp 64–5
14 Bultman, Rudolf, *History and Eschatology*, p 45

15 Armstrong, Karen, *A History of God*, p 151
16 Baldock, John, *private correspondence*
17 Pagels, Elaine, *Adam, Eve, and the Serpent*, cover blurb
18 Ranke-Heinemann, Uta, *Putting Away Childish Things*, p 294
19 Pagels, Elaine, *Adam, Eve, and the Serpent*, p 150
20 Armstrong, Karen, *The First Christian*, p 97
21 Ibid
22 Pagels, Elaine, *The Gnostic Gospels*, p 123
23 Ibid, p 126
24 Ibid, p 127

15 THE PARAGON DISMANTLED

1 Kelly, Peter, *Searching for the Truth*, p 120
 2 Ibid, p 142
 3 Ibid
 4 Ibid, p 143
 5 Ibid
 6 Ibid, p 144
 7 Rahner, Karl, *Theological Investigations*, p 25
 8 Ibid
 9 Ibid
10 Ibid, p 26
11 Schonfield, Hugh, *Those Incredible Christians*, p xv
12 Ibid
13 Rahner, Karl, *Theological Investigations*, p 33
14 Kelly, Peter, *Searching for the Truth*, p 143
15 Rahner, Karl, *Theological Investigations*, p 38
16 Ibid
17 Ibid, p 37
18 Ibid, p 26
19 Ibid, p 28
20 Ibid, p 29
21 Cupitt, Don, 'The Christ of Christendom', in *The Myth of God Incarnate*, p 134
22 Young, Frances, 'A Cloud of Witnesses', in *The Myth of God Incarnate*, p 34
23 Ibid, p 37
24 Ibid, p 40
25 Ibid, p 38
26 Rahner, Karl, *Theological Investigations*, p 25
27 Young, Frances, 'A Cloud of Witnesses', in *The Myth of God Incarnate*, p 39

28 Ibid, p 18
29 Ibid
30 Ibid, p 21
31 Ibid, p 24
32 Wright, N T, *Who was Jesus?*, p 79
33 Ibid
34 Ibid
35 Schonfield, Hugh, *Those Incredible Christians*, p 117
36 Ibid, p 118
37 Wright, N T, *Who was Jesus?* p 57
38 Ibid
39 Ibid, p 100
40 Ibid
41 Ibid, p 49
42 Lefebure, Leo D, 'The Wisdom of God: Sophia and Christian Theology', Christian Century, Vol III, No 29, 19 October, 1994

EPILOGUE

1 Cupitt, Don, 'Final Comment' in *The Myth of God Incarnate*, p 205
2 Jung, Carl, *Modern Man in Search of a Soul*, p 226
3 Ibid, p 227
4 Ibid
5 Young, Frances, 'A Cloud of Witnesses' in *The Myth of God Incarnate*, p 15
6 Ibid, p 16
7 Ibid, p 27

Bibliography

WORKS CITED AND BACKGROUND READING

Allen, Thomas, *Possessed*, BCA/Doubleday, London 1993

Aquinas, Thomas, *Summa Theologica*, vol IV

Armstrong, Karen, *The First Christian: St Paul's Impact on Christianity*, Pan, London, 1983

— *A History of God*, Mandarin, London, 1994

Baigent, M, Leigh, R and Lincoln, H, *The Holy Blood and the Holy Grail*, Jonathan Cape, London, 1982

— *The Messianic Legacy*, Jonathan Cape, London, 1986

— *The Dead Sea Scrolls Deception*, Jonathan Cape, London, 1991

Bainton, Roland H, *Early Christianity*, Van Nostrand Reinhold, New York, 1960

Baker, Roger, *Binding the Devil*, Sheldon Press, London, 1974

Ballou, Robert O, *The Other Jesus*, Doubleday, New York, 1972

Bermant, Chaim, *The Jews*, Sphere Books, London, 1979

Bettenson, Henry, *The Early Church Fathers*, Oxford University Press, New York, 1991

Boettner, Loraine, *Roman Catholicism*, Presbyterian & Reformed Publishing Company, Philadelphia, 1964

Brasher, Joseph S, *Popes Through the Ages*, Van Nostrand, New York, 1959

Brennan, J H, *Occult Reich*, Futura Publications, 1974

Bultman, Rudolf, *History and Eschatology*, Edinburgh University Press, Edinburgh, 1957

— *Jesus and the Word*, Fontana Books, London, 1958

Burrows, Millar, *The Dead Sea Scrolls*, Secker & Warburg, London, 1956

Carroll, John, 'A Western Crisis of Belief' and 'Time for a Recovery' *The Age*, 20 June 1996

Charlesworth, James H, *Jesus and the Dead Sea Scrolls*, Doubleday, New York, 1993

Churton, T, *The Gnostics*, Weidenfeld & Nicholson, London, 1987

Clark, Mary T, *Augustine*, Desclee Company, New York, 1958

Cohn, Norman, *Europe's Inner Demons*, Paladin, London, 1976

Corbin, Henry, *The Man of Light in Iranian Sufism*, Shambala, Boulder, 1978

Craveri, Marcello, *The Life of Jesus*, Grove Press, New York, 1970

Crossan, John Dominic, *Jesus: A Revolutionary Biography*, Harper, San Francisco, 1994

— *The Essential Jesus*, Harper, San Francisco, 1994

— *Who Killed Jesus?*, Harper, San Francisco, 1995

Cupitt, Don, 'The Christ of Christendom', in *The Myth of God Incarnate*, edited by John Hick, SCM Press, London, 1977

Daniel-Rops, H, *The Church of Apostles and Martyrs*, J M Dent & Sons, London, 1948

— *The Church in the Dark Ages*, J M Dent & Sons, London, 1959

— *Jesus in His Time*, Eyre & Spottiswood, London, 1961

— *The Catholic Reformation*, J M Dent & Sons, London, 1962

de Chardin, Teilhard, *The Appearance of Man*, Collins, London, 1965

— *Hymn of the Universe*, Collins, London, 1965

— *Letters to Two Friends 1926–1952*, Fontana, London, 1968

— *Let Me Explain*, Collins/Fontana Books, London, 1974

Doane, T W, *Bible Myths*, University Books, New York, 1871

Doresse, Jean, *The Secret Books of the Egyptian Gnostics: An Introduction to the Gnostic Coptic Manuscripts Discovered at Chenoboskion*, Hollis & Carter, London, 1960

Dulles, A, *The Survival of Dogma: Faith, Authority, and Dogma in a Changing World*, Doubleday, New York, 1973

Durant, Will, *The Age of Faith*, *The Story of Civilization* series, Simon & Schuster, New York, 1950

— *Caesar and Christ*, *The Story of Civilization* series, Simon & Schuster, New York, 1944

Eisenman, Robert, *The Dead Sea Scrolls and the First Christians*, Element, Shaftesbury, 1996

Eisenman, Robert and Wise, Michael, *The Dead Sea Scrolls Uncovered*, Element, Shaftesbury, 1992

ERANOS, Bollingen Series XXX, vol 5, edited by Joseph Campbell, Pantheon Books, New York, 1964

Ferguson, John, *Jesus in the Tide of Time*, Routledge & Kegan Paul, London, 1980

Filoramo, Giovanni, *A History of Gnosticism*, Blackwell Publishers, Boston, 1992

Fox, Robin Lane, *Pagans and Christians*, Penguin, London, 1986

— *The Unauthorized Version*, Penguin, London, 1991

Friedman, Richard Elliott, *The Disappearance of God*, Little Brown & Co, New York, 1995

Gartner, Bertil, *The Theology of the Gospel of Thomas*, Collins, London, 1961

Gaster, H Theodor, *The Scriptures of the Dead Sea Sect*, Secker & Warburg, London, 1957

Geivett, Douglas R, *Evil and the Evidence for God*, Temple University Press, Philadelphia, 1993

Grant, Michael, *Jesus*, Sphere Books, London, 1978

Grant, Robert M, *Gnosticism: An Anthology*, Collins, London, 1961

Graves, Robert and Patai, Raphael, *Hebrew Myths*, Cassell, London, 1964

Hastings, Macdonald, *Jesuit Child*, Reader's Union, Lewes, 1972

Hick, John H, *Philosophy of Religion*, Prentice Hall, New York, 1973

— 'Jesus and World Religions', in *The Myth of God Incarnate*, edited by John Hick, SCM Press, London, 1977

Hodson, Geoffrey, *The Kingdom of the Gods*, Theosophical Publishing House, Madras, 1952

Hoeller, Stephan A, *The Gnostic Jung and the Seven Sermons to the Dead*, Theosophical Publishing House, Wheaton, 1985

— *Jung and the Lost Gospels*, Theosophical Publishing House, Wheaton, 1993

Holl, Adolf, *Jesus in Bad Company*, Collins, London, 1972

Jaynes, Julian, *The Origins of Consciousness and the Breakdown of the Bicameral Mind*, Houghton Mifflin, Boston, 1990

Johnson, Paul, *A History of the Jews*, Phoenix, London, 1994

— *The Quest for God*, Weidenfeld & Nicolson, London, 1996

Jonas, Hans, *The Gnostic Religion: The Message of the Alien God and the Beginnings of Christianity*, Beacon Press, Boston, 1963

Jung, C G, *Modern Man in Search of a Soul*, Kegan Paul, Trench, Trubner, London, 1933

— *Memories, Dreams and Reflections*, Collins and Routledge & Kegan Paul, London, 1963

— *Aion*, Bollingen Series XX, Princeton University Press, 1979

— *The Spirit of Man in Art and Literature*, Collected Works, vol 15, Routledge & Kegan Paul, London

Kahl, Joachim, *The Misery of Christianity: A Plea for Humanity Without God*, Pelican Books, London, 1971

Kelly, Peter, *Searching for the Truth*, Collins, London, 1978

Kepel, Gilles, *The Revenge of God*, Polity Press, Oxford, 1994

Kersten, H and Gruber, E R, *The Jesus Conspiracy*, Element, Shaftesbury, 1994

Kingsland, William, *The Gnosis or Ancient Wisdom in the Christian Scriptures*, George Allen & Unwin, London, 1954

Klausner, Joseph, *Jesus of Nazareth*, The Macmillan Company, New York, 1925

Knight, Christopher and Lomas, Robert, *The Hiram Key*, Century/Random House, London, 1996

Kuhn, Alvin Boyd, *Shadow of the Third Century: A Revaluation of Christianity*, Theosophical Publishing House, Wheaton, 1949

Layton, Bentley, *The Gnostic Scriptures*, Doubleday, New York, 1987

Ling, Trevor, *A History of Religion East and West*, The Macmillan Press, London, 1982

Maccoby, Hyam, *The Myth Maker*, Weidenfeld & Nicolson, London, 1986

Mack, Burton, L *The Lost Gospel, The Book of Q and Christian Origins*, Harper, San Francisco, 1993

Martin, Malachi, *The Decline and Fall of the Roman Church*, G P Putnam's Sons, New York, 1981

— *The Jesuits*, Touchstone Books, New York, 1987

— *Hostage to the Devil*, Arrow Books, London, 1988

McLynn, Frank, *Jung: A Biography*, Bantam Press, London, 1996

Mead, G R S, *Fragments of a Faith Forgotten*, University Books, New York, 1960

Messadie, Gerald, *The History of the Devil*, New Leaf/Boxtree, London, 1996

Miles, Jack, *God: A Biography*, Simon & Schuster, London, 1996

Moore, James, *Gurdjieff*, Element, Shaftesbury, 1991

Moule, C F D, *The Birth of the New Testament*, Adam & Charles Black, London, 1962

Murphy, John L, *The General Councils of the Church*, Bruce Publishing Company, Milwaukee, 1960

Neumann, Erich, *The Origins and History of Consciousness*, Bollingen Series XLII, Routledge & Kegan Paul, New York, 1973

Noel, Gerard, *The Anatomy of the Catholic Church*, Hodder & Stoughton, London, 1980

Oppenheim, A Leo, *Ancient Mesopotamia*, University of Chicago Press, Chicago, 1964

Osman, Ahmed, *The House of the Messiah*, HarperCollins, London, 1992

Pagels, Elaine, *The Gnostic Gospels*, Vintage Books, New York, 1981

— *Adam, Eve, and the Serpent*, Random House, New York, 1988

— *The Origin of Satan*, Random House, New York, 1995

Paglia, Camille, *Sexual Personae*, Penguin, Harmondsworth, 1991

Perowne, Stewart, *The Life and Times of Herod the Great*, Arrow Books, London, 1960

— *Caesars and Saints: The Evolution of the Christian State*, 180–313 AD, Hodder & Stoughton, London, 1962

Petrement, Simone, *A Separate God: The Origins and Teachings of Gnosticism*, Harper, San Francisco, 1995

Pike, Nelson, *God and Evil*, Contemporary Perspectives in Philosophy series, Prentice Hall, New Jersey, 1964

Post, Laurens van der, *The Story of Our Time*, Penguin Books, London, 1978

Purcell, Mary, *The First Jesuit*, Newman Press, Westminster, Maryland, 1957

Quick, Oliver C, *Doctrines of the Creed*, Fontana, London 1971

Quispel, Giles and Scholem, Gershom, *Jewish and Gnostic Man*, Eranos Lectures 3, Spring Publications, Texas, 1987

Rahner, Karl, *Theological Investigations*, vol. 17, Darton, Longman & Todd, London, 1981

Ranke-Heinemann, Uta, *Eunuchs for Heaven*, Andre Deutsch, London, 1990

— *Putting Away Childish Things*, Harper, San Francisco, 1994

Raven, C E, *Teilhard de Chardin, Scientist and Seer*, Collins, London, 1962

Robinson, M James (ed), *The Nag Hammadi Library*, Harper & Row, San Francisco, 1988

Romer, John, *Testament: The Bible and History*, ABC Books, Sydney, 1988

Rosa, Peter de, *Vicars of Christ*, Corgi Books, London, 1989

Ryle, Gilbert, *The Concept of Mind*, Penguin, Harmondsworth, 1976

Salibi, Kamal, *The Bible Came From Arabia: A Radical Reinterpretation of Old Testament Geography*, Pan Books, London, 1985

— *Conspiracy in Jerusalem: The Hidden Origins of Jesus*, I B Tauris, London, 1988

Schonfield, Hugh, *Jesus, a Biography*, Banner Books, London, 1948

— *The Authentic New Testament*, Dennis Dobson, London, 1956

— *The Politics of God*, Henry Regnery Company, Chicago, 1971

— *The Essene Odyssey*, Element, Shaftesbury, England, 1984

— *Those Incredible Christians*, Element, Shaftesbury, 1985

— *The Passover Plot*, Element, Shaftesbury, 1993

Schubert, Kurt, *The Dead Sea Community*, Adam & Charles Black, London, 1959

Scott, Sir Walter, *Demonology and Witchcraft*, George Routledge & Sons, New York, 1884

Shanks, Hershel, *Understanding the Dead Sea Scrolls*, Vintage Books/Random House, New York, 1993

Silberman, Neil Asher, *The Hidden Scrolls*, William Heinemann, London, 1995

Sitchen, Zecharia, *The 12th Planet*, Avon Books, New York, 1976

— *Genesis*, Bear and Company, Santa Fe, 1991

Smith, Morton, *Jesus the Magician*, Victor Gollancz, London, 1978

Smith, Prof P, 'The Renaissance' in *Encyclopedia Britannica*, vol 19, William Benton, London, 1968

Spengler, Oswald, *The Decline of the West*, George Allen & Unwin, London, 1980

Spong, John Shelby, *Born of Woman: A Bishop Rethinks the Birth of Jesus*, Harper, San Francisco, 1971

— *Resurrection: Myth or Reality*, Harper, San Francisco/New York, 1994

Star, Leonie, *The Dead Sea Scrolls: The Riddle Debated*, ABC Books, Sydney, 1991

Stein, Murray, *Jung's Treatment of Christianity: The Psychotherapy of a Religious Tradition*, Chiron Publications, Wilmette, Illinois, 1986

Suhr, Elmer G, *The Ancient Mind and its Heritage: Exploring the Hebrew, Hindu, Greek and Chinese Cultures*, Exposition Press, New York, 1960

Szekely, Edmond Bordeaux, *From Enoch to the Dead Sea Scrolls*, Academy Books, San Diego, 1975

Sutherland, Stuart, *Irrationality: The Enemy Within*, Penguin, Harmondsworth, 1994

Talbot, Michael, *The Holographic Universe*, Grafton Books/HarperCollins, London, 1991

Tarnas, Richard, *The Passion of the Western Mind*, Ballantine Books, New York, 1993

Thiede, Carsten Peter and D'Ancona, Matthew, *The Jesus Papyrus*, Weidenfeld & Nicolson, London, 1996

Thiering, B E, *Created Second: Aspects of Women's Liberation in Australia*, Family Life Movement of Australia, Sydney, 1973

— *Redating the Teacher of Righteousness*, Theological Explorations, Sydney, 1979

— *The Gospel of Qumran*, Theological Explorations, Sydney, 1981

— *The Qumran Origins of the Christian Church*, Theological Explorations, Sydney, 1983

— *Jesus the Man*, Doubleday, Sydney, 1992

— *Jesus of the Apocalypse*, Doubleday, Sydney, 1995

Vermaseren, M J, *Mithra, the Secret God*, Chatto & Windus, London, 1963

Vermes, Geza, *Jesus the Jew: A Historian's Reading of the Gospels*, Fontana/Collins, London, 1981

Vogt, Joseph, *The Decline of Rome*, Weidenfeld and Nicolson, London, 1993

Weiss, Johannes, *Earliest Christianity: A History of the Period* AD *30–150*, vol 11 Harper Torchbooks, Harper, New York, 1965

Weizsacker, Carl Friedrich Von, *The Ambivalence of Progress: Essay on Historical Anthropology*, Paragon House, New York, 1988

Westman, H, *The Springs of Creativity*, Routledge & Kegan Paul, London, 1961

Wilber, Ken, *The Atman Project: A Transpersonal View of Human Development*, Theosophical Publishing House, Wheaton, 1989

Williams, N P, *The Ideas of the Fall and of Original Sin*, Bampton Lectures 1924, Longman Green, London, 1927

Wilson, Bryan, *Religion in Sociological Perspective*, Oxford University Press, New York, 1983

Wilson, Edmund, *The Dead Sea Scrolls 1947–1969*

Wilson, A N *Jesus*, Flamingo/Harper Collins, London, 1992

Wilson, Ian, *Jesus, the Evidence*, Weidenfeld and Nicolson, London, 1984

— *Holy Faces, Secret Places*, Doubleday, Ontario, 1988

Wright, N T, *Who Was Jesus?*, SPCK, London, 1994

Young, Frances, 'A Cloud of Witnesses', in *The Myth of God Incarnate*, John Hick (ed), SCM Press, London, 1977

Index

Abelard 73
Abraham 18, 46, 247
  and Isaac 150–3
Acts of the Apostles 59, 64, 157, 169,
  180, 182, 185–6, 188, 199
Adam/Adapa 247
Adam and Eve, Books of 17
Agamemnon 152
Akkad 234
Alacoque, Margaret Mary 135
Alexander Jannaeus 163
Alexandria 41, 44, 46, 64
  library at 170, 214
Alexian Brothers 106, 107
Allen, Thomas 101–2, 104, 107, 108,
  109, 111
Ananias 171, 186, 188
Anatolia 234
angels 17–18, 113, 114, 133, 138, 239, 276
  rooted in consciousness 131
Anglicans 267
Annunciation 105
anthropology 86, 94
Antioch 41, 44, 46, 64, 175, 195, 196,
  200, 218
apocryphal gospels *see* gospels,
  apocryphal
apostolic continuity 5–6, 29–31, 44–5,
  55–6, 188–9, 232
Arabia 185, 188–9, 193, 197
Arabic language 171, 192
Aramaic (Hebrew) Gospel 59
Aramaic language 134, 192
archaeology 151
Archbishop of Alexandria 117
archetypes 19, 130, 151–2, 202–4,
  206–7, 291
Armstrong, Karen 41, 142–3, 254, 255,
  262, 265, 269, 270
Arrupe, Pedro 99, 103, 136
Asaph 202–3
Asia Minor 63, 182
Assyria 233
  mythology 98–9, 99–100

Athanasius 211, 213, 294
atonement 182, 263
Atrahasis 240
Augustine 18, 76, 88, 102, 149, 269
Australian, The 134
Australian Broadcasting Commission 173

Babylon 63–4, 233
Babylonians 247
Bacon, Roger 73
Baker, Roger 52
Baldock, John 266
baptism 52, 171, 194
  Jesus' 160
Baptists 58, 231
Bar Kochba 57, 231
BBC World Service 27
belief 5, 37, 278–9
Belloc, Hilaire 13, 27
Benedict IX, Pope 13
Benedict XV, Pope 15, 33
Berning of Osnabrück, Bishop 14, 72
bicameral mind 219, 235–8, 241, 249
birkat ha-minim curse 116, 195, 209, 226
Birmingham Post 27
Bishop, Raymond 101, 103, 104, 105–6,
  109, 110
Blatty, William Peter 98, 104
Boettner, Loraine 61, 63, 64
Bones, David 'M' 35, 36–7, 51, 84–5, 87,
  90, 92, 93, 94–5, 153–4, 243
Boniface VIII, Pope 75, 277
Bowdern, William S 101, 104, 105–7,
  108, 109, 110, 134–5
Brasher, Joseph 4
Brennan, J H 20
Buddhism 50
Bultmann, Rudolf 143, 264
Byzantine theology 255

Calvin, John 140
Caraman, Philip 28, 30, 31, 74
Carpocratians 184
Carroll, John 139–42, 145

Cathars 14
Catherine the Great 25
Catholic Church
    betrayed by Jesuits 27
    conflation of Sophia and Mary 293
    deception and distortion 5–7, 37–8, 45,
        47, 48–9, 62, 63
    doctrinal entrapment 89–90,
        266–7, 273–4
    and exorcism 34, 101
    founded by God personally 65
    hierarchy 133, 135, 136
    in India 88–9
    Jesus' four levels of knowledge 275–6
    in the Middle Ages 73–5, 78–80
    missionary work 103
    origins 214
    parallels with Third Reich 12, 14,
        20–1, 72, 302
    persecution of Jews 14–15, 21
    preoccupation with suffering 268–9
    and the Reformation 139, 140
    and the Renaissance 68–9
    repression of learning and scholarship
        3–5, 15–16, 19, 32–3, 35–7, 41,
        52–3, 143
    rise of the papacy 13–14
    as saviour of civilization 49–50
    and scientific progress 82, 84–5,
        94–5, 136–7
    today 29–30
    world of the Compact 102–3
    see also Jesuits; Roman Church
Cave, William 63
Cave of Machpelah, Hebron 150
Chalcedon, Council of 144
Charles II 63
Charlesworth, J H 172, 173
Children of Israel 133
Children of Light 161, 162, 166
Christ of Golgotha 74
Christianity
    current crisis 139–43
    dualistic conception of good and evil
        2–3, 11–12, 16, 19–20, 24, 120,
        122–4, 126, 138–9, 148
    essence of 287–9
    fear of criticism 173–4, 187
    fundamentalism 121
    growth of the clergy 125–7
    integral to Western consciousness 212–13
    and Judaism 116–17, 122, 124, 168,
        169, 176–7, 195–6, 197, 209

Mesopotamian background 233–4
    mysticism 50
    and the nature of Jesus 275–94
    orthodox and Gnostic 124, 213–15,
        219, 228–9, 270, 271–3
    and paganism 122
    preoccupation with sin 268–9
    radical and ultra-radical 127–32
    today 1–3, 30, 89–91, 212–13,
        232, 266–7
    two contemporary versions 145–50
    see also Catholic Church; Protestant
        Church; Roman Church;
Christology 40, 157, 190, 193, 194, 196,
    206, 210, 282–3, 284–6, 287–8,
    289–90, 291–2, 295–6, 301, 303
Chronicles 22
Chronos 152
Cicero 78
Clement XIV, Pope 25
Clement of Alexandria 184, 160
Clement of Rome 62, 125, 126, 198
Clementine Homilies 60
Clementine Recognitions 69
Code of Canon Law 7, 47
Cohn, Norman 18, 22, 23
consciousness
    of consciousness 242–3, 297–9
    effects of fasting 113
    evolution of 238–40
    and matter 82, 88, 90–6, 130–1
    self-transformation 153–4
    sleep of 220–3, 237–8
Constantine, Emperor 38, 42, 43, 44, 46,
    47, 50, 52, 54, 76–7, 122, 210
    Donation of 46–7
Constantinople 46, 70
Coptic Egyptian 192
Corbin, Henry 262
Corinth 125, 200
Council of Chalcedon 144
Council of Nicea 190
Councils of the Lateran 14
Craveri, Marcello 114–15, 253, 254
Crispus 54
Cupitt, Don 286–7, 297, 299

Damascus 208
    Nazarenes 186, 218
    Paul in 171–72, 185, 188
Damascus I, Pope 77
D'Ancona, Matthew 116, 159, 191–2,
    194, 195, 197, 198, 204–5, 207, 209

Daniel 148, 164
Dante 21, 75
David 22, 23, 56, 178
  House of 164
Davies, Paul 130
Davies, Philip 172
de Chardin, Teilhard 35, 36, 50, 81–4,
    86–90, 91–2, 93, 103, 111, 124,
    131, 136, 137, 146, 276
de Gaulle, Charles 82
de Guzman, Domingo 14
de Luca, Marianus 74–5
Dead Sea Scrolls 53, 166, 171, 173
Decretum see Code of Canon Law
della Mirandola, Pico 88
demonic possession 28, 30–1, 31–2, 33–5
  David 'M' Bones 36–7
  Father Jonathan 92–6
  'Jamsie' 99–101
  and psychiatric phenomena 108–9
  Robbie Manheim 101–2, 103–11
  Teilhard de Chardin 85
demons 17, 18, 122–4, 148–9, 194, 239
  rooted in consciousness 131
Descartes, Ren, 86
desposyni (blood relatives of Jesus) 38,
    39, 41, 42, 44, 48, 170, 209
Devil (Lucifer, Satan)
  as adversary of God 19, 22, 65–6,
    68–9, 70–1, 103, 111, 123,
    124, 182
  as corrupter of the faith 3, 18,
    32, 137–8
  evolution of 21–3, 121
  expulsion from heaven 17–18
  Jesus and 113–32
  literal existence 101–2
  manifest in possession 33–4, 101,
    104–5, 110
  as metaphor 102
  Old Testament 19, 22–3, 119–20
  as one force with God 130
  origin of concept 233
  as personification of the I-making
    impulse 23
  progressive and conservative
    views 148–9
  survives death of Jesus 16
  temptation of Jesus 113–17
Dezza, Paolo 26
disciples 254
  as exorcists 194
  at the Resurrection 207
  at the Transfiguration 258
  see also names of disciples
divine revelation 77
Domitian, Emperor 57, 231
Donation of Constantine 46–7
Doresse, Jean 217, 218, 219, 220,
    221, 228
Dostoevsky, Feodor 174
Dublin Evening Herald 27
Duchesne, Louis 19
Duns Scotus 88
Durant, Will 75, 77, 175, 176, 198,
    199, 200

Ebionites 40–1, 58–9, 173, 176, 177, 200,
    215, 227, 230, 261
Ecclesiastes 148
Egypt 216
Eisenman, Robert 172, 173
Elijah 159, 160, 253, 254
Enki 247, 248
Enoch, Book of 17, 164
Ephesus 41, 44
Epiphanius 176, 220, 227, 231
Essa 169, 190, 192, 195, 197
Essean-Essen (Holy Ones) 58, 124
Essenes 58, 162, 164–7, 171–2, 202, 231,
    265, 293
  cleanliness and purity 263
  conception of Satan 130
  Jesus and 165–7, 171, 260, 263–4
  John the Baptist splits from 165
  links with Gnosis 215, 217
  and Pharisees 164–5
  at the Transfiguration 254
ethical choices 131
Eucharist 128
Eusebius 38, 39, 46, 62, 63, 231, 289
evil
  attributable to Satan 148–9
  incarnate 38, 102, 121, 138–9
  intrinsic 28, 30–1, 34
  power of 33
  as tangible presence 23
  willed by God 24, 138
  see also good and evil
evolution 35, 36, 82, 88, 95, 137
exorcism 33–4, 34–5, 95, 101, 104,
    105–8, 109–10,
  by disciples 194
Exorcist, The (book) 98–9
Exorcist, The (film) 101
Ezra 167

faith 165–6, 254–5, 303
feminists 293, 294
Ferguson, John 253, 256, 257
fish symbolism 171, 202
Franciscans 73
Fraticelli spiritualists 73
Frederick II, Emperor 79–80
Frederick the Great 25
free will 147–8, 149, 153–4
Freemasonry 25, 26
Freud, Sigmund 238
Friedman, Richard Elliott 24, 241
fundamentalism 121, 267

Gabriel, Archangel 105, 144
Galilee 160, 167, 172
Galileo Galilei 82
Ganss, Father 67
Geivett, Douglas 142, 145–7, 149–50
Genesis 77, 110, 247–9
    Gnostic interpretation 219, 220
Gentiles 39, 160, 175, 179, 189, 196,
        208, 268
    and Jewish Law 40, 45
    Paul son of 177
    Paul's mission to 63, 64, 122, 188
    Peter and 40, 45, 200
Gesland, Henri 35
Gilson, Etienne 30
Gnosis 202
Gnosticism 268, 271, 289, 213–16
    approach to Sophia 294
    and Clement of Alexandria 184
    influence on Paul 176, 180
    and orthodox Christianity 124,
        213–15, 219, 228–9, 270, 271–3
    spiritualization of Jesus 261
    true meaning of 129, 218–19
    use of symbolism 228
God
    and Abraham 150–3
    absence of 1–2, 23–4, 50–1, 53–4,
        84, 142
    as adversary of the Devil 19, 22, 65–6,
        68–9, 70–1, 103, 111, 123,
        124, 182
    of Christian orthodoxy 277, 278
    and Church authority 12, 15, 52–3,
        72, 76, 133
    embodied by Constantine 46
    evolution of Jewish 247–50
    experience of 129
    and history 297

Jesus' relationship with 251, 254, 257,
        261, 287
    Old Testament 19, 22–3, 119, 241
    as one force with Satan 130
    otherness 283, 299
    as a 'person' 250, 287
    progressive and conservative views
        145–8, 150
    stripped of projections 288–9
    as the Word 250–2
gods and goddesses 123
    as organizations of central nervous
        system 238
    proliferation and disappearance 240–5
    visions and voices of 235
Goethe, Johann Wolfgang von 22, 269
good and evil
    as cosmic opposites 2–3, 11–12, 16,
        19–20, 24, 120, 122–4, 126,
        138–9, 148
    as interdependent pairs 128–9
gospels, apocryphal 6, 119, 194, 212, 299
    Acts of Peter 262
    of Mark, secret 184
    of Philip 128–9, 130, 131
    of Thomas 117–18
gospels, New Testament 45, 117,
        119, 178
    anomolies and contradictions
        144–5, 157
    'creatures of Satan' 121
    date 177
    divinity as form of consciousness 141
    Jesus' brothers and sisters 134
    literalism and myth 205
    self and relation to God 129
    see also John; Luke; Mark; Matthew
Grant, Michael 253
Gratian 45
Greece 234
Greek language 62, 134, 160, 171, 192
Greeks 148, 160
    bishops 39, 41, 44
    culture 69, 160, 163
    gods 79
    science 77, 78
Gregory III, Pope 47
Gregory VII, Pope 73
Gregory IX, Pope 73
Gregory XIII, Pope 25

Hadrian 41, 42, 43
Halloran, Walter 101, 107

hallucinations 234–8
Hammurabi Law 245
Hanson, A T 203
hasidim 163, 164
Hastings, Macdonald 25, 26, 29, 49
hatred 166
Hebblethwaite, Peter 27–8
Hebrew (Aramaic) Gospel 59
Hebrew language 134, 160, 194
Hebrews 59, 246–50
Heer, Fredrich 269
Hegesippus 57, 231
hell 31, 147–8
Hellenism 176
Hellenization 160
heresy 4, 5, 15, 18, 26, 176, 290
heretics 14, 53, 73–5, 116, 120, 121,
        125–7, 190, 211–12, 214–15
    Jesus as 171, 173, 183, 186,
        217, 218
Herod the Great 161, 194
Herodian party 260
Herodian period 173
Hick, John 88, 145–7, 148–9
Hillell 160
Himmler, Heinrich 20, 71
history
    God and 297
    and mythology 118–20
    transcending 297–9, 302–3
Hitler, Adolf 12, 14, 19–21, 71, 72
Hobbes, Thomas 13
Hodson, Geoffrey 23
Hoeller, Stephen 194, 195, 202–3, 206–7,
        214, 215, 217
Holocaust 1, 11, 15, 21, 50
Homer 123
Hughes, Albert 107, 109
humanism 140, 142
Huxley, Aldous 50

Ignatius of Antioch 50
Ignatius Loyola 25, 26, 32, 35, 50, 67–8,
        71, 83, 103, 109
    Spiritual Exercises 67, 71, 72
Iliad 239
India 88–9
Innocent III, Pope 14, 277
Inquisition 14, 73–4
Intermediate Period 240
Iphigenia 152
Irenaus 40, 58, 59, 62, 88, 126, 128, 129,
        229, 273

Irish Times 27
Isaiah 164, 167
Islam 203, 286
Israel 166, 251, 293
    crucifixion as atonement for 226
    early monotheists 130
    government by Nazarenes 223
    heritage 165
    Messiah of 41, 56, 115, 120, 175, 178,
        185, 196, 208, 218, 231, 255,
        258, 265, 267–8
    national purity 182
    nationalism 261
    New and Old Covenants 264
    as Son of God 292
Israelites 203, 250

James (the Just), brother of Jesus 6, 39,
        55, 57, 62, 143, 145, 160, 190,
        230
    Ebionite affiliations 113, 227
    highly regarded by Gnostics 228
    and Jesus 184, 207, 208
    and Judaism 168, 173, 176, 196,
        199–200
    leader of Nazarenes 40, 42, 45, 48, 59,
        60, 64, 178, 195, 217, 224, 228,
        265, 284, 281
    and Nassenes 217, 218
    and Paul 157, 171–2, 175, 182, 183–7,
        200–1, 224, 225
    rejection of Temple 227
    as Teacher of Righteusness 172
    at the Transfiguration 253
Jamnia 195
Jaynes, Julian 219, 234–40, 240–1,
        242–4, 249
Jeremiah 158, 159, 160
Jerome 62–3, 143
Jerusalem 44, 46, 163, 167
    Church 39, 43, 60, 170, 171, 174,
        176, 177, 178, 183, 189, 195,
        217, 230
    Council 60, 64, 200, 209, 224
    destruction 116, 119, 196, 198, 209,
        226, 270
    developed by Herod 161
    Essenes in 172
    Nazarenes banned from 41, 42–3
    Nazarenes flee 230
    Paul in 175, 181, 183, 185, 188, 199,
        200–1, 208, 224
    see also Temple at Jerusalem

Jesuits (Society of Jesus) 20, 25–6, 27, 35,
    68, 70, 71, 82, 85, 89, 99, 101, 104,
    109, 111, 133, 135–6
Jesus
    as Alpha and Omega 36
    as archetype 41, 202–4, 206–7, 284,
        290–1, 301
    character 159–60, 162, 166–7
    crucifixion 1, 2, 3, 16, 18, 30, 137,
        253, 255, 260, 267, 269
    divinity 88, 141–2, 194–5, 197, 202,
        204, 205–6, 215, 224, 300–1
    as emperor 12–13, 19, 300
    and Essenes 165, 166–7, 171, 172–3,
        260, 263–4
    family 134, 143–4, 145, 160, 173,
        184, 257
    four levels of knowledge 275–6
    genealogy 56–7
    at Gethsemane 257, 261
    as God 40, 41, 58, 120, 174, 190,
        205, 230, 252, 255, 258, 275,
        280–7, 301–2
    Gnostic version 221, 261
    in the Gospel of Thomas 117–18
    as heretic 171, 173, 183, 186,
        217, 218
    humanity 256–9, 275, 279
    meetings with Paul 157, 168–9,
        179–80, 187, 188, 207,
        217, 264–5
    as Messiah 6, 40, 41, 56–7, 115, 116,
        117, 175, 178, 181, 185, 196,
        208, 218, 224, 231, 255, 258–9,
        265, 267–8, 280, 292–3
    moral demands 299–300
    moral perfection 301–2
    Muslim version 286
    the Nazarene 58, 113, 171, 173,
        174, 192
    as Omega Point of consciousness 84,
        93, 94, 131, 137
    the paragon dismantled 275–94
    relationship with God 251, 254, 257,
        261, 287
    Resurrection and after 168–9, 178–81,
        182, 187–90, 204, 207–8,
        216–17, 224–5, 255, 260–1, 265,
        270, 279
    Sacred Heart 135–6
    Satan and 113–32
    secret teachings 184, 190
    Sermon on the Mount 270

    significance of name 191–5
    spirituality 296
    suffering revered 50
    temptation in the wilderness 113–17,
        118–20, 131–2, 162, 181, 191
    theology 160
    transcends history 297–9
    Transfiguration 253–74
    as the Word (Logos) 176, 284, 285,
        293–4, 301–2
Jesus Seminar 120, 295, 296
Jesus the Heretic (Lockhart) 48, 193, 286
Jewish Apocrypha 17
Jewish Nazarene Church 38–9, 41–2, 43,
    59–60, 61–2, 215
Jews
    demonology 23
    diaspora 160, 161
    and the Holocaust 1, 11, 50
    join Nazarenes 38–9, 201, 223,
        231, 284
    magical deification 194
    national purity 182
    persecution by the Church 14–15, 21,
        120, 121
    Peter's mission to 63, 64
    want to kill Paul 185–6
    war with Romans 198
    see also Hebrews; Judaism
Joachim of Flora 73
Job 22, 119
John (disciple)
    gospel 16, 251, 293
    at the Transfiguration 253
John XXII, Pope 277
John XXIII, Pope (Angelo Roncalli) 15,
    19, 28, 29
John the Baptist 159, 160, 165, 171, 173,
    194, 215, 217, 251, 258
John of the Cross, St 35
John Paul II, Pope 15, 26, 88,
    134–5, 144
Johnson, Paul 150–1, 152–3, 160, 162,
    163, 167, 168, 247–8, 250
Jonathan, Father 92–6
Joseph (Jo-Asaph) 202–3
Joseph, husband of Mary 57, 144, 207
Josephus 64
Joses 160
Joshua (three figures) 202
Jospeh 160
Judah, brother of Jesus 160
Judah the Galilean 162

Judaism 167, 203
  archetypal images 202–4
  and Chrisitanity 116–17, 122, 124,
     168, 169, 176–7, 195–6,
     197–8, 209
  early history 164–5
  early view of Satan 119
  evolution of God 247–50
  Jesus and 160, 268
  Mesopotamian background 234–5, 247
  Nazarenes and 42, 57, 58, 116–17,
     132, 175, 177–8, 195–6,
     199–202, 209, 210, 218, 223–4,
     225–6, 227
  ritual slaughter 263
  scrambled by God as the Word 251
  Shekinah (presence of God) 293
  Sheol (underworld) 148
  Sophia (Wisdom) 293, 294
Judas Iscariot 120, 295
Jude 57
Judea 115, 172, 300
  Roman invasions 6, 161, 209
Jung, Carl 5, 16, 19, 206, 207, 297,
    298, 302
Justin (Roman philosopher) 123–4
Justin Martyr 40

Keane, Michael 27
Kelly, Peter 279–83, 284, 285, 294
Kingdom of God 157–8, 181–3, 208, 221,
    258, 260, 261, 262–6, 290, 296, 303
Knight, Christopher 170, 171, 172, 174,
    217, 244
Koester, Helmut 117

La Colombiere, Claude 135
Lactantius 77
Lagrange, Père 19
language 242
Lanz, Adolf 20
Lateran, Councils of the 14
Latins 255
Law of Moses 234, 245, 264
  Jesus' attitude 160, 165, 166, 168,
    184, 263
  Menelaus attempts to abolish 163
  Nazarene observance 40, 173, 175,
    202
  Paul's disregard 168, 176, 200
  in secular affairs 161
le Bougre, Robert 73
Lefebure, Leo 293

Leigh, Richard 14
Leo XIII, Pope 75
Leo the Great 13
Lewis, C S 282, 284
Linus 62
Llull, Ramon 88
Logos 176, 291, 293–4, 301
Lomas, Robert 170, 171, 172, 174, 217,
    244
Lot 17
Lucifer *see* Devil
Luke, gospel 113, 114, 117, 119, 126,
    144–5, 254, 277
Luther, Martin 46, 104, 140

Maccabean martyrs 148
Maccoby, Hyam 176–8, 179, 180, 181,
    182, 183, 196, 197, 200, 208, 210,
    224
Mack, Burton 174
Malingo, Cardinal 112
Mandeans 215–19, 227, 230, 261
  consider Jesus heretic 171, 173, 183,
    186, 217, 218
Manheim, Robbie 101, 103–11
Marcus 128
Mark, gospel 114, 194, 277, 290
  secret 184
Marlow, Christopher 22
Martin, Malachi 27, 75, 79, 110, 121,
    141, 147, 149, 262, 277
  *The Decline and Fall of the Roman
    Church* 38, 39, 42, 44, 47–8,
    49–50, 52, 76, 231
  Hostage to the Devil 27, 28–9,
    30–1, 31–2, 33–7, 51, 84–5,
    92–6, 99–100, 111, 136–8, 154,
    243
  The Jesuits 65–6, 67, 68, 70–2, 82–3,
    85–90, 102–3, 133, 135–6
Mary (mother of Jesus) 105, 160, 207
  association with Sophia 293
  considers Jesus mad 145, 173, 184
  as Queen of Heaven 266
  saves John Paul II's life 134–5
  virginity 134, 144–5
Matthew, gospel 59, 113, 114, 116, 117,
    119, 126, 166, 174, 191–3, 259,
    277, 301
Maximus the Confessor 255
Mead, G R S 212, 214, 229, 232
Menelaus 163
Merton, Thomas 50

Mesopotamia 38, 43, 170, 233–4, 235, 243, 247
Messadie, Gerald 233, 240
Messiah
  as Archetypal Man 41, 284
  Hitler as 12, 72
  Jesus as 6, 40, 41, 56–7, 115, 116, 117, 175, 178, 181, 185, 196, 208, 218, 224, 231, 255, 258–9, 265, 267–8, 280, 292–3
Messiahship 118, 206, 207, 255, 258, 263, 264, 265
Michael, Archangel 106, 109–10, 111
Middle Ages 18, 69, 72–5, 78–80
Milton, John 22
modernism 4, 15, 19, 32–3, 36, 99, 103, 121, 136, 141, 147
  fatal thread of 81–97
monotheism, development 22, 249
moral law 129–30
Moranis, Bishop 73
Moses 203, 253, 254
Mount Hermon 253, 256, 258, 262
multiple-personality disorder 108
mysticism 50, 214
mythology
  Assyrian 98–9, 99–100
  Christian discomfort with 174
  and history 118–20
  myth maker 174–8

Nag Hammadi 206–7
Nasara 189, 198, 197, 284
Naassenes 217, 218, 219, 220, 228–9, 230
naturalism 79
Nazarenes 38–45, 56–60, 113, 170–90, 261, 271
  appeal to Sylvester 38, 41, 43–4, 47–8, 54–5, 76, 170, 209, 210, 215
  confusion with Christians 42, 171, 179, 195–9, 215, 216, 281, 284
  dilemma of 223–6
  displaced by Roman Church 48, 119, 170, 189
  early government of Roman Church 61–2, 64, 175
  fragmentation 226–8
  Gospel 59, 193, 227
  heterodox branch (Christian precursors) 186, 197, 202, 204, 218, 223–4
  and Jesus' Resurrection 208

  and Judaism 42, 57, 58, 116–17, 132, 175, 177–8, 195–6, 199–202, 209, 210, 218, 223–4, 225–6, 227
  later relationship with Roman Church 6, 38–45, 57–8, 59–60, 230, 231–2, 292
  militant branch 116, 162, 180–1
  origins 192–3, 204
  Paul and 42, 43, 168, 175, 179, 196, 199–201, 218, 223–4, 231–2
  Peter's role 59–60
  regrouping 228–32
  survival 209–10
  see also Ebionites; Mandeans; Nassenes; Ophites
Nazareth 113, 192
Nazarites 113, 173, 182, 196, 215
Nazism 20, 50
Nero 45, 62, 179, 197, 198, 209
Neumann, Erich 222, 223
New Age 90, 93
New Testament 285
  account of Jesus 117–18, 120, 132, 159, 193, 257, 258, 277, 291, 302
  conception of Satan 22
  divine mandate 85, 121
  literalism and metaphor 158–9
  mistaken explanations 173
  reference to Peter 55, 56, 61, 64
  spirituality 296
  studies 175, 191, 217, 288
  textual tamperings 6, 157, 180, 181, 184–7, 260
  three viewpoints 62
  two faces of Paul 210, 269–70
  voices and visions 235
  see also gospels, New Testament
Newman, Cardinal 149
Nicea, Council of 190
Nicene Creed 289, 291
Nicholas I 74
Noah 248
Noel, Gerard 13, 15

obsessive compulsive disorder (OCD) 108, 109
occultism 19–20
Oedipus 152
Old Testament 290
  angels 17–18
  conception of Satan 19, 22–3, 119–20

Jesus in 203
links with Mesopotamia 247
as myth 150–1
voices and visions 235
Ophites 218, 219, 220, 228–9, 230
Order of the New Templars (Ordo Novo
    Templi) 20
Origen 18, 88, 262
Orthodox Church 34
Osman, Ahmed 203
Osterreich, T K 35
Owen, Richard 134

paganism 52, 68, 69, 79, 88, 152
pagans 53, 70, 120, 121, 122, 123–4
Pagels, Elaine 116, 117, 121–2, 123, 125,
    128, 131, 132, 179, 182, 195, 268,
    269, 271, 272
palaeontology 84, 86, 92, 94, 95
Palestine 38, 39, 43, 113, 115, 170, 172,
    209, 257, 278, 284, 300
papacy
    alleged descent from Peter 45, 61,
        62–3, 65
    censorship 19
    corruption and brutality 13–14, 27–8,
        73–4, 75, 277
    demand for obedience 70, 71, 75
    divine mandate 12, 65, 133
    election methods 13, 77
    forgery 46–7
Paul 39, 53, 174–8, 230, 267
    in Arabia 185, 188–9, 193, 197
    background 177
    beliefs 16, 118, 119, 165, 166, 167,
        168–9, 174, 176, 178–9, 179–80,
        188–90, 196, 203, 261, 264,
        265–6, 273–4, 291, 292
    double nature 269–70
    dual view of the Devil 102
    epistles 57, 61, 62, 63, 125, 126, 157,
        175, 177, 185, 188, 264, 269, 274
    execution 197
    and Gentiles 63, 64, 122, 160, 188
    and Gnosticism 176, 180
    and James 157, 171–2, 175, 182,
        183–7, 200–1, 224, 225
    in Jerusalem 175, 181, 183, 185, 188,
        199, 200–1, 208, 224
    and Judaism 45, 176, 181, 200, 202
    meetings with Jesus 157, 168–9,
        179–80, 187, 188, 207,
        217, 264–5

and Nazarenes 42, 43, 168, 175,
    179, 196, 199–201, 218,
    223–4, 231–2
and Peter 55, 145, 185, 188–9,
    199, 200
Roman citizenship 182–3
in Rome 61, 63, 175
Paul VI, Pope 102
Pazazu 98–9, 100
Peace of Westphalia 54
Pekin Man 86
Pepin, king of the Franks 46, 47
Peratae 218, 229, 230
Persia 233
Persians 148
Peter 57, 196, 230
    Acts 262
    and apostolic continuity 6, 44, 45,
        55–6, 188–9, 232
    bones in Rome 39
    Epistle to Rome 61, 125, 264
    execution 197
    and Jesus 178, 217, 258, 259
    and Judaism 45, 175, 176, 199, 200
    legend of Roman episcopacy 42,
        45, 61–3
    and Paul 55, 145, 185, 188–9,
        199, 200
    and the Resurrection 208
    role in Nazarene Church 59
    at the Transfiguration 253, 262
Petrement, Simon 202, 203,
    215–16, 228–9
Pharisees 116, 162, 163, 164–5, 166,
    260, 265
Philip, Gospel of 128–9, 130, 131
Pius VI, Pope 25
Pius VII, Pope 25
Pius IX, Pope 14
Pius X, Pope 3–4, 19, 32, 36
Pius XII, Pope 4, 19
Plantinga, Alvin 149
polytheism 240
poor, the 167
possession *see* demonic possession
Powys, David 139–40, 141
Presbyterians 267
Priestly, J B 22
Protestant Church 34, 104, 112, 293
Purcell, Mary 67
Purcell, Terry 173, 174

Qumran 164–7, 171, 172, 206, 217, 265

Rahner, Karl 26, 282, 285–6, 287, 289–90, 294
Ranke-Heinemann, Uta 40–1, 46–7, 50, 58, 125–6, 143–4, 148, 197, 268–9
Ratchford, Bill 27
Rayner, R C 281
Rebecca 150
Reformation 139, 140, 141
religion 142
  and war 148
Renaissance 67, 68, 69–70, 72
repentance 251
Revelation, Book of 16, 57, 63, 204, 264
Richards H K 27, 28
Rigorists 161, 164, 165, 264
Ritter, Archbishop 108, 111
Roman Church
  adoption of Peter 55–6, 59–60
  displaces Nazarene Church 48, 119, 170, 189
  early government by Nazarenes 61–2, 64, 175
  and Gnosticism 214, 219, 229, 270, 271–3
  later relationship with Nazarenes 6, 38–45, 57–8, 59–60, 230, 231–2, 292
  rise to power 44, 54, 76–7, 122, 210, 261–2, 270
  and Roman Empire 12–13, 46
  view of Jesus 41, 58, 118, 119, 170, 174, 177, 190, 284
  see also Catholic Church
Roman Empire 12–13, 21, 43, 46, 55, 64, 70, 80, 180, 214, 261
Romans 56, 116, 145, 157
  arrest of Paul 175
  crucifixion of Jesus 118, 160
  culture 69
  destruction of Jerusalem 170, 226, 270
  gods 79
  invasion of Judea 6, 161, 209
  persecution of Christians 123–4, 197–8, 300
  persecution of Nazarenes 42–3, 57, 179, 197–8, 199, 209
  war with Jews 198
Rome 161, 234
  Jesus meets enemies of 131–2
  mass exorcisms 112
  Paul in 61, 63, 175
  Peter in 45, 61–3, 64
Roncalli, Angelo *see* John XXIII, Pope

Rosa, Peter de 7, 14, 15, 27–9, 30, 31, 37–8, 45, 47, 50, 55, 62, 63, 73–4, 75, 79, 121, 198

Sacred Heart 135–6
Salibi, Kamal 189, 197, 284
salvation 150, 168, 301
Samaritans 58, 231
Samuel 22
Sanhedrin 161, 223
Sarah 150
Satan *see* Devil
Schiller, Johann 269
schizophrenia 235–6
Schonfield, Hugh 171, 173, 176, 193, 209, 215, 294
  Those Incredible Christians 6, 48, 53, 55, 56, 58, 59, 223, 224, 227, 230, 231, 292
  The Passover Plot 39, 189, 262–3
Schubert, Kurt 117, 165, 166
Schulze (Lutheran minister) 104
science 32, 35, 82, 84–5, 86–7, 137, 141
Scott, Walter 60
Scotus Erigena 73
self
  as barrier to spiritual comprehension 129
  denial of 245–6
  see also bicameral mind; subjectivity
separateness, delusion of 23–4
Sermon on the Mount 167
serpent symbolism 110, 218, 219, 220, 229
Sethians 218
Shammai school 162–3
Shekinah (presence of God) 293
Shelley, Percy 93
Sheol (underworld) 148
Sicarii 161–2
Simeon 39, 230
Simon, brother of Jesus 160
Simon Magus 60
sin 268–71
Smith, Morton 184, 194
Smith, P 78–9
Society of Jesus *see* Jesuits
Socrates 123
Sodom and Gomorrah 17–18
Sol Invictus 261
Sophia (Wisdom) 293–4
Spengler, Oswald 205, 206
Sperling, David 121

spirituality 296
New Age 90
popular 140
SS (*Schutzstaffeln*) 20, 71–2
Stephen III, Pope 46
subjectivity
emergence of 219, 238–40, 242
sleep of 221–2, 242–3
suffering 268–9, 300
Jesus' adored 50
Sumer 233, 234
Sumerians 247
Sunday Press 27
Sunday Times 28
Sunday Tribune 27
Swinburne, Richard 149
Sylvester I, Pope 13, 42
Donation of Constantine 42, 46
Nazarenes' appeal to 38, 41, 43–4,
47–8, 54–5, 76, 170, 209,
210, 215
Syria 38, 43, 170, 216, 234

Tacitus 198
Teacher of Righteousness (Essene) 165–6,
172, 202, 263
Templars 73
Temple at Jerusalem 115
destruction 116
Herod rebuilds 161
Jesus' antagonism 162
Nazarene worship 177–8
Paul's purification 175, 181–2, 183
ritual slaughter 263
Tertullian 126, 128, 129, 273
theology
and history 296–7
inhuman 268–71
and intellect 70, 77
tug-of-war 32–7
Theosophy 90
Theudas 128
Thiede, Carsten Peter 116, 159, 191–2,
193–4, 195, 197, 204–5, 207,
209, 301
Thiering, Barbara 173, 180, 216–17, 254
Third Reich 11–12, 14, 20–1
Thomas, Gospel of 117–18
Thomas Aquinas 74, 108
Time magazine 295

Times, The 134
Timothy 125
Titus 43, 198
Toldoth Jesu 227
Torah 161, 293
as access to God 251
attempted reform 163
James' adherence 196
Jesus' attitude 160
Nazarene observance 177, 179, 197,
218, 223, 225
Paul's disregard 181, 196, 200
Peter's adherence 199
repudiated by Paul's Christians 224
Tourette's syndrome 108
transcendence 297–9, 302–3
Trinity 133
Tusculum, counts of 13

Unam Sanctum (Papal Bull) 75
unconscious, the 129, 221, 222
unconsciousness 222, 237–8, 298
Ur 247, 248

Valentinus 127–8, 130
Valla, Lorenzo 46
van Biema, David 295
van der Post, Laurens 16, 19
Van Roo, William 107–8
Vatican 33, 112, 134
Vatican II 26, 29, 103, 293
Virgil 78
Vogt, Joseph 46

water 171
Weber, Max 141
Weston, H 153
Whitehead, Alfred North 188, 189
Wise, Michael 172
women 52, 56, 125–6, 128
Wright, N T, Dean of Lichfield 91, 250,
280, 291–2, 292–3, 294, 296
writing 241, 244

Yahweh 22, 167, 194q
Young, Frances 288, 289–90, 294, 301

Zealots 115, 116, 117, 120, 131, 161,
162, 196, 226, 261, 270–1
Ziusudra 248